MW00638351

THE
ASTROLOGY
GAME

THE ASTROLOGY GAME

The inside story:
The truth about astrology

Malcolm Dean

Beaufort Books, Inc.

New York   **Toronto**

Library of Congress Publication Data
   Dean, Malcolm, 1948-

The Astrology Game

Bibliography: p.

ISBN 0-8253-0002-9

1. Astrology   I. Title

BF1708.1.D42   133.5   C80-094374-0

Published in the United States
by Beaufort Books, Inc., New York

Printed in Canada   First Printing

ISBN 0-8253-0002-9

Contents

Preface

The truth about astrology — the real truth, that is — is that neither its critics nor its proponents want to let the cat out of the bag. There is solid evidence of planetary influences in everything from gold stocks to short-wave radio conditions, not to mention human behavior. But both critics of astrology and traditional astrologers are squirming because the truth about astrology is going to upset everybody's apple-cart.

This book is one result of a search I undertook some twenty years ago. Once I recognized my interest in astrology, I became determined to get right to the bottom of it, no matter how long it might take. At first I studied all the usual textbooks and practiced reading horoscopes just like any other student practices a new craft. But years later, I became dissatisfied and intensely uncomfortable with the subject. Why were critics so adamant in their belief that there was nothing to the idea of planetary influences? Why did astrology seem to work for some, but not others? Why were there so many schools of thought within astrology? Was it possible that it was all nonsense? Was it possible it was all quite true? For years, I vacillated between these positions, torn between my own experiences with astrology and the often elusive evidence for it. At times it was very tempting to abandon the search in favor of more practical pursuits. Yet something kept me going. There was enough to convince me to dig deeper.

Now I know the answers. Now I know — at least in outline — why people have come to so many conflicting conclusions over the millennia. The issues are many and fascinating. There are more things in heaven and earth than can fit in this tiny volume. Here we will concentrate first upon astrology as a social phenomenon, and then upon its contemporary condition. For two main reasons I am reserving an examination of the broad range of evidence for cosmic influences in our daily lives for a future volume. First, it is important that you come to a better understanding of what traditional astrology is, how it developed, and where it has led us. Too often people engage in lengthy conversations about astrology without realizing they don't know the first thing about it. Knowing nothing, it is difficult to ask fruitful questions. Secondly, although the available scientific evidence shows that we live in a universe far more intimate and interconnected than we realize, it is often argued that scientifically accepted cosmic influences have nothing to do with astrology. Therefore, it is equally important for you to see just how close to traditional astrology some recent statistical investigations have come. To underline the implications of this research to society at large and to the skeptical scientific establishment in particular, Chapters Ten and Eleven outline these investigations and the treatment they have received by various self-appointed arbiters of scientific truth.

I said this book is one result of my search. Another result manifested itself in 1977 as I approached my goal. My work as a freelance broadcast journalist led me into many fields outside my usual interests and introduced me to many investigators in these fields. I became aware that evidence must be sought in many ways and in many places. Perhaps, I reasoned, only by bringing together discoveries from many fields would it be possible to piece together a complete picture of astrology. But who would be interested in such a work? Certainly not those scientists who have decided that planetary influences are impossible, and therefore cannot exist. And probably not many astrologers, who are quite content to construct their horoscopes in the traditional

manner, never raising their eyes to the new heavens which
are opening even now. Obviously, the problem was to
interest open-minded individuals in both camps who might
be awakened to the implications of new discoveries in many
fields which may appear to be unrelated, at first glance, to
astrology.

My solution to this matrix was *Phenomena: The News-
journal of Cosmic Influence Research*. Now supported
by a small, worldwide network of the best and brightest
researchers in this field, *Phenomena* led me to survey
regularly thousands of scientific and popular journals in
search of discoveries which might reveal something of our
relationship to the universe. I condensed the results of this
search into regular issues aimed at uncovering the con-
cordance between ancient traditions and modern discoveries.

At the same time, I wrote thousands of letters, seeking out
researchers in many countries, requesting information,
following leads to publications few have heard of, and
groups most people don't even know exist. While others
spent their salaries on cars, televisions, and insurance
policies, I disbursed much of a meager income on postage,
stationery, subscriptions, and xeroxes. While others were
filling in time-cards and collecting regular paychecks, I was
"wasting my time" in libraries and second-hand bookshops.
My search frequently drove me to despair, and almost out of
house and home.

Eventually, the patterns became clear. One could
discern the direction, if not the ultimate destination. Now, I
know where I stand on this question which fascinates so
many of us. And if this book confirms your position for or
against astrology, or causes you to think again, or expands
your conceptual horizons, it will have served its purpose.

Acknowledgments

Ronda Clanfield
Russ Germain
Patricia Stewart
Eric Tarkington
Robbie Terris
Lorne Tulk
and especially
Mom and Dad

Graph p. 180 courtesy of Mr. Sam Crawford
Map p. 40 courtesy of Dr. Geoffrey Dean
Diagrams pp. 232, 233, 236, 245, 246, 249, 250, 254, 255
courtesy of Dr. Michel Gauquelin
Astro*carto*graphy Map p. 318 courtesy of
  Mr. Jim Lewis
Diagrams pp. 79, 80 courtesy of Mr. Neil Michelsen
Horoscope p. 220 from *Spica*, Vol. 1 No. 1
All other diagrams are the property of the author

Introduction

This is an honest book! In a field dominated by True
Believers, it is refreshing to see someone take a realistic and
objective look. Malcolm Dean neither inordinately
condemns nor whitewashes modern astrology. He
recognizes its flaws and is critical where it is appropriate. On
the other hand, he also documents a case that is quite
damaging to astrology's critics, showing them to be often
guilty of slipshod science and victims of their own belief
systems, systems which are in several instances made
obsolete by the best of modern science.

In addition, Malcolm Dean shows us the best of modern
astrological research and reveals it to be competent by
scientific standards. And this research is found both to
validate the essential astrological principle, the linkage
between individuals and cosmic cycles, and at the same time
to be inconsistent with some of astrology's most cherished
methods.

What makes this book most interesting is that the author
has been very closely involved with both the people and the
events that he describes. Therefore his reporting of the facts
is especially accurate. This is not a work typical of many
journalists who report hearsay and rumor as if it were hard
fact. Mr. Dean knows whereof he speaks.

Robert Hand

One

Who's There?

Everyone has an opinion about astrology, but few people really know much about it, let alone *why* they hold the particular opinion they do. If you persist in asking people at parties or over the lunch table why they believe or don't believe in astrology, they suddenly become irritable. The topic is often shrugged off with a small joke. Only the ardent adherents and the serious skeptics will offer their opinions. These will be final, often based on one or two incidents, such as a friend who visited an astrologer, an item in the newspapers, a brief fling with a ninety-five-cent pocket horoscope, or the conclusions of a respected colleague. Few and far between are those who have really looked into astrology with an open mind, without a prior bias.

Take this five-minute test. Before you read any further, take a sheet of paper and jot down your opinion of astrology and why you think you hold that opinion. Put the sheet away somewhere until you've reached the end. It will be interesting to see if your viewpoint changes, how and why.

Most of us, when you come down to it, are True Believers. We believe or do not believe in astrology without ever having looked into it. Few of us like to have our cherished beliefs (or disbeliefs) challenged. And since almost everything written about astrology is by True Believers, or True Disbelievers, there are hardly any books which treat astrology as a valid and interesting study in and of itself. For, from the birth of civilization to the birth of the modern Americas, and even today in the birth of a new age, astrology has always been a part of society. Sometimes venerated, sometimes mocked, sometimes officially acknowledged, sometimes cloistered, but always to be found somewhere.

There's a second test I'd like you to perform before we go any further. How would you answer these questions: How many astrologers are there? How much is the astrology business worth, in your country and in the world at large? The reason I ask you these questions is because your opinion of astrology is, to some extent, founded on an impression you have concerning the extent of astrology in our society and its effects on society.

"One thing that has struck us," said Prof. Paul Kurtz, who was editor of *The Humanist* magazine in 1975 when it led a media campaign against astrology, "is that we find a mounting tide of belief. Astrology is part of a larger picture that is developing. I call it a magical world-view."[1]

We will examine the quality of the arguments and statistics offered by the most vocal skeptics of astrology in Chapter Eleven. But the charges are familiar ones. Thousands of innocent citizens are relinquishing their freedom by abandoning reason and embracing cults, gurus, and teachings contrary to those held by most modern academics. In 1970, members of the Science Faculty of the University of Montreal even petitioned the Canadian broadcasting authority, the Canadian Radio-Television Commission (CRTC), to ban astrology from radio and television.[2] Their brief claimed "psychological harm" could result from astrological predictions. Prof. Gilles Beaudet, principal author of the brief, claimed "the people who are setting themselves up as astrologists know it is nonsense. They are nothing but charlatans." Similar calls for the banishment of astrology from the media were issued in England and the United States.

Further down the newspaper item, Prof. Beaudet admitted that the University of Montreal had not undertaken any special research for their brief. They had drawn, he said, "from a number of studies." One of the local Montreal astrologers, John Manolesco, countered with his own accusation: "These people are intellectual frauds who have never stuck their noses inside an astrology text. They would like to replace my show with their own educational shows. If people want to get educated, they can go to school."

Whom are we to believe? Scientists have been complaining for years that they have had no easy access to the public through the media, a complaint which has only partially been answered by a spate of science programs on television and radio. If astrology makes no sense to such scientists — most of whom have never spent time examining the evidence for or against it — might not Manolesco be right? Might not some scientists simply be expressing sour grapes in saying, "See how these crackpots get their own shows on television, and we have a hard time exposing our serious research to the public!" And where were the studies proving that horoscopes could do "psychological harm"? Were the scientists themselves behaving in a scientific or an emotional manner by making these charges?

The truth of the matter is that aside from the obligatory sun-sign column in your local newspapers, astrology has had a much rougher ride from the media than have the questionable aspects of science or academia. Much like the court fool, the astrologer is one of those disenfranchised individuals who is invited to do his piece, then asked to get out of the way quickly and quietly. This was driven home to me during a convention of Canadian astrologers in Toronto in 1974. Local reporters descended on the convention one afternoon, seeking an item for the usually thin weekend newscasts. At one point, I found myself at the center of a circle of microphones, with the reporters anxiously listening for an angle on which to base their news reports. They dutifully remained silent while I commented upon the responsibility of the media to report on positive evidence, and the pejorative and sensational tone that most media items use when covering astrology. I also mentioned that it was the feeling of the more responsible astrologers — humanistic astrologers, as they call themselves — that astrology is not best used as a predictive science, but rather as a counseling tool for personal development and understanding. All these points were recorded on tape while the reporters stood waiting for me to finish speaking. Then the reporter from the largest rock music station in Toronto eagerly jumped in to ask me if I had any predictions for the coming year. Stunned for a moment, I paused, and answered No. The reporters literally groaned, and immediately turned away, in search of someone else who would oblige them with an interview which would fit their image of astrology, *and what they thought the public would want to hear in an item on astrology*.

Back in 1960, it was *Life* magazine's turn to take potshots at astrology.[3] An article by Henry B. Darrach Jr. began:

> On a recent bright, sunny morning a prosperous U.S. astrologer strolled into his walnut-panelled office. Shooting his emerald-studded cuffs, he swung a pair of custom-made brogues aboard an ormolu writing table and smugly smiled at a priceless bodhisattva that inscrutably smiled back at him. Whereupon he flipped the intercom and gave his secretary good morning. "I see by my chart," he announced contentedly, "that Jupiter is entering the Second House. Call my broker."

The image is just too neat. Was Darrach there in person to witness that sunny morn? Is he implying a relationship between the sunny morn and Jupiter entering the second house? Why does the bodhisattva smile "inscrutably"? And is Darrach suggesting some kind of complicity between a Buddhist religious symbol and the astrologer? Would Darrach have been allowed to publish the same paragraph if his astrologer had winked at a statue of the Virgin Mary?

I must confess that during thirteen years of active interest in astrology, during the many interviews I have recorded with astrologers from around the world, and during the major astrological conventions I have covered in Canada, the U.S., and England, no one has ever mentioned such an affluent astrologer to me. And certainly, anyone who telephoned their broker on the basis of Jupiter entering their second house alone would be asking for disappointment.[4]

"Like most of his somewhat peculiar sort," Darrach continued, "the astrologer had good cause to be content with his second house (business ventures and finances). For several years now the U.S., to the horror of many rational people, has been caught up in the biggest callithump since

Belshazzar saw the handwriting on the wall." Darrach claimed that the number of working astrologers in the U.S. had "swelled to more than 5,000" since World War II, and the number of customers had "multiplied from about three million to more than 10 million — perhaps a full million of them hard-core cultists who religiously run their daily lives on celestial schedule." During the period 1946-1960 Darrach reported that astrology columns in newspapers increased from 185 to nearly 1,000 newspapers with a daily circulation of 40 million. Half a dozen popular astrology magazines had a circulation of about 550,000. With his demonstrated ability at *ad hominem* innuendo, Darrach allowed that "about 7,000 truth-seekers, powermongers, bunko artists, lonelyhearts and wallflowers last year enrolled in more than 30 U.S. academies of astrology, where they were presumably edified by their instruction in solar biology, . . . cosmic politics, stellar dietetics and how to give absent treatments."

Many of the facts and criticisms Darrach cited were correct. The best astrologers agreed with him on many points in 1960, and even more would agree today. The question is simply this: If we can show that there is evidence for some of the claims of astrology and that these claims might lead to beneficial discoveries for society, what damage is being done to serious researchers when such blanket innuendo and bias is applied to the subject? Why is it so necessary for critics to mock astrology superciliously as foolishness while in the same breath citing it as a dangerous cult? If the evidence were simple and clear cut, surely a consistent appeal to reason and the facts would suffice?

Apparently not.

Darrach did, however, allow three accurate predictions to creep into his article:

—in 1922 astrologer [Marc Edmund] Jones recorded a prediction that in the fall of 1942, when Neptune entered Libra, an event would occur that would drastically change the course of world history. In the fall of 1942 the first controlled nuclear chain reaction took place in Chicago, and the atomic age began.

—In April 1953, after studying Georgi Malenkov's horoscope, astrologer Carl Payne Tobey predicted that on July 10, 1953, an event of major importance would take place in

the Kremlin. On that day the Russian government announced
the overthrow of the chief of the secret police, Lavrenti Beria,
who was arrested and later liquidated.

—On Dec. 21, 1957, astrologer Willi Bischoff announced
that "Pope Pius XII is under unfavorable aspects. A maximum
disturbance, which gives rise to grave misgivings, occurs in
full power on 10 October, 1958." On Oct. 9, 1958, the Pope
died.

Unconvinced, Darrach noted that astrologers have a
tendency to overlook the predictions that go wrong. True.
But Darrach also overlooked the fact that the two American
astrologers he quoted as giving correct predictions were also
acknowledged authorities in their field. One does not make
judgments on the value of an idea by its less competent
adherents.

"Such is the peculiar status of the ancient art of astrology
in the middle of the 20th Century," Darrach concluded, "a
ghost come back from the dead to haunt the modern mind. Is
the ghost a meaningless chimera or a great world spirit,
a superstitious reversion or a creative influence?" A balanced
point of view, considering his opening paragraph. But his
final sentence confirmed Darrach's position, " 'Astrology is
in dispute all right,' says a scientific authority, 'but not
among scientists.' "

Or should we say, not among True Believers?

By all accounts in the media, astrology was booming in
the late sixties. The Toronto *Globe and Mail* was able to
publish an article entitled "Astrology: An ancient cult on a
billion-dollar binge."[5] All the usual figures were trotted out.

"Say the newsstand and subscription sales of astrological
publications in Toronto [population then about 2.1
million] add up to 200,000 copies, at an average of 50 cents
a copy. But that is only a start. The magazines are full of
advertisements for related occult wares, ranging from crystal
balls at from $10 to $75 to gold-plated 'gambler's amulets'...."

You can almost hear the cash registers ringing.

The Globe then quoted Prof. Donald McRae, University
of Toronto, Department of Astronomy, who succinctly
defined astrology as "a device by which unprincipled
people take advantage of the ignorant to perpetrate a fraud
for monetary gain."

But *The Globe* was not about to take astrology too seriously. The writer concluded that the best example of how to take astrology in one's stride came from a London pub during the end-of-the-world scare in 1962. While the "British astrological faithful" were seeking refuge on a mountain in Lancashire, he reported, "the pub, named The World's End, stayed open."

Cute, but not accurate. The small group who ascended the mount did not represent the British astrological faithful, but a group of occultists. Few Western astrologers, who use different methods and a different zodiac, could see what the fuss was about. The media, having blown the story up out of all proportion, and in ignorance of the details, repeatedly twisted it around for their own ends.

Two years later, it was *Time's* turn.[6] Eschewing the well-heeled astrologer shooting his fancy cufflinks, *Time* opened with a Hollywood epic:

> Equally mindful of his aged bones and exalted station, Berosus the High Priest slowly mounted the stone ramp that spiraled seven times around the great ziggurat and brought him into the presence of the Beings. They blazed and glittered in the night sky above the sleeping city of Babylon far below . . . the signs, he saw, were good . . . . On the morrow, he would tell the king that the time was opportune to move against the Assyrians.

But another cute opening fails to satisfy. Perhaps *Time's* attitude to ancient astrologers was defensible in the 1960s, but as we will see later, the ancients were capable of incredible precision in their calculations, and on some points of astrology, they were probably closer to the truth than modern astrologers are.

Time reported that there were perhaps 10,000 full-time and 175,000 part-time astrologers in the U.S. in the late sixties. Zolar, a former clothing salesman named Bruce King, was distributing more than fifty zodiacal and occult items and publications all over the world, ranging from $200 horoscopes to $25 stock-market forecasts. Astrology columns were published by 1,200 of the 1,750 daily newspapers in the U.S., California's Midpeninsula Free University offered no less than five courses in astrology, including one entitled "Out of the Aquarium and into the Aquarian."

In Japan, popular bookstores were well-stocked with *Koyomi*, a bestseller with a circulation in the millions. These guides are often referred to as "astrology," but are really Japanese oracles, calculated from three repeating cycles of nine, ten, and twelve days. A cycle of ten days combines with the number twelve to produce sixty-day and sixty-year patterns, regardless of celestial happenings. The nine-day cycle is used independently to produce a different cycle of symbols. Thus, 1980 is the year of the monkey, of positive metal, monkey being the ninth of twelve signs, and positive metal being the seventh sign out of ten. At the same time, 1980 is called the "Second-Black," being the second of a nine-color series.

The whole thing is precise as a five-dollar four-function calculator and as cold, lifeless, and groundless as biorhythms, which the Japanese are also quite fond of. Such systems of fortune-telling are quite independent and different from astrology as it is practiced in the West and India. But the Japanese are also fond of their Western-style daily sun-sign forecasts. At least ten Western-style astrology booklets are commonly available throughout the country, some of them translations of Western publications.

In France, things weren't much different. In 1954, 30,000 offices devoted to occult and astrological consultation were reported to be in operation. About $450 million was reportedly spent on magic every year. Paris alone had 3,460 registered offices of astrology which had declared an income of more than $5 million since 1935.

The French psychologist, Michel Gauquelin, whom we will meet later, was moved to comment, "Well over a million dollars per day for this adventure — much more than is spent on scientific research! With the money the French spend in a year for predictions of the future, it is said that over 600 miles of highway could be built."[7]

Before we go any further, it should be pointed out that the total *daily* military expenditures for the world are over $1,000 million dollars. The scientific and academic communities benefit directly and indirectly from these funds, and France is one of the world's major military suppliers, often supplying military dictatorships and other unsavory regimes. For a real killing, horoscopes are not where it's at.

We could go on with these statistics against astrology, but it would be meaningless. Meaningless because these figures are rarely compared to the funds generated by many other common social activities which are ultimately just as frivolous. One could as easily complain about the money wasted in commercial sports, race track betting, jukeboxes, and teenagers' makeup. To quote figures in the millions and billions as evidence of a black tide of superstition rising to engulf society is silly. It is to fail to recognize that there are dozens of "junk" markets which rely as much on statistical responses to advertisements as on any real need. We see advertisements for interesting but ultimately useless gimmicks all the time, and it is well known that advertisers depend on attaining a certain statistical level of impulse response to an ad in order to make a profit. They don't care if people need what they are selling, and they don't want to know if there is even a real need for their product. They simply want to make a profit. Dollars.

Quoting the million-dollar argument against astrology is meaningless because it has nothing to do with real astrology. And I can prove it to you.

Who's really interested in astrology? Let's see.

For all the fuss made about astrology, there have been precious few studies of it by academics and public opinion polls. I have been able to locate only three major European surveys, and two more recent American surveys. Between 1950 and 1956 the German Demoscopic Institute under Prof. Hans Bender (who is still involved in astrological research today) surveyed the attitudes of Germans toward astrology. Here is a summary of the results:[8]

30% over eighteen years of age believe in planetary influences
20% do not think planetary influences are impossible
7% had a personal horoscope cast

In 1963, the French Institute of Public Opinion (IFOP) conducted a survey for *France Soir*.[9] The results are always quoted in slightly different versions, but the most interesting follow:

30% believe in astrology
58% know their sun sign

53% read their daily horoscope in the newspaper
38% would like to have a personal horoscope analysis
43% classify the astrologer as a scholar rather than a charlatan or doctor
37% believe their personality corresponds to their sun-sign description
23% say the predictions of daily horoscopes are remarkably accurate

Of those who know their sun sign, read their daily horoscope at least sometimes, and believe there is an element of truth to astrology:

21% are male
39% are female
38% 20-34 years old
33% 35-49 years old
24% 50-64 years old
20% over 65 years old
34% are professionals, executives
36% tradespeople
46% employees
29% workers
15% agricultural employees
30% retired or no profession
40% live in a city of more than 100,000
21% live in a city of less than 2,000

Only 6% were interested in predictions of the future of the world or other individuals, which is a sad comment on something.

The average astrological client is a young female, between 25 and 35, who has a good income. She wants to know about her love, her money, and her health.

In 1963, Ires Marketing obtained these results on a larger sample:[9a]

50% of men read daily horoscopes, at least sometimes
70% of women read daily horoscopes, at least sometimes
71% are age 18-25
less than 50% are over 55 years of age
44% of farmers read horoscopes, but
60% of all other categories read their horoscope

only 4% of the women had purchased an astrology magazine
only 2% of the men had purchased an astrology magazine
three times more women than men consult astrologers

In 1979, I published an analysis of two American surveys by Francis Fullam of the Survey Research Laboratory at the University of Illinois.[10] The Gallup and Roper surveys Fullam discusses were much more simple than the ones quoted so far. They were basically interested in finding out how many people "believe" in astrology — whatever that means.

When Gallup asked its question in 1975, 22% said they believed in astrology, but 69% said they didn't. The rest probably didn't understand the question. Fullam calculates that 32 million adult Americans believe in astrology. The Roper Organization tried to ascertain how people feel about astrology. They asked a two-phase question: "How do you feel about astrology? Would you say you believe in it strongly, in some aspects, or not at all?" They found that 6% were strongly interested in astrology, 39% believed in some aspects of it, 50% didn't believe in astrology at all, and 5% didn't know how they felt.

If you simply add the figures, it looks like Roper found twice as many people interested in astrology as Gallup did (45% vs. 22%). In other words, if 22% equals 32 million, then 45% would be about 66 million. And if each of these 66 million Americans spend one cent per day on astrology for thirty years . . . . It reminds me of the old horror stories about China's latest secret weapon. The idea was that everybody in China (about one quarter of the world's population) would build a stand about six feet high. When the time came, each citizen was to climb up on his stand, and jump down when the signal was given. The resulting shock wave from millions of Chinese hitting the earth almost simultaneously was supposed to send a shock wave which would tear California loose and flood the west coast of North America.

Fullam believes the difference in the Gallup and Roper findings is due to the emotional weighting of the question. Some people don't feel strongly enough to answer one question a certain way, while the other question gives them an option which they can accept. Fullam calculated a composite profile of the American public's belief in astrology:

	Believe Strongly	Believe Some Aspects	Not At All	Don't Know
Roper	6%	39%	50%	5%

	Yes		No	Don't Know
Gallup	22%		69%	9%

	Believe	Believe Some Aspects	Interested	Don't Believe	Don't Know
Composite (Aprox. %)	5%	15%	25%	50%	5%

So roughly one in three persons believes in astrology. What kind of hay do our academic friends make of it?

In 1966, Jacques Maitre discussed the results of the IFOP poll in the journal *Diogenes*.[11] Maitre thinks many people believe in astrology because they are having difficulties adapting to industrial civilization. Witness the lower percentage of farmers interested in astrology. Farmers are less exposed to the popular media, the bright lights of the local "apple." Established religion has lost ground, Maitre says, while technology has gained. "Between . . . there remains a no man's land all the larger because the new ways of life in turn engender new hazards." And into the vacuum, according to Maitre, rushes astrology and all sorts of occult interests. He admits that calculating a complete horoscope is an arduous task: " . . . even the pure charlatans find this difficult." But for Maitre, astrology has taken precedence over other occult interests because it fits in so well with newspapers. Sun-sign astrology deals with twelve simple categories, so it's easy to find "you." And since astrology is based on astronomical and hence calendrical cycles, it fits in well with the periodical appearances of magazines and newspapers. Astrology permits you to ignore your areas of ignorance, saves you from having to decide why events occur to you, helps you to avoid making decisions, and gives you fast, fast relief from the industrial revolution.

Or, as Maitre quotes Karl Marx: "The daily press . . . which spread their stories in an instant throughout the world, fabricate more myths in a day (and the bourgeois herd accepts and diffuses them) than could have been produced in a whole century in earlier times." Marx obviously subscribed to *Pravda*.

A much more positive attitude toward astrology is exhibited by Edward Tiryakian of Duke University. Tiryakian is one of a small group of sociologists who have finally realized that since so many people are interested in astrology and the occult, sociologists ought to be studying it. He believes that many ideas which we now call "modern" and "scientific" in fact originated from thinkers who were deeply involved in astrology and other so-called "occult sciences."

"Esoteric culture [is] a seed-bed cultural source of change and wide-ranging innovations in art, politics and even science," Tiryakian argues. People involved in this esoteric culture "are major inspirational sources of cultural and social innovations."[12]

That's a long way from a "cult on a billion-dollar binge." Why is Tiryakian's attitude so different from what you usually read about astrology? Tiryakian follows what I call the Occult Conspiracy theory of history. This theory suggests that in each age a small group of thinkers have studied various teachings which were made available to them, and out of this matrix of ideas and symbols, new discoveries have emerged. The discoveries often take form in society as technological innovations, and through this medium, the general population have a chance to absorb the "teachings."

Sound far out? Don't forget that the alphabet and numbers were once occult teachings passed down through the ranks of secret societies. These days, writing is so common we have a hard time understanding that long ago, it had the potential of being a top military and state secret. The advantages enjoyed by an army which used couriers with papyrus dispatches to coordinate military campaigns quickly became apparent to ancient Egypt's neighbors!

Tiryakian says the groups which mediate these ideas, between the occult source and society at large, "tend to operate in socially invisible or secret social organizations." Sometimes they have to, simply to preserve their skins. Long ago, it might have meant burning at the stake to be exposed as a member of such a group. Today, we are much more modern, and in some ways more effective — we just laugh at people with crazy ideas like astrology. And this climate leads to a kind of official version of history which is quite different from what may have occurred. Tiryakian says there is an "undue reliance on records of government and other institutional agencies which have sought to repress these esoteric groups."

Even these days, occult ideas can be found at the root of important modern movements such as communism, psychoanalysis, and modern science.

Karl Marx is often thought to have gained most of his ideas from the philosopher, Hegel. But in 1968, Ernst Benz published his discovery that behind Hegelian and Marxist thought there were many esoteric and mystical sources.[13] One full generation before Marx a German theologian named Octinger predicted that society would enter a Golden Age in which state, private property, and money would disappear in a communism of equality and love.

The Jewish mystical tradition of the Kabbalah is behind a good deal of Freud's psychology.[14] And even some of Freud's theories about sexuality came from a man others called a pseudo-scientist, a mystic, and a buffoon. As Dr. Frank Sulloway shows in his *Freud: Biologist of the Mind*, Freud's concepts about infant sexuality came from a book by Wilhelm Fleiss, entitled, *On the Relations Between the Nose and the Female Sexual Organs*. Fleiss believed as well in a kind of biorhythm of "human periodicity."[15] Freud was also interested in hypnotism, which was introduced by the occultist, Mesmer. Freud's one-time heir apparent, Carl Jung, made extensive studies in alchemy.

"Alchemy and astrology may also have been of importance in the rise of modern medicine," says Tiryakian, "with Paracelsus being another key figure mediating between esoteric culture and modern scientific thought .... Astrology and theosophy were also part of the cultural baggage which was utilized rather than rejected by modernizing scientists such as Kepler and even Newton. The very social organization of modern science, in the form of academies of science, owes much inspiration to Francis Bacon's *New Atlantis* ...."

The fact that some of the top Nazis were involved with astrologers is often used by critics as proof that astrology is negative and dangerous. But Tiryakian looks upon this kind of historical turning-point more positively:

> In the historical unfolding of Western civilization, occult revivals have attended such critical periods of transition from one cultural matrix to another. The waning period of the Roman Empire is a case at hand, with a great flourish of esoteric culture and symbols. The Renaissance/Reformation is another major one shifting cultural paradigms . . . . It is during this period . . . that there was a major occult revival, with esoteric culture becoming a major vehicle of new expressive symbols and belief systems, a source of new value orientations.

Today, critics accuse believers in astrology of being in a "retreat from reason." But Tiryakian says these retreats from reason into the occult are retreats in the sense of *religious retreats*, "a temporary withdrawal for inspirational meditation which provides a restoring of psychic energy to be used in re-entering the everyday life with greater vigor."

And remember all the jokes you've heard about the Age of Aquarius which is supposed to be dawning? A number of articles in the papers have made fun of it. But, concludes Tiryakian, "if we come to perceive the occult revival of today not as an ephermeral fad of mass society, but as an integral component in the formation of a new cultural matrix . . . we will see the Age of Aquarius as a major sociological happening."

And if you think about the changes which came over society and science during the Renaissance, and during the time of Kepler and Newton, and the changes and turmoil of today, it is plain to see that the Age of Aquarius is no joke, even if you don't believe in astrology.

Another sociologist who has studied astrology and the occult extensively is Prof. Marcello Truzzi. Truzzi was one of the more important figures in the current attack on astrology, but we'll get to his story later. He grew up with circus people and learned stage magic, so it was natural for him to develop an interest in the sociology of the occult along with a great tolerance for the beliefs and interests of others. Unlike a lot of people, Truzzi does not automatically equate an interest in unicorns with a desperate need for psychiatric treatment.

"Since things unknown to science today can become known to it tomorrow," says Truzzi, "things occult can, and often have, been incorporated into science."[16]

Truzzi says some occult groups have been right when they believed that their "truths" would eventually be accepted by everyone. "These groups serve important functions for science," Truzzi says. "They often act as data repositories and reminders of the existence of anomalies for the expanding and adapting legitimated sciences."

For instance, Truzzi says that if a Loch Ness monster is actually found to exist, the data gathered by the various groups who have studied Loch Ness for all these years while under fire from debunking critics for their "irrational" beliefs would be of great importance for scientists once the existence of the monster had been demonstrated. "All such groups perform the valuable function of acting as storehouses for incongruous events," Truzzi believes.

But these are the hard-core believers. Most people interested in astrology, Truzzi says, "take a highly irreverent, almost playful attitude. To most of these people, astrology is fun; it is a non-serious, leisure-time element of popular culture, *not* a spirtual searching for Karmic meaning."[17]

Belief in astrology is inevitably compared with other beliefs which cannot be "proven" according to the rigors and extremely limited scope of current scientific techniques. In 1978, Laura Otis, a student at the University of Toronto, surveyed public beliefs and superstitions. Otis's thesis was entitled "A Survey of Extraordinary Beliefs," which is odd considering she found that the majority of the public believes in ESP. (It would rather seem that *dis*belief in the paranormal is extraordinary.) Her results were reported by *The Toronto Star* under the grabby headline, "God is losing ground to occult, survey shows."[18]

The headline was bound to bring out any resident hostility toward the paranormal among religious readers. But it was unjustified, because the only figures quoted did not compare public belief at a previous time with the current beliefs in 1978. In fact, God wasn't doing too badly in

Toronto that year, for while 85% of the 713 persons interviewed believed in ESP, 73% believed in God. With a sample
of that size, God was running neck-and-neck, it would seem.

Otis compared the public belief with the beliefs held by
university professors and students. Only 33% of the
academics believed in ESP, while students were only a little
behind the public, with an 80% acceptance of ESP. The
question is important, because academics continually hold
themselves as authorities on subjects outside their particular
specialities. And, as with any club, members of academic
circles are not always willing to endure the curious glances
which a professed belief in ESP or astrology creates.

In 1973, however, a survey of university faculty members
across the United States showed that professors are favorable
to the existence of ESP by a two-to-one ratio![19] Obviously
the "rising tide of belief" and Freud's "black tide of
occultism" have a healthy foothold in academic circles. But
the breakdown is interesting: While professors in the arts,
humanities, and education (all fields depending upon sensitivity and human interactions based on personal judgments)
were 77% positive toward ESP, natural and social science
professors (whose fields involve more statistics and
empirical experiments, and much less personal sensitivity
and judgment) were only 55% positive. At the bottom of the
list were psychologists, only 34% of whom believe in ESP.

Why? Consider these facts. Professors in the arts and
humanities more often cited personal experiences as the
basis of their belief, the same evidence which most astrologers will give as the basis of their belief in planetary influences. The social scientists turned to books and scientific
articles as the basis of their beliefs, books and articles
already biased by current prevailing attitudes in academic
circles. Natural scientists — physicists, astronomers, and the
like — were found to rely more on hearsay and a priori
reasons, and they were also found to have read very few books
on ESP and similar subjects. An a priori reason is rather
like saying, "Astrology is ridiculous and cannot be true,
therefore it is not true."

In another study, the biases of the most negative group,
the psychologists, were revealed.[20] The psychologists were
given a research study in astrology which reported either

positive or negative results. Those who received the study reporting negative results rated the study as more valid and better designed than those who received the same study with positive results inserted. Younger psychologists accepted the positive results more easily than older ones. And many of the questionnaires used in the study were returned with emotionally charged comments in the margins, indicating that opinions were based more on personal feelings (based in turn on what?) than on any objective, or scientific, studies.

As I said, whether we like it or not, we're all True Believers. Ultimately, each of us has to take the plunge and decide where we stand on a multitude of issues which neither science, scientists, nor our loved ones can really help us with. They're all in the same ocean, on different rafts.

One of the main reasons for the common impression that astrology is a real money-maker is the success of a very few popular books such as Linda Goodman's *Sun Signs*. In my opinion, this and similar books are aimed at an audience which treats astrology more like a gossip column than a serious attempt to describe personality traits. This audience is willing to purchase short and shallow descriptions of behavior, but doesn't want any in-depth analysis of motivations and no details or theory to complicate matters.

Thus, it was with much fanfare that the press around the world reported that Goodman's second book, *Love Signs*, sold for the highest price ever paid for a nonfiction manuscript — a cool $2.25 million. The sale took place in early December, 1978, during a two-day auction to New York publishers. A further $500,000 was paid for hardcover rights, plus $250,000 for British publication rights. The first print run was 150,000 copies.

If even one-tenth of these figures applied to other astrological books, perhaps the critics would be justified in their complaints. As it was, Henry Weingarten, a leading New York astrologer and publisher was moved to comment: "Obviously this perpetuates the false media impression of astrology and may encourage more 'scientific' criticism; other greedy publishers will publish more Sun sign nonsense." But Weingarten felt that there would also be some favorable fall-out. "More people will become astrology-

annual entitled *Your Future.* Now it publishes purse books, *Old Moore's Almanac, Horoscope Yearbook,* and a new quarterly called *Zodiac,* for a total of thirty publications per year. Purse-book publication began in 1962 and now reaches several million per year in the U.S. and Canada alone. Editions in current translation include Portuguese, Italian, Japanese, and Finnish.

But popular astrology publishing is not without its perils. New magazines occasionally enter the field with imitation covers designed to fool the casual buyer. It is reported that *Starcraft,* a now-defunct Canadian sun-sign magazine was first issued in digest format. Eventually, its appearance closely rivaled the large American magazines. As a result, Dell's cover includes a warning: "Beware of imitators! See that Dell is in the upper left-hand corner."

In India, things are not much safer. Dr. B.V. Raman, editor of *The Astrological Magazine,* published since 1895, was forced to take legal action in 1979 to stop publication of a rival magazine which adopted the same logo and title. One of Raman's regular columnists complained that his articles were being translated into one of India's many languages for a pirate astrological magazine, but somehow the pseudonym under which he is usually published was replaced with his real name![23]

Contrary to the French findings discussed earlier, some astrology editors fear they are losing readers in the twenty-to-thirty age group. A composite reader profile, obtained from interviews with several sun-sign magazine editors during the late seventies, shows that about one-third have read their particular magazine for over fifteen years. A further quarter have followed them for over six years. About half of those who read sun-sign magazines have been interested for over fifteen years, and fully three-quarters have attended college. Nearly half are in a comfortable income-bracket (over \$14,000 per annum in 1979), and work at a skilled or professional job. One-third are homemakers or retired. Most readers of sun-sign magazines are middle-aged or older, and nearly half are married. About eighty-five per-cent are female.

But a real clue to the nature of the popular astrology

market is contained in the annual publishing statements required by the U.S. Postal Service. The January, 1980 issue of Dell Horoscope provides the following figures:

Dell Horoscope — Average Circulation, 1979

Total copies printed	334,023
Paid subscriptions	25,914
Store sales	150,966
Returns from agents	143,838

What those figures are saying is that for every sun-sign magazine sold, roughly one other copy is returned by the newsagent, unsold. Junked. It's a fifty-fifty business, which indicates that sun-sign magazines rely heavily on impulse buying. Mrs. Homemaker visits the corner store and decides that it's worth one dollar to read about her future for this month, or she sees a grabby headline on the cover and becomes curious. But she's not a devoted reader. Those number only 26,000 out of a total population of over 250 million North Americans, and this is for the leading popular astrology magazine!

That proportion is repeated once again when we compare the number of persons involved in serious astrology to those who may be interested in popular astrology. Confusion over the actual number of astrologers in the world abounds, especially in anti-astrology articles. The most fantastic figures are presented as proof that the world is losing its soul to irrational beliefs. One such example was provided by Dr. George Steiner, Extraordinary Fellow of Churchill College, Cambridge University and Professor of English and Comparative Literature at the University of Geneva.

"Even Yeats, with his weakness for ectoplasm, table-rapping and theosophy, could not have anticipated the menagerie that has come slouching and mincing out of Twentieth Century unreason," Steiner asserted in one newspaper article.[24]

"There are three times as many registered astrologers in Europe and the United States as there are chemists . . . ."

I wrote to Dr. Steiner, seeking the source for his figures.

"Apologies, but I can't help," Steiner replied. "That

figure came via an article in the *New York Times* about four years ago. But I have heard others cite it."

I feel this is weak scholarship. For starters, there is no such thing as a "registered astrologer." Although there are a few courses which offer degrees in astrology, there are no official registers, and only in a very few local municipalities must an astrologer obtain a license in order to practice. Just as the regular subscribers to *Horoscope* are a tiny proportion of the population of North America, so the proportion of serious astrologers, "registered" or not, represent a tiny fragment of those interested in astrology.

Serious astrology magazines do not contain sun-sign predictions. In fact, they regularly publish editorials roundly condemning the sun-sign magazines for demeaning, as they see it, a highly complex and skilled art through over-simplification and appeal to prurient interests (love, money, all that jazz). Most of the serious magazines are published by organizations in their various countries, so their readership is close to the actual membership of the organizations. In 1978, the world's largest astrology organization, the American Federation of Astrologers, reported a net income of only $76,000. Income before expenses from memberships and its biannual convention (the world's largest astrology event) was $108,000. Divided by the fifteen-dollar-yearly-membership fee and the ten-dollar new-membership enrollment fee, we find a probable average membership around 3,000 to 5,000. The only other surviving national organization in the United States as of 1980 was the National Council for Geocosmic Research, with a membership of about 500.

The second-largest astrology organization on the planet is the Astrological Association, with a membership of about 1,500, mainly in England. From there, it's all downhill. There are roughly eighteen major associations of astrologers in eight European countries.[25] But throughout the world, there are only about forty journals dealing with serious astrology, and their average circulation must be roughly 500 or less. In Canada, there were only three astrological organizations in 1980, the most active one being the British Columbia Astrological Society, with its journal, *The*

Ecliptic, and a membership of about 100. The Toronto Guild of Astrologers has a similar membership, but has never published its own journal. And the Fraternity for Canadian Astrologers has a small and widely scattered membership throughout the world's second largest country, with only a small newsletter for a publication.

The standards of these journals and organizations are a real shocker to newcomers. I remember how I felt during my first visit to a major astrological convention. Grossly over-weight housewives wearing huge multi-colored dresses and sporting ten-year-old perm styles wandered the halls in pursuit of young astrology authors, hanging on their pronouncements regarding past lives and karma. A very serious young man who lectured on a German system of astrology which uses hypothetical planets never seen by any telescope was profoundly shocked when other astrologers did not take his astrological revelation seriously. Discussions of setting professional standards or the scientific evidence for and against astrology were poorly attended in favor of how-to classes offering free example readings for beginners.

Of the major astrological organizations in the world, only two are actively concerned with research, although this interest is more on the part of individual members than of the organization as a whole. In the United States, the National Council for Geocosmic Research, with about 500 members across the country, has managed to gather the best and brightest of the younger astrological generation into a loose network. But the NCGR shows an almost schizophrenic tendency to confuse its scientific orientation with psychic fairs and the less responsible sides of the occult. This ability of various astrologers and astrological groups to invoke the "scientific" aspects of their art while in the same breath they promote or attach themselves to the most dubious features of the occult subculture is a constant source of wonder even for many serious astrologers.

The public is not aware that within the ranks of those who call themselves astrologers, a struggle goes on between those whom we might call the "popularizers" and the serious astrologers. The case of the popular Canadian television show "Beyond Reason" is a good example. The brain-child of Allen Spraggett, "Beyond Reason" uses a three-member panel in soundproof booths, who must guess the identity of the guests based on questions and statements derived from a horoscope, a palm print, and a personal object. The astrologer, the palmist, and the psychic on the panel are isolated from each other and do not hear what the other panelists say, or the answers to questions other than their own. Dubbed by *The Toronto Star* as "Canada's top authority on the occult," Spraggett had left an earlier career as a United Church Minister to write newspaper columns and do daily radio dialogues on the paranormal in Toronto.

During 1976, Spraggett was attempting to clinch a deal with the Canadian Broadcasting Corporation for "Beyond Reason." I was at that time involved in the Toronto Guild of Astrologers, who sponsored a series of lectures by Dr. Zipporah Dobyns, a psychologist and well-known astrologer. Spraggett attended a lecture along with his associate, Dr. Logan Stanfield, now a Calgary psychoanalyst. At one point, Spraggett called me over and outlined his plans for the televison show. I was horrified. I could see all the charges of sensationalism and hucksterism which might be aimed at such a program by the skeptics. For his part, Spraggett felt the show would provide an ongoing demonstration of the ability of astrologers, palmists, and psychics to detect the identity of his guests using only their occult arts.

But Spraggett's next request bowled me over. He requested permission to speak to the assembly and outline his plans for the television series. He was having problems convincing the CBC executives to take his program, and he wished to have those present share in a few moments of concentration aimed specifically at those program executives. In short, he was requesting that the serious astrologers present partake in an act of magic. Naturally, I refused and presented Spraggett with a copy of the Guild's constitution and Code of Ethics, which specifically forbade publicizing or promoting astrological practice in a sensational or undignified manner. Spraggett declined to accept the documents from me, and I pressed them upon Dr. Stanfield instead. As it turned out, Spraggett didn't need help; "Beyond Reason" still enjoys good ratings.

Among most astrology groups, there seems to be an almost suicidal urge to discredit themselves through ill-conceived actions, immature behavior, and a lack of any concerted research efforts. And the picture does not get any better out in the "boonies." Outnumbering those in organizations by at least ten-to-one, there are thousands of amateurs who really know almost nothing about their field, or that there even exist astrological organizations and serious journals to which they might profitably subscribe. Yet they hang their shingle out, place an ad in the *Yellow Pages*, and even willingly appear on the local radio station to discuss astrology.

The average homegrown astrologer, it is not too harsh to say, is a wide-eyed, well-meaning innocent, naively awash in a sea of philosophical, psychological, and astronomical questions which have occupied the sleepless nights of many great thinkers. Unfortunately, the erudition necessary to deal effectively with these questions rarely if ever filters down to the basic texts used by even the serious students and practitioners, let alone the sun-sign publications.

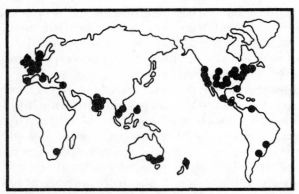

Major astrological organizations are found in only a few areas of the world. Contrary to popular opinion that astrology is a mass movement, total worldwide membership in these organizations is not much more than 10,000.

As for all those "astrological hordes" the critics worry about, forget them. Total worldwide membership in astrological organizations is probably around 10,000. And as for the number of individuals who successfuly earn their living through astrology, the United States leads the sweepstakes with probably 1,000. Most European countries probably have 100 or fewer full-time astrologers. Canada probably has around 50, along with England, Japan, and Argentina. And no one really knows how many astrologers there are in the East, because most of them aren't much more than local fortune-tellers and witch-doctors.

Compare these figures to the attendance at a major league hockey or baseball game. Compare the total gross *budget* of the American Federation of Astrologers ($743,00 in 1978) with the *profits* from only one baseball game! And to put the icing on the cake, look in your local *Yellow Pages* under "Astrologer." In some places you won't find them listed because the telephone company won't allow it, but where they are listed, try phoning a few and ascertaining whether they are full-time or part-time, and how much they earn from astrology. I'm willing to bet that it's a lot less than you earn.

Now let's go back and examine some of those huge figures quoted earlier. How can you get a billion-dollar industry out of a community of perhaps 1.0,000 astrologers? Obviously, someone is making money, but it's not the astrologers. The answer is simple: Astrology is widely viewed as a gimmick, and businessmen see no reason why they shouldn't take advantage of impulse buying when it comes to astrological products.

So if you have any complaints to level against astrology, don't aim them at the serious researchers. They'll probably agree with you. Aim them at the newspapers which regularly print irresponsible attacks on astrology while hypocritically continuing to publish sun-sign columns. Aim them at the amulet-makers, the crystal-ball manufacturers, the computer-horoscope "free offer" distributors, your local grocer who sells sun-sign magazines. Aim your complaints anywhere else except at the extremely tiny group of researchers who are attempting to bring astrology out of the Middle Ages.

Because when it comes to the real thing, who's there? Hardly anyone.

Two

The True Believers

It is the true believer's ability to 'shut his eyes and stop his ears' to facts that do not deserve to be either seen or heard which is the source of his unequaled fortitude and constancy. He cannot be frightened by danger nor disheartened by obstacle nor baffled by contradictions because he denies their existence. Strength of faith, as Bergson pointed out, manifests itself not in moving mountains but in not seeing mountains to move. And it is the certitude of his infallible doctrine that renders the true believer impervious to the uncertainties, surprises and the unpleasant realities of the world around him.

Eric Hoffer, The True Believer,
Copyright 1951 by Eric Hoffer. Reprinted by
permission of Harper & Row Publishers, Inc.

The first thing you must know about astrology is that there is a battle for your mind being waged continually through the media. For some reason, astrology is never mentioned in neutral terms. Even though it's been around for thousands of years, it doesn't have the unquestioned stature of motherhood and apple pie as a part of our cultural heritage.

Right now, you are being presented with facts designed to modify your attitude toward astrology. But at least I'm being honest. I'm telling you why I'm telling you these facts.

Serious astrologers — that tiny community of only 10,000 or so — believe that the media have given them a rough ride. Just before World War II, the American film producer, Will Hays, planned twelve films on astrology, but organizations of scientists protested against the projects. The war made the debate irrelevant.[26]

We've already taken a brief look at the treatment astrology has received from major newspapers and magazines, plus the attitudes of several sociologists toward astrology. Major television networks have approached astrology much more timidly. ABC in New York was gathering interviews for a documentary at one point, but the project was shelved. BBC-TV's "Horizon" program ("Nova" in the U.S.) only in late 1979 resuscitated a planned examination of the evidence for astrology after the show had spent several years gathering dust on the shelf due to internal pressure against it. Researchers on these programs often spend their time interviewing "experts" *about* astrology, giving the serious astrologers short shrift. Where media documentaries avoid treating astrology with outright mockery, they often water it down to the point of apparent absurdity. At the other extreme, of course, there are independent film producers who make a good income every year by filming "documentaries" on Atlantis, ghosts, and goblins, complete with sensational reenactments.

Scientists, too, have voiced concern over the treatment the media have given certain topics. But they find themselves on the other side of the astrological fence and not always for the clearest and best of reasons. Realizing that we are being engulfed by a new industrial revolution, by new discoveries which threaten our very existence if they are not controlled and employed wisely, and by ever-more sophisticated military technologies, scientists see that the public is increasingly left behind — sometimes way behind — the tide of modern discoveries. And where the media report science stories, they are often aired in a sensational or incompetent manner. Science items are not being aired for their intrinsic value; more often they must have some kind of political overtone before news editors will include them. And of course, there's always that cute little "better mouse-trap" item they include by interviewing the local nutty inventor.

This often allows the anchor man to get off air without leaving the impression that things are as bad as they really are. He can grin while observing, "That, too, is reality" or "That's the way it is."

But is it? As part of the battle for your mind, many scientists have come to the conclusion that the reason they are not getting through to the public is that the public is too soft between the ears. As one of astrology's leading critics, astronomer George Abell of UCLA wrote:

> Is belief in astrology not a harmless pastime? I think that depends on the degree to which one relies on it for making important decisions, or how strongly one allows his psychological perception of himself to be frustrated by astrological inconsistencies.
>
> On a larger scale, though, I believe that democracy is jeopardized by irrational and uncritical thought and decision-making by its constituents. Hitler was well aware of the power to be gained by exploiting the irrational beliefs of people. And as Voltaire said, men will cease to commit atrocities when they cease to believe absurdities.[27]

Are Abell's comments justified?

For any given concept, there is always a spectrum of opinion, ranging from "that is true" to "that is not true." Astrology is true. Astrology is not true. And the position of any observer can be placed somewhere along this spectrum, closer to one position than the other. In time, the entire spectrum changes slowly, as those holding one position die or become disinterested. The spectrum might disappear from history entirely, even though the particular issue being disputed remains relevant to the pursuit of knowledge. Or, the spectrum might outmode itself at one point by revealing a new, more fundamental set of issues.

For instance, it is often argued that astrology represents a medieval world-view and is therefore no longer relevant to any among us but historians. Thus, those holding to the negative end of the astrological spectrum would like their side to win by sending the whole issue into a historical oblivion, a mere passing fancy in the history of world culture. This position would be difficult to accept, even if astrology were shown to be completely without foundation, for the simple fact that in practically every ancient culture there were priests and wise men who spent their lives attempting to ascertain the nature of cosmic cycles and what their influence was here on Earth. To ignore the immense role which astrology played throughout man's cultural history is to ignore one of the foundations of civilization itself. We will take a closer look at recent discoveries which emphasize this point later on.

The particular theme which is central to any given spectrum of opinion goes through various characteristic phases. As astrologer and psychologist Dr. Zipporah Dobyns notes:

> The people who are attacking astrology today are going to look very foolish in a matter of a few years, when is it finally accepted. They'll say, "Oh, we knew it all the time." The process of scientific acceptance goes through several very clear and obvious stages. The first stage is to say that something is total nonsense, and only crazy people have anything to do with that. It's an illusion, or a delusion, or a fraud. Then the second stage is to say "Well, there's something there, but it's not really important." The third stage is to say, "It's really important, the people who have it don't know what they're doing with it. We're going to take it over, and take charge of it. But we knew it all the time."[28]

Dobyns points to hypnosis as one example. Once lumped in with all sorts of occult practices, it is now firmly in the hands of the medical establishment. "And that's where astrology will be — in the hands of psychologists, psychiatrists and other researchers within a few years if the astrologers don't clean up their act and come out of the Middle Ages," Dobyns asserts.

Then there is the case of meteorites. Once upon a time it was heresy in scientific circles to believe that stones fall from the sky. It was obvious to everyone but the simple-minded that since objects fall down, stones could not possibly fall from the sky. How could they get up there in the first place? Here the argument was against those who had observed stones falling personally — shepherds, farmers, and others known by sophisticated city-dwellers to be simple-minded. The established scientific community had no time to waste gazing up at the sky, waiting for a stone to fall.

Similarly, one of the leading critics of astrology, Dr. Bart Bok, stated: "At one time I thought seriously of becoming personally involved in statistical tests of astrological predictions, but I abandoned this plan as a waste of time unless someone could first show me that there was some sort of physical foundation for astrology."[29]

Thus, the claim offered by psychologists, psychiatrists, astrologers, and many critical clients — that astrology seems to work and is worth investigating — is brushed aside, unless some evidence for astrology can be offered within the presently accepted model of reality. Not so long ago meteorites, rockets, and travel faster than thirty miles per hour were rejected as nonsense simply because there seemed to be no known way that they could be true at the time. But it is one thing to say, "We do not see how this could be so," and another to say, "This is not only impossible, it's ridiculous." And, as we shall see later, those who hold to this most negative end of the spectrum are quite likely to fall in to not only self-propagandizing, but also in to publicly propagandizing for their cause. This is a dangerous occupation for a scientist, whose emotional biases are supposed to be held at a clinical arm's length, lest they contaminate his evidence.

Buckminster Fuller fingered one aspect of the problem when he described his research method: ". . . I ruled that I must always answer the questions from experience. My answers must not be based on hearsay, beliefs, axioms, or seeming self-evidence." But Fuller also accepts that he can trust the reporting of some other individuals as reliable sources. "For instance, I could include the experimentally derived data of scientists."[30]

Yet, as Fuller notes elsewhere: "Science has found no *up* or *down* directions of Universe, yet scientists are personally so ill-coordinated that they all still personally and sensorially see 'solids' going up or down — as, for instance, they see the Sun 'going down.' "[31]

So at some point, we each must choose who, along the

spectrum of opinion, we are going to trust. Shall we believe the astronomers, who believe that their telescopes have not detected any influences from the planets, even though their telescopes were not built to search for such influences? Or shall we believe psychologists and psychiatrists who have actually learned to do what the astrologers are doing, and report some positive results? Who shall we listen to, and why? In deciding this, we tend to take a position ourselves, and to become at once more or less a True Believer, a card-carrying member of one portion of the opinion spectrum.

Robert Hand, one of the world's most competent astrologers, has often pointed to this problem:

> *Hand:* "An important point which must be understood here is that, for whatever reasons, a person who studies astrology does not find that daily experience contradicts what his astrology shows him. If that were true, there would be no astrology. It is not blind self-delusion which makes people feel that astrology works. There may be aspects of astrology in which self-delusion is involved, to be perfectly honest. But to ascribe the whole thing to self-delusion is, in fact, self-delusion."
>
> *Dean:* "But on what basis can you say that there is something to astrology? Just on the collective opinions of astrologers and their clients?
>
> *Hand:* "Let me rephrase what you said to what it really means . . . the collective opinions of the only people who have really bothered to study it. The opinion of an astronomer who has in fact not ever studied astrology has about as much weight as the opinion of a plumber. Because he thinks that he has studied the physical parameters of the solar system and the galaxy, he assumes that he is totally aware of everything that has to do with that field of study. But how can he be aware of something he hasn't ever bothered to look at? Astrological observations are horribly unrigorous, I admit. But astrology has been going on a long time. The meanings of the signs and houses and planets have been derived over roughly three thousand years of observation, which to be sure, has not been systematic. But the unanimity is quite amazing, considering that we're dealing with something which is so subtle that there ought to be almost no unanimity at all. Of course, in the fine details of astrology there are hundreds of opinions, but in the gross symbolism of astrology

there is remarkably little divergence, considering that we are dealing with something which is allegedly, according to some people, a figment of our imagination."[32]

If you were to ask your local pet scientist if anti-gravity is possible, you'd probably get a mildly negative response. Cars floating through the air have been hanging around science-fiction stories ever since the 1800s, not to mention some ancient scriptures. As an appealing literary device, anti-gravity vehicles have provided countless hours of innocent fun for Trekkies and Star Wars fans. But of course, we all know that the law of gravity cannot be repealed, even though during the last federal election in Canada, the Rhinoceros Party held this as one of the major planks in their platform.

But the process to which Dr. Dobyns referred earlier has already started. Scientific journals have now moved from the "it's impossible" stage to the "there's something there, but it's not very practical" position.

"Physicists have often found themselves explaining to enthusiastic people exactly why it [anti-gravity] is impossible," reported *Science News* in March, 1980, "now perhaps they may have to begin explaining how it is possible."[33]

The suggestion is based on an article by a Parisian scientist who has attempted to formulate a new theory of gravity, a goal which scientists have been chasing for decades. After explaining the necessary mathematical contortions and scientific wand-wavings necessary to allow anti-gravity into the arena of acceptable topics for discussion, *Science News* was quick to point out how it will probably not be very important or meaningful: "Antigravity may thus exist, but it does not seem as if it will ever power a speeding spacecraft. Its effects as calculated . . . lie somewhat beyond the reach of current experiment so nothing can be inferred from their not having been seen. If experiment ever gets good enough to find antigravity, the procedure is more likely to cost money than to make money."

Or, if we turn out the lights and have a good night's sleep, everything will seem fine in the morning. Despite our worst fears, the universe is still safely under control. We need fear no further shocking revelations.

The True Believers 49

A little closer to our astrological home-base, there is the recent case of the British astronomer Fred Hoyle, who has outrageously suggested that comets may possibly cause epidemics here on earth. This has been an astrological tradition since earliest times, when comets were often held to be harbingers of famine and war. So naturally such a suggestion was treated with appropriate contempt and disdain in scientific journals. Hoyle had "flipped his lid," a young astronomer flatly informed me, since the days when his earlier theory of a Steady State universe had been discounted in favor of the current Big Bang theory of the origin of the universe. In Hoyle's Steady State, atoms were thought to appear out of nowhere in the depths of space, which does sound rather magical, when you think of it.

It all began in November, 1976, in the prestigious science journal *Nature*, with an article illuminatingly entitled, "Primitive grain clumps and organic compounds in carbonaceous chondrites."[34] Hoyle had developed a theory with Dr. N.C. Wickramasinghe suggesting that complex organic chemicals might exist in clouds deep in space. Because amino acids, vital chemicals in the life process, had been discovered in meteorites, Hoyle and Wickramasinghe suggested that the "dense interstellar molecular clouds . . . may well be the cradle of life."

A follow-up article made the implications of this theory a little more clear: "Does epidemic disease come from space?" Hoyle and Wickramasinghe asked in *New Scientist*, a kind of *Time* magazine for British scientists.[35]

"Comets have almost invariably been regarded as bad omens," Hoyle noted, arguing that "a cometary impact on the Earth could have led to the start of terrestrial life. Even today, the periodic influx of cometary debris in the form of micrometeorites may be responsible for waves of disease which sweep the planet."

Hoyle suggested that organic chemicals might have formed even before the planets, early in the history of the solar system. At that time, much of the material we today see in the Sun and planets had not condensed, and Hoyle thinks that comets might have stored these organic chemicals. As the planets formed, they would have been bombarded by comets occasionally, and "infected," as it were, by the basic chemical forms necessary for life. Since comets are still orbiting the Sun, sometimes coming near to Earth, Hoyle's theory suggests that epidemics might be the result of new and strange "extraterrestrial biological invasions."

It is commonly believed that epidemics such as influenza are random mutations which are transmitted from person to person. But Hoyle says it is therefore surprising that epidemics usually only last about a year and don't spread throughout the entire population. Early plagues as described by residents of ancient Athens, for example, do not seem to correspond to diseases known today. The first reference to the common cold was in the fifteenth century A.D., and the first clear description of influenza occurred in the seventeenth century A.D. Hoyle thinks that the primary infection from cometary dust when a comet passes near the Earth is the most lethal. Subsequent infections passed from person to person become progressively less virulent, and the epidemic eventually dies out on this "foreign" planet.

The reaction from the scientific community was predictable. Only two weeks later, one astronomer and biologist stated that the Hoyle-Wickramasinghe theory was "full of contradictions and inaccuracies."[36] Doubt was cast on the discovery of organic molecules in outer space, and the idea that a comet might be a safe harbor for primitive life was rejected. The orbit necessary for a comet to survive over long periods of time and then deliver its organic cargo to earth was ridiculed. Flaws and fallacies were found throughout Hoyle's theory.

But Hoyle didn't give up, and neither did other scientists who worked with him. In one project, Hoyle discovered that if the Earth's upper atmosphere was covered by dust from passing comets, the climate would be strongly affected, with sometimes calamitous results.[37] Another project showed that even in the 1890s, scientists knew that influenza did not spread slowly, but seemed to affect an entire population simultaneously.[38] Modern air travel has not affected the spread of influenza, yet the person-to-person contact theory remains solidly entrenched.

"Some will find it hard to believe that Hoyle and Wickramasinghe can possibly believe their own comet theory," said one astronomer.[39] "If it was a political ploy to attract attention to their more serious work on organic space chemistry . . . it may well have backfired." Another researcher concluded that Hoyle's theory "smacks more of science fiction than of science."[40] But he supported its publication, saying "I would hate to think that unorthodox views could be suppressed . . . ." Fred Whipple, Prof. of Astronomy at Harvard, pronounced himself "charmed but not impressed by the picture of life forms developing in 'warm little ponds,' protected in their icy igloos from the cruel cold and near vacuum of open space . . . ."[41]

Sorry, folks, the invasion has been called off. You can go back to sleep now.

Or has it?

None less than the former editor of *New Scientist*, Dr. Bernard Dixon, has come to support Hoyle's position.[42] Dixon writes that the three main objections to Hoyle's theory can be answered "not just plausibly, but devastatingly." The idea that tiny microbes cannot survive space doesn't explain why earth-bound microbes have highly efficient mechanisms to repair damage caused by wavelengths of light which are filtered out by Earth's atmosphere. And why should such defenses have survived millions of years of evolution if they were not needed? Hoyle says they are needed so the microbes can journey safely to Earth. And don't the standard textbooks explain quite satisfactorily how plagues spread? No, says Dixon, pointing to recent medical papers which admit there is still no proper evidence to show how flu viruses survive. The papers suggest that the flu *does not* spread from person to person. Could the flu virus's elaborate mechanisms to penetrate and take over body cells indicate that it is indeed a terrestrial being? Dr. Dixon concludes that the reason we may not want to accept such an extraterrestrial origin is that we would have to acknowledge our inability to deal with plagues and to face a universe full of new microorganisms in deep space.

Most of the papers referred to in this dialogue are part of the usual give-and-take of the scientific paradigm. It's great fun for all concerned, and even more fun to watch if you can crack the jargon used. It's good, clean fun unless a few diehards try to suppress ideas they find too preposterous.

But are we simply dealing with comets and possible germs

from outer space? We are not. Lyall Watson's *Lifetide* points
to some fascinating background items in this area of
research.[43] Watson shows that about two percent of the
meteorites which fall to Earth are called carbonaceous
chondrites because they contain organic matter. About 0.1
percent of all the matter which has fallen on Earth during
its history was organic.

Not much, you say? The total weight of the organic matter
now on the Earth is only 0.0000001 percent of the Earth's
total mass.

"This means," Watson says, "that meteors are coming
from somewhere that is a million times more organic than
the Earth itself."

Perhaps we live on the cosmic equivalent of a desert
island, not the lush garden of Eden amidst a barren and
hostile vacuum, as we have been told. Life may literally be
raining down upon us from the cosmos.

Now observe the attitude these researchers have taken.
They have spoken of dangerous epidemics, and the possibility of infection from space. Remember how carefully the
first lunar astronauts were isolated and decontaminated
upon their return? But if life has been falling to Earth
from distant regions of space for millions of years, surely we
are in some way already accustomed to our cosmic environment? Surely we can now see that life has even managed to
bridge space itself? Perhaps the life and intelligence which
increasing numbers of astronomers admit must exist out
there is not so different from us after all. And perhaps in
some appropriately scientific way (none of that mystic
mumbo-jumbo now!) all life is One.

Scientists are perfectly correct and justified in examining
the evidence as closely as possible. But in their close and
skeptical examinations, they often fail to see trends which
more intuitive minds perceive and project to their inevitable
conclusion. Thus, it is easy for scientists to write papers
condemning ancient and medieval astrologers for their
belief that comets might cause epidemics, but they do so only
because their unspoken consensus view of reality says that
things must be so. These are statements of belief, not scientific knowledge. And they are made, not on the basis of proper
investigations, but upon *pre*judice, judgment before the

fact, and before all the facts are available. If one were to adhere strictly to the scientific method, one would have to admit that we know virtually nothing with certainty. And that's a big admission for just about anyone to make. Even astrologers have a very hard time admitting they don't know very much about astrology!

In any discussion, it is important that people state their bias plainly, and discuss how it affects the kind of evidence they rally to their support and the way in which they treat that evidence. Many problems in modern science are due to the refusal by many scientists to see that one model of reality cannot possibly encompass reality itself.[44] How can that which is contained, contain or describe the container, except from the point of view induced by its experience of containment? The training of a modern scientist does not include any special exercises in observation, objectivity, or a study of the effects of consciousness and attitudes upon experiments. They are picked up haphazardly, often unconsciously. The Eastern monk studies matter by carefully meditating on it; the Western scientist assembles vast and expensive equipment to tear particles apart. Is either way more valid than the other? Or does each way have its own, built-in range of possible experiences and conclusions?

More important than any particular view of reality and nature are the attempts by various individuals to find a harmony between apparently variant models. We find such efforts in books like *The Tao of Physics,* where a Western physicist attempts to demonstrate a basic identity between modern discoveries and ancient Eastern doctrines.[45] Such works are invariably pooh-poohed in the establishment journals — journals devoted exclusively to their own, unstated paradigms. They are rejected as "bad physics," or "bad science." One rarely sees a review which suggests that even if such approaches prove unacceptable, nevertheless they produce interesting thoughts and open up new avenues for investigation. For, and this is my explicit bias, many scientists, and unfortunately among them many leading, established scientists, have for so long practiced the art of testing and retesting evidence with extreme caution that they have become habitual naysayers. Like any group, those most vocal represent a kind of club with its own group view of reality, its own carefully screened evidence to justify that view, and a set of prepared responses to any viewpoint or alternative evidence which does not fit that reality.

This is very much the position in which modern astrologers find themselves. There are all sorts of True Believers running around, shouting hosannas every time an experiment turns up evidence to support their particular points of view. Few individuals in the dialogue have attempted to understand *in depth* why the opposition thinks the way it does, and what implications this might have. Few can honestly say they have attempted to bridge the gap between the paradigms. And thus few can honestly say they have examined *all* the evidence, because the definition of acceptable evidence varies according to the view of reality being entertained at the time.

An interesting example of one observer who momentarily crossed the boundary between the paradigms is found in Ellic Howe's book *Urania's Children*.[46] During World War II, Howe was employed by the Political Warfare Executive. The department's activities, Howe recounts, were divided into "black" and "white" operations. While "white" operations had an openly British origin, such as BBC broadcasts to occupied Europe and leaflets dropped on Germany, the "black" operations were designed to appear as if they originated within the Nazi empire itself. Howe became involved in one such campaign when he was asked to assist in producing fake issues of a Germany astrological periodical. Once the war ended, he forgot about astrology. But in 1958, Howe's curiosity was aroused when he came across references to astrology in the works of Jung. Howe pursued his interest in the same haphazard way most people explore it; he purchased copies of the popular sun-sign magazines and quickly came to the not-very-unusual conclusion that it did not make sense to read a prediction for one-twelfth of the entire population.

In North America and various other countries, astrologers usually insist on having a client present during a reading (humanistic astrologers would make this a prerequisite), but in England it is common to see advertisements offering a written horoscope analysis by mail. The astrologer never meets the client, thus preserving the sanctity of personal privacy to which the British are so passionately attached.

"My astrologer sent me five pages of typescript," Howe recalls. "In the first paragraph he made a strikingly accurate observation about one of my more pronounced personality traits. This was very much to the point and I was impressed. He also offered a number of vague short-term predictions, eg. I would do well financially in June, meet with unexpected obstructions in September and would travel abroad in October. I was never conscious that any particular prediction had been fulfilled, but I did go to France at short notice in November."

Intrigued, Howe decided to step a little more deeply into these strange waters. By chance, a qualified astrologer, Phyllis Naylor, gave a lecture at an organization which Howe often attended, and he soon established a lasting friendship:

> In February 1959, Mrs. Naylor taught me how to cast a horoscope and the elements of interpretation. The mathematical side was easily learned but I could not match Mrs. Naylor's skill in describing the psychological characteristics of the people (whom I knew well) whose horoscopes I produced for her inspection. She had no idea of their identity. By degrees, however, I became fairly adept at this "blind diagnosis" business. Most of my attempts at "prediction" were wide of the mark and I imagine that my few successes in this direction — one or two of them were quite impressive — were achieved more by chance than virtuosity.
>
> I fared better with "prediction in reverse", meaning the identification of past events from a person's horoscope. The late Arthur Gauntlett, a well-known professional astrologer, challenged me to tell him what had happened to him on two specific days of his life. He said that none of his professional colleagues had succeeded in describing the events in question. In order to solve this puzzle I used the German "Hamburg School" system . . . and succeeded far beyond our respective expectations. Some years later Mr. Gauntlett sent me a "testimonial" which read: "On the 30th January 1961 you gave me the answers to my questions, and you were so extraordinarily close to the actual events that, had I not known otherwise, prior knowledge might have been suspected." I could not

guarantee to repeat the performance today, and cannot explain why I succeeded in 1961.[46,47]

So astrology *can* work, even when a skeptical mind is applying the system. Howe has since lost his interest in astrology; although his book is one of the few competent histories of twentieth-century astrology, he now speaks of astrology in the same way one speaks of a distant land, visited long ago and nearly forgotten. He crossed the barrier between paradigms, observed astrology at work before his very eyes, yet continued to write of it with skepticism and mild sarcasm.

It's curious to observe that those who insist there is obviously *nothing* to astrology are those who have never managed to learn to read a horoscope. Negativity toward astrology precludes any conscious suspicion that there might be something to it. But as Howe demonstrates, a general disinterest in or lack of sympathy with astrology does not preclude astrology actually doing what astrologers claim it does. This is no proof of astrology. But it is a strong indication that, whatever the case, there is something to it which ought to be investigated. Obviously, such investigations cannot proceed in an atmosphere of sensational and negative claims against astrology from those devoted to debunking and exposing this "pseudo science."

But the usual attitude to such examples, depending upon your paradigm, is "Wow! It really works!" or "Such nonsense! This could all be explained by chance, or as the fantasy of the astrologer, or as a *post hoc* explanation of some kind, or as a result of information subliminally communicated to the astrologer by the client."

Politics, they say, is the art of the possible. Compromise is always necessary, and the ideal is never (or rarely) achieved. Similarly, no model of reality ever achieves more than an approximation of selected aspects of reality. This indicates that an either/or approach to evidence is not always the most productive or desirable. And it seems that this is the case with astrology.

There are other possibilities. We could suggest that the astrologers are on to something. Perhaps there are, indeed, cosmic influences based on the mutual angles between the planets as seen from our particular location on Earth. But suppose that the astrologers don't really have the correct methods of determining what these influences are? Suppose they merely possess a general outline, an extremely rough model, then what?

Obviously, if the *general idea* of astrology were correct (and we will see that, indeed, the astrological heritage has performed its role; certain facts about our relationship with the cosmos have been buried in the astrological garbage heap, just as Kepler once supposed), but if the *particular methods* and *interpretations* that astrologers use are off the mark, we would have a system which produces the results we see today, results which we will examine in later chapters. The net result would be a system which sometimes produces results, and sometimes does not. If we tested the system by strict statistical methods, employing only the most skeptical researchers possible, we could then confidently publish all sorts of research papers claiming to have "disproved" astrology (as if that would make any difference!). We could follow the example of others and hold press conferences, publish books, and give interviews stating flatly there is "no evidence whatsoever" that astrology works.

And to many this would be comforting indeed. But it's not the real issue. The issue would be that if this were true about astrology — that the general idea is correct but the particulars need a great deal of research and refinement — if this were true, we would be guilty of inadvertently discouraging research into a promising and fruitful new area of scientific discovery. And all this, of course, in the name of science, democracy, motherhood, and apple pie. Not to mention The American (British, Canadian, French, German, fill in the blank) Way.

I suspect the weatherman — everybody's favorite whipping-boy — must feel the same way astrologers do at times. He can tell you his satellite pictures and network of meteorological stations around the globe help him to predict when a storm might move into your area. But he might miss completely at times. The storm might dissipate, or it might veer to the north and leave your area high, dry, and sunny. The storm might arrive late, or not as advertised. The weatherman might predict much rain on the basis of his information, but you might experience only a small sun-shower in your location.

On the face of personal experience, you might say there is as little reason to believe in the efficacy of weather prediction as in astrology. You'd be wrong, of course, because once you begin to study weather-prediction models, you become aware of the complexities with which the weatherman is faced in making his prediction. A wise weatherman couches his language with cautious terms, and explains that one or more scenarios might occur, each with a particular result for your location. His predictions might be specified as valid for the next few hours, days, or months. And the longer the predictions reach into the future, the less accurate we expect them to be. We do not mind the weatherman admitting mistakes now and then, either. He is free to update his predictions on a daily basis, according to the new information which has reached him since his last prediction.

"Ah," I hear you thinking to yourself, "I can see the parallels. It's true that if astrology were true, the data astrologers use must be very complex and difficult to interpret. But weather is physical. We can touch it, and it touches us in a direct fashion."

On a microscopic level, however, we find other mysteries. Those immense patterns of weather are composed of gases and liquids. Gases and liquids, in turn, are composed of molecules and atoms. Atoms, in turn, are composed of various particles which are held together by forces which physicists can observe. And beyond this, lie dragons. We do not know what gravity and electromagnetism are. Effectively, we live in ignorance of the fundamental forces of nature. Like the weathermen, we observe an immense universe without comprehending its fundamental essence. We can only describe certain broad patterns upon which a handful of experts have agreed. Whether we are attempting to close in on the mysteries of subatomic particles, or expanding our attention to include the entire known physical universe, we are ultimately dealing with something as mysterious and dim as a fog. And any scientist who tries to argue to the contrary is arrogant, or silly, or both.

So physical evidence, even though we are used to thinking of it as being "concrete," is ultimately just as nebulous as the alleged influences of the stars. When you think about it, we exist and perceive only within a narrow spectrum. Cats and dogs hear higher sounds than we do. We have to speed whale songs up twice in order to hear them clearly. The floor which supports you appears solid, yet its atoms are almost entirely composed of empty space. You cannot see a bullet travel out of a pistol, yet in that split second, a computer can perform many thousands of operations with total accuracy. Meanwhile, you would have to observe the sky for thousands of years before you could perceive any motion in the vast clouds of stars in other galaxies. Our reality, and even our weather, are highly selective. Upon examination, we find that our normal consciousness is only faced with a certain tiny range of data, out of a vast spectrum. And from this evidence we attempt to predict, that awful word again, the nature of the whole.

Mind you, the astrologers could have smartened up and taken a lesson from the weatherman. They could have couched their predictions in cautious language and spoken of probabilities and alternatives, instead of fated certitudes. Astrologers could have issued periodically revised forecasts and devoted their journals to analyses of their many failures to predict correctly, instead of piling new mistakes upon old ones. They could have applied statistical analyses to their systems years ago, rather than waiting for their most bitter critics to attack them with numbers. Astrologers could have ceased attempting to woo the gullible public with mysterious references to "karma," "fate," and other borrowed mystical concepts which they so obviously don't understand. They could have long ago instituted professional organizations and standards and actively worked to expose and discredit the charlatans who prey on public interest in astrology. They could have refused to publish inconsequential predictions in the *National Enquirer* every year. They could have ceased to publish system upon system, many mutually exclusive, each claiming to be an infallible solution to certain problems in astrology. Astrologers could have admitted long ago that they are not perfect. They could have told the public that their art, like medicine, can only predict the general function and location of an organ, not every intimate detail of its size and individual peculiarities.

Instead, the astrologers have shrieked "eureka" and rushed into the street, thoroughly convinced they possess a new key to the mysteries of the universe. Maybe they do, but they do not comprehend that a wet bath-towel is not proper dress for a scientific conference! And the public already perceives they are half-naked. That's a curious mode of dress, most people think, but perhaps that's the way these starry-eyed natives are accustomed to appearing. Still, it displays an eager naiveté and a social ineptness which is characteristic of astrologers and their societies all over the world. They perceive that their paradigm is a misfit in today's predominant world-view. And their feelings of inferiority lead them to act like the emperor who must claim the finest plumage in the land, even if it is based on premature conclusions provided by a dishonest tailor.

Not only do astrologers and their critics disagree on the kinds of evidence permissible to support the astrological model, they also disagree on the need for some explanation of how astrological influences might work. Astronomers justifiably complain when astrologers offer various kinds of magnetic, gravitational, and radiational models to explain the effects they observe in horoscopes, because the astronomers and astrophysicists know about such things. The kind of influence which astrology requires would have to behave in a very peculiar fashion, unlike anything known in classical physics. For instance, it is not related to the distance of a planet from Earth, or its size. Tiny Pluto, located millions of miles distant at the edge of the solar system, is held by astrologers to be just as powerful as giant Jupiter, which contains a great deal of the solar system's planetary mass. Similarly, Mercury appears to the untrained eye just like a tiny dot on the face of the Sun when it crosses in between the Sun and the Earth. Yet its effects in horoscopes are held to be distinct from its massive, fiery neighbor, even when it is on the far side of the Sun. Even the tiny asteroids, many smaller than Manhattan Island, are used by some astrologers with success in horoscopes. Furthermore, astrologers can relate the positions of planets today with the positions at your birth to describe current conditions (transits), as if both positions were real and concrete. Astrologers even use systems where planetary motions are slowed down like a special effect in the movies, so that every day after birth equals one year of daily experience. From this artificially slowed motion (secondary progressions, as they are called) astrologers say they can predict major crisis points in the life. These three sets of positions — the actual ones in the sky today, those current at the birth, and the positions derived by slowing planetary motion down to the rate of one day/year — are frequently used *simultaneously,* thus ignoring normal concepts of time and space. Clearly, the kind of universe perceived through astrological symbols is very different from the one we were taught about in physics class.

But there are cases in the history of science where such impossible tales came true, after all. Stones falling from the sky (meteorites) is one example. Similarly, only the most naive and ill-informed astrologers today insist that their art is perfect and true in its entirety. Most would be profoundly relieved if some critic would demonstrate to them a mechanism whereby their art could operate.

The discovery of a mechanism whereby astrology might work is not out of the question. Things once held to be impossible are occurring all the time. Critics of astrology have often argued that the gravity of the planets is so weak that they could not possibly have any effect on individuals here on Earth. Lee Ratzan, a mathematician at the New Jersey Medical School in 1975, calculated the gravitational effects on a newborn child of the doctor present at birth and the planets.[48] He concluded that the Moon exerts the greatest gravitational force, then Jupiter, then the doctor at 0.5 meters distance, then Saturn, Venus, the doctor again at 1 meter, and then Mars. The gravitational effects are so mild that they don't even move one cell the length of its diameter. Ratzan concluded that astrologers ought to calculate the configuration of the personnel in the delivery room, rather than celestial configurations. And for extreme accuracy, he urged that astrologers also take into account the magnetic field from the overhead light!

"But then under what sign would the individual be born?" he asked. "Clearly either the dollar sign (depending upon the obstetrician) or the 'Oxygen in Use — No Smoking' sign."

But in 1975, a Mexican scientist published a remarkable report which comes very close to describing an astrological origin for cyclones, earthquakes, volcanoes, and sun spots.[49] Angel Calvo Mijangos noted that the Earth and the Moon perform a balancing act as they spin around the Sun. The Moon attempts to spin away from the Earth, but the Earth's gravity holds it back. Similarly, the Sun attracts both the Earth and the Moon, but their orbital motion balances this force. All three bodies are related by common centers of gravity. In the case of the Moon, the balance point is not at the center of the Earth, but some hundreds of miles below the surface. Mijangos believes that phenomena such as earthquakes are the products of "remnant forces" left over during this continual balancing act and tug-of-war between the celestial bodies. In other words, it may not be direct gravity which is behind some phenomena, but the subtle left-overs. Nature does not always respond to absolute values, but sometimes a subtle change in a given value can mean a great deal.

Mijangos suggests that it is not gravity, but the centrifugal forces which oppose gravity, which might be the important factor. At each point on Earth there is a particular remnant force resulting from the balance of forces along each of two lines — the Sun-Earth line and the Moon-Earth line. Each of these pairs can be considered an individual system with a unique balance between gravitation and centrifugal force. When two bodies appear to conjoin from the point of view of a third (conjunction), Mijangos believes there would be no remnant forces. Thus, the relative positions of the celestial bodies become a possible measure of the remnant forces in the cosmic balancing act. In astrology, these angles have been called "aspects," and researchers in other fields have concluded that the angles between planets are important factors in measuring cosmic conditions. Furthermore, as the Earth turns each day, the angle between a given location and these celestial bodies would change, just as we perceive the Sun and Moon rising and setting.

"The remnant of the centrifugal force is more important than that of attraction," says Mijangos, "and it is the force that intervenes decisively in the creation and government of geophysical phenomena such as tides, winds, cyclones,

tornados, earthquakes, and volcanic eruptions, magnetic
and electrical tides, and sun spots. The planets help the
Sun and the Moon to produce geophysical phenomena."

And since it is possible to calculate where the planets will
be, far into the future, Mijangos claims "it is possible to
predict accurately the occurrence of geophysical phenomena
and their intensity on a long-term basis." Even on the Sun,
Mijangos suggests, a similar mechanism may be responsible
for producing sunspots through the remnant centrifugal
forces of the whole solar system.

Such intimate planetary relationships may sound far-
fetched, but even orthodox scientists are discovering close
relationships between the planets. When Apollo astronauts
deposited seismometers, sensitive instruments designed to
detect "moonquakes," on the Moon's surface, it became
possible to study the rate at which such events were occurring on Earth's satellite. It quickly became apparent the
Moon experiences its own version of earthquakes in a
regular, cyclic pattern. The question was raised — is there a
similar pattern in earthquakes? The detection of such
patterns is sometimes akin to finding a distant radio station
with an old radio. There's lots of static and interference.
But two American scientists have managed to detect such a
cycle in earthquakes, and on top of that, they have shown
there is a relationship between earthquakes and moonquakes. Dror Sadeh and Kent Wood report that moonquakes
occur in a 27.2-day cycle.[50] This is the lunar nodical period,
also known as the draconitic month, or the time the Moon
takes to cross the Earth's equator, travel once around its
orbit, and return to the same relative position again. On
Earth there is an earthquake cycle exactly half this period —
a 13.65-day cycle. The American scientists have concluded
that monthly changes in the tidal forces the Earth and Moon
exert on each other explain the main pattern. And, like
Mijangos, they emphasize that it is the directional relationship, rather than the actual distance between the Earth and
the Moon, which is the important factor.

The important point here is that even within known laws
and mechanisms, there remain possibilities to explain how
the planets might affect conditions here on Earth. There is
still some distance between these influences and those which

traditional astrology suggests, but having taken one step on a journey, each subsequent step seems easier. Thus, critics have absolutely no business, even by the rules of their own game — the so-called "scientific method" — in categorically stating that there is no mechanism whereby the planets may affect conditions on Earth. A true and cautious scientist may only state at this point that the evidence which he has chosen to examine up to this point does not show him how planetary influences might operate. To go further than this is to become a True Believer, confirmed in the belief that astrology is not possible.

We all find ourselves playing the role of True Believers, confidently stating that such and such is impossible, and if it were true we'd eat our hat. Yet the daily paradigm we share and feel so confident about is even now outmoded by developments in physics. As Fritjof Capra points out in his illuminating book, *The Tao of Physics,* by the 1920s

> it became clear that even the subatomic particles were nothing like the solid objects envisioned by classical physics. Depending on how we look at them, they appear sometimes as particles, sometimes as waves . . . it was found matter does not exist with certainty at definite pinpointable places but rather shows "tendencies to exist." These tendencies are expressed in quantum theory as probabilities, and the corresponding mathematical quantities take the form of waves. . . . This is why particles can be waves at the same time. They are not "real" three-dimensional waves like sound waves or water waves. They are "probability" waves, abstract mathematical quantities related to the probabilities of finding the particles at particular points in space and at particular times.[51]

Our illusion of daily reality is buoyed along on a sea of quantum probabilities.

To Capra, the language of modern physics is revealing to the Western mind what Eastern mystics have known for thousands of years: The universe is one, all is in flux, the basic nature of "concrete" objects is essentially emptiness. "I believe that the world view implied by modern physics is inconsistent with our present society, which," Capra notes, "certainly does not reflect the harmonious interrelatedness we observe in nature." His solution: "Mystical experience is necessary to understand the deepest nature of things, and science is essential for modern life. What we need, therefore, to cope fully with life is a dynamic balance between mystical intuition and scientific analysis. The survival of our whole civilization may depend on whether we can bring about such a change. It will depend, ultimately, on our ability to adopt some of the *yin* attitudes of Eastern mysticism, to experience the wholeness of nature and the art of living with it in harmony."

You can almost hear the howls of derision which must have escaped from thousands of pimply-faced physics undergraduates when they read that passage. Another California snowflake from Berkeley telling impossible and seductive tales. Just imagine modern science actually supporting ancient mumbo-jumbo.

Yet even the staid and highly conservative *Scientific American* has published articles extending this type of argument. Most of us think of daily reality as something "out there," independent of our state of consciousness. We act as if the world would get along quite well without us, never blinking an eye if we were to disappear without a trace. But consider this subtitle from one article on quantum physics: "The doctrine that the world is made up of objects whose existence is independent of human consciousness turns out to be in conflict with quantum mechanics and with facts established by experiment."[52]

Without batting an eye, in that wonderfully calm and dry manner which academic journals adopt while they are considering questions of literally cosmic importance, physicist Bernard d'Espagnat proceeds to recount the experiments which have led him to conclude that ". . . in some sense all objects constitute an indivisible whole. Perhaps in such a world the concept of an independently existing reality can retain some meaning, but it will be an altered meaning, and one remote from everyday experience. . . . A discovery that discredits a basic assumption long held and seldom questioned, is anything but trivial. It is a welcome illumination."

But the implications of such discoveries on a personal, daily basis still escape the physicists involved in such research. They are rather like a virgin abandoned on purpose by her friends at a party, knowing that sooner or later the dialogue must begin, and who knows where it all will end?

A young student of astronomy once described his reaction to his quantum physics courses by pointing out that at the beginning of the course, various assumptions were given, along with their experimental background. Building on this, the professors proceeded to develop the equations used in quantum mechanics until the theory was complete and up-to-date. "After this," the student commented, "I looked back at those initial assumptions, and I had to wonder about the whole thing."

He had discovered what it is to be a True Believer. Just like the rest of us, just like physicists, we are predisposed to accept or reject some things in life, even before we realize we can make up our own minds. Ellic Howe's experience in successfully reading a horoscope — even though he "officially" doesn't believe in astrology — shows how these annoying little anomalies can sneak through our world view. And you should know that astrologers, too, sometimes look back on the chain of assumptions they have made while reading a horoscope and question what they are doing. This is why astrologers so often say, "We only know that we can do certain things with astrology. We haven't a clue how it works."

Yet here we have the physicists, warning us in plain English that our prevailing paradigm will not be able to deal adequately with the implications of their discoveries. Capra has clearly stated that our ability to deal with the oneness and interrelatedness of everything may be a decisive factor in deciding the (not guaranteed) survival of our civilization.

In later chapters, after we have studied more about basic astrology and how astrologers work, I will outline some of the most spectacular evidence for cosmic influences in human behavior. I think that anyone who approaches the question with a truly open mind will see that even if traditional astrology is not confirmed, at least the general idea behind astrology, and some of its specific points, are well on the way to vindication.

Three

Your Daily Fix

When one thinks that each year there are millions of readers who desperately gobble up what they can of the astrological forecast for the year, when one thinks that they are all hoping and praying for a break they will not get . . . what is an astrologer to say to himself, how is he to regard humanity? . . . Even if one can read the stars like a book, even if he can read palms like a timetable, even if one has fortune on his side, there are still too many traps, too many pitfalls, too many hazards, too many impossible-to-foresee occurrences in life for one ever to be certain of anything.

Henry Miller in
Sydney Omarr's Astrological Guide for 1973
by Sydney Omarr.

What does your horoscope say today? Admit it! You've been seen doing it, just like everyone else! Over lunch, on the way to work or home, relaxing after a meal, just like everyone else, you've turned to the horoscope page, just in case there was something there for *you*.

Though they are often denigrated by skeptics and serious astrologers alike, popular daily horoscopes are a fine place to begin your investigation of astrology — provided you go deep enough. All the basic questions are to be found there, in a microcosm, along with some of the answers.

Gullibility

The first question you ask yourself when reading your horoscope is: Is it right? But what you should really be asking is:
How can I judge? Psychologists and sociologists have long
been interested in this problem, because they so often use
questionnaires in their research. Along with the standard
skeptical attitude of academics, the fact that astrology
appears to make predictions about your character and behavior makes it a juicy target for tests designed to illustrate
how poorly it works.

In 1974, one psychologist gave the same general horoscope interpretation to three groups of students.[53] One group
was informed that the interpretation was true for most
people, while the second group was told the interpretation
was based on the year and month in which they were born.
The third group was told that the interpretation was based
not only on the year and month of their birth, but also on the
exact day of birth. All the students received the same horoscope, hand-written by students who were impersonating
astrologers. But the original text was taken from Linda
Goodman's *Sun Signs*, one of the most popular and widely
read books on astrology. The students had to rate the
accuracy of the horoscope reading they received on a scale of
one to five.

Results: All students in the three groups rated the reading
they received as fairly accurate. But those who were told
that the horoscope was specifically for their day of birth felt
it was more accurate than those who were told it was just for
anyone. You can fool some of the people all of the time, but
the way to do it is to tell them that a horoscope is "just for
them."

"The ultimate problem in astrology is essentially practical," says Dr. Geoffrey Dean, an Australian chemist who
recently published one of the first scientific surveys of
astrological writings.[54] "Are astrological interpretations
true or not?"

Dr. Dean believes that much of astrology's apparent
validity can be explained by the combined gullibility of
both practitioners and clients alike. His vast survey of
astrology, entitled *Recent Advances in Natal Astrology*,

1900-1976, refers to many studies by both astrologers and skeptics who attempted to test popular horoscopes. One typical experiment by Michel Gauquelin involved placing an ad in the popular magazine *Ici-Paris:* "Totally Free! Your Ultra-personal horoscope! A ten-page document — benefit from this unique experience. Send your name, address, date and place of birth. . . ."

Every one of the 500 respondents received the same horoscope, which was in fact an analysis of the chart of Dr. Petiot, a notorious French criminal who murdered dozens of people and dissolved their bodies in lime. Dr. Petiot's horoscope had been generated by a computer program written by one of France's leading astrologers, and it spoke of ". . . instinctive warmth . . . a worthy, right-minded, middle-class citizen . . . altruistic sacrifice. . . ."

Along with the horoscope, there was a questionnaire and reply envelope. Those who accepted the invitation to reply said they found the fake horoscope to be 94% accurate. Another 90% found that their friends and family confirmed the accuracy of the reading. Dr. Petiot was, by that time, unavailable for comment.

For years, psychologists have been exploring the ability of most people to find themselves in descriptions of almost universal validity. In study after study, subjects have rated fake analyses based on astrology, graphology, and other psychological tests as good or excellent. You are more likely to accept an analysis of yourself if you are told it is quite specific to you, if the description is short, and if there is a good degree of mystery involved.

But it doesn't end there! When subjects were given fake readings and then asked to compare them with actual readings obtained by using psychological tests of good standing, the fakes were rated as good as or better than the accepted test. And it didn't matter whether the subjects were judging their own results from the tests, or it was their friends and family, or even strangers who were asked to compare the results. People who have had even a little exposure to sun-sign astrology (and aren't we all contaminated already?) adjust their self-image to conform to the typical descriptions of their sign.

Statements of universal validity — applicable to most

people — such as "you enjoy a certain amount of change and variety in life" and "you are forceful and well-liked by others" tend to be accepted easily as personal descriptions. We're all human, and they touch our common experience of being human.

The results, says Dr. Dean, suggest that an "accurate" reading is based on three factors: "Be as general as possible. Be as mysterious as possible. Demand data that is as accurate as possible." Consequently, Dean is not surprised that most astrologers are convinced that astrology works. "Under these circumstances," he says, "it could hardly do otherwise."

The problem is an ancient one: Know thyself. But how do you describe what you know to other people, in language which everyone understands? Psychologists have been working on this problem for several decades now. Vast statistical tests, some given to tens of thousands of subjects, have permitted some progress toward standardizing the ways some tests detect "personality dimensions." That is to say, it is now known that some psychological tests will perform in specific ways when given to large numbers of people. From this information, scientists have been able to detect personality features which satisfy the stringent criteria of scientific evidence.

The drawback is that people are so complicated, and there are so many theories in psychology, that the personality features which have been detected in this fashion achieve their scientific respectability by being quite one-dimensional. It's quite easy to describe chemical reactions in scientific terms — they almost always occur the same way in identical circumstances. But human beings can vary tremendously, even within tightly knit family groups. So how is it possible to describe a given individual's personality in terms which can be detected using modern statistical and psychological methods?

We usually describe people with trait words, such as "aggressive," "introverted," and so on. The problem is that one person's pie is another's poison. You might enjoy an aggressive person's behavior, while another might find it offensive. You might describe the aggressive person as "outgoing," while someone else might describe him as "intrusive." About one percent of the words in English are, in fact, trait words with meanings which can vary more or less according to their usage, and the time and region in which they are used.

As Dr. Jim Williamsen, a mathematician and founding member of the harmonics school of astrological theory, points out:

> As ordinary individuals engaged in informal conversation, we all feel quite comfortable in using trait words to describe human behavior. Thus, two people who know a third . . . can quite successfully communicate about the third person's honesty. . . . The situation is very different, if, for example, we ask the psychologist to devise a test . . . which will discriminate between honest and dishonest people generally. . . . If we ask two psychologists to define "honesty" in terms of other trait words, we would find important differences, and even apparent or real contradictions.
>
> Things are equally tenuous in dealing with astrologers. If you ask two of them which horoscopic factors indicate honesty or its opposite, you will get two different lists of factors. They may share items in common, but there will be some which will be contested to the death!
>
> What is it about trait words that makes their systematic . . . application so difficult? . . . Psychologists have wrestled with them for years. To my knowledge, most astrologers are not aware that there are deep and serious problems here. They seem to think that trait words are transparent and show their meaning quite clearly. . . . Others think that the psychologists have it all worked out; it only remains to find the astrological correspondences. Still others think that the psychologists are confused; all they need do is look at horoscopes and all will become clear.[55]

If astrologers are not aware of the "deep and serious problems" in horoscopes and personality descriptions, what about the public? Innocently turning to the daily horoscope, almost no one is aware of the can of worms they have uncovered, both within astrology and psychology!

The Astronomy of Your Daily Fix

Some astronomers will no doubt erupt violently at the above subtitle. According to them, there is no basis to planetary influences, and astrology is merely a conglomeration of misunderstandings and misinterpretations of ancient astronomy. Then, too, it is often pointed out that there are only twelve signs of the zodiac for Earth's billions of inhabitants. Not everyone under Leo experienced an "emphasis on creative endeavours, significant changes, relations with children," on May 30, 1980! And even for those daily horoscope columns which include a reading for your birthday, how could one personality profile describe the hordes which accompanied you into life on Earth on your birthday, and every year prior to and subsequent to your year of birth?

Good questions. But before you attempt to arrive at a balanced answer, you should know a few basics about astrology and daily horoscopes. The diagrams which accompany this chapter provide you with a short course in the astronomical basis of astrology. It takes a little work before you understand the three-dimensional picture in your mind, but everybody has to go through it sooner or later. So many fields of interest are closed to us because "experts" tell us that it would be quite difficult to understand for ourselves. Thus, we are often urged to accept the received opinions of the experts and do no investigation for ourselves. Astrology is often one such field, where True Believers and True Non-Believers spend much of their time voicing their firm beliefs in the hope that you will unquestioningly accept them. In other words, don't be discouraged if you can't grasp the astronomy right away. It just takes a little time and effort.

Practically all astrology proceeds from two fundamental astronomical facts: the planets revolve about the Sun in their particular orbits; and the Earth turns on its axis once a day. Take a look at Diagram 1. You are standing on the equator, with one foot in the northern hemisphere and one in the southern. The Sun rises vertically in the east at morning on the first day of spring and fall (Aries and Libra). But as you remember, the Earth is tilted in its orbit. Just like a top, it spins along at an angle. And this makes the Sun appear to be sometimes higher, and sometimes lower in the sky, producing our seasons. So, if you came back to the same spot every day of the year, standing on the equator facing east each morning, you would notice that the Sun is rising now a

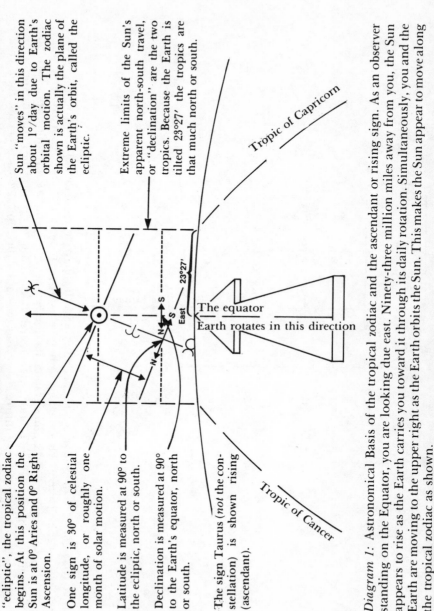

Where the Earth's equator crosses its orbital plane, or "ecliptic", the tropical zodiac begins. At this position the Sun is at 0° Aries and 0° Right Ascension.

One sign is 30° of celestial longitude, or roughly one month of solar motion.

Latitude is measured at 90° to the ecliptic, north or south.

Declination is measured at 90° to the Earth's equator, north or south.

The sign Taurus (*not* the constellation) is shown rising (ascendant).

Sun "moves" in this direction about 1°/day due to Earth's orbital motion. The zodiac shown is actually the plane of the Earth's orbit, called the ecliptic.

Extreme limits of the Sun's apparent north-south travel, or "declination", are the two tropics. Because the Earth is tilted 23°27' the tropics are that much north or south.

Tropic of Capricorn

The equator

Earth rotates in this direction

23°27'

East

Tropic of Cancer

Diagram 1: Astronomical Basis of the tropical zodiac and the ascendant or rising sign. As an observer standing on the Equator, you are looking due east. Ninety-three million miles away from you, the Sun appears to rise as the Earth carries you toward it through its daily rotation. Simultaneously, you and the Earth are moving to the upper right as the Earth orbits the Sun. This makes the Sun appear to move along the tropical zodiac as shown.

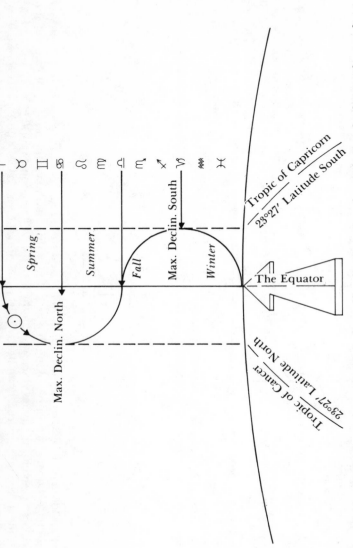

Diagram 2: As the Sun moves through the zodiac, it appears to rise to the north, then to the south, in a regular pattern. This diagram shows the rising position of the Sun for each day of the year. The sine curve traces the Sun's gradual motion between the solstices (Cancer and Capricorn) and the equinoxes (Aries and Libra). This apparent motion is due to the tilt of the Earth in its orbit. By dividing this annual cycle into twelve phases, the signs of the tropical zodiac are established. Your sun-sign is a product of the Earth's orbital position during this yearly cycle. Your rising sign (ascendant) is a product of Earth's daily rotation which makes the Sun appear to rise in the east

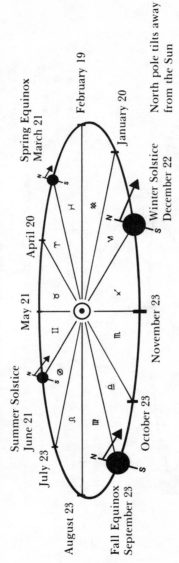

North pole tilts toward the Sun

Summer Solstice
June 21

July 23

May 21

August 23

Fall Equinox
September 23

October 23

November 23

April 20

Spring Equinox
March 21

February 19

January 20

Winter Solstice
December 22

North pole tilts away
from the Sun

Earth is always tilted in the same direction. Here the tilt is at right angles to the Sun, which therefore appears to be above the equator in Aries and Libra.

Diagram 3: Your sun sign, the tropical zodiac, and the seasons are all a result of the Earth's axial tilt. At one point of its orbit, the Earth's north pole tilts toward the Sun. At the opposite point, the south pole is nearest the Sun. In between, the Earth's direction of tilt is at right angles to the Sun, which appears to be over the equator. Seen from Earth, this produces the sinusoidal motion shown in Diagram 2.

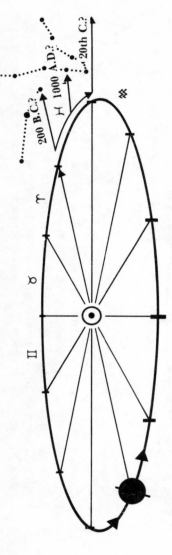

Diagram 4: Precession of the equinoxes creates two kinds of zodiacs. Each year the Earth arrives just short of where the previous spring equinox occurred. This *precession* (opposite of procession) moves the tropical signs backward through the constellations as shown. The definition of each constellation has changed through time, so it is debatable where each begins and ends. The astrological ages, such as the infamous Age of Aquarius, are one way of indicating approximately against which constellational background the current spring equinox occurs. Thus, when any astrological age begins or ends is a matter of opinion, not based on astronomical fact. Zodiacs based on stellar positions or constellations are called sidereal zodiacs, each beginning at a different stellar position. There are two main astrological sidereal zodiacs (one used by Hindu astrologers, another proposed by the Irish astrologer Cyril Fagan), and the unequal constellations marked on astronomical star-charts which in some cases differ significantly from the ancient constellations.

The zodiac is often shown with Aries at the left (east or ascendant). This is called the natural zodiac.

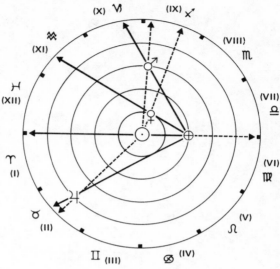

Diagram 5: Once the position of the zodiac is established, the zodiacal longitudes of the planets can be derived. Looking down from above, this simplified diagram (not to scale) shows only Venus, Earth, Mars and Jupiter orbiting the Sun. Positions as seen from Earth, solid arrows, are called "geocentric," those from the Sun are called "heliocentric." Geocentrically, the Sun is shown at the spring equinox as in Diagrams 1 and 4. Heliocentrically the Earth is "in" Libra. Note different positions each coordinate system produces. Geocentrically, Venus is "in" Aquarius, heliocentrically "in" Sagittarius. As distance from Sun increases, difference between positions decreases. For Mercury and Venus, 180° of difference is possible. For distant outer planets, only one or two degrees is possible. The orientation of the zodiac as shown (Aries at ascendant, east, left) is called the "natural" zodiac. The significance of each sign in these positions is often transferred to the house in the same position. Thus, Aries is often used interchangeably with the first house (I), Taurus with the second (II), etc.

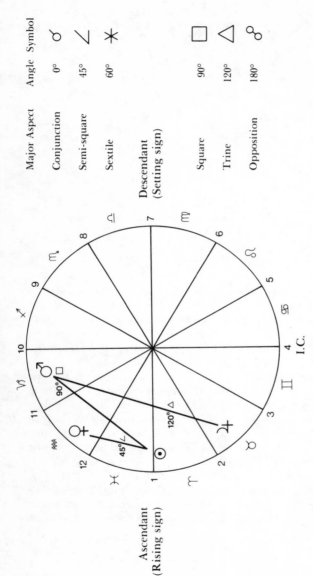

Diagram 6: Final step in deriving a horoscope. The planets are shown "in" the signs determined geocentrically in Diagram 5. Earth is at the center, and the ascendant is Aries. The "cusp" or beginning of each house is numbered, as in "1st cusp" or "cusp of 10th." Aspects are significant angles between planets. Here Sun is 45° or semi-square to Venus, and 90° or square to Mars. Mars is 120° or trine Jupiter. The combination of a planet in a sign, in a house, in significant angle to another planet in its sign, and in its house, produces a wealth of interrelated data for the astrologer to interpret. Major symbolic themes in the chart must be repeated several times before the astrologer can be sure they are dominant factors in his or her analysis.

M.C. or Midheaven

Ascendant
(Rising sign)

Descendant
(Setting sign)

Major Aspect	Angle	Symbol
Conjunction	0°	♂
Semi-square	45°	∠
Sextile	60°	✳
Square	90°	□
Trine	120°	△
Opposition	180°	☍

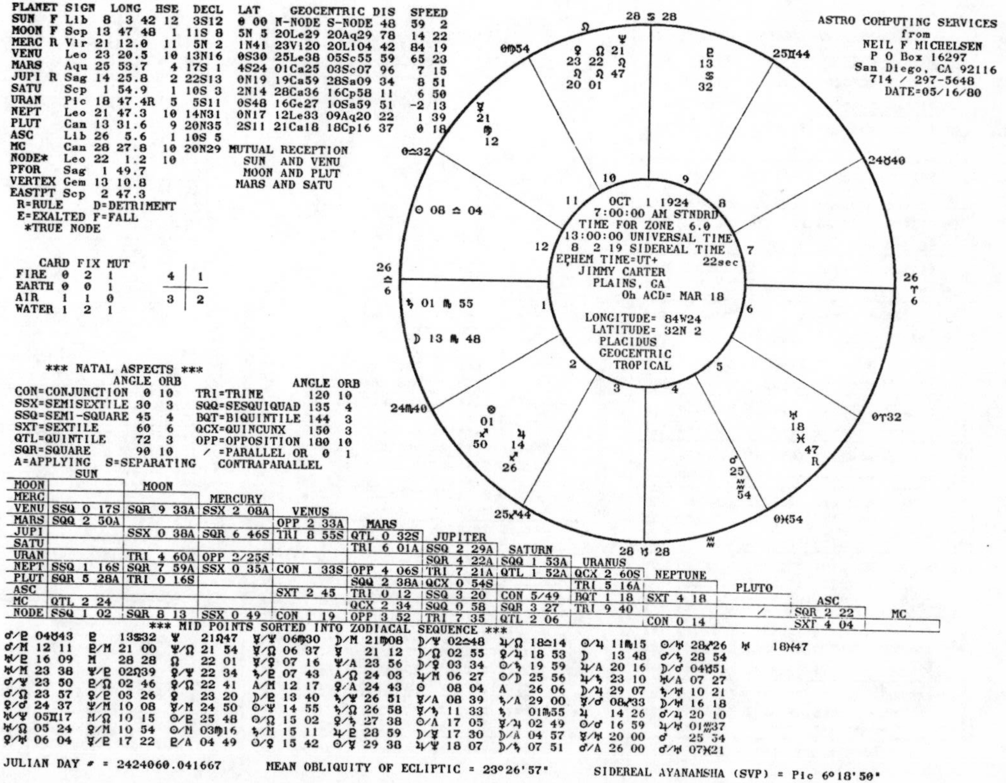

Diagram 7: A complete horoscope as used by contemporary astrologers. The astrologer has provided the time and place of the event, along with the type of zodiac and house system preferred, and what kind of chart should be derived from the data (there are many). The computer calculates and prints the entire page shown in a matter of seconds. Original data is in the center of the horoscope. Each planet and house cusp is annotated with the exact degree of the zodiac. *Top left:* complete positional information on planets and the angles of the chart. *Left of ascendant:* table of elements and quadrants of chart. *Below horoscope:* table of aspects between planets. *Extreme bottom:* table of midpoints between planets. The total array of data shown is considered the bare minimum by contemporary astrologers.

NOVEMBER 1982

LONGITUDE

DAY	SID. TIME	☉	☽	☽ 12 Hour	MEAN ☊	TRUE ☊	☿	♀	♂	♃	♄	♅	♆	♇
	h m s	° ′ ″	° ′ ″	° ′ ″	° ′	° ′	° ′	° ′	° ′	° ′	° ′	° ′	° ′	° ′
1	2 39 49	8♏ 14 2	1♉ 7 44	8♉ 12 21	7♋ 5	5♋ 53R	26♎ 38	7♏ 27	0♑ 2	18♏ 6	26♎ 45	3♐ 18	25♐ 6	27♎ 19
2	2 43 45	9 14 3	15 20 45	22 32 11	7 2	5 44	28 16	8 42	0 46	18 19	26 53	3 21	25 8	27 22
3	2 47 42	10 14 6	29 45 53	7♊ 1 2	6 59	5 37	29 55	9 58	1 31	18 32	27 0	3 24	25 10	27 24
4	2 51 39	11 14 11	14♊ 16 54	21 32 43	6 56	5 32	1♏ 34	11 13	2 16	18 45	27 7	3 28	25 11	27 26
5	2 55 35	12 14 17	28 47 51	6♋ 1 44	6 53	5 30D	3 13	12 28	3 1	18 59	27 14	3 31	25 13	27 29
6	2 59 32	13 14 26	13♋ 13 54	20 23 57	6 50	5 30	4 52	13 43	3 46	19 12	27 21	3 35	25 15	27 31
7	3 3 28	14 14 37	27 31 36	4♌ 36 39	6 46	5 31	6 30	14 59	4 31	19 25	27 28	3 39	25 17	27 33
8	3 7 25	15 14 50	11♌ 38 57	18 38 25	6 43	5 32R	8 8	16 14	5 16	19 38	27 35	3 42	25 19	27 36
9	3 11 21	16 15 5	25 35 1	2♍ 28 42	6 40	5 31	9 47	17 29	6 1	19 51	27 42	3 46	25 20	27 38
10	3 15 18	17 15 22	9♍ 19 28	16 7 19	6 37	5 29	11 24	18 45	6 46	20 5	27 50	3 49	25 22	27 40
11	3 19 14	18 15 41	22 52 14	29 34 10	6 34	5 25	13 2	20 0	7 32	20 18	27 57	3 53	25 24	27 43
12	3 23 11	19 16 2	6♎ 13 5	12♎ 48 56	6 30	5 19	14 39	21 15	8 17	20 31	28 4	3 56	25 26	27 45
13	3 27 8	20 16 25	19 21 39	25 51 11	6 27	5 11	16 16	22 31	9 3	20 44	28 10	4 0	25 28	27 47
14	3 31 4	21 16 50	2♏ 17 27	8♏ 40 25	6 24	5 3	17 53	23 46	9 48	20 58	28 17	4 4	25 30	27 50
15	3 35 1	22 17 16	15 0 3	21 16 22	6 21	4 55	19 30	25 1	10 34	21 11	28 24	4 7	25 32	27 52
16	3 38 57	23 17 45	27 29 24	3♐ 39 14	6 18	4 49	21 6	26 17	11 19	21 24	28 31	4 11	25 34	27 54
17	3 42 54	24 18 14	9♐ 45 59	15 49 50	6 15	4 44	22 42	27 32	12 5	21 37	28 38	4 15	25 36	27 56
18	3 46 50	25 18 45	21 51 3	27 49 53	6 11	4 41	24 17	28 47	12 51	21 51	28 45	4 18	25 38	27 58
19	3 50 47	26 19 18	3♑ 46 42	9♑ 41 53	6 8	4 40D	25 53	0♐ 3	13 36	22 4	28 52	4 22	25 40	28 1
20	3 54 43	27 19 53	15 35 53	21 29 11	6 5	4 40	27 28	1 18	14 22	22 17	28 58	4 26	25 42	28 3
21	3 58 40	28 20 28	27 22 20	3♒ 15 53	6 2	4 42	29 3	2 33	15 8	22 30	29 5	4 29	25 44	28 5
22	4 2 37	29 21 4	9♒ 10 26	15 6 37	5 59	4 44	0♐ 38	3 49	15 54	22 44	29 12	4 33	25 46	28 7
23	4 6 33	0♐ 21 42	21 5 4	27 6 26	5 56	4 45R	2 12	5 4	16 40	22 57	29 18	4 37	25 48	28 9
24	4 10 30	1 22 21	3♓ 11 21	9♓ 20 27	5 52	4 45	3 46	6 20	17 26	23 10	29 25	4 40	25 50	28 11
25	4 14 26	2 23 1	15 34 19	21 53 32	5 49	4 44	5 21	7 35	18 12	23 23	29 31	4 44	25 52	28 13
26	4 18 23	3 23 42	28 18 33	4♈ 49 48	5 46	4 42	6 55	8 50	18 58	23 37	29 38	4 48	25 54	28 16
27	4 22 19	4 24 25	11♈ 27 35	18 12 4	5 43	4 39	8 28	10 6	19 44	23 50	29 44	4 51	25 57	28 18
28	4 26 16	5 25 8	25 3 19	2♉ 1 12	5 40	4 35	10 2	11 21	20 30	24 3	29 51	4 55	25 59	28 20
29	4 30 12	6 25 52	9♉ 5 28	16 15 39	5 36	4 30	11 36	12 36	21 17	24 16	29 57	4 59	26 1	28 22
30	4 34 9	7♐ 26 38	23♉ 31 9	0♊ 51 14	5♋ 33	4♋ 26	13♐ 9	13♐ 52	22♑ 3	24♏ 29	0♏ 4	5♐ 3	26♐ 3	28♎ 24

DECLINATION and LATITUDE

DAY	☉ DECL	☽ DECL	☽ LAT	☽ 12hr DECL	☿ DECL	☿ LAT	♀ DECL	♀ LAT	♂ DECL	♂ LAT	♃ DECL	♃ LAT	♄ DECL	♄ LAT
1	14S15	7N33	4S36	10N10	8S44	1N39	13S 8	0N55	24S51	1S24	16S24	0N51	8S13	2N16
2	14 34	12 41	3 56	15 2	9 24	1 34	13 34	0 54	24 51	1 24	16 28	0 51	8 15	2 16
3	14 53	17 11	2 60	19 4	10 4	1 28	13 59	0 52	24 50	1 24	16 32	0 51	8 18	2 16
4	15 12	20 40	1 52	21 56	10 44	1 23	14 24	0 50	24 50	1 24	16 35	0 51	8 20	2 16
5	15 31	22 50	0 36	23 21	11 23	1 17	14 49	0 48	24 49	1 24	16 39	0 51	8 23	2 16
6	15 49	23 28	0N42	23 12	12 2	1 11	15 14	0 46	24 47	1 24	16 43	0 51	8 25	2 16
7	16 7	22 33	1 56	21 33	12 40	1 4	15 38	0 44	24 46	1 24	16 46	0 51	8 28	2 16
8	16 25	20 13	3 2	18 35	13 18	0 58	16 2	0 42	24 44	1 24	16 50	0 51	8 30	2 16
9	16 42	16 42	3 57	14 37	13 56	0 51	16 25	0 40	24 42	1 24	16 54	0 51	8 33	2 16
10	16 59	12 21	4 37	9 57	14 33	0 45	16 48	0 37	24 40	1 24	16 57	0 51	8 35	2 16
11	17 16	7 26	5 1	4 52	15 9	0 38	17 11	0 35	24 37	1 24	17 1	0 50	8 37	2 16
12	17 33	2 15	5 8	0S22	15 44	0 31	17 33	0 33	24 35	1 24	17 4	0 50	8 40	2 16
13	17 49	2S56	4 59	5 30	16 19	0 25	17 54	0 31	24 31	1 24	17 8	0 50	8 42	2 16
14	18 5	7 58	4 35	10 20	16 53	0 18	18 15	0 29	24 28	1 24	17 11	0 50	8 45	2 16
15	18 21	12 34	3 57	14 39	17 26	0 11	18 36	0 26	24 24	1 23	17 15	0 50	8 47	2 16
16	18 36	16 33	3 8	18 15	17 58	0 4	18 56	0 24	24 21	1 23	17 18	0 50	8 49	2 17
17	18 51	19 45	2 11	21 1	18 29	0S 2	19 15	0 22	24 16	1 23	17 22	0 50	8 52	2 17
18	19 6	22 2	1 9	22 48	18 60	0 9	19 35	0 19	24 12	1 23	17 25	0 50	8 54	2 17
19	19 20	23 18	0 5	23 33	19 29	0 16	19 53	0 17	24 7	1 23	17 29	0 50	8 56	2 17
20	19 34	23 31	0S59	23 13	19 58	0 22	20 11	0 15	24 2	1 23	17 32	0 50	8 59	2 17
21	19 48	22 40	2 1	21 52	20 25	0 29	20 28	0 12	23 57	1 23	17 36	0 50	9 1	2 17
22	20 1	20 49	2 58	19 33	20 52	0 35	20 45	0 10	23 52	1 22	17 39	0 50	9 3	2 17
23	20 14	18 3	3 47	16 22	21 17	0 42	21 1	0 8	23 46	1 22	17 42	0 50	9 5	2 17
24	20 26	14 29	4 27	12 26	21 42	0 48	21 17	0 5	23 40	1 22	17 46	0 50	9 7	2 17
25	20 38	10 14	4 56	7 54	22 5	0 54	21 32	0 3	23 33	1 22	17 49	0 50	9 10	2 17
26	20 50	5 26	5 11	2 53	22 27	1 0	21 46	0 0	23 27	1 22	17 52	0 50	9 12	2 18
27	21 2	0 15	5 11	2N26	22 48	1 6	21 60	0S 2	23 20	1 21	17 56	0 50	9 14	2 18
28	21 12	5N 8	4 54	7 49	23 8	1 12	22 13	0 4	23 13	1 21	17 59	0 50	9 16	2 18
29	21 23	10 26	4 18	12 58	23 27	1 17	22 25	0 7	23 6	1 21	18 2	0 50	9 18	2 18
30	21S33	15N20	3S26	17N30	23S45	1S23	22S37	0S 9	22S58	1S21	18S 5	0N50	9S20	2N18

DAY	♅ DECL	♅ LAT	♆ DECL	♆ LAT	♇ DECL	♇ LAT
1	20S42	0N 7	22S 7	1N14	4N54	16N29
5	20 45	0 7	22 8	1 14	4 51	16 30
9	20 47	0 7	22 8	1 13	4 48	16 30
13	20 50	0 7	22 9	1 13	4 46	16 31
17	20 53	0 7	22 9	1 13	4 44	16 32
21	20 56	0 7	22 9	1 13	4 42	16 33
25	20 58	0 7	22 10	1 13	4 40	16 34
29	21S 1	0N 7	22S10	1N13	4N38	16N35

☽ PHENOMENA			
d	h	m	
1	12	57	○
8	6	39	☾
15	15	11	●
23	20	6	☽
d	h	° ′	
5	22	23N29	
12	10	0	
19	17	23S34	
27	1	0	
5	11	0	
11	22	5N 8	
19	2	0	
26	12	5S13	

VOID OF COURSE ☽ LAST ASPT		☽ INGRESS		
2	5am 3	3	♊	0am23
4	9pm49	5	♋	2am 0
7	0am 3	7	♌	4am11
9	3am43	9	♍	7am41
11	4am32	11	♎	12pm46
13	4pm28	13	♏	7pm43
15	9pm23	16	♐	4am52
18	1pm59	18	♑	4pm22
21	3am57	21	♒	5am21
23	4pm30	23	♓	5pm43
25	7pm31	26	♈	3am 8
28	8am20	28	♉	8am32
30	1am37	30	♊	10am36

d	h	
4	10	PERIGEE
20	11	APOGEE

DAILY ASPECTARIAN

Day	Aspect	Time
1 M	☿☌♄	2am 2
	☽#♄	3 0
	☽⚻♅	3 42
	☽#☿	6 8
	☿☌♇	10 23
	☽☍♀	11 46
	☉☍☽	12pm57
	☽⚼♆	3 14
2 T	☽⚼♂	0am45
	☽#♀	4 49
	☽☍♃	5 3
	☉#☽	10 18
	☽⚻♆	4pm21
	☽⚻♄	7 22
	☽⚻♇	8 4
	☽#♃	8 11
	☉∠♆	10 11
3 W	☽⚻☿	0am17
	☿ ♏	1 11
	☽⚻♂	3 4
	♀∠♆	3 56
	☽☍♅	6 3
	☽⚻♀	6pm27
	☉⚻☽	6 36
	☽⚼♄	8 24
	☽⚼♇	8 57
4	☽#♅	0am31
Th	☉☌♀	2 2
	☽⚼☿	4 15
	☽⚻♃	7 30
	☽#♆	2pm16
	☽☍♆	6 4
	☿⚹♂	6 43
	☉⚼☽	9 14
	☽△♄	9 23
	☽⚼♀	9 36
	☽△♇	9 49
5 F	☿⚺♅	4am42
	☽☍♂	7 23
	☽⚻♅	7 52
	☽△☿	8 16
	☽⚼♃	8 43
	♂⚺♅	5pm40
6 S	☉△☽	0am 1
	☽△♀	0 54
	☽⚼♅	8 59
	☽△♃	10 8
	♂∠♃	7pm30
	☽⚻♆	8 12
	☽□♄	11 54
7 Su	☽□♇	0am 3
	☽#♆	5 27
	☽△♅	10 24
	☽⚻♂	12pm30
	☽□☿	5 13
	☽#♅	7 14
	☽⚼♆	9 42
8 M	♄☌♇	1am51
	☉□☽	6 39
	☽□♀	8 38
	☽□♃	1pm56
	☽⚼♂	3 39
	☽#♃	10 53
	☽△♆	11 35
9 T	☉#☽	0am 2
	☽#♀	1 34
	☽⚹♇	3 34
	☽⚹♄	3 43
	☿∠♆	8 27
	☽#☿	1pm48
	☽□♅	2 18
	☽△♂	7 16
	☉∥♃	8 19
10 W	☽⚹☿	4am10
	☽∠♇	5 55
	☽∠♄	6 13
	♀∥♃	11 25
	☉⚹☽	3pm 8
	☽⚹♀	6 22
	☽#♄	6 24
	☽⚹♃	7 20
11 Th	☽□♆	4am32
	♀☌♃	6 57
	☽⚺♇	8 41
	☽⚺♄	9 9
	☽∠☿	10 31
	☽∥♇	12pm22
	☽⚹♅	7 52
	☉∠☽	8 11
	☽∠♃	10 43
12 F	☽∠♀	0am 4
	☉∥♀	0 16
	☽□♂	3 59
	☽⚺☿	5pm32
	☽∠♅	11 20
13 S	☉⚺☽	1am49
	☽⚺♃	2 35
	☽⚺♀	6 26
	☽#♇	8 28
	☽⚹♆	11 19
	☉☌♃	2pm16
	☽☌♇	3 38
	☽☌♄	4 28
14 Su	☽⚺♅	3am20
	☽∥♄	3 54
	☽⚹♂	3pm 2
	☿∥♃	3 8
	☽∠♆	3 29
15 M	☽☌☿	9am51
	♀⚺♆	10 0
	☽☌♃	12pm 2
	☉☌☽	3 11
	☽⚺♆	8 16
	☽☌♀	9 23
	☽∠♂	9 35
16 T	☽⚺♇	0am48
	☽⚺♄	2 1
	♀∠♂	2 4
	☽∥♃	5 15
	☿☌♃	5 20
	☽∥☿	11 45
	☽☌♅	1pm 6
	☉∥☽	3 53
	☽∥♀	7 19
17 W	☽⚺♂	4am53
	☽∠♇	6 17
	☽∠♄	7 43
	♀⚺♇	7 57
	☽∥♅	10 38
	♀⚺♄	11pm 7
	☽⚺♃	11 59
18 Th	☽∥♆	1am32
	☽⚺☿	5 38
	☉⚺☽	7 35
	☽☌♆	7 36
	☉⚺♆	7 50
	☉∥☿	9 22
	☽⚹♇	12pm20
	☽⚹♄	1 59
	☽⚺♀	3 34
	☿⚺♆	8 41
	♀ ♐	11 8
19 F	☽⚺♅	1am12
	☽∠♃	6 47
	☽∠☿	4pm38
	☉∠☽	4 44
	☉☌☿	6 24
	☽☌♂	9 20
20 S	☽∠♀	1am36
	☽∠♅	7 51
	☿⚺♇	9 2
	☽⚹♃	1pm54
	☉⚺♇	5 39
	☽⚺♆	8 39
21 Su	☿⚺♄	0am37
	☽□♇	1 27
	☉⚹☽	2 10
	☽□♄	3 31
	☽⚹☿	3 57
	☿∥♀	7 39
	☽∥♆	7 59
	☽⚹♀	11 49
	☿ ♐	2pm29
	☽⚹♅	2 34
	☉⚺♄	7 51
	☽∥♅	10 44
	☽∥☿	11 36
22 M	☽∥♀	0am35
	☽∠♆	3 14
	☿∥♅	4 18
	☉∥☽	7 12
	☿∠♂	8 7
	☽⚺♂	2pm31
	♀☌♅	2 47
	☉ ♐	3 24
	♀∥♅	5 7
23 T	☽∥♃	2am32
	☽□♃	3 48
	☽⚹♆	9 26
	☽△♇	2pm 7
	☽△♄	4 30
	☉□☽	8 6
	☽∠♂	10 25
24 W	☽□☿	1am19
	☽□♅	2 55
	☽□♀	6 50
	☿☌♅	2pm19
	☽⚼♇	7 29
	☽⚼♄	9 59
25 Th	☿∥♆	5am 2
	☽⚹♂	5 20
	☽∥♄	5 33
	☽△♃	3pm 4
	☽□♆	7 31
	☽⚻♇	11 54
26 F	☽⚻♄	2am28
	☽#♇	3 41
	☉△☽	10 10
	☽△♅	12pm 0
	☽△☿	5 54
	☽⚼♃	7 11
	☉∥♅	7 39
	☽△♀	9 17
27 S	♂∠♅	4am 5
	☉☌♅	11 24
	☽⚼♅	2pm59
	☉⚼☽	3 15
	☽□♂	3 35
	♀∥♆	6 21
	☽∥♇	9 48
	☽⚻♃	10 13
	☽⚼☿	11 58
28 Su	☽△♆	1am36
	☽⚼♀	2 28
	☿∥♂	4 3
	☽☍♇	5 40
	☽☍♄	8 20
	☉∠♂	8 50
	☽⚻♅	5pm 1
	☽#♄	6 43
	☉⚻☽	7 10
29 M	☽⚼♆	3am15
	☽⚻☿	4 44
	☽⚻♀	6 28
	♄ ♏	10 33
	♀∠♇	2pm50
	☽△♂	9 27
30 T	☽☍♃	1am37
	☿∠♇	3 43
	☽⚻♆	4 10
	☽⚺♇	8 0
	☽⚻♄	10 47
	☽#♃	3pm48
	☽☍♅	6 53
	☽⚼♂	11 16

Diagram 8: Page from a modern astrological ephemeris, or table of planetary positions. The entire page has been generated by a computer and printed directly by a plotter. *Top:* Daily positions of the planets in the zodiac. The daily sun-sign is shown in column three, under the sun symbol. The next four columns give lunar data, followed by the planets in order of distance from the Sun. *Middle:* Daily positions of the same planets are here given in two

little more north, now a little more south, than it did on the previous day.

Meanwhile, the Earth would have been continuing in its yearly orbit about the Sun. One way to mark out this progress is to observe which stars are near the Sun as the seasons proceed. The Sun appears to travel against the background of the stars, but really it is the Earth which is moving around the Sun, now viewing it from one position, then another. So, while the Sun is busy rising to the north or south of the equator, it is also slipping through the star fields and rising each day against a slightly different celestial background. In Diagram 1, the Sun is shown at 0° Aries. But two weeks later, it would be halfway through Aries, and you can see how far north it would be by tracing the line of the zodiac. This movement forms an annual cycle which is shown in Diagram 2, and it is this cycle which most astrologers use to establish their zodiac.

So now you have some idea of how the zodiac is derived. It's not simply an arbitrary division of the year into twelve sections. The zodiac most, but not all, astrologers use is based on the same cycle as our seasons. And since there is growing evidence that there are some seasonal influences on people, we might stop to observe at this point that in a general way, the astrologers' zodiac might have originated from the suspicion that the seasons affect many natural cycles in plants, animals, and humans.

By examining Diagram 3, you can gain an overview of the Earth orbiting the Sun. The pie-shaped signs of the zodiac mark out the seasonal (technical term: "tropical") sign against which the Sun would be observed during that portion of the year. Going around the circle, you'll find the approximate dates at which the Sun enters each sign of the tropical zodiac. Notice also, that the Earth is always tilted

---

other co-ordinates, showing their distance above or below the zodiac or the equator. Box at far right contains phases of the Moon and other phenomena. *Bottom:* Daily aspectarian gives times at which planets form aspects (important angles) to each other, plus times of ingresses (when a planet enters a new sign).

The page shown is for the period of minimum arc between all planets in the solar system (see Chapter Twelve for discussion). From *The American Ephemeris* by Neil F. Michelsen.

in the same direction. Thus, at one point, the Sun appears to be over the northern hemisphere, while at the opposite point it is over the southern hemisphere. At the two mid-points, it is over the equator. We call these mid-points the equinoxes, which means that day and night are equal because the Sun is rising over the equator. At the other points in its orbit, the Sun is nearer one pole of the Earth, and we speak of solstices, during which the difference between night and day are maximum. In the summer, we are used to long days and short nights because the Sun is more northerly in the sky. In the winter, the Sun is more southerly, and hence the horizon tends to cut our daylight down somewhat. In the northern hemisphere we therefore expect shorter days and longer nights in the winter. In the southern hemisphere, the opposite is the case. Thus, your birthday approximately locates the Earth in its orbit around the Sun and tells us which sign you are born under.

But not quite. The Earth's orbit is not exactly 365 days. It is more like 365.24219 days. And since you're not expected to go to work for .24 of a shift or to spend .24 of a night sleeping, we save up these fractional days until we have a leap year, at which point another day is added to the calendar to catch up with the astronomy of the Earth's orbit. The problem arises that if you are born near the end of one sign and the beginning of another (technical term: "cusp"), you have to determine the *precise* position of the Sun in the tropical zodiac (actually, the precise position of the Earth in its orbit around the Sun) in order to find out which sign the Sun was "in" at your birth. If you simply go by those tables of dates which are published in horoscope columns, you could be off by one sign! Similarly, the time when the Sun appears to leave one sign and enter the next is measured in seconds, not hours or days. So on some days, the Sun rises "in" one sign and "enters" the next sign by nightfall. In order to provide an average reading easily accessible by casual readers, astrologers have simply listed the dates closest to those on which the Sun changes sign, although some lists differ from each other.

Of course, most of us are not born "on the cusp," so we don't worry about these things. We blithely plunge ahead and seek free answers to our daily concerns which we then casually accept or reject. After all, it doesn't cost you a penny just to look. But you can see that the astronomy of sun-sign columns is probably just as confused as the problems we encountered with trait words in character descriptions.

It sometimes comes as a shock to potential believers to find out that in astrology even the zodiac is a point of hot dispute. Often skeptics and disbelievers argue that the signs used by astrologers are not the real signs in the sky. This argument is essentially silly, but it's not obviously silly. To understand more, turn to Diagram 4. Remember that when we began this series of diagrams, the stellar background against which the Sun appears to move was used as a kind of graph. The ancient people must have used prominent stars and the patterns they form (constellations) as markers much like explorers use prominent peaks to mark their way. Thus, thousands of years ago on the first day of spring, it was possible to state that the Sun rose near a certain group of stars. Eventually, however, it became clear that the position of the Sun on the first day of spring (vernal equinox) was actually moving backwards in the sky. At first, ancient astronomers were not sure whether this was a regular motion or simply a temporary deviation from a norm. Once it became known that the equinoxes were moving backward (precessing), astrologers had a new cycle to work with. They could use the zodiac to chart the motion of the Earth around the Sun, as we have already seen, but the new cycle observed in the precession of the equinoxes suggested that there was a kind of larger zodiacal background, that of the constellations.

Hence, the astrological ages. The infamous Age of Aquarius is marked out by the backwards entrance of the vernal equinox (0° Aries) into the constellation of Aquarius. The problem is, no one knows precisely where the constellation is. The ancients sometimes left imprecise records, and even in modern times, the boundaries between constellations have been changed around. The motion of precession is actually a product of changes in the Earth's axial tilt, and the nature and extent of this cycle are still not completely understood. The cycle lasts about 25,000 years, but many sources differ on its precise length. There are almost as many dates given for the beginning of the Age of Aquarius as there are astrological authorities, ranging from the eighteenth to the twenty-sixth centuries.[56]

To make matters worse, not only the length of the constellational zodiac cycle is in dispute, but astrologers also disagree regarding where the constellational zodiac begins. Indian astrologers use a different zodiac from most Western astrologers. Some astrologers use a zodiac called the sidereal zodiac, reputed to be a reclaimed zodiac used in ancient Egypt, and discovered by Cyril Fagan, an Irish astrologer. A very few others use unequal signs in their zodiac, some signs having more or less than 30°.

So why is it silly to use the objection of the many zodiacs against astrology? For several reasons. First of all, when skeptics use this argument, they are really appealing to your prior belief in signs. They say that the signs are not really where astrologers say they are, and thus they are using the signs in their argument as if they were concrete entities. Tropical zodiac astrologers simply respond that they are studying the zodiac based on the annual cycle of the Sun and that seasonal effects are well-known to scientists. More are being discovered all the time. Thus, to tropical astrologers, those who use the constellations have been simply left behind, as it were. And besides, the signs are not concrete entities, in terms of stellar groupings, sources of radiation, or anything else. Tropical astrologers see them more as phases of cycles, used to chart the positions of the planets. Thus, skeptics who say that the astrological signs are not the same as constellations are often quite ignorant of the proper astronomical basis of the tropical zodiac. You can't argue that an ancient zodiac should correspond with the astronomical constellations as found on modern star-charts and determined by modern astronomers.

Secondly, when astrologers from the different schools of thought speak of the signs of the zodiac, they are not necessarily speaking of the *same* signs. The constellations which form the sidereal zodiac are not described in the same way as the signs of the tropical zodiac. The sign of Cancer means something essentially different to each school of astrology. So the debate between astrologers becomes which zodiac works best rather than which one is "right."

It might come as another small shock to discover that to the best astrologers, the zodiac is not that important, anyway. The more technically competent an astrologer is, the less he or she relies on the zodiac, and the more emphasis is placed on other factors in the horoscope. Finally, it is not completely clear what the function of the zodiac is in astrology. Later on, we will see that there is very strong evidence that the general outline of astrology is correct, but the evidence for signs is weak or even negative. Yet while astrologers often interpret charts based only on signs, they find themselves blind using charts with everything else *except* the signs. I will only suggest at this point that the true function of the zodiac in astrology has not been recognized by either astrologers, skeptics, or scientific investigators. But this is a fascinating topic which must wait for another volume.

Once the zodiac has been established, we now have a way of measuring the motions of the other planets in relation to Earth. Diagram 5 shows only the Sun, Mercury, Venus, Earth, and Jupiter, but it gives you an idea how this is done. The Sun is shown on the first day of spring, 0° Aries. The solid lines show the positions in the zodiac at which the planets are seen. Since these positions are judged from the point of view of the Earth, they are called geocentric. The dotted lines are the positions at which the planets would be observed from the point of view of the Sun. These positions are sometimes used in more technically advanced forms of astrology and are called heliocentric. You can imagine that as the planets go around their fairly circular orbits, they draw a path through the zodiac. These positions at your birth, are the ones that astrologers refer to when studying your horoscope.

In fact, the word "horoscope" is a misnomer. Originally, it meant the sign which is rising in the east. Remember that in the first diagram, the Sun was shown rising in Aries, but just below this, a portion of the sign, Taurus, was visible on the horizon. A person born at this moment would be said to have Sun in Aries, with a Taurus ascendant. The Greek astrologers called the rising or ascendant sign *horoskopos*, but in modern times the word has been taken to mean an entire chart of planetary positions erected for a specific time and place. The rising sign is a product of the Earth's daily rotation on its axis, so that each sign rises once during each day. Beyond simple sun-sign astrology, many astrologers enjoy studying personality portraits developed from the simple combination of the sun sign, the moon sign, and the ascendant. These are usually held to be the most prominent factors in a chart.

But the ascendant does more than this. It effectively places the zodiac, along with the planets in their signs, in a particular orientation. This orientation (the word refers to the east and displays an astrological heritage in language) is one of the most important in astrology, since it relates the planets to the horizon. You see the Sun in the morning when it rises over your horizon. And similarly, all the planets, even though we can't see them during the day, rise, climb to a "high noon" position, set in the west, and pass more or less beneath us. In traditional astrology this angle between the local horizon and the position of a planet is measured roughly by placing the planet in a "house."

The origin of the astrological houses is shrouded in mystery, but later on we will examine some evidence that, just as leading modern astrologers have suspected, it is this angle between a planet and the horizon which is one of the most important facets of astrology. There are twelve signs, and in most astrological systems, there are also twelve houses. Obviously, it is tempting to find a parallel between the two sets of symbols, so astrologers have often related the first sign, Aries, with the first house. The roman numerals in Diagram 5 indicate the number of each house. The purpose of a house in astrology is to provide a general sphere of mundane experience. Thus, your Sun in Aries might show you to be outgoing, sometimes impulsive, and often eager to open new fields of experience. But placed within a particular house, the specific way in which this facet of your personality might best be developed is revealed.

Those seeking profundity in the traditional meanings given to the houses as shown above are likely to be disappointed at first. The range and depth of house symbolism can be quite profound, matching anything in current psychological or psychiatric theory, but the mundane descriptions found in popular astrology books are as facile

Planets appear to rise in the east and set in the west due to Earth's daily rotation.

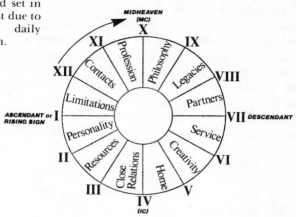

Diagram: The astrological houses each have a traditional sphere of influence in the life of the "native" or subject. As the Earth turns each day, the planets rise and set as shown. Thus, the moment of birth determines the houses in which the planets will be found on that particular day. This permits the astrologer to describe mundane conditions in which the planetary and zodiacal symbols are likely to manifest. (After Marc Edmund Jones, *How to Learn Astrology*.)

and mundane as they at first appear to be. Basically, the purpose of this tool in astrology is to link the more psychological indications derived from the signs with worldly spheres of activity. You see this aspect of astrology at work when your daily horoscope refers, for example, to "professional superiors" (sixth house), "family affairs dominate your personal scenario" (fourth house), "accent on fulfillment of hopes and desires" (ninth house).

But we are getting ahead of ourselves. Obviously, if the rising sign or ascendant depends upon the Earth's daily rotation, even a few minutes can make a difference in a horoscope. So how do the daily horoscope columns attempt to create a general reading for everyone born in one sun sign? By two methods. First, an "average" reading is created by using one specific degree of each sign. Remember that the Sun moves through the zodiac each day (really, the Earth is orbiting the Sun). Since there are 360° in a circle and 365 days in the year (or to be precise, 365.24219), the Sun moves roughly 1° per day. You were born, therefore, in one of 30° of your particular sun sign. Sun-sign columnists usually attempt to make readings not for any specific degree of the signs, but for the entire 30° segment of the zodiac. And when a degree is necessary, they usually choose either 0° of the sign, or 15°, which is the middle of the sign. Thus, "your personal horoscope" not only averages you in with every other native of your sun sign, but also treats your particular degree of your sun sign according to an arbitrary average degree. Sydney Omarr, for example, tends to use the 0° (first degree of a sign) standard in his popular sun-sign column.

The second method sun-sign astrologers use in their attempt to describe the general daily conditions of your life is called "solar houses." The diagrams we've studied have shown how an individual horoscope is erected — one for a specific individual born at a specific time and place. But the sun-sign astrologer attempts to be equally specific — in a general sort of way, that is — for everyone born within a given sign. This is accomplished by arbitrarily creating a set of houses which have nothing to do with the local horizon. In its most crude form, the "solar houses" are created simply by counting your sun sign as the first house and proceeding around the zodiac, each sign being the next house in this sense. Since a house has to begin somewhere and end somewhere in the zodiac, here is where the arbitrary 0° or 15° standard comes in. To take the 0° standard for the first three signs, we would obtain general horoscopes which look like the ones opposite.

You have already seen how the planets move around the Sun, and how this motion can be described as passage through the zodiac. The positions of the planets at your birth are called "natal positions," while those which are happening while you are reading this paragraph are called "transits." A planet "transits" a sign in your horoscope. And since the solar houses allow the sun-sign astrologer to equate each sign with a house, these planetary transits can be related to one particular sphere of your life.

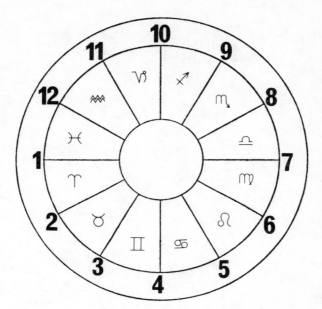

Solar houses for Aries ♈

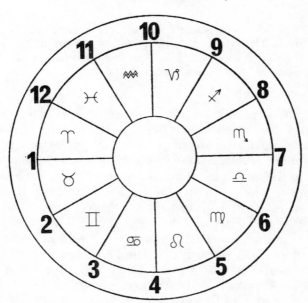

Solar houses for Taurus ♉

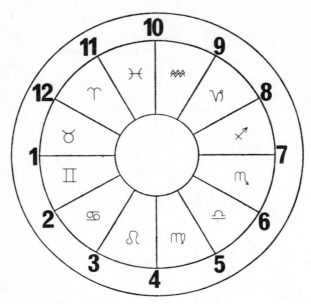

Solar houses for Gemini Ⅱ

Diagram: The solar houses for the first three signs. Here the first house ("self," "personality") is equated with your sun sign, and the other signs are then used as arbitrary houses.

The final pieces of our astrological puzzle are the meanings attributed to the planets. We have seen that the signs may have originated in seasonal cycles observed by ancient man, and that these symbols may have been adapted later into the astrological houses. But how was ancient man to ascertain the influence of a particular planet? Often, explanations are as simplistic as "Mars is red, and so is blood. Blood is only visible when shed, so Mars relates to violence and aggression." Such an explanation ignores the power of symbols when applied and employed by interested minds over thousands of years. The symbolical and mythological background of the planets is rich and vast, so we cannot explore it in this discussion. Let me simply note that in Chapter Ten we will examine the first evidence that, whatever astrologers are doing (or think they are doing) with horoscopes, they have, in fact, been able to detect planetary influences which modern statistical methods have independently confirmed. The problem is, however, that it is still not clear if *all* the planets have an astrological influence, and it is now clear that at least in the case of Jupiter, the astrologers have the wrong idea about its influence.

Nevertheless, the received tradition, dating back many centuries, suggests that a rudimentary list of planetary influences goes something like this:

☉	Sun	= Purpose
☽	Moon	= Feeling
☿	Mercury	= Mentality
♀	Venus	= Acquisitiveness
♂	Mars	= Initiative
♃	Jupiter	= Enthusiasm
♄	Saturn	= Sensitiveness
♅	Uranus	= Independence
♆	Neptune	= Obligation
♇	Pluto	= Obsession

(after Marc Edmund Jones, *How to Learn Astrology*)

Like all traditions, the meanings of the planets cannot be easily reduced to simple key-words or one specific interpretation. Students must usually spend some time discussing them with others and reading various texts before their particular characters are distinguished. But you already know some of this symbolism. It has come down to us in such words as jovial, saturnine, martial, lunatic, mercurial.

Thus, equipped with the basics of astrology in a highly condensed and simplified form, we can turn to Sydney Omarr.

The Secrets of Sydney Omarr

Sidney Kimmelman was born on August 5, 1926, in Phila-delphia, when Libra was rising. Apparently, no one pre-dicted that he would become the world's most widely syndicated astrologer, and one of traditional astrology's most effective spokesmen in the American media.[57] Yet, at an early age he displayed a great interest in magic and numerology. At the age of fifteen, he wrote a book on numerology and sold an article on the "number signs" of movie stars to a popular magazine. It was for numerological reasons that he changed his name to Sydney Omarr. His first trade name was Kimball the Great, but when he saw Victor Mature's performance in *Shanghai Gesture*, where Mature played a charming scoundrel named Omar, Sidney Kimmelman was left behind forever.

Omarr's adolescent interests were stage magic and boxing. His predictions came to the attention of the *Philadelphia Record*, whose sports editor decided to take up his challenge and publish them. Omarr's prediction of Joe Louis's defeat in 1947 gained a great deal of attention, and step by step, astrology and numerology became the central interests of his life. Soon after his eighteenth birthday, Omarr enlisted in the U.S. Army. Placed in the air force branch, he continued to write astrology articles in his spare time. In a search for a typewriter he could use, he came to the attention of the editor of an army sports newspaper, and once again he found himself predicting the outcome of boxing matches. His fame spread, and eventually a weekly advice show entitled "Sydney Omarr's Almanac" was broadcast once a week on Armed Forces Radio Service. Omarr became the first and only (publicly at least) U.S. serviceman assigned to full-time duty as an astrologer!

Now firmly set in his direction, Omarr returned to public life at twenty-one and began publishing a trade journal for astrologers. This might seem to be a logical thing to do, considering that most fields have their trade journals and considering the amount of money most people think astrologers earn. Surely there would be a good advertising and subscription base for such a journal? But in fact, even today, astrological magazines regularly appear and die out due to lack of subscriptions. Few astrologers subscribe to any astrological journals, and often the one or at most two they support are not the best. To most observers, Omarr was cruising for a financial bruising. His *Astrology News,* however, did succeed in setting off a small furor between two sun-sign magazines, and he became more widely known in the astrological community. About the same time, he published his *Thought Dial,* a kind of numerological oracle which sets forth his ideas on numbers and their predictive powers. *Astrology News* suffered the fate of most astrological journals and went the way of the buffalo. The *Thought Dial* is still in print these days.

Omarr also decided to extend his education with the aid of the G.I. Bill, and his experience in writing boxing and astrology columns suggested that journalism might be a good field to study. One of his teachers assisted him in obtaining a job as a CBS newscaster in Hollywood and besides his newsroom duties, a successful practice for celebrities was soon underway.

In more recent years, Omarr's daily horoscope column has become the most widely syndicated astrology feature in the world. His annual booklets of predictions for each sign, his *Thought Dial,* and other publications have supported a comfortable life in one of Los Angeles's more expensive districts. His regular appearances on the Merv Griffin Show have provided millions of viewers with the only exposure they may ever have to a serious and articulate astrologer. On one of these shows, he correctly guessed the identity of two mystery guests, based on their horoscopes. The producers decided to pull the segment because no one would believe it was possible. Omarr eventually won the battle, and the mystery guest idea became a hit. But his accuracy was too much for some guests. It is reported that Dr. Joyce Brothers, the popular psychologist, went into a "seething rage" and suggested that Omarr had prior knowledge of her presence on the show. Later, on the Johnny Carson show, a portion of the program was bleeped because of the U.S. National Association of Broadcasters. Omarr had been discussing some serious research which appears to support astrology, but the NAB guidelines do not permit discussing astrology in such a way as to support its credibility.[58] A similar incident occurred on the Mike Douglas Show. Omarr reports that his appearance was not broadcast because he was too accurate![59]

Since astrology has been my beat for several years, I decided to meet Omarr personally. From Toronto, I obtained permission for an interview and moved on to Los Angeles as part of an interview tour. But by the time I arrived, Omarr had changed his mind. "Really," he said, "I don't see people."

Discouraged, I noted that Mercury had been retrograde (traveling backward) for a few days now, and this sort of thing was to be expected. The trade language did the trick. I was granted permission to visit, but my bus arrived late. Once past the security staff of his luxurious apartment building overlooking the Pacific, I entered his crowded living room. The walls were adorned with photographs and pictures, and Omarr sat at his desk, facing the door. It was the night of an early primary, and Ronald Regan and John Anderson were holding forth from a large television near the kitchen. Now confined to his chair, Omarr motioned me to sit beside him. The television stayed on, turned up. No sensitive, intimate interview was going to emerge from this meeting. Friends were arriving every few minutes, and we discussed politics, the recent attack on astrology, and his sun-sign column, amid constant interruptions.

Omarr recalled his prediction that Pierre Trudeau would return to power in Canada after the brief Conservative government of Joe Clark in 1979. But he allowed that Clark was too young to be counted out forever.

Like most sun-sign astrologers, he defended popular astrology as an introduction to serious astrology. "If it weren't for popular horoscopes," he insisted, "there would be no astrology in America today. It was the sun-sign columns which supported many serious astrologers, so that they could get on with their work."

More friends arrived. The noise level increased. We briefly discussed the leading astrologers of his day and mine. Then it was time to go. He turned to his admirers, and I said good-bye. I was left wondering why someone who had so ably defended popular astrology in the media didn't want to talk about serious astrology with someone who knows the field. I recalled it was equally difficult to initiate a serious conversation with another Los Angeles superstar — Timothy Leary. *Sic transit gloria Hollywood.*

Omarr did reveal that insofar as his daily column requires it, he uses the 0° standard in his calculations. He also mixes numerology with his astrology. Yet of all the sun-sign columns I have studied and which are commonly available, his is most worthy of study. First of all, he writes systematically. This means that his astrology is based on method, not pure intuition. And it means that if his system works, it will work regularly. Some sun-sign columnists simply write what comes into their heads, without realizing that there have been several attempts by leading astrologers to find a successful formula for such daily predictions. Other columns by brand-name astrologers are neither systematic nor written by the persons in whose name they are published. As part of general cutbacks, newspapers are firing the few good astrology columnists in favor of cheaper syndications written by astrologers no one knows and who may simply be incompetents. There have even been cases of newspapers which simply repeated the same predictions year in, year out!

Armed with the foregoing basics in astrology, it is possible to decode some of Sydney Omarr's columns, so as to illustrate how your daily horoscope is derived. Taking once again only the first three signs, I have extracted arbitrarily selected sun-sign forecasts for May 18, 1980. The solar houses are shown for Aries, Taurus, and Gemini, this time with the positions of the planets on that particular day.

As the planets move through the zodiac, they form angles with the Earth as the vertex. For centuries, astrologers have agreed that the angles shown in the table on Diagram 6 are significant indicators of "energy-flows" between planets. Areas of tension and ease in personality and interconnections between the various spheres of life are held to be shown by planets "in aspect" to each other. Below the solar-house charts for Aries, Taurus, and Gemini, I have marked the significant aspects which the Moon formed on May 18, 1980,

Diagrams: Solar horoscopes for May 18, 1980 for
Aries, Taurus, and Gemini.

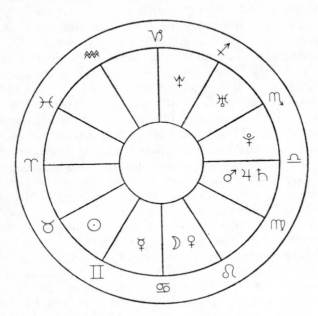

Aries: **Home repairs, domestic duties command
attention. Aim for security, check values, perceive
needs of one close to you.**

read directly from an astrological ephemeris, or table of
planetary positions.* Translated into English, the symbols
show that the Moon formed 45° angles, or semi-squares,
with Mercury, Mars, and Jupiter at different times that day.
This is held to be a stressful and dynamic aspect. The Moon
also formed a sextile with Saturn, a positive, beneficial
aspect. Another beneficial aspect, the trine, was formed
between the Sun and Uranus. Two stressful, difficult
aspects, the quincunx and the square, were formed with
Neptune and Pluto respectively. As you can see, these
aspects not only link planets to one another, but also connect

*Pronounced eff-'emm-er-is. The plural is ephemerides, pro-
nounced eff-emm-'air-id-ees.

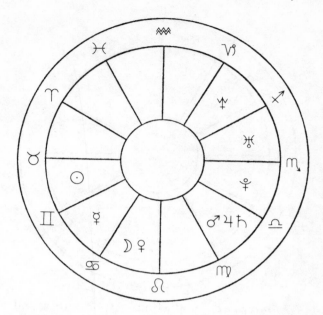

Taurus: Define meanings, steer away from wishful thinking, be positive, sift through ideas, eschew unsolicited advice from anxious relatives.

Lunar aspects: $☽∠☿, ♂, ♃ ; \ast ♄ ; △ ♅ ; ⊼ ♆ ; □ ♇$

solar houses, thus providing further material for the astrologer to work with.

For Aries, note the emphasis on home and domestic concerns. The Moon spends only about two and a half days in each sign, so its passage of Cancer, the fourth solar house for Aries, prompts this message. Conjoining Venus in that house, in a sign and house which underline the domestic theme, the message is taken even further, to the point of concern for security. The stressful aspect with Neptune in the ninth house, where values and philosophy are found, shows that there is a possibility of misunderstanding. And the square aspect with Pluto in the seventh house, which traditionally signifies partnerships, adds up to the recommendation to "perceive needs of one close to you."

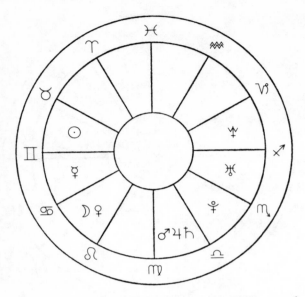

Gemini: Love, production, responsibility and money dominate this powerplay for you. Check assets, be aware of values, get valid appraisal and accounting.

For Taurus on that day, the Moon and Venus fell not in the domestic fourth house, but in the communicative third. The same aspect between the Moon and Neptune displays a possibility of misunderstandings, so the reading cautions the reader to "define meanings, steer away from wishful thinking." It suggests that readers "be positive, sift through ideas," probably because of the aspect with Mars and Jupiter in Taurus's fifth solar house of Virgo. Virgo is a symbol of analysis, or sifting, and Mars and Jupiter together symbolize rapid growth. Hence, the indications are positive for critical and creative thought, but daydreaming should be avoided.

For Gemini, the planets move around the circle into the next house once again, and we observe that the Moon and Venus now fall into the second house. Hence money is an important theme of the day. Now Mars, Jupiter, and Saturn are found in the fourth house, symbolic of the home, so the reader is cautioned to check his assets and responsibilities.

The Moon-Neptune aspect is valid for each sun sign that day, so there is a caution to get a valid appraisal and accounting.

Gemini is also informed that a powerplay is in effect on that day. You will also notice occasional references to your "cycle" being high or low. The cycle referred to is the monthly lunar cycle, during which the Moon passes through all twelve signs of the zodiac. Obviously, at one point during the month, the Moon transits your sun sign, and this is held to be a good time for you to make your desires known or to achieve your goals. The reasoning is that since everyone experiences the same transits, those with a natal (birth) position now being transitted by the Moon stand to benefit from their lifelong experience with that lunar position. Conversely, when the Moon is in the sign opposite to your sun sign, it is not a good time to sign contracts or make requests. The very nature of the "opposition" (an aspect of 180°) suggests that the other person will get his or her way.

Does it all work? You decide. Is it simply a matter of generalities which can be applied in so many ways they always seem valid? Or is there a residuum of coincidence which piques your imagination and leads you to believe that there is something to it, after all? How is it that every so often, one day's reading seems so *right?*

I'm convinced that planetary influences do, indeed, exist. And I'm equally convinced that most astrologers don't know what they're talking about. Most of them are so innocently ignorant it has never even begun to occur to them that this is the case. So when I decided to delve into daily horoscopes, I was skeptical and like many readers, predisposed to negativity. There seem to be spells when they don't work, but many days, the general theme discussed does seem to be present in my daily experience. But given the research we discussed at the beginning of this chapter, is this simply coincidence and gullibility?

It is important to note that many serious astrologers think so. For them, sun-sign astrology is so simple it is ridiculous. They agree totally with the common criticism that nothing so general could apply to you personally. The leading American astrologer, Carl Payne Tobey, an early friend of Sydney Omarr, conducted his own astrological research from this point of view. Then he noticed that his mail-orders for horoscopes tended to be highest when the Moon was in his sun sign, and lowest when the Moon was opposite his sun sign. He claimed that in over seventeen years of business records, this cycle was discernible, although in specific cases the pattern might not be followed.[60]

The point is that most astrologers are as uncomfortable with daily sun-sign predictions as are skeptics. To many serious astrologers, sun-sign columns are a demeaning phenomenon which cheapens an intricate and highly symbolic art which is difficult to acquire, but terribly easy to parody. This point is driven home if we simply examine one page from a typical modern astrological ephemeris. An ephemeris is a table of planetary positions for given dates, and thus it is one of the primary tools of the astrologer. Diagrams 7 and 8 show both a contemporary horoscope and one page of a contemporary astrological ephemeris. Both have been entirely generated by computer using complicated astronomical formulas. It quickly becomes obvious that there is a great deal more information available to a competent practicing astrologer than the sun sign. In fact, if you examine the sample page from the ephemeris closely, you'll find the current sun-sign in the upper left-hand corner under the symbol for the Sun. As I have shown, your daily horoscope is based on a reading of the Sun's passage through one sign of the zodiac, during a thirty-day period at the time of your birth. Yet, here is a table of precise positions for the major planets for each day in several coordinate systems, along with a chronological listing of the daily aspects or angles they form with each other.

Do sun-sign horoscopes work? You decide. If they don't, with all those generalizations built in, it's not surprising, really. But if they *do* appear to work now and then, despite the severe limitations in which the sun-sign astrologer is forced to operate, what does that suggest about the power of astrological symbolism?

> The fault, dear Brutus, is not in our stars,
> But in ourselves, that we are underlings.

Four

The Sign of Baloney

Sex and the Stars

One thing you must never assume is that the astrology you are exposed to is real astrology. It might not even be a serious attempt to imitate real astrology. This point was driven home when I came into contact with the author of *Sex and the Stars*, Martin Pentecost. This slim 184-page paperback was originally published in Toronto in 1973, but I didn't obtain a copy until 1978.[61] And it was the author's son, a buddy from high school, who told me that his father, John Hearn, was working on an astrology book. This surprised me, because the author was known to me as a former executive of a Toronto chemical firm, a budding playwright and freethinker, and a prominent member of the Unitarian Church. Astrology was certainly an atypical interest.

"The research which produced this book occupied many pleasant years," Pentecost wrote on the jacket of his book. "Not all of it is first-hand, but by no means was all of it hearsay. The evidence will not be denied . . . it is only fair to admit that more of the evidence was obtained from the bedroom than the night sky."

Pentecost then uncovers the supposedly true sexual natures of the twelve signs of the zodiac for his unsuspecting but eager audience. First, twelve sections delineate the "Twelve Signs of Woman."

"Aries woman is first and foremost an actress . . . . One of the most stubborn and discredited clichés of male mythology is that a woman will always go back to a man who has brutalised [*sic*] her. This is almost completely untrue for everyone except Aries . . . . Once she surrenders to her own genitals her capacities are voracious and violent."

"Twelve Signs of Man" follow. "A married Scorpio is a model husband as far as his penis and his wallet are concerned, but his wife must expect nothing else from him. Her job is to keep house for him, and act as an incubator and nursemaid for his children while he gives the best of himself to his male friends and continues the remorseless cycle of courtship, seduction and discard in a series of adulteries . . . ."

Human curiosity being what it is, the unsuspecting reader would naturally look for a section describing his/her current, intended, or desired relationship. So Pentecost provides short sections detailing the 144 possible combinations between each of the twelve signs of man and the twelve signs of woman. For a Sagittarius woman/Aquarius man combination, Pentecost's comment is short but not sweet: "No!"

On the other hand, he views a Leo woman/Capricorn man combination with misgivings: "His early affairs with Leo will be 90% emotion, 8% affection and 2% sex — which is about as bad as it can get . . . . Leo has a good instinct and performs her part perfectly; the unmarked Capricorn is almost too easy to scalp for her, and the experienced one is a man to avoid."

Naturally, this sort of heavy breathing is hard to resist. Nearly anyone would be attracted by the word "sex" in the title, and the word "stars" might mean either astrology or those Hollywood heartthrobs who provide continual fodder for the pages of *The National Enquirer*. Once you've lifted the book off the shelf in the store, you soon find yourself checking up on your own sign (but were you checking up on your own performance, or on the accuracy and scholarship of the author?) and then your current and past sexual relationships. The book, in short, is a sure sale.

And sell it did. Over one quarter of a million copies in the United States. Healthy sales in Canada. A translation into French. And in Israel, *Sex and the Stars* hit the bestseller list!

There's just one little problem. Pentecost doesn't even know how to cast a horoscope. In an interview with me, broadcast coast-to-coast across Canada, Pentecost was quite clear about his methods.[62]

"As far as I was concerned," he said, "I wasn't writing about astrology, I was writing about people. There's one sort of free-for-all subject that anyone is prepared to talk about at any time, and that's their love life. It's great soap-opera stuff. Sometimes people would say something like 'typical Scorpio' or 'typical Libra,' and I had no idea what a typical Scorpio or Libra was. But really, I was working from people to astrology, not from astrology to people. Nor did I ever attempt to check whether my observations in the field bore any resemblance to what were standard opinions of astrologers. I wasn't interested."

"How did you choose the name 'Martin Pentecost,'" I asked.

"Oh, that was out of the blue," Hearn replied. "I thought it sounded sort of appropriate to the subject."

And in fact, Hearn/Pentecost had left a trail of under-spoken clues to reveal his true opinion of astrology. "Astrologically, the manual is far from foolproof," he noted on the back cover. "Some people appear to be governed by their Sign of Conception, others confuse the issue by being premature, and some do not fit at all." When it came to facing the problems of the Gemini woman/Capricorn man combination, perhaps Hearn also came face to face with some regrets about his methodology.

"No one can write on astrology without being aware that they are perpetuating a cruel hoax. All we know is that there is SOMETHING, some loose set of possibilities which have slightly more chance of being right than not." (This from someone who publicly admits never having studied the subject.)

Hearn's approach consisted of simply talking with friends and friends of friends, whose sun signs he duly noted. By gathering notes and making some direct observations (if you think it's easy to find all 144 combinations among your acquaintances, just try), Hearn was able to assemble an astrological textbook superficially similar to hundreds of other pulp productions — many of them written by authors just as knowledgeable and competent in the field.

Even if we confine ourselves to traditional astrology, it is likely that Hearn was unaware of the technical issues his writings avoided. Any first-year student of astrology would point out that a personality or sexual profile, or a compatibility analysis, must proceed from an examination of the entire horoscope, not just the sun signs of a few friends and former flames. Your local astrology bookstore may stock several books on compatibility, and astrological theories on sexuality date back to the early 1800s. The Florida astrologer, T. Pat Davis, speat many months gathering and analyzing sexual assaults.[63] While her subject is almost the opposite of Hearn's, so is her attitude to astrology. In scholarly fashion, Davis provided chapters on general considerations behind her study, clear outlines of her methods, and results.

In general, astrological tradition holds that couples with strong affinities to each other have important points in their horoscopes in "conjunction" (at the same point in the zodiac), or a "major aspect" (an angle of 60°, 90°, 120°, or 180° to each other in the zodiac). But because the symbolism of astrology is so detailed and complex, a simple yes/no, good/bad judgment as given by Pentecost approaches the ridiculous. It is demonstrably easier for a competent astrologer to describe the *nature* of a given relationship. And just as a psychiatrist would be foolish to prescribe a therapy for a patient on the basis of one test-result, without a direct consultation with those involved, so a serious astrologer requires a *context* in which to examine the astrological symbols. This is usually provided by the question the client asks, such as, "Why are we having arguments these days?" Most astrological theories of compatibility have yet to be tested by statistical methods. Some have never attained any popularity among astrologers, probably because they don't work. After all, astrologers depend on positive results to stay in business. Not all clients are gullible. In Chapter Ten we will examine some evidence that the cumulative feedback astrologers have received over the centuries has, in fact, allowed them to detect some planetary influences. Furthermore, at least one academic degree thesis now in progress has obtained initially positive results for astrological compatibility.

But Pentecost, by his own admission, was not interested in finding out what serious astrologers might have written about these concerns. At one point, he describes Aries as "too mercurial to control," even though Aries is traditionally ruled by Mars. Was Pentecost's astrological vocabulary simply too limited for its task? And why would someone with no background in the field pick a name out of the blue and write such a book?

"To what extent I looked at astrology," Hearn told me during our broadcast interview, "I rejected it totally, because all the astrologers are doing is studying one another. When was the last time anyone did any field work? One thing I claimed about this book is it's the only book I know of where anybody's done any field work."

I have already shown that this is completely untrue. Later chapters will only serve to underline the fact. Even a passing knowledge of the field and current research would indicate that Pentecost's statement is totally inaccurate. Since Hearn rejects astrology, he assumes that astrologers are merely parroting each other. He does not realize that serious astrological works are read critically by other astrologers, who have their own cases and files with which to test any new hypothesis. Word gets around fast when someone has simply copied a major author's opinion. And just like any art, the finer points of scholarship and technique are quickly perceived as missing.

What of Pentecost's audience? Dozens of letters flooded in from different countries. He received responses such as "you described my situation perfectly," and letters of gratitude for the helpful advice. All given, of course, in good faith that a sincere astrologer and counselor was behind the delineations.

"Do you cast horoscopes, or do you know how to do that?" I asked Pentecost.

"No, I don't . . . no," he responded.

I would only ask, even if astrology was totally without foundation, if there was not a single piece of evidence pointing to cosmic influences in human behavior, if astrology had been conclusively shown to be a hoax, would it still be morally justifiable to use the innocent concerns and questions of the public to earn money from such a book as *Sex and the Stars?*

All the Diamonds in the World

"At last, there is something new under the sun!" crooned the dust jacket of a new astrology book in 1973. "An updated, believable system of popular astrology intended for the devotee, the skeptic, and those with a curious interest in a fascinating field."

Sky Diamonds: The New Astrology burst on the astrology scene like a firecracker.[64] Author Owen S. Rachleff, who has taught religion, humanities, and the occult at New York University since 1969, unveiled his new "vastly expanded" system of sidereal astrology. The reader was about to be treated to a new revelation in astrology.

You will recall that in Chapter Three, Diagram 4 illustrated how the position of the Sun on the first day of spring is moving backwards through the constellations. Diagram 1 also showed how the most commonly used astrological zodiac is determined by the apparent passage of the Sun over the equator at this spring equinox. I mentioned that most, but not all, astrologers use this zodiac, which approximates obvious seasonal cycles and reflects the changing durations of night and day.

For Rachleff, such a position was untenable. "There is no such thing as an original point . . . on any circle," he informed his readers. "Contemporary astrologers insist that the influence of Aries somehow remains in the sky at the March 21 point, even though the real stars of Aries have shifted thirty degrees to the west. This is absurd and illogical."

For Rachleff, astrology is supposed to be a study of the effects of stars upon people. Therefore, one cannot expect influences to come from *signs* which no longer correspond to the *constellations* after which they were named. "How can *nonbodies* — that is signs — do any influencing?" Rachleff asked. He acknowledged that one small school of astrology had attempted to return to the ancient zodiac, but noted that his "vastly expanded" system was superior, because he planned to use not only the zodiac, but all of the constellations.

Rachleff sympathized with the possible traumatic effects of the sudden realization that you are not an Aries, but a Pisces. "But before resisting, out of hand, such a change," he cautioned his readers, "one should read the Sky Diamond definition [of the signs]."

Like the Lone Ranger, with a hearty "*Ad astra!*" Rachleff was off on a cosmic tour of his new revelation. "To use the Sky Diamond System," he wrote, "one must be willing to accept the facts of cosmic reality. . . . Prophetic and daily use of this sytem is possible and will doubtless be explored in other books about the Sky Diamond approach." What was to follow was astrology "updated, refined, expanded and revolutionized."

Rachleff's revelation consisted of over 200 pages of adapted sun-sign readings, allegedly interpreting your character as based not only on the constellations in the zodiac, but also the constellations near them, to the north and south in the sky. The related myths, literary references, and historical anecdotes were to give you a picture of the great significance of each Sky Diamond, as he named each group of constellations. Not only the traditional planets, but even a few particular *moons* of planets were to figure in his astrological calculations. There was also room for an asteroid for which even astronomers have not published ephemerides (tables of celestial positions).

And there were the obligatory character analyses. For Sagittarius, that is the re-scheduled Sagittarius from December 18 - January 21, Rachleff suggested: "You are the dynamic bowman, the ambitious Archer . . . . You are a reliable guardian . . . a resourceful and intelligent individual." How helpful.

As for actually putting this new revelation to use, Rachleff devoted an entire six pages to instructions for calculating one of his Sky Diamond horoscopes. First you must consult an astronomer's ephemeris, not an astrological one, which is not based on "cosmic reality." Then, you must determine which constellational "diamonds" the planets were in at a given date. Then, you would attempt to calculate the predominance of positive or negative influences. There were no instructions for adjusting the data to the actual time of birth; only the positions taken directly from the ephemeris were discussed. There was no mention of rising and setting signs of planets, and there were no instructions for calculating whether a planet was inside or outside the diamond-shaped limit he arbitrarily set on each constellation, limits which even an astronomer would have difficulty dealing with, I suspect. "The constellations themselves are always of primary importance in any horoscope, regardless of planetary effects," he insisted, contrary to the cumulative experiences of thousands of astrologers over as many years. There was no mention of aspects, houses, or any advanced astrological techniques. And especially no mention of any tests of his system on actual cases.

What is an innocent browser to make of this book, stuffed on a shelf in the occult section along with numerous other candidates for your hard-earned cash? And what is one to make of Owen Rachleff's expertise in astrology?

The dust jackets of Mr. Rachleff's books reveal that he is an Assistant Professor in Liberal Studies at New York University, where he teaches courses on the occult and religion. His course entitled "Witchcraft, Magic, and Astrology" is held to be one of the most popular. He has taught at the New School for Social Research and at Cooper Union. He has written for *TV Guide, Midstream, Horizon,* and *Scientific American.* His books include *Rembrandt's Life of Christ* (a Book of the Month Club dividend), *Great Bible Stories and Modern Paintings,* and *The Occult Conceit.*

Wait a minute . . . *The Occult Conceit?* Yes, friends. And there's another book as well, entitled *The Secrets of Superstitions,* subtitled *How They Help, How They Hurt.*[65] If you needed a further clue to Rachleff's attitude toward astrology and his own Sky Diamonds, you can find it on page 129:

" . . . Even a 'corrected' system (as I mischievously advanced in an enterprise called *Sky Diamonds: The New Astrology*) does not change the premise. Astrology basically remains a superstition, since it would depend in any form on myths and magic formulas long since depropagandized. We at long last know, for example, that the body called Mars does not drip blood and therefore might as well be called Gandhi or XYZ . . . ."

In Chapter Eleven we shall see the same argument being raised against the very strong evidence for planetary influences which is presented in Chapter Ten. But considering that both Pentecost and Rachleff have had great fun at the expense of astrology and its serious students, I think it is completely fair to question their work.

Sex and the Stars merely includes a statement on the copyright page allowing that "This is a work of fiction. All the characters in this book are fictional and any resemblance . . . ." and so on. *Sky Diamonds* simply states on the back cover that Rachleff, "a critic of the occult and erroneous astrology . . . has sought to offer logical alternatives to the outdated superstitions."

Even a casual glance reveals that the authors only have a superficial knowledge of the actual positions held by astrologers. Both of them hold to one or two simplistic and misinformed objections and proceed to blow them up into what they hope are terminal revelations.

Genes and the Stars

Beyond imitation lies improvement. Hence we are blessed or inflicted — your choice — with a crop of books purporting to reveal new astrologies, astrologies which have escaped the attention of both astrologers and skeptical scientists. These are for readers who fancy themselves to be more "scientific" and perhaps slightly above all that superstitious sun-sign nonsense. They discuss new theories of weather prediction, cycles of all kinds — anything with a dash of science and a liberal sprinkling of somewhat occult ideas. It has become fashionable to say that the ancients were not so wrong, and not so right, but here's the real story.

In 1976, Edmund van Deusen, a former Associate Science Editor for *Fortune* magazine, published *Astrogenetics*.[66] "This book is written in the belief that both astrologer and scientist are right — and both are wrong," van Deusen stated.

For him, astrology had performed a valuable function in keeping alive the idea that character is in part determined at birth.

While skeptical of astrology's fortune-telling image, van Deusen allowed that "there *does* seem to be a common quality to all Sagittarians . . . . Arians *are* self-centered . . . the total amount of truth may be very small, compared to astrology's other outrageous claims, but . . . it has been enough to keep astrology ticking . . . ."

van Deusen is right on one score. "Seasonality" as it is called, is now a widely accepted topic of scientific study. Seasonal cycles have been detected in all kinds of plant and animal life, and in humans as well. An entire field, known as biometeorology, is emerging into greater and greater prominence as researchers realize that climate, magnetism, radiation, and some extra-terrestrial influences are affecting mankind. Psychologists are beginning to acknowledge that these factors have to be taken into account in their work. At least two scientific journals are devoted exclusively to this research, and advanced thinkers are realizing that they must now combine previously unrelated fields, such as biology, astronomy, meteorology, and physics, in order to get a clear picture.

In a vague outline, these results support the general idea, but not the specific theories, of astrology. So it is tempting to argue that astrology has simply preserved one or two grains of truth which can now be acknowledged in their pure, scientific form. Such research has often been held back by fear of its possibly neoastrological aura.

So naturally, both astrologers and skeptics were interested when van Deusen set out to test his theory that there might be differences in personality and career according to sun signs. To test the "astro-genetic expression" as he called it, he decided to use sun-sign definitions as "a first approximation of the effect of season of birth on personality." By taking, for example, 2,000 journalists and editors from *Who's Who in America*, van Deusen found a below-average representation of Capricorns and an above-average representation of Scorpios. Hence, it was possible to argue that the "natural inquisitiveness of Scorpios" who are "willing to dig for the facts because knowledge is its own reward" led to their prominence in the list of journalists and editors. Thirty-six other lists followed, each showing peaks in zodiacal signs which might correspond to astrological traditions.

Chapter Six of *Astrogenetics* summarizes "what it means to be" each of the signs of the zodiac, via edited excerpts from *The Compleat Astrologer*, along with lists of the various professions which scored above or below average in van Deusen's calculations. Finally, there was a complete explanation of the methods used in the surveys and calculations.

Obviously, van Deusen was not in the same camp as our two previous authors. He had developed a new hypothesis, done his research, and reported his results. For the casual reader, it might appear that all was well in lotus-land. Astrological tradition had been confirmed, and True Believers might continue firm in their convictions.

But in April, 1977, van Deusen received a letter from Dr. Michel Gauquelin, a leading researcher of planetary effects whose work is reviewed in Chapters Ten and Eleven. Gauquelin wondered how van Deusen could have gathered data for the same professional groups which he had studied only to find no evidence of seasonal patterns. "The results of my observations have been published several times during the past twenty years, and we published our data in 1970," Gauquelin told van Deusen. "What do you think about these discrepancies? As far as I know, you did not write about them in your book."

Gauquelin pointed out that van Deusen had not corrected his data for the effects of socioeconomic levels, year of birth, and country of birth. Other researchers have established that seasonal patterns of birth vary widely with these other factors, so they must be taken into account before a genuine seasonal effect can be detected.

Then there was the problem of matching the results with traditional astrology. Edmund van Deusen found a maximum of baseball players in Libra, a sign traditionally ruled by Venus, not the athletic and aggressive Mars. Then, too, the astrological signs are discrete zones, whereas van Deusen's graphs rose and fell in patterns which did not abruptly change at the cusp of the signs. This fact was also noted by van Deusen, but he still attempted to link the sun-sign readings he borrowed with his astro-genetic results.

Finally, Gauquelin wondered, where did the "astro" of astro-genetics come from? Edmund van Deusen had not provided any link with the planets or stars — simply a possible seasonal effect in various professional groups. As we will see, Gauquelin performed "genetic" experiments on several thousand sets of parents and children, with no positive results for the signs of the zodiac (although there were other positive results). And finally, there was a dis-agreement over the probability levels which van Deusen published.

"I would be happy to know your feelings about the above comments," wrote Gauquelin.

No reply was ever received. What has become of astro-genetic research, no one seems to know. Eventually, I published Gauquelin's letter to van Deusen in *Phenomena*[67] along with a similar statement from astrologer Cary Franks.

"I read the book and was amazed at its claims," wrote Franks. "So this July and August, we checked some of these categories that van Deusen uses, and I also did tennis professionals as well. I found *no* statistical significance...."

What is the answer? Reading between the lines of his book, I suspect that van Deusen conducted his experiments honestly, but had not realized the full complexity of the statistical problems he was facing. Nevertheless, we are faced by his silence, and until van Deusen enters into a dialogue on his research — an obligatory ritual in science — we may never really know.

Astrogenetics remains in print, with not a hint of the questions and controversy it raised in the minds of both astrologers and skeptics.

Biorhythms

Life does have its ups and downs. I couldn't believe my eyes when I attended my first astrology convention, only to observe neophyte astrologers calculating biorhythms as well as horoscopes. To many skeptics, one chart is as ridiculous as the other, but a closer look reveals some significant dif-ferences between astrology and biorhythms. So if I am not out to protect you from the heresy of planetary influences, allow me to save you from the blunders of biorhythms.

Just as many phenomena have seasonal cycles, the human body has shorter cycles of its own. *Body Time*, by Gay Gaer Luce (Bantam Books) will give you a good idea of current progress in this field of research. Back in the 1880s Wilhelm Fleiss was busy observing cyclical changes in the lining of the nose, in an attempt to relate them with neurotic symptoms and sexual abnormalities. Fleiss believed everyone had a male cycle of twenty-three days and a female cycle of twenty-eight days. Fleiss even treated Sigmund Freud by applying cocaine to the "genital cells" inside his nose, as part of a therapy he developed from his investigations.

In the late 1800s, psychologist Hermann Swoboda noticed rhythms in his patients and began to keep records on their illnesses. His work was lost to history during World War II, but around the same time, a teacher at Innsbruck claimed to have observed a thirty-three-day mental cycle in some of his students.

But biorhythms were on their way to popularity. George Thummen's early book *Is This Your Day?* claimed that researcher Rex Hersey had also found evidence for a thirty-three-day cycle, but Hersey's original paper concerned emotional cycles, and his data showed that the cycles were not of a constant length. Each individual had a different cycle.

Today, biorhythms are available in most of the same places you find horoscopes. They are not quite so popular, because they are not quite so convenient. While it's easy to remember your birthday and read your daily horoscope, biorhythm columns usually involve some kind of calculation to combine the three most popular cycles and determine your reading for the day. You can buy electronic calculators which do your biorhythms for you, and there are many computer services which will gladly send you reams of cycle charts which a computer can produce rapidly and inexpensively.

The idea is simply that everyone has three cycles relating to their physical, emotional, and mental well-being, of exactly twenty-three, twenty-eight, and thirty-three days in length. When the cycles are up, you're up, you lucky thing.

And when they're down, you're down. Just like the nursery rhyme:

> The brave old Duke of York,
> He had 10,000 men;
> He marched them up to the top of the hill,
> And marched them down again.
> And when they were up, they were up.
> And when they were down, they were down.
> And when they were only halfway up,
> They were neither up nor down.

Just like sun-sign astrology, biorhythms are free, and *just for you*. It's great fun to have your suspicion confirmed that today is, in fact, a high point for you. And it's comforting to discover that today is the bottom of the cycle; it's all uphill from here if you can only last until the office closes for the day.

The problem is simply this: The Universe is not a Swiss watch. Nature is no respecter of timetables. That's why we have so much trouble predicting earthquakes, weather, and a whole host of events which are part of our experience. We know we can expect hot weather in the summer, but precisely when, and how much? We know California is going to have a big earthquake, but when, and how big?

Nature operates strictly within limits. But within those limits, there is always room for individual variations. Modern science has developed statistics to deal with the broad patterns which are observed in nature, but it fails dismally when it comes to predicting unique events. Natural cycles are known to invert their phase suddenly, or they might skip a cycle, or delay a little extra. Only Mother Nature knows. And she's very reluctant to talk.

So is it really possible that in this universe where everything varies now and then, where even the motions of the planets cannot be described *precisely*, where everything must be described with built-in margins of error, is it really possible that you have three cycles which begin the moment you are born and continue henceforth, regardless of age, traumatic experiences such as accidents, nutrition, profession, health, always perfectly in phase and period?

In a word: No.

Yes, you do have cycles and rhythms within you and without you. And it is a very good thing to become increasingly aware of life's tides. Perhaps if we were more in tune with the concept of cycles and tides, we could even begin to control wars, depressions, and famines.

But unless you aspire to imitate the inner workings of a Swiss watch, forget your biorhythms. Many studies of accident patterns, body cycles, and other phenomena have simply failed to produce any evidence that such totally regular and predictable cycles exist.[68] If biorhythms appear to work one day, it is a chance phenomenon similar to reading your daily horoscope. Only there is less supportive evidence for strictly regular biorhythms than there is for some kinds of planetary influences.

And as far as traditional astrology goes, it must be noted that all of the astronomical cycles on which it is based vary in their length and combinations. In fact, astrologers have often pointed out that the rich complexity of these cycles appears to behave much as a living organism. Thus, they feel at liberty to seek out parallels between cycles in the heavens and observed phenomena on Earth. Then, too, astrological techniques generally allow predictions only to within a few days or weeks. Biorhythms attempt to predict a high for a special day.

It is possible that each of us does have general rhythms in our personalities, emotions, and bodies. But these must be established on a personal basis and may be subject to change at any time.

The moral of the story is simply this: Most of what passes for astrology is not good astrology, and some of it is not even astrology. In the world of science, there are journal referees and vigorous debates. In the marketplace there are consumer reporters and standards associations. In professional fields such as medicine, law, and architecture, there are degrees and standards which must be obtained and respected.

But since no one really believes all that stuff about the planets influencing us, astrology and astrologers are in a real pickle. They can't study in accredited institutions, because the institutions reject astrology. And since, therefore, anyone can hang a sign claiming to be an astrologer, we now observe a field where 99% of those practicing are effectively incompetent and naive. Therefore, the demand for quality publications in astrology is close to nil. Junk publications manage to survive, while serious ones die out with the uncanny regularity of biorhythms!

Somewhere in astrology, there is a solid meat. But most of what you read is sheer baloney.

Five

The Electronic Analyst

The Computer Reveals All

"How well do you know yourself?" the computer-horoscope firm inquires. "Would you like to know when your luck is going to change?" How about a horoscope "just for the two of you"? Or a "personal horoscope just for you plus your biorhythms"?

At prices ranging up to fifteen dollars on average, you can now obtain not just a general daily reading for everyone born in your sun sign, but a properly calculated and completely delineated horoscope based on the same accurate data which a professional astrologer would use. You receive from 5,000 to 20,000 neatly printed words generated from a prestigious brand-name computer, often handsomely bound in a presentation folder, delivered to your personal residence by a uniformed representative of the federal government (the postman).

When the astrology boom arrived in the sixties, computers were just beginning to come down in price and size. With a sufficient volume of business, it became economically feasible to store masses of text in a computer and instruct it to assemble a horoscope based on your birth data. From early computer services in New York City, the idea caught on and today such horoscopes are available from firms in the U.S. and several European countries. Actually, there are fewer services than you might expect; some companies simply repackage the print-outs they receive from a major computer service and advertise it in their own name. Altogether, I estimate that there are less than a dozen astrological computer services which have been in business for more than two years.

What do they provide, and how do they work? Just fill in the form which says, "I want to know about my real self." Give the computer your accurate birth-data, including precise time and place of birth, along with enough money to grease the computer's palm. You can charge it, if you like, and there's a full refund if you're not completely satisfied.

Computer horoscopes are expanded and highly detailed versions of your daily sun-sign column. Rather than depending on one astrological factor, the computer has been programmed first to calculate your entire basic horoscope. This includes the position of the Sun, Moon, and planets, the sign rising and culminating at birth, and other data which are commonly found in horoscopes. The computer then searches its memory and retrieves a section of text which has been written for each planet or horoscopic factor in each sign and each house of the chart. These sections are then assembled into an epistle which is printed, bound, and mailed off to you in due course.

It all sounds quite impersonal, considering that you were to find out all about your inner self. But one sophisticated English horoscope service has taken things a step further. The computer has been instructed to pick up your name and insert it occasionally in order to give you the impression you're having a conversation with an old friend. "As I was saying, *Fred*, your Moon in Sagittarius inclines you to philosophy and . . . ." The computer even picks up on the fact that you included the title "Mr.," "Miss," "Ms.," or "Mrs." before your name and uses this as a clue to your character.

Computer horoscopes are based on some not-so-unreasonable assumptions, if you believe in traditional astrology. Over the centuries, astrologers have come to a general agreement on the significance of the planets, signs, and houses. It is assumed that everyone with a given combination in their birth chart, or natal horoscope as it is called, shares a given set of characteristics and experiences in their life. So, through personal experience, through experiences observed in the charts of clients, and theoretical extrapolation where observations have not been made, the astrologer employed by the computer service prepares a series of texts. All that is left is for the computer to retrieve those portions applicable to your horoscope and assemble them for print-out.

The weak links in this chain of events are obvious. What if the astrologer was incompetent? Did the employer take care to select the best astrologer available? Did he really care about the quality of his product, or was it simply another business rip-off in the guise of sincere astrology? Did the astrologer personally observe the circumstances he described, and if so, on how many cases? How much of the text was simple extrapolation from untested astrological tradition?

All the old problems of gullibility, statements of universal validity, self-knowledge and character descriptions remain in computer delineations. Since the astrologer has generalized his interpretation, or written it with some average client in mind, each planetary position must be discussed without reference to specific issues in your particular life. It is the question-and-answer process, the process of inquiry, which any therapist depends on to perform a counseling service. Obviously, this is lacking in computerized interpretations.

The particular philosophical school held by the astrologer also makes a difference. Some schools usually take a hard-line predictive approach, often with an emphasis on the fatalistic. For them, it is important to describe physical circumstances in your life. The psychological causes or remedies are of lesser importance. Astrologers of the humanistic or holistic school, on the other hand, place the emphasis on your inner development. The signs are interpreted in a psychological and symbolic manner, and predictions of precise events are held to be a debasement of the true significance of astrology. Since the public is largely unaware of such philosophical divergences among astrologers, the businesses which supply horoscopes do not take pains to point out the background, qualifications, and orientations of their staff astrologers.

But the pot-luck aspect of computer horoscopes has its balancing factor; a personal reading by an astrologer costs from thirty-five dollars up these days (you can add inflation as this book ages), whereas your personal computer horoscope usually costs about fifteen dollars. If you're too skeptical to put up the money for a competent astrologer, but curious enough to want to see what an astrologer might tell you, the computer horoscope might be your cup of tea.

The largest computer-horoscope firm on the planet is Para Research, located in Massachusetts. In the early 1970s, Frank Molinsky, then a young businessman in his late twenties, purchased a bankrupt and very primitive computer-horoscope service and set about expanding and improving the program. Prominent American astrologers were hired to write interpretations, and the computer output was offered to other similar firms. Today, Para Research's computer output appears through several American outlets, plus England and Europe. A Spanish version of the natal horoscope is available for the American market. Para's gross income from its computer plus book publishing is reported to be near $1 million per annum, but any company can have difficulty even at that level of cash flow, so it is hard to use this figure to support the astrological rip-off theory.

Para Research offers five computer outputs, each mainly written by one astrologer. The general interpretation of your birth chart was written by Bob Pelletier, a Boston astrologer. Robert Hand of Cape Cod, a leading American astrologer, provided texts which describe planetary transits, a youth portrait aimed at teenagers, and a composite analysis which shows the relationship between two horoscopes. New York astrologer and editor, John Townley, provided a text for a "love portrait." Some of these texts are available in book form, and your local astrology bookstore will probably have a series of books entitled *Planets in Transit*, *Planets in Youth*, and so on. This popular series has found a market among amateur astrologers who need assistance in interpreting symbols now and then. They can look up the relevant passage and compare their understanding of the symbols with a general reading by a more prominent astrologer.

As a business venture or as traditional astrology, computer horoscopes cannot be counted as a success. In both fields, they squeak by with barely passing grades, and that's about all. The best that can be said of them is that they interest a few people, make a little money, and have a degree more connection with good astrology than do sun-sign horoscopes.

Fun and Games

If the steadily increasing power and decreasing cost of large computers spawned automated horoscope readings, the advent of the microprocessor has created a new era of portable electronic astrology. You'll recall the earliest hand-held calculators were expensive, clumsy, and somewhat stupid. Yet within only a few years, they had practically wiped slide-rules off the market with their ability to perform trigonometric functions. A few years later, electronic toys with microprocessors, speech synthesizers, and lots of blinking lights began to catch on. Suddenly, manufacturers were looking for new products based on the new technology — items which could be manufactured for pennies in Hong Kong and Korea, and sold for a good profit in department stores at Christmas time. Department stores were only too happy to oblige. Suddenly the toy departments had a new specialty counter, stocked with all sorts of automated amusements, plus a good supply of batteries.

It was not until 1979, however, that a hand-held astrological computer was to be marketed. It took several years for the development of components small and sophisticated enough to handle a few basic planetary calculations without help from the operator. And it took businessmen a while to seek out the expertise they needed to develop product concepts for what they thought would be a lucrative market.

First to take the plunge was Kosmos (motto: "Helping people to better understand themselves"), a manufacturer of biorhythm calculators. A professor of astronomy at a southern university was hired to prepare a computer program which would calculate the positions of the Sun, Mercury, Venus, and Mars on a given date. Since the program had to fit inside a hand-sized package, only positions for midnight could be provided by the machine. Atlanta astrologer, Jeff Jawer, was directed to design and produce a package which would allow the user to punch in his birth date and read the signs (not the precise degrees) in which those four planets were located at birth. This information is stored, and the user can then punch a second set of birth data into the machine. Once this calculation is complete, a push of a button sets a light glowing beneath each planet. A green light shows compatibility between the positions of that planet in each horoscope, while yellow shows that there might be some friction or incompatibility. The pre-dominance of one color over another — three out of four lights, for example — shows the general tone of the relation-ship. These predictions are based on the classical aspects (angular relationships of 60°, 90°, etc.) between the *signs*, not the precise positions, of the four planets which have been calculated.

ASTRO, as the calculator was named, performs other astrological operations as well. You can compare one planet in one horoscope with a different planet in the second horoscope by entering an astrological formula into this electronic oracle. For example, you can compare the posi-tion of the Sun in one birth chart with the position of Mercury in the other horoscope, to ask the question, "Do you understand my goals?" The green or yellow light provides the answer. By comparing Mars in one chart with Venus in the other, you ask the question, "Do you like my style?" Since there are four planets in two charts, sixteen combinations are possible. When ASTRO is not calculating planetary positions, it serves as a four-function calculator. ASTRO sells for about fifty dollars, and though North American sales are not as healthy as predicted, worldwide volume has made it a viable product.

Such question-and-answer formulas might be generally agreeable to many astrologers, as far as they go. But Jawer himself is quick to point out that a proper astrological reading involves the other factors of the horoscope as well. The machine could suggest everything is rosy, as far as the four planets it is capable of calculating, but the other signs might not look so favorable. Then, too, ASTRO has bitten off quite a big mouthful. Not only does it calculate birth positions for one person; it analyzes compatibility between two individuals. This is an area which has already become the subject of scientific tests. Should any statistically positive results emerge in the near future, it might be possible to program a new calculator along the lines of ASTRO in conformance with the available evidence. As it is, this lack of empirical evidence for the formulas which have been programmed into the machine, and the omnipresent possibility that other factors in the horoscopes might contradict what ASTRO indicates, means that results often have little meaning.

Coleco, a major toy manufacturer, recently learned about the astrological market the hard way. Their astrological machine was designed to provide the sign positions of all the planets. By using number codes and a manual, the user could obtain a basic reading of his horoscope. Searching for this machine at a recent consumer-electronics show, I was informed by a Coleco salesman that the machine had been withdrawn. One factor contributing to its demise may have been its poor accuracy.

If the market for specialized astrological toys is somewhat risky, astrology is always one of those "options" calculator and computer manufacturers throw into their sales packages. After all, if they can provide some astrological abilities as part of their product at a low cost, a few extra sales might be gained. Those who are not impressed by the astrological options might at least be happy to know that one is available. Thus, when programmable calculators entered the marketplace and began to plummet in price, even prestigious firms such as Hewlett-Packard and Texas Instruments helped to distribute astrological programs developed by some of their customers. (Just in case the dollar signs are still rolling in your eyes, no one made a cent out of these arrangements.)

However, large toy manufacturers had been keeping a beady eye on developments in calculators and home computers. Mattel decided in the late seventies to set up a new branch called Mattel Electronics aimed specifically at computerized games. Their first entry into the marketplace has been named Intellivision, for intelligent television. The Intellivision unit looks like a flat typewriter. The master unit includes two hand-held control panels so that two users can play electronic soccer, golf, hockey, checkers, space battle, and many other games. Each game is programmed into a cartridge which can be inserted much like a cassette. Once this master unit is placed within the keyboard unit, the toy becomes much more like a full-fledged home computer. You can compute your taxes, analyze your stocks, study guitar lessons, take conversational French, and calculate your horoscope!

Yes, with Intellivision in your home you can calculate "your personal horoscope — accurately, scientifically!" The "world-famous astrologer and prognosticator" Jean Dixon has done it all for you. The user inputs his or her complete birth data, and Intellivision displays a correctly calculated horoscope. The ten planets are seen in their correct houses and signs, then the screen changes to an interpretation of the chart, much along the lines of the Para Research books discussed above. Once a natal chart has been stored in the machine, you can request a yearly forecast beginning on a date of your choice. The computer calculates the positions of the outer planets, Jupiter through Pluto, and determines on which dates significant angles or aspects will be formed with the stored natal positions. Once again, texts provide an analysis of the requested period. Various other charts and comparisons of two charts are also offered.

Jean Dixon is certainly a talented and enterprising lady! Not only can she write a daily horoscope column, prepare recorded messages for a telephone forecast-service (complete with commercials), and consult with clients, but it appears she has also managed to pick up a little computer programming on the side.

In fact, however, Jean Dixon is largely unknown to serious astrologers. Many even doubt if she knows how to calculate a horoscope. It is a name which is being marketed, and it is a measure of the public image of astrology that Mattel sought out a brand-name astrologer rather than making it clear that their astrological programs were, in fact, designed by a young Los Angeles astrologer for a few thousand dollars. The irony is that he prefers not to use this type of zodiac in his professional work.

Through commercial ploys such as this, the public

remains unaware that there *are* serious astrologers, that there are leading philosophers, theorists, and practitioners who study an art far more complex than the astrology which business interests casually flaunt for their own profit. One simply cannot expect the basic issues to be examined and developed properly, one cannot expect the best astrologers to receive the hearing they deserve both from the public and astrological amateurs, while serious astrology is hidden behind the skirts of various media personalities for maximum profit.

But business interests are not entirely to blame. If astrologers have inherited a "divine science" and protected a cosmic revelation against the slings and arrows of outrageous criticism, they have sold their heritage for a mess of potage. And even astrologers have said so.

Dr. Zipporah Dobyns, a clinical psychologist and leading humanistic astrologer, says she sees no use for popular astrology, except to make money. "That it does," she says. "It makes money for the people who write it, and sometimes they really need the money, so they have to excuse their action. I think it's a debasement of what astrology is really about. Astrology is enormously complicated . . . the scientist sees this stuff put out as if people are just one of twelve signs and naturally says it's nonsense, because it *is* nonsense."

Dr. Dobyns believes popular astrology continues because the public demands it. "I've been told by people in newspaper work that if they remove any one feature from a newspaper, the feature that gets the most complaints is the comics, and next to that is astrology. People don't know any better, and apparently people are so desperate for any kind of guidance they will grasp at any kind of straw. The average person isn't ready for something that is as complicated, as time-consuming, as difficult and abstract, as true astrology."

But, like astrology, the argument goes in circles. Those involved in popular astrology can point to the increasing sophistication of the astrology which is reaching the public, thanks to this electronic revolution. Formerly confined to daily sun-sign columns or monthly pulp magazines, accurate astrological calculations are now more readily available. Popular astrologers hope that experience with a basic calculator such as ASTRO or the fairly complete interpretation offered by Intellivision may serve to introduce the complexities of astrology to a wider audience.

If they are right, their gamble will have succeeded. If they are wrong, a serious and mature investigation of astrology may in fact have been held back by fun and games.

Professional Services

Simultaneous with the emergence of computerized horoscope readings, computer services aimed at professional astrologers entered the marketplace. Calculating a horoscope is an involved and tedious affair, often taking several hours. Since astrologers tend to the intuitive and poetic modes of thought needed for symbolic interpretations, they are often poor in mathematics. Rare, indeed, is the person who is thoroughly versed in computer programming, mathematics, psychology, symbolism, and counseling. Yet this is precisely what serious astrology demands. Most clients, on their part, do not take astrology seriously enough to pay an astrologer sufficient money to make hours of calculations worthwhile. Few and far between are those clients who can afford to pay an astrologer what a psychoanalyst, for example, would earn for similar efforts. The net result is that many horoscopes are calculated with one or more errors, and the more calculations that are involved, the more errors there are likely to be. Computerized calculation services for professional astrologers were clearly a godsend.

In 1972, Astro Computing Services was founded by Neil Michelsen. Michelsen had always been interested in metaphysics, and although he is not an astrologer, his background as a computer programmer for IBM gave him a unique perspective of the possibilities for a computer service aimed at serious astrologers. In his spare time, he began developing computer programs to transform astronomical positions as used by astronomers into astrological formats. Three years later, he resigned from seventeen years of service with IBM to devote himself full-time to astrological computing. ACS's biggest plus was the printer Michelsen chose to employ; you can see the horoscope of Jimmy Carter in Chapter Three for an example. While most computer services were making do with primitive dot-matrix printers or typewriter-style output, Michelsen purchased a costly Versatec electrostatic printer. In one fell swoop, this unit solved the problems one faces in computerized astrology: how to draw the circle of the horoscope and print those glyphs and symbols which are not readily available. The Versatec printer is capable of doing all of these, so that Michelsen's computer could calculate, format, and print a complete horoscope such as Carter's in a matter of seconds.

To his endless credit, Michelsen eschewed popular astrology. His computer has never been programmed to provide interpretations; it only provides the raw data from which a professional astrologer makes his or her interpretations. This meant that Michelsen carefully had to analyze not only what techniques were in common use by astrologers, but the best way to go about them. As a result, in several cases, technicalities which had puzzled astrologers of lesser competence have been resolved. Refinements which might involve a few extra minutes in calculations are no longer tempting to avoid, since it takes just as long to order a precise chart from the computer as an imprecise one. And the astrologer is freed to concentrate more on two vital areas of astrology: securing accurate birth-data and providing a competent interpretation. Accurate birth-data has always been a problem, but astrologers were often tempted to fudge by calculating approximate charts by hand. The computer does not approximate; it provides an accurate chart for any time requested.

As for the interpretation, Michelsen's computer is already having an influence on the style of modern astrology. Look again at the sample horoscope of Jimmy Carter. At the bottom you will find a list of what are called mid-points. These are the points in the zodiac midway between two given planets in the horoscope. In the first half of this century, two German schools of astrology developed systems of interpretation based on formulas built up from these mid-points. In true Teutonic style, they laid the emphasis heavily upon their predictive value. Today, both schools or styles of astrology have active adherents in the U.S. and other major centers of astrological activity. Obviously, the calculation of such an array of sensitive points takes quite a while, and the possibility of error is great. At the same time, the techniques which employ these mid-points tend to use a much smaller orb (the astrological equivalent of a margin of error) than traditional techniques do. So precision is even more important. Astrologers who were interested in these points were therefore oriented to "number-crunching" and predictive applications of astrology. But since Michelsen's computer provides all these calculations, not only accurately but also neatly sorted into zodiacal sequence, as a basic service for a few dollars, astrologers in other schools have also become interested in experimenting with them.

A second example of this effect of technology on astro-logical techniques and styles occurs in the case of what are called progressions and transits. These are essentially ways of updating a horoscope in an attempt to describe current conditions, or conditions at any selected time in the life of the subject, or "native," as the Victorian astrologers had it. Transits are the actual positions of the planets at the selected time. The angles these positions form with respect to the birth or natal positions allow for interpretation of current trends. Progressions come in many styles and varieties, but the most widely used system, called secondary progressions, moves the planets at the proportionate rate of one day per year, so that the first day of life symbolizes the first year, the second day the second year, and so on.

To calculate the precise dates of these events, one by one, and carefully tabulate them in chronological order for all planets was a task almost beyond the most fervent number-crunchers. Thus, there was no way to put these systems to a real test, either in terms of traditional astrology or statistics. But for a few extra dollars, an astrologer can now request progressions and transits for an entire lifetime, all neatly calculated, formatted, and printed in a few seconds by Michelsen's computer.

An information revolution is underway in astrology. As has been often pointed out, computers quite happily produce reams of information which can be totally erroneous. One mistake in the input can produce thousands of accurately sorted, neatly printed mistakes. Now astro-logers were to experience the possibilities first-hand. One after another, Michelsen expanded his services to include practically every technique in the basic astrological canon, and then some. The print-out which can be generated for one birth-chart alone runs into many yards of charts and tables. While on one hand, this means that astrologers can experiment with techniques which were previously beyond their mathematical ability, this also means that they are faced with a vast and complex array of analytical methods which are probably beyond their competence, on average. Even in terms of traditional astrology, the careful testing of one method of prediction against known events in the lives of clients demands a special combination of detective work and intuition. Since there are no rigorous training methods available, and few senior teachers with this kind of special expertise, most astrologers do not realize how poorly they are equipped to face the information explosion. On the other hand, scientists who are currently investigating astrology have not even begun to test these methods of prediction. They are still busy with the basics of signs, houses, and aspects.

Elsewhere in this volume, you will see an example of the next logical step in this information revolution. The standard reference for astrologers is a table of planetary positions or an ephemeris. In ages past, astrologers had to calculate their own ephemerides. Thus, it is no surprise that most of the early astrologers were astronomers. (Astronomers would prefer to tell their historical tale the other way around.) It was the search for accurate astrological information which led to the development of astronomy. But by modern times, a split was effectively underway in contemporary thought; the symbolic and intuitive elements were moving aside for an intellectual and materialistic push ahead. Thus, astrologers found themselves dependent on calculations made by astronomers for non-astrological purposes. These had to be converted out of astronomical frames of reference into those used by astrologers. The calculations had to be done by hand, and then typeset by hand, leading to many errors. Then, too, the astronomers were not always interested in the same time periods as the astrologers, and often did not calculate complete ephemerides of some bodies. Astrologers found themselves picking up what crumbs of information they could obtain, hoping that the astronomers would soon provide them with information they desperately wanted but couldn't ask for.

To make a long story short, in 1976 the *American Ephemeris* was published. You can see from the sample page in Chapter Three the amount of information provided for any given day listed there. Even if the coordinate systems and symbols are all Greek to you, you'll be able to appreciate the information explosion which is occurring in astrology today. You can find the sun sign in the third column in from the upper left corner. Michelsen's computer was recently programmed to provide the entire page as computer print-out, practically at the push of a button. Now it is possible to request various forms of specialized ephemerides for particular techniques or schools of astrology. The information is printed without error, and in the most convenient format possible. Not only ephemerides, but also other commonly used reference works such as tables of houses, which are employed in determining the angular positions of planets in a horoscope, can also be produced with a greater accuracy than ever before, custom-tailored to a specific location. Before this innovation, astrologers who did not live in a major city were often forced to use two tables, one for a major city to the north and one for another to the south, and interpolate between the answers thus obtained.

During the mid-seventies, Michelsen joined forces with a new astrological organization called the National Council for Geocosmic Research. This was initially intended to be an organization aimed at the most technically competent and advanced astrologers in the U.S. Although the NCGR has never fully completed any proper research and has tended to stray back toward the occult and less scientific aspects of astrology, one project initiated through this involvement has already borne rich fruit in terms of a scientific examination of astrology. In Chapter Ten, you will read about the research of two French scientists who have been examining planetary effects in human behavior for thirty years. The thousands of cases gathered by Drs. Michel and Françoise Gauquelin were obtained by Michelsen and entered into his computer, in the hope that astrologers might use them for research. The Gauquelins were quite understandably concerned about this, at first. As you will read, they had spent many years and a small fortune on their research, only to be accused of being charlatans. Wasn't it possible that if skeptical scientists learned that their data was being used for research by astrologers that they would only use this fact against them? Several years of initial hostility passed away, however, and by 1979 the Gauquelins actively began to employ Michelsen's computer to further their research. Now that their data has been entered into the computer, checked and rechecked, experiments can be performed more rapidly and more accurately. An astrological revolution is well underway, as you will see. But who is prepared to accept the results? Whether traditional astrologers or skeptical scientists are prepared to adapt to evidence which shows they are both in error to some degree remains to be seen.

The next step in the astrological revolution was obviously to give each student of astrology access to this kind of computing power whenever it was needed. And only a personal computer could accomplish this. There were two ways to approach the goal: a specialized machine devoted entirely to astrological calculations or specialized programs for the increasingly sophisticated home computers which were entering the market.

So, in 1975 a new firm called Digicomp Research of Ithica, New York began developing the world's first desk-top astrological computer, the DR-70. Dr. Om Gupta, an electrical engineer and computer specialist, gathered a development team consisting of astrologer Tim Smith, Prof. David Lewis, Jim Elkins, and Jeff Cox. Each handled a particular aspect of the programming and mechanical design. The result was a machine about the size of a typewriter which contains a "dedicated" microcomputer. That is to say, the DR-70 is built for astrology, and astrology is all it does. Planetary positions over an incredible period of ten thousand years can be calculated. The DR-70 can produce any desired information from the basic canon of astrological technique. The user has a choice of zodiacs, can compare different horoscopes, can search for aspects in a chart, can update a horoscope to any desired time and so on. The machine is ruggedly built and designed for continual professional use. Unveiled at the biannual convention of the American Federation of Astrologers in 1978, Digicomp has subsequently sold 400 DR-70's to professional astrologers at a price approaching $3,000. These are people who constantly calculate charts, who often cannot afford to wait for a computer service to mail their horoscopes back to them, and who have a sufficient volume of business to make the price competitive with an outside computer service. An optional printer and battery pack for in-car operation are also available, and the DR-70 is being marketed in Canada, Australia, and Europe. Obviously, no company could survive on such sales as the DR-70 has attained. Besides their astrological interests, Digicomp Research also has U.S. Government contracts through the Department of Defense, and is developing a new Pascal package (a computer language).

But for some, the price is too high, and being limited to astrological calculations too restricting. While the DR-70 was in development, Commodore, Radio Shack, and many other companies were entering a race for the home-computer dollar. While at first, home computers were thought of as an expensive novelty (like most inventions), they are now being perceived as an essential part of daily life and business. And as the market grows, so does the ability of the microcomputer to compete in many ways with full-size computer systems.

One of the first serious astrologers to realize the exciting potential of home computers was Michael Erlewine. Erlewine had already carved a reputation for himself through his innovations in using various systems of celestial coordinates in astrology. His carefully compiled annual astrological calendar can be found hanging near the desk of many a budding astrologer. Erlewine had combined a spiritually oriented philosophy with the most technically advanced methods of astrology. So when machines which could perform these calculations swiftly and accurately came along, Erlewine found his place in the revolution.

Erlewine believes that the cost of home computers will continue to drop, putting serious astrology within reach of anyone who is interested. He was the first to prepare basic astrological programs specifically for the major brands of home computers. Pop a Matrix Software cassette into your machine, and you're ready to become an astrologer!

Erlewine's advanced journal, *Matrix*, publishes astrological, astronomical, and statistical programs for computers, along with technical articles for computer-astrology buffs. But like Digicomp, Erlewine has found that computer astrology does not a rich man make. He supports his astrological research and publications in part through developing computer games and other software for business interests.

But old-fashioned mechanical calculators were not to be supplanted so easily. Even in this day of electronic calculator-watches, old-fashioned Swiss watches maintain their allure. In this case, however, it was not a Swiss but a Dutch watch, produced by Almere Projects. Astrologer Jacob Venker assisted in designing a pocket watch which is set to run on sidereal time, the measure of time which is used in astrology and astronomy to determine which stars and planets are rising. The conventional clock face was replaced with a zodiac, a basic star-map, and lines indicating the horizon at different latitudes on Earth. For the first time, astrologers were able to reach into their pockets and see immediately which degrees of the zodiac might be rising or culminating overhead. But this demands a word of explanation.

Astrology is often explained as a kind of clock with many hands. One set of hands goes around the dial extremely slowly. These are the outer planets, which take hundreds of years to orbit the Sun. As you gradually come closer to the Sun, the planets move faster and faster in their orbits. Jupiter takes roughly twelve years, while Mars takes about two, and Earth only one year to orbit the Sun. You know that the Moon only takes about a month to orbit the Earth. But even faster than this cycle is the daily rotation of the Earth. We speak of planets rising and setting, but what is really happening is that the Earth is turning on its axis, bringing them into view above our location. The horizon and the line which passes vertically through your location are called the "angles" of your horoscope, and to astrologers these are among the most important factors to be considered. Their rapid motion gives them great importance, because they change with every passing moment. There is a tradition among astrologers that, for instance, when a roomful of people suddenly falls silent, when people say "an angel just passed," what really happened was that a planet just rose or set, or the angles changed signs in the zodiac.

I observed this kind of phenomenon once during my student days. I was supporting my studies by working in a large office and from my desk I could observe most of the employees on my floor. Every day I would place on my desk a list of times when a new sign or planet would rise, or when an aspect would form exactly between two planets. I did it just as a casual investigation; there were no statistics involved and no record was kept. But I remember one afternoon how the office had been quiet for some time. It was strange how everyone seemed to have been at his desk for quite a while. My timetable said that Mars was about to rise. And nearly everyone rose with it. Typewriters suddenly became busy, people were on their way to the xerox machine, to drop off a letter, to consult with their manager, to visit the john. And I remember wondering at the time why no one else noticed the sudden change which came over the entire office.

Explain this as you wish. Later on, we will see that Mars rising is perhaps one of the best confirmed astrological ideas — at least when it was rising at birth. There have been hardly any scientific studies of current planetary positions, or transits, although one scientific research project by a major research laboratory which found correlations between planetary positions and accidents was dropped like a hot potato. But I'm saving that story for a rainy day.

The Astrowatch provides instant access to information for such experiments. Since most astrology is calculated from the Earth as a center, there is no planet Earth in a regular horoscope. Astrologers sometimes refer to the angles of the current horoscope, the transitting angles as a kind of Earth in the chart — only with four points in the zodiac, instead of one. There would be the transitting (or current) ascendant, descendant, midheaven, and I.C., just as with the horoscopes we have already studied. The only difference is that this horoscope is the one for *now*, and it is constantly shifting and changing. The Astrowatch and similar devices allow an astrologer immediate access to this information.

But like the information revolution as a whole, this is a double-edged sword for astrology. Astrologers like to argue that it is the transitting ascendant or midheaven which might have triggered off a sudden, unexpected event such as a car accident. Rather like a combination lock, the transitting angles are often spoken of as the last number, the last tumbler to fall into place. So it's tempting to think that at last, here is a tangible way to study astrological influences.

But if you look at those reams of computer output, the dozens of charts you can produce from one single set of birth data, the transitting ascendant whirling around your horoscope once a day, and all the many signs and symbols which come pouring out like the horn of plenty, it quickly becomes obvious that so much is happening that it is nearly impossible to tell if anything really correlates with anything else. If the dials whirl around fast enough, and hit enough significant points in the horoscope, who is to tell whether there is a genuine astrological effect or not?

There are three answers to this question. The skeptics say there is nothing to it. The astrologers are simply imagining that the planets have effects; they are simply studying random symbols and becoming a little dizzy-headed in the process. The astrologers say you have to experiment with the symbols to see astrology work. If you can't suspend belief, at least suspend your disbelief (which is a kind of belief). Get involved with the symbols, they say, and you, too, can see astrology work for yourself. You're both wrong, say the research scientists. The only way to check it out is with large numbers of cases, special statistical methods, and computers, if possible. Only when all the basic hypotheses of astrology are checked out in this way, will it be possible to state that astrology has a scientific foundation.

And so, having passed beyond sun-sign columns into the fun-and-games world of electronic toys, and from there into the world of serious astrology and computers, we find the same basic question. Does astrology really work? Do planetary influences really exist? Whose opinion can you trust and why? And why do you hold the opinion you presently have regarding astrology?

Perhaps it's all written in the stars . . . .

Six

Archaeoastrology

Astrology has had a lot of hard things said about it ... and yet, it was not simply a misapplication and distortion of astronomy; it was linked with the main impulses and needs driving men to study the stars; astronomy could not have developed without it ... to isolate it from the complex of ideas in which it played a vital part, and to consider only what was irrational in it, is to show total irresponsibility as an historian of culture.

Jack Lindsay, Origins of Astrology,
Barnes & Noble, 1971
(Rowman & Littlefield)

Maps once displayed ornate dragons peering out of the ocean depths to show where current knowledge of the world ended and imagination took over. Knowing our world better each year, we now find such attempts to extrapolate into the unknown somewhat quaint and amusing. Yet today, we are really no better; old dragons have simply been replaced with new ones. Where formerly geography and early history were major mysteries, vast unknowns, these days establishment thinkers are busy creating dangerous dragons out of occult traditions and concepts which have survived despite their best efforts to mock and disprove them out of existence.

Officially proscribed traditions such as Atlantis, advanced

knowledge in ancient Babylonia and Egypt, worldwide travel in ancient times, knowledge which even this arrogant age might not yet comprehend, these ideas have circulated in occult and minority groups for centuries, refusing to be buried and forgotten. This is not surprising. Only a few decades ago, "official" histories held that the world was created in one day some few thousand years ago. Once evolution became an accepted theory, it was still difficult to believe that man's history went back very far. Newer "official" histories had us emerging almost instantly from the jungles and deserts, suddenly finding the ability to erect pyramids, to invent mathematics, music, writing, and efficient bureaucracies. Yet even if all this incredible genius did erupt in the space of only a few blinks of the eye of history, ancient man was still discussed as if he were somewhat dull and stupid. Historians could accept his genius in some things, but still spoke in sneering terms of ancient myths, science, and especially astrology.

It is often difficult to understand something unless we know a little of its origins. Astrology has always been a difficult subject to penetrate, not only because of all the incompetent nonsense which is written under its banner, but also because the reasons for its emergence and its great importance to virtually all ancient societies were little known and poorly understood. Moreover, modern writers make tremendous, and tremendously arrogant, assumptions in dealing with ancient consciousness. Finding ourselves suddenly in a world populated with increasingly sophisticated machines, asphalt roads, and instant communication, a world totally out of touch with its environment, we no longer understand how intimate our ancestors were with Nature. We no longer comprehend how ancient minds attempted to deal with the world which surrounded them. And most especially, modern minds have great difficulty in understanding the symbolic and intuitive modes of thought upon which ancient minds based their vast and impressive achievements.

Against this background of modern arrogance, ignorance, and official religious positions which discouraged the study of ancient pagan beliefs, it is not surprising that the true history of our world has been virtually ignored until recently. Scholars are now seriously considering ideas which only occultists have dared to preserve, heresies even worse, in some ways, than astrology.

It is a particularly delicious irony that one of establishment science's most holy of holy scriptures, the prestigious journal, *Nature*, was in some way responsible for this quiet revolution. *Nature's* founder and first editor, Sir Norman Lockyer (1836-1920), a distinguished astronomer and the discoverer of helium, became interested in using astronomy to assist archaeologists in determining the dates of ancient monuments. In 1894, he published a monumental work on the subject, *The Dawn of Astronomy: A Study of the Temple Worship and Mythology of the Ancient Egyptians.*[69] Lockyer knew from the works of contemporary archaeologists that the Egyptian temples had been constructed only after a ceremony called "the stretching of the cord." The pharaoh, accompanied by the goddess Seshat, the mistress of the laying of the foundation stone, would hold stakes connected by a cord. When the cord was aligned perfectly with a star or the sun, the stakes were driven into the ground, and this line became the main axis of the temple. Thus, each temple and major monument in Egypt was aligned to a particular celestial object or event.

Now remember that in Chapter Three we saw how the star fields shift against the yearly tropical cycle of our Sun, yielding what we call the precession of the equinoxes. The entire cycle takes thousands of years, so a period of centuries must pass before there is any appreciable difference between a given event and the stellar background against which it is observed. But Egypt is, in fact, not only one of the oldest known civilizations, but also one of the longest-lived, spanning thousands of years from its earliest times to the Greek era. Thus, any monument erected according to one alignment would, after some time, no longer be oriented to the original celestial object. If a temple had been aligned toward a certain star, after 300 years the light of that star would no longer shine down through the carefully aligned pillars to the shrine. If the Egyptians were attempting to "tune" their temples to given celestial cycles, the temples would unavoidably slip "out of tune" through the natural motions of the Earth.

Knowing this, Lockyer showed that it was possible to date temples and monuments accurately by calculating where the stars would have been thousands of years ago. Since the motion of the precession is known, a simple calculation would allow one to find the star or celestial event to which the temple was dedicated and aligned. Later calculations of this sort led Lockyer to date Stonehenge at 1500 B.C., a date which has been confirmed as substantially correct.

More than this, some Egyptian temples were so old, even in their own time, that the degree to which the stars had shifted was clearly visible to those who populated them. Lockyer showed that the ancient Egyptians must have known the precise length of Earth's year, probably measured from the solstices or equinoxes. Temples were aimed at the solstices[70] and the autumnal equinox, but stars which rose at those times, not the solar event itself, were the important factor. As we know, these stars would shift due to precession, making a temple obsolete. Lockyer showed that not only Egyptian temples, but also the Greek Parthenon, had been reconstructed or added to along the new lines necessary to allow for the precession of the equinoxes. New wings or additional lengths were added to the temples at different angles, clearly showing at which star the monument was being aimed throughout the centuries.

The consequences of this sophisticated ancient knowledge for current models of history was too devastating for archaeologists to accept. Egyptologists had a good chuckle, and Lockyer's work disappeared for many years.

In his foreword to the modern edition of Lockyer's book, Giorgio de Santillana writes that even in 1953, Zbynek Zaba of Prague was unable to locate Lockyer's work for his paper on the orientation of the pyramids. As a result, says Santillana, Zaba "found it necessary to argue at length against the current opinion that the accuracy [of the orientation of the pyramids with the points of the compass] is purely coincidental . . . . Zaba accepts without examination the opinion that the temples are oriented by nothing more than practical convenience . . . . Had he been able to read Lockyer, he would have changed his mind."

Even today, Egyptologists are not required to read Lockyer. Most do not recognize that the Egyptians discussed the precession of the equinoxes in their myths and religion, not in explicit astronomical treatises — an example of modern mentation unable to grasp ancient symbolic and intuitive genius.

Decades passed, and it was only due to the interest and commitment of independent thinkers, some related to occult movements, others isolated scholars and amateurs, that the idea of sophisticated astronomical knowledge in prehistoric and ancient times was kept alive. Establishment archaeologists and astronomers continued to pooh-pooh the idea as absurd, the evidence as fabricated, the investigators as charlatans, and so on ad nauseum. A tired, old record which we will see replayed in later chapters.

But not all ears were deaf and not all eyes were winking in derision. In the early 1950s Alexander Thom, professor of engineering at Oxford, began to publish papers in mathematical and astronomical journals, showing that many ancient sites throughout the British Isles were used as observatories, particularly lunar observatories. Thom had trudged over hill and dale with a heavy theodolite on his back in order to survey accurately the standing stones which are so common in some parts of Europe. By 1967, he was able to publish a summary of his surveys of over 600 such sites.[71] As you would expect of an engineer, his work was precise, careful, and cautious, at first attracting little attention.

If you've tried to follow the motions of the Moon for a few nights, you know it's very complicated. Not only does the Moon have phases, but it rises and sets like the Sun. Sometimes it appears high in the sky, and at other times it appears far to the south. Even to many amateur astronomers, its complicated cycles remain a mystery beyond their ability to observe. But as Thom has pointed out, ancient Britons understood the moon's motion very well:

> . . . these people had it taped. They knew exactly that it came up at one time of year very far up in the heavens, and set in the north, and a fortnight later it was setting equally far in the south. Now by a careful study of these extreme limits, they found that superimposed on the regularity, there was a small wobble of the orbit. The question has arisen, could these people have observed this wobble? And undoubtedly they could. The technique they used was to stand at the ring, or at

the backsight as we call it, look to a distant mountain, and watch the Moon setting behind it. They moved themselves sideways slightly to such a position that the edge of the Moon just trickled down the edge of the mountain. And that was a very exact method of getting the position of the Moon in the sky that night. They repeated it next night, and then from a study of these over a period they found this little wobble. Now the importance of the wobble is that when it is at its maximum, that was the time when there might be a solar or lunar eclipse.[72]

The fact that ancient Britons could detect motions of the Moon which most moderns have never even heard of should be allowed to sink in. But there is more. Many ancient sites have arrays of stones or stone-holes located nearby (including Stonehenge). Why would the ancients spend their time lugging heavy stones about the countryside? Prof. Thom explains:

Now in studying the motion of the Moon as it came up along the horizon farther north every night, there came a night when it turned back. Now that maximum was probably in between two of the observing periods, which were of necessity at the moonset. Therefore, they had to add on a little bit to their position on the ground to get where it would have been had they observed the maximum directly. Now to do this today, we take a slide rule and make a simple calculation. But these people, instead of using a slide rule, had rows of stones set out in fan-shape on the ground. And they carried out a construction on that by walking about and observing.

The ancients had their graph papers, constructed by rows of stones, circles of monoliths, tiles on the floors of temples. Ancient man, the simple savage, was becoming an ancient astronomer. This would be a comfortable conclusion to reach, since modern astronomers enjoy their status, as they see it, as one of our earliest and preeminent sciences. But gradually, scholars are realizing that the reason why they objected so vociferously to the whole idea of sophisticated ancient astronomical knowledge is precisely because it means that all their theories about ancient society are wrong. If ancient Britons were constructing Stonehenge from as early as 3000 B.C. to 2000 B.C., how was it possible to argue that civilization arose in the Middle East and only gradually spread north through Europe? What kind of land, indeed, did the Romans "civilize" when they conquered Britain?

This question is considered and answered in part in Dr. Euan MacKie's book, *Science and Society in Prehistoric Britain*.[73] Thom's evidence for ancient astronomical observatories, says MacKie, "leads inescapably to the conclusion that some very advanced astronomical and geometrical knowledge has been accumulated in Britain and Brittany well before the beginning of the Bronze Age, to such an extent that it is hard to believe that there was not at the time a learned and skilled professional order of wise men — perhaps already very old — whose members were able to pursue their studies full time while supported by the rural population . . . ."

Based on his investigations of Mayan civilization, MacKie suggested that there were highly organized, stratified, theocratic societies in the ancient prehistoric world. The accepted scientific image has been one of simple tribes of hunters, and later, farmers. On the other hand, the popular image has been one of white-robed Druids leading fair virgins to the altar stone for sacrifice under the Full Moon. MacKie points out that many of these ancient stone circles include remains of domestic buildings where priests and the devout would have mingled and studied the heavens.

John Michell in his *Little History of Astro-archaeology* takes this line of thought to its logical conclusion.[74] The old writers have been vindicated, he says, despite the proscription their researches received from establishment scientists. Not only are many ancient monuments, including Stonehenge, astronomically oriented, they are also connected to each other over many miles by "straight track" or ley lines which are still visible. Some can be seen from aerial survey photographs, while others can still be followed along hedges separating modern farm fields. The network they create goes all over Britain and connected hundreds of ancient sites to each other like a modern highway system connects cities and villages.

Michell writes: "Stonehenge was no longer an isolated monument, but the centre of a vast system of astronomically placed stations extending far across the Wessex landscape

. . . . Nor is it the only such system. Its outlying stations must have served as marking points for other astronomical centres, and thus the entirety of Neolithic 'ritual' sites in northern Europe may be seen as the relic of an ancient scientific enterprise, conducted over many centuries and presumably directed by a central college of astronomer-priests whose authority was everywhere accepted."[75]

Is it possible that ancient science was far more exact and pervasive than we have been led to believe? In 1971, Peter Tompkins published a book entitled *Secrets of the Great Pyramid.*[76] Besides a review of the well-known and widely mocked occult theories of mathematical and numerological teachings in the Great Pyramid of Gizeh, Tompkins included as an appendix a fascinating paper by the late Prof. Livio Stecchini, "Notes on the Relation of Ancient Measures to the Great Pyramid."

While a student at Freiburg, Stecchini attended lectures by the philosopher Heidegger, the father of existentialism. Hitler did not approve of the activity at Freiburg, so Stecchini returned to Italy, where he obtained a doctorate in Roman law. He had already studied under professors whose sole specialty was contracts of sale in ancient times, and one of his early papers concerned the length of the mile in Syrian and Roman law. The war forced Stecchini to go the U.S., where he decided to obtain a doctorate in ancient history at Harvard. But he found that historians of the ancient world, in contrast to his professors of ancient law, did not believe in precision of measurement in ancient times. They spoke to him of "the spirit of the ancients" as if the ancients were "in a constant state of alcoholic stupor."

I interviewed Prof. Stecchini several years before his death, as part of a radio documentary series on ancient Egypt:

> I have always been interested in ancient measurements. I wrote my Doctor's dissertation at Harvard on the subject "The history of money in Greece." And I was able to show that the standard of the mint in Athens was based on a grain, which is the modern English grain. The Greeks could be accurate to one-eighth of an English grain in calculating weights.
>
> People were very sceptical about such perfection. Then, I began to think . . . where did they get these measurements? And I found out that the basic measurements were made by the

ancient Egyptians. I found out how the Egyptians measured, which kind of records they had about the size of their own country. And I came to the conclusion that all the measures used in Egypt, Mesopotamia, Assyria, Babylonia, the Old Testament, Greece, Rome, and down to the present English measures, were all derivatives, and simple derivatives, of the Egyptian calculation of the length of Egypt. That was the basis of all measures in the world. The Egyptians had measures about the size of the Earth which in modern times were not achieved until about 1910.

Then I came to the problem of the pyramids. And my conclusion about pyramids is this. A pyramid is basically a representation of the northern hemisphere in scale. So you take a hemisphere, you flatten the sides out, and you get a pyramid. At Gizeh, there are three pyramids. And I was able to determine that the three pyramids form a system. You get all sorts of data about the Earth, its dimensions, the volume and surface, and everything you want by combining the three pyramids. And the three pyramids form a system.[77]

Stecchini's work remains little known and incompletely published. As with the entire field of ancient and prehistoric sciences, few and far between are the scholars who combine such a knowledge of ancient law, measurements, and archaeology.

Thus, if it is not already established, at least the serious possibility has been raised of advanced astronomical knowledge in earliest historical times. The "dawn of history" appears to have been more like the morning coffee-break! What, then, are we to say of early man? Would the club-swinging brutish Neanderthal stereotype survive recent discoveries unscathed?

Curiously, it was NASA, the folks who brought you the Moon live on prime-time television, who were responsible for. the discovery of the origins of astrology. In 1962, Alexander Marshack was contracted to write a history of man's efforts to reach into space. During his research, Marshack became aware of significant gaps in the standard version of man's early history. In *The Roots of Civilization,* he writes:

"Searching through the historical record for the origins of the evolved civilizations, I was disturbed by the series of 'suddenlies.' Science . . . had begun 'suddenly' with the

Greeks . . . mathematics and astronomy had appeared 'suddenly' among the Mesopotamians . . . writing had apparently begun 'suddenly' with the cuneiform of Mesopotamia and the heiroglyphs of Egypt . . . ."[78]

Marshack already had a suspicion that the rituals ancient man performed in his caves had seasonal overtones. Authorities agreed with this idea in general, but no one knew how to interpret the drawings the early cave-dwellers left behind or their carved bones. Why would a hunter, 10,000 to 30,000 years ago, have kept a bone with him, occasionally scratching on its side? Some bones appeared to have marks going around their diameter, much like a decoration. Others seemed to have small holes in them as if a child had stabbed them with a pencil many times. And no one had ever ascribed more to those markings than simple decoration or absent-minded amusement like whittling wood.

Marshack's curiosity led him to examine some of the ancient bones more carefully. Through a low-power microscope, he determined that the markings had been made in a certain order. Furthermore, there were groups of markings which clearly belonged together. They formed number patterns, as if someone had been counting. More than this, they appeared to be counting off the days of the lunar month!

Thus, dating back to what is now our dawn of history, we have evidence that early man carried with him tally-sticks in order to keep track of the lunar cycle. His cave paintings celebrated the seasons, depicting the wildlife which populated his world at various times.

In a more recent paper, Marshack discusses the available evidence for the language and meaning which must have accompanied these decorations.[79] At a site in France that is approximately 300,000 years old — a time when man was not yet homo sapiens, but was already building huts — intentional pattern engravings of bone have been discovered. Marshack's microscope permitted him to see that a series of festooned double-arcs carved by these distant ancestors was "precisely like the tradition that appears later throughout the full 25,000 years of the Upper Paleolithic [period]."

Scholars are correct in their cautious approach to such discoveries. It is their duty to treat them with a view to establishing precisely what the evidence truly shows. But as outside observers, we are also within bounds to note that the dawn of history has now receded by as much as 300,000 years in the past century! Obviously, we still have a great deal to learn and integrate into our current view of our history.

The 1970s witnessed a further step in this revolution. Stonehenge became a popular topic, Erich von Daniken successfully amused the public and outraged scholars with his ancient astronauts and Nazca runways for alien spacecraft. King Tut went on a tour of North America and Europe, giving thousands an opportunity to view firsthand the sophistication of ancient art and culture. Thor Heyerdahl continued his series of cross-ocean voyages in replicas of ancient ships, proving that the ancients could have visited distant continents. Dozens of books were published on each of these topics, a few making bestseller lists. Obviously, the old preconceptions about ancient and primitive man were crumbling away. But what new images were being exposed?

Nineteen seventy witnessed the birth of a fascinating journal entitled the *Journal for the History of Astronomy*. Under the editorship of M.A. Hoskins, this journal began publishing articles concerning the origins of astronomy. At last, there was one vehicle through which the phenomenon of astronomy itself could be studied. Hoskins was quick to begin publishing Prof. Thom's most recent papers on standing stone sites in Britain and Brittany, and he was also quick to put down the expected attempts to scoff at prehistoric astronomy. Although he was willing to publish serious discussions on issues, pro and con, "in this journal," Hoskins wrote, "polemical contributions are unwelcome."[80]

Across the ocean and in isolated areas around the world, scholars were now uncovering ancient astronomical sites with regularity. North America, South America, China, and central Asia were bearing witness to sophisticated astronomical knowledge in many ancient civilizations. A new interdisciplinary science was emerging, and researchers were just beginning to find themselves not alone, but in a small and vital community scattered around the world.

American astronomers were naturally interested in the

astronomy of the ancient Americas. While advanced astronomical observatories from the ancient Middle East and Europe were widely known, the astronomy of the Mesoamerican pyramids was still hotly disputed. Stone circles, not so ancient as Stonehenge and quite primitive in comparison, were located all over North America, especially in the prairie provinces of Canada and the southwestern U.S. By 1977, Dr. John B. Carlson of the University of Maryland began to publish a newsletter to keep researchers informed of the many investigations, books, and conferences. Researchers from fields as diverse as anthropology, archaeology, architecture, art history, astronomy, geography, history, the history of science, physics, and prehistory were eager to have a means of keeping in touch with events in their new field. *Archaeoastronomy Bulletin* lasted only five issues before the amount of new research, conferences, and publications demanded a full-scale journal. Simultaneously, a Center for Archaeoastronomy was established at the University of Maryland, and the archaeoastronomy of the ancient Americas began to yield rich fruits. So rich, in fact, that back in England, the *Journal for the History of Astronomy* now found it necessary to publish a supplementary series entitled *Archaeoastronomy* to accommodate the specialized papers which were emerging and which might not interest those concerned with more recent times.

At the University of Texas Press, particular attention is being paid to the culture of the Mayans who flourished to the south in what is now Mexico and Central America. New works such as *Deciphering the Maya Script*,[81] *Archaeoastronomy in Pre-Columbian America*,[82] and *Native American Astronomy*[83] show that something important is happening to our historical perspectives.

"It takes little imagination to see that there is much in this subject which has not been, and cannot be, explained from a purely materialistic point of view," writes Michael Coe in his foreword to *Native American Astronomy*. "For instance, the astonishing markings in the desert pampa of southern Peru, or the strange Building J at Monte Alban in Mexico, or the crescent moons and stars in the rock art of the American Southwest. It is clear that there were powerful currents of thought at work among the early inhabitants of the New World which went far beyond economic, political, and social needs."

Both volumes on archaeoastronomy mentioned above were edited by Anthony Aveni, professor of astronomy at Colgate University, a leading authority on ancient Mayan astronomy.

In 1978 I interviewed Prof. Aveni about his research:

> *Aveni:* "There's no question that the ancients were interested in the heavens. They were interested primarily in following their gods across the sky, and they wanted naturally to master nature by understanding the cycles of these gods. Now once they established a writing system they could record these observations. And lo and behold, maybe after a few lifetimes they could see that certain phenomena like eclipses recurred at regular intervals. Now the discovery of the recurrence of eclipses for an ancient person . . . oh, that would be like our putting a man on the Moon. It would have been a stupendous scientific achievement. And it would have led to further interest in the celestial cycles. After all, the ancients fully believed that the heavens controlled crop cycles, they determined when fertility periods occurred, when to plant, when to harvest. So in a very direct way I think ancient man was in contact with his environment. That's why he was studying astronomy."
>
> *Dean:* "It sounds like you've almost discovered ancient *astrologies*, not astronomies."
>
> *Aveni:* "Yes, I think that's fair to say. Astronomers used to think of astrology as a demeaning term, and wash their hands of it. And I think for the ancient Maya, the people that I study, astronomy *was* astrology. Let's face it, there's no doubt that these people were motivated by religious forces, and I think that we have not appreciated their astronomy fully because we thought of religion as a drag force, rather than the impetus which pushed them on. That has caused us to demean their astronomy relative to the Greek astronomy which comes to us through the Renaissance, and which gives us our scientific view of things.
>
> "We have to realize that just because religion was driving them, that this is no reason to think that they weren't too accurate. We tend to view things too much in the present, and too much in the context of our own culture. For that reason, I

think we're a little chauvinistic, and we should try to erase that."[84]*

And so we have come, not only to the source of astrology and religion, but also to a great turning point in our understanding of our buried past, and the earliest stages of a new understanding of ourselves, our modern culture in a crisis of transformation. We have discovered not ancient astronomies, but ancient *astrologies,* even at the dawn of human culture. Little wonder that these discoveries are gathered under various names — ancient astronomies, astroarchaeology, archaeoastronomy — anything but what they really were, which is astrology in its pure, original form.

---

*In the light of Chapters Ten and Eleven, some of Prof. Aveni's points take on a new aspect. There, I discuss modern evidence which closely parallels modern traditional astrology, and the current attack on astrology by a small but dedicated, high-profile group of media personalities in the academic community. Their argument in general has been that a belief in the occult, and hence in astrology, leads inevitably to "irrationalism and obscurantism" and therefore is a bad influence on society in this "enlightened" and so-called scientific age. They interpret history as a difficult struggle on the part of a few rational thinkers who gradually broke free from superstition, religion, and political oppression. Thus, reality can only be established through rationalism and science. Spiritual experiences, too, must be explained in terms of currently accepted scientific methods and concepts. And since astrology has no currently acceptable explanation, it must be rejected as part of our magical baggage, along with any evidence which might hint at a core of truth to such a dangerous idea.

It should be made clear that most contributors to this attack on astrology are avowed atheists. For them, any religious connection or origin is an undesirable one. Religion, according to their view, has not been a positive, progressive force in the development of human culture.

This position was once defensible; it emerged from eighteenth- and nineteenth-century materialism, precisely when man was embracing new technologies for which classical religions had not prepared him, and to which they could not adapt. This led inevitably to an essentially mechanistic world-view in which consciousness itself, and especially symbolism, are still great unknowns, and even greater "ignoreds." I have already touched briefly upon some of the contradictions this world-view is facing from recent discoveries in quantum physics.

One result of the rationalist-materialist world-view is that spiritual experiences are not accepted as *real.* They are discussed as "deep feelings" or "dehumanizing beliefs." Scientists reject them as completely and

This does not make sense until we remember that the essential ideas of ancient astrology have been largely confirmed by modern science. Today the interactions of the terrestrial and cosmic environments with crops, wildlife, and even human populations are being studied in another new field called biometeorology. The first textbook devoted exclusively to human biometeorology was published in 1963 by the Dutch scientist, Dr. S.W. Tromp.[85] There, he cited 4,400 research papers on the effects of climate and weather on humans and their environment. These effects include solar radiation, electrostatic and electromagnetic fields, cosmic radiation, gravitational fields, seasonal diseases, the month of birth — all factors which astrologers both modern and ancient have attempted to deal with. An update of this original textbook to cover the period up to 1973 added 3,500 more research papers and involved about 100 new contributors to review the entire field of biometeorology.[86] In a recent paper, Tromp has gathered and discussed studies suggesting a wide variety of extraterrestrial influences, ranging from effects of the Sun and planets, to cosmic rays, the influence of the Moon, and so on.

---

irrationally as others accept them without question. Hence, according to the rationalist-materialist view, all aspects of what is now called the paranormal must be vigorously rejected. Hence, the current attack on astrology discussed in Chapter Eleven.

In contrast, note Prof. Aveni's positions that the ancients were in direct contact with their environment in a way which must remain mysterious to most urban residents, that religion was an impetus, a valuable coherent model of the natural forces which surrounded ancient man and which led him to greater precision in observing natural cycles. Religion was not a drag force against cultural and scientific development.

Even if spiritual experiences, as real events involving higher realms of consciousness and energy, do not exist, even if we choose to explain them simply as "religious feelings," the evidence shows that in ancient times there was no split between religion, science, art, and society. The split is, in fact, a product of the decline of modern religions which have themselves slowly turned away from and denied spiritual experiences.

No wonder, then, that astrology is so automatically reviled, and evidence for it so vehemently rejected. Ancient man was obviously familiar with, and saw himself as living within, a kind of astroecology — a unitary and organic world-view which is inherently frightening and repulsive to modern thinkers who have already suffered from our modern cultural schizophrenia, long before it occurs to them to attack or investigate astrology.

Current research "strongly suggest(s) the existence of unknown forces in our environment," says Tromp, "either electromagnetic radiation, corpuscular radiation or gravitational waves, each of which has an extra-terrestrial origin. They could affect the biosphere either directly or indirectly."[87]

Another modern field of research which has come perilously close to vindicating the general idea of astrology is that of cycle research. In 1971, Edward R. Dewey published his book, *Cycles: The Mysterious Forces That Trigger Events,* in which he summarized years of research into the cyclical behavior of crop yields, stock prices, wars, life insurance sales, and just about everything else.[88] Dewey even discovered a 9.18-month cycle in ton-miles of the Canadian Pacific Railway between 1860 and 1960! "During World War II," he wrote, "the cycle almost vanished . . . but after the war it reasserted itself on the same time schedule, same wavelength, and same calendar timing as before the war!"

Dewey is survived by his Foundation for the Study of Cycles, located in Pittsburgh. Some members of the foundation represent one of astrology's most clandestine populations. Their journal, *Cycles,* has published many articles on economic trends (with obvious implications for investment programs). But it's amusing to see some articles making occasional reference to planetary positions and even quoting from the writings of leading astrological thinkers — all while carefully tiptoeing around any possible connection with astrology, of course.

To their great discredit, modern astrologers are virtually totally ignorant of research in biometeorology and cycles. The majority of them are not really capable of grasping what these fields are about, quite frankly. Otherwise, there would have been some significant movement within their ranks to incorporate fresh findings and new methods. But this has only emerged as a definite trend in astrology since roughly 1975, and only a few dozen astrologers are involved in the movement.

At the same time, biometeorologists and archaeoastronomers have not put their heads together to explore the possibility that the ancient astrologers might have been on to something. We could just dismiss the whole idea by saying that the ancients were correct in their suspicions, but totally wrong in their astrological methods and assumptions. That would be a comfortable conclusion. But in Chapter Ten, we will examine evidence that indicates it might not be a long-lived one.

At least, we can now attempt to outline what the earliest astrologies were like, and what they attempted to achieve. We know that ancient man was closely in touch with nature and continually attempted to understand the forces which faced him. The seasonal character of crop cycles, the abundance of wildlife, and the weather must have rated top priority in terms of research — much like our nuclear defense programs today. If there were any way to predict when it would be more productive to hunt or fish, ancient man would have eventually found it.

His earliest astrological preoccupation appears to have been with the lunar phases, counting off the days of the month on his tally-bones, and drawing pictures of the wildlife he depended upon for sustenance. There is some evidence, not accepted in academic circles as yet, that even at these early stages, man was exploring the numerology of astronomical cycles and developing calendars to deal with them. Some of the earliest figurines could have been representations of planetary gods.

As man's understanding of the motions of the Moon developed, he began to erect structures (observatories) which permitted him to make detailed and long-term studies. Whereas modern astrologers are almost totally concerned with the Moon's motion through the signs of the zodiac, ancient astrologers studied other aspects of the Moon's cycles. They were interested in the times when it appeared most northerly or southerly on the local horizon. Their astrology was developed from direct and continual observation of both celestial and terrestrial cycles, not a modern book of tables such as a planetary ephemeris. They were very concerned with eclipse cycles — about which modern astrologers are fairly confused — knowing that they had some relation to invisible radiation which can blind the on-looker, that they were connected with earthquakes and eruptions of the Earth from time to time, and so on. And they studied the cycles of the seasons in order to understand more deeply how heat follows cold, plenty follows famine, rain follows drought. Indications are that the earliest astrologers were an elite and highly educated class of society, whose function was not only to improve knowledge of celestial cycles continually, but also to lead society into a harmony with them.

Two things ancient astrologers did not do: They did not tell fortunes or write ego-flattering sun-sign columns in newspapers. An astrology of the individual did not exist until ancient Greece. Early astrology was preoccupied with the welfare of the tribe, only later personified through a personal astrology for the monarch.

What, then, is the truth about archaeoastrology? We could simply discount it as an early attempt to deal with natural cycles, biometeorological phenomena, and the cosmic influences we will discuss in Chapter Ten. This conclusion is comforting to most archaeoastronomers for several reasons. It allows them to maintain the official line that astrology was/is simply superstitious nonsense which encumbered early scientists. Thus, they can search early star maps and translate early texts purely for records of eclipses, solar spots, novas, and comets. As a result of this, the vast bulk of astrology's literature remains untranslated and inaccessible. The history of astrology per se is buried and widely held to be unworthy of study. Not one single university in the world permits degree studies in the history of astrological theory.

We might adhere to the position that while cycles and climatic effects are known, astrology is silly and archaeo-astrology best left to the archaeoastronomers. This position ignores the fact that clear links have already been shown to exist between planetary positions and personality, while other effects of extraterrestrial origin are now under study.

Or, we might take the astrological bull by the horns, so to speak, and take up the position held by esoteric thinkers such as John Michell (quoted above), who suggests that ancient monuments were part of a coordinated scientific endeavor designed to interface directly with the forces of the Earth and other celestial objects. That is to say, astrology really can be put to some practical uses, once it is properly understood.

That is clearly a difficult task. We have already begun to see how many layers of nonsense must be peeled away before anything like serious astrology begins to emerge. Most astronomers are now beginning to accept the idea that the ancients were capable astronomers, but that there might actually be some kinds of cosmic influences (even non-astrological, biometeorological ones) remains an uncomfortable thought. Most biometeorologists are comfortable with their seasonal effects and their electromagnetic-field studies, but that these might be responses to a larger cosmic environment seems to be pushing things a little too far, too fast.

Yet the trends are quite clear. Once the barriers between these various disciplines come tumbling down, once enough bright and open minds begin to grasp the implications of all the available evidence, cosmic influences along roughly astrological lines will be on their way to acceptance. Horrifying as this possibility must seem to some critics and skeptics, the indications are that this may well happen before the century is out. Thus, in archaeoastrology we see not only the origins, but also the destination of serious astrology, biometeorology, and astronomy. Astrology has often been called astronomy's poor cousin. Apparently it is both parent and bride-to-be.

Seven

Sex, Money, and Health

Astrology simply isn't for everyone. Most people are not really concerned with the "why" of reality. After all, the greatest astrologer in the world still can't tell you what's going to happen to him tomorrow. He can tell you "why" it will happen, and he can tell you the meaning of its happening, or she can. But to actually say "tomorrow at 12:15 a bus will collide with a taxi cab in front of my house" is beyond the powers of any astrologer. And most people don't want to know "why" or "how" anything is occurring in the universal or cosmic sense. They simply want a convenient way to avoid more thinking. And of course, this brings into being the type of astrology that we see in the sun-sign columns, which will undoubtedly always be popular with the public.[89]

Jim Lewis, astrologer

"How's your love life?" the television commercial inquires.

One way or another, your sex life, your money, and your health are the three great concerns of life. Thousands of business concerns are built on your concerns. Feeble, doubt-ridden creatures that we are supposed to be, we are offered all sorts of potions and medicaments, all the way from shampoos and automobiles to magic charms, astral por-traits, and psychic readings. Beer commercials feed on our supposed feelings of inferiority and alienation from others, preaching the amazing social grace which proceeds from the communion of a Saturday evening session "with the boys." Automobile manufacturers invariably manage to sprawl an expensively clad blond over their cars. Cosmetics manufacturers offer their products tacitly as aphrodisiacs and surefire hooks to "get that man." You are a social eunuch if you don't participate in these paradigms in some way. People without cars are in some way suspicious. Girls without makeup are plain janes. If you think commercial sports are ridiculous, there's got to be something wrong!

Yes, sir, just step right up, and we'll fix you for good. You can't decide what your goals are in life? You don't know which lifestyle fits you best or gets you ahead the fastest? The commercial interests of the world offer their free services "just for you." Remember that phrase from an earlier chapter? Why, if you can't provide your own imagery, they'll do your mental interior decorating for you. Just stare at this advertisement. . . .

The point is that we are faced on all sides by interests which prey upon our feelings and offer ways to modify them. Most of these interests are vast multinational corporations, beyond reproach because their fortunes employ thousands and help to fuel national economies. At the other end of the spectrum are the "free offers," "how to be a millionaire," "your personal four-leaf clover," and sad but true, various astrological offers promising "the secrets of instant success."

We have already taken a look at the dimensions of popular astrology in this regard. It is quite doubtful that great amounts of money are being removed from the purses of the gullible by purveyors of astrological charms and horoscopes. Certainly, rumors abound of occasional charlatans making small fortunes from one-dollar "free" offers. But the scale of such scams pales in comparison to those regularly perpetrated by some of the industries mentioned above.

Serious counseling of all kinds, too, often centers on these three areas of human need. Somehow we imagine that if we could experience sexual and emotional fulfillment, have unlimited amounts of money, and perfect health, that would be the end of our wants. What many people do not realize is that counselors from many schools of thought do not aim to make you a superman or superwoman. Their practical aim is most often simply to assist a client or patient to return to normal functions within society. That is, a patient often emerges from a therapy with all the somewhat unfulfilled needs, all the money and health problems that normal people have. The value of the therapy is simply judged by how well an individual adjusts to these perfectly normal conditions, how well he or she functions on a day-to-day basis.

Most of us are brought up automatically to think that others can help us in some way. The authority of teachers, the church, the peer group, the boss at work, the authority of authorities in many fields outside our own expertise — these encourage us to seek solutions and answers from others. But in contrast, there is a school of thought in contemporary psychology which suggests that no one really benefits from a therapy or counseling session. Some psychologists maintain that psychoanalysis or psychotherapy are as unscientific, in their way, as astrology is held to be. They aren't surprised when someone enjoys or appears to benefit from a horoscope reading. After all, they say, psychiatric patients appear to benefit from their psychotherapy sessions as well. And they claim there is no strong evidence to indicate that therapy or counseling really works. It's impossible to tell if treatment accomplished the healing, or if the patient was already on the way to spontaneous healing and then sought out some kind of therapy or counseling once the process had begun.

Isn't it nice to know that the "experts" are just as confused as the rest of us? With these points in mind, and remembering our discussion of gullibility and statements of universal validity, we can now take a look at astrology in action. How do counseling astrologers work, and what other applications is astrology being used for?

There are lots of reasons why you should have the experience of a horoscope reading from a competent astrologer. First of all, you might just be curious. Curiosity is a wonderful thing: it has led man all the way from the primitive jungle to our modern asphalt jungles! If you would like to know something about astrology, no one, including the rabid skeptics who are trying to convince you that astrology is dangerous to society, has the right to keep you from satisfying your curiosity.

But how to do it? Do you simply walk in the door and "have a reading"? This is not the best approach. You should be clear on the real reasons why you have decided to have someone read your horoscope. Do you want to test astrology? That's a valid reason, and a reading is certainly one way for you to see for yourself if there is anything to it. But often, a client who on the conscious level does not believe in astrology will request a reading and desperately search for some clues within the astrologer's words regarding a pressing concern.

If this is the way you approach an astrologer, you're doing everyone concerned a disservice. Any counselor first clarifies what the actual questions and concerns of the client may be. Then, answers may be sought. But if you smugly try to discount astrology during a reading, while within there is turmoil and unanswered questions, you are simply wasting time, money, and ultimately denying your own needs.

If you wish to test astrology by having a reading, tell the astrologer you have selected. He or she will be quite happy to give you a reading while showing you how a horoscope works, how he is deriving statements from the symbols written on the chart, and how predictions are made. That way, you not only have a chance to see if there's any validity to astrology, but you also come out of the experience with a personal introduction to the subject.

How should you select an astrologer? Surprisingly, many people don't realize that astrologers are listed in the *Yellow Pages* in many cities. The telephone companies in some areas still refuse to take ads for astrologers, but since astrologers have won practically every court case and bylaw prosecution thrown their way, this prejudice is slowly crumbling away. The size of the ad in the *Yellow Pages*, or even the fact that the astrologer has an ad there, is not a good guide to the quality of the astrologer.

Do not assume that because Astrologer So-and-so is on your local radio or television station that he or she is a good astrologer. Radio and television programs are often only a small step above sun-sign magazines, and it demands a special kind of showbiz mentality to make astrology interesting to a general audience. This is not necessarily the kind of sensitivity you need to have a fruitful counseling session.

Remember that you're up against a field where over 90% of those involved are sheer, unadulterated amateurs. And most of them don't even know it. The overwhelming representation of females in astrological circles (85% of sun-sign magazine readers are female) indicates that a "housewife syndrome" is operative. Astrology is a great hobby for some homemakers, but a qualified homemaker is not necessarily a qualified spare-time counselor.

In countries such as England, many astrologers do all their business by mail, never seeing their clients. Generally, the astrologer is contacted through a newspaper or magazine ad or by a reference from an acquaintance. You submit your precise birth-data, along with the fee, and await a written report which usually gives you a character reading along with the general trends for the next few months. Since you never see the astrologer, and the astrologer never sees you, this approach is often pot luck and rejected by many serious astrologers for that reason. But if personal attendance at a reading is inconvenient, or if you are not that curious after all, mail-order astrology is a step above the automated variety of horoscope readings we discussed in the last chapter. At least, if you have further questions, you are dealing with a human. Once having said his piece, the electronic analyst has nothing more to add.

While satisfying the renowned British penchant for privacy, such arrangements are virtually unheard of in North America, where clients are expected to attend in person. Written reports are sometimes available at extra cost, but clients are usually welcome to bring a cassette to tape their horoscope reading. And since astrologers, like medical specialists, are sometimes victims of court cases based on their counseling, don't be surprised if you are requested to sign a legal-release form before the reading begins.

There are several criteria which will assist you in eliminating some of the incompetent astrologers in your area, although they will not necessarily lead you to the best. There may be a local astrological organization. A telephone call will determine if they have a code of ethics and established standards for practicing members. If they act as if they've never heard of such an idea, hang up and go elsewhere. Be aware that many "institutes," "schools," and "societies" are simply shingles for an individual astrologer. Generally, the more pretentious the title, the lower the quality of the astrologer. Inquire if the organization is a democratic and legally incorporated entity. Some organizations have a list of practitioners who adhere to their code of ethics, and they will assist you in reaching those on that list.

Once you have several names to choose from, you should talk to each astrologer, in order to establish what fees are paid for what services. How long has he or she been involved in astrology? A minimum of ten years is often needed to produce a fairly competent professional astrologer. Does the astrologer specialize in any particular applications of astrology? How long has he or she been actually counseling? Does the astrologer have another profession? Does the astrologer have any relevant background in counseling, psychology, or business? And most important, on the basis of your conversation, do you feel you have a personal rapport with this particular astrologer?

If all you are seeking are snappy predictions and character analysis, do not pass Go, return to Chapter One, and begin all over again. Lots of people get a bit of a shock when they attend a reading expecting trite sun-sign astrology and are suddenly confronted with unrequested details of some personal concern about which the astrologer should not know anything. You can get your ego-flattering jollies much more safely from a computer.

How much should you expect to pay? High fees do not guarantee a high quality of astrological competence. But by the same token, a very low fee might indicate an amateur astrologer, an apprentice, or someone who doesn't care enough to do a thorough job. You should also remember that one astrologer might charge extra for a service which another includes in the basic fee. As of 1980, thirty-five to fifty dollars was an average first-time charge for a general horoscope reading with perhaps up to one year's analysis of trends.

What happens next? Astrology is based on timing, and for an accurate natal horoscope or birth chart to be calculated, it is necessary to know as precisely as possible when and where you were born. In some countries it is not legally required for a doctor to record this information. They rarely make a point of stopping during the delivery to record an accurate hour and minute. Relatives are often quite forgetful about the time of home deliveries or weren't present in the hospital delivery room. So you must inquire carefully and obtain as much precise information as possible. A conscientious astrologer may go so far as to require you to present a copy of your birth certificate, so he knows that the data you present is accurate. Without this documentation, some refuse to do any work on a horoscope. And conversely, if an astrologer accepts the birth information casually over the phone, without inquiring as to its precision or its source, you should cancel the arrangement then and there — he or she doesn't know or care enough to be precise.

Some astrologers will accept approximate birth-data, but insist that a reading can't be done until a "rectification" has been performed. The theory of rectification goes like this: As you will see in a few pages, horoscopes are not static; they change continually throughout the life. There are various systems in astrology which attempt to describe these varying conditions. Obviously, if astrology is valid, you would expect significant symbolic combinations to occur at the times of important events in the life. So, by reversing the process, the astrologer can work with a chart in order to compare a given list of important events with what would have happened in a particular horoscope, if the birth had been at one time or another. By carefully working within the known time-span during which the birth occurred, it is theoretically possible to determine which chart would be the correct one.

To make this clear, remember that in Chapter Three we observed how a horoscope is derived from the astronomical conditions at birth. You know that the fastest changing factor is the daily rotation of the Earth, which places every planet in relation to the local horizon. In traditional astrology, this is judged by the zodiacal sign rising in the east at the time of birth and the sign overhead at the noon point, the Midheaven. The houses of the horoscope are divisions of the circle of the zodiac based upon one or both of these points, depending on the system used. The astrologer has several events, then, to judge against known events in the biography which he has requested from his client. He might see that the earliest possible birth-time would mean that one sign was rising, but a later possibility would have produced another sign as the ascendant. Each possibility might place the planets in different houses, or it might produce different angles (aspects) between the ascendant and the planets. The first clue, then, would be to see which chart, out of the various possibilities, fits the observed character of the client best.

Then, with a likely candidate in mind, the astrologer can begin to see what would have happened in that chart at the age of a known important event. If a significant astrological event matches up with the actual event in the biography, the chart begins to appear to be valid. Another event is tested, and another, and another. Thus, with some detective work, a skilled astrologer maintains that he can detect a real birth-time from a false one. But the emphasis here is on skill. It takes a certain kind of astrological talent to be able to work with the dynamic systems of astrology, to be able to see how the chart would have moved *in time* during the period of the given biography.

Obviously, this would be a potent test of astrology. Even if particular astrologers failed it, there would still remain the possibility that a computer could begin to judge when the astrological systems are making significant hits versus known events in a given biography. Yet there have been no formal tests of rectification, probably because most critics of astrology don't know enough about the subject they are criticizing to see the possibilities rectification offers as an important test of traditional astrology. Certainly, most advanced astrologers can recall cases where they received confirmation of a rectified birth-time when a client came across accurate information long after the initial reading was requested. We'll come to the dynamic methods used in rectification in a few pages; I only mention it here because so many people don't have accurate birth-data, and because this is often the first process an astrologer will apply to a horoscope of a client.

Once the birth data is accurately established and the horo-scope calculated, the astrologer usually studies the chart and makes notes before the actual reading. With practice, it is possible to gain an impression of the kind of personality a horoscope represents fairly quickly, although at this point there are no inherent indications of sex, intelligence, background, or important life events. If it is a "blind test" of astrology which you are seeking, it might be better to deal with a mail-order astrologer. But if you wish to obtain a meaningful and relevant reading, giving the astrologer personal details and outlining areas of immediate concern will be of great assistance. Naturally, critics will pounce on this idea and suggest that astrology is nothing more than "cold reading" — picking up hints from the client and cleverly feeding them back in a new form. Serious counselors of all kinds will respond by pointing out that counseling proceeds from human interaction; one could not expect a valid reading from a psychological personality test without a counselor's interpretation, either.

The astrologer works with three main elements in a chart, plus a fourth. As we saw, a horoscope is constructed from the positions of the planets at birth, and these are measured in terms of house and sign positions. Thus, planets, signs, and houses are the three basic sets of elements in astrology. The fourth element comprises the aspects, or angular distances between points in the zodiac, within the chart.

The planets represent patterns of behavior and styles of acting. They are the dynamic forces in a chart, which indicate what type of activity is to be expected. We speak of martial music, mercurial wit, and so on, each representing some characteristic style of action and energy.

The signs are passive environments which modify these modes of energy. In traditional astrology, signs do not in themselves indicate dynamic patterns, but they can modify energy with which they interact. It is difficult to speak of a sign without explaining it in a context. Usually the context is that of sun sign. Or we might speak of the ascendant or rising sign, the sign on the Midheaven, and so on. An astrologer might ask, "Where is your Mars?", but one rarely hears the question, "Where is your Libra?" There are books which discuss the archetypal symbolism of the signs of the zodiac, but again, most of these books refer to the sun sign as a kind of lifelong path of development which each person born in or under that sign experiences. Other discussions of the signs tend to view them in terms of their myths or their origins in history. So the signs are at once the most mysterious and most essential issues in modern astrology. Their importance in advanced astrology is vastly overrated by the public and by amateur astrologers. Indeed, there is a tendency amongst the most advanced theoreticians nearly to abandon them. Unfortunately, the public rarely hears about this level of astrology.

Houses are the third main element of traditional astrology, and there is broad agreement that they are several times more important than the signs. These are also a twelve-fold division of the sky, but the division is based on the horizon at the time of the horoscope, not on the zodiac. Each house is held to represent a particular area of the "native's" or subject's life. The origin of this system is not well known or understood, particularly because establishment scholars have never really interested themselves in this aspect of astrology. As we saw in the previous chapter, they often simply extract the astronomical basis of astrology for their historical research. Thus, most of the essential historical documents which might help modern researchers determine how houses developed remain untranslated and inaccessible to serious astrologers. One school of thought holds that the houses represent mundane analogues of the signs. Thus, Aries would be similar to the first house, Taurus to the second, and so on. Other astrologers maintain that the houses must be considered as quite distinct from the signs. In this century, there have been attempts to link the system of astrological houses with the mandalas which Jung studied. Thus, the bottom of the chart, the I.C., might represent the Unconscious of Jungian psychology, while the line formed by the ascendant and descendant signs would represent the conscious level.

Another great problem which astrologers love to dispute is the method which is used to obtain the house cusps or points in the zodiac where each house begins. The most commonly used method today is that of Placidus, a seventeenth-century astrologer. This method is being used with success in statistical research today because it divides the daily arcs of the planets into equal portions of time, avoiding statistical problems which other house systems produce for re-searchers. Those a little more technically oriented often favor a similar system invented by the twentieth-century German astrologer, Dr. Walter Koch (1895-1970), called "birthplace" houses. What the different systems do is to change the degree of each house cusp, or starting point, in the zodiac. In extremely northern latitudes, some house systems cease to work, which has led to great debates on the astrology of people born in those regions. Like those in so many other fields, astrologers will often shrug off all these problems, saying simply "it works." But even though you don't have a clue about these problems, it's an interesting test to ask the astrologer you've chosen which house system he's using, how it works, and why he chose it. If you get a blank look, you might have an amateur on your hands.

When you put these three elements of the chart together, astrology begins to work. You have a planet, in a sign, in a house. Or, a mode of action, modified by a sign, working through a certain sphere of life activity. Each such combina-tion allows the astrologer to make a statement about some aspect of the personality represented by the chart. Then, the fourth element, the angular relationships between each such statement comes into play. Each planet, in its sign and house, is in aspect to another planet in its sign and house. Thus, each area of the chart is naturally connected to other areas, allowing for complex symbolic statements describing psychological complexes and mundane experiences. With all these combinations and permutations, as Robert Hand points out, "There are more possible horoscopes than there have ever been human beings."[90]

Amateur astrologers will often read a chart by taking out "cookbooks" and going through the various analyses given by authors for each combination of planet, sign, house, and aspect. But a skilled astrologer will study the chart to see which symbolic statements keep emerging from all the combinations. Any important personality trends will be stated repeatedly in the chart through different combi-nations.

One point rarely appreciated by the public is that horoscopes are not as specific as they are often held up to be. We have the image of the showbiz astrologer who appears to know all about you, all the intimate details of your inner life, through your personal horoscope. Yet, many people are born at roughly the same time as others, and in the same places, and therefore have similar horoscopes. Thus, a counseling astrologer will often emphasize that besides the horoscope, there are the other conditioning factors to be considered — heredity, family background, order of birth, education, life experiences, and so on. Through a continual process of feedback and questions, the client and astrologer can quickly narrow down any fields of interest and their relevant symbolism in the chart. This is why an open and honest approach to the experience of a reading is best. There is no way a serious astrologer can predict how you are responding to your early conditioning, including the astrological conditions present at your birth. But once the counselor understands what level you are working on and what your current areas of concern are, the information which can be retrieved from a horoscope can become quite detailed and useful indeed.

At this point, no doubt, there is a skeptic grumbling that it's all a matter of cold reading, gullibility, and showmanship. This is something you'll have to determine for yourself if and when you have your chart analyzed by an experienced astrologer. But it is worth remembering that a growing number of psychiatrists are becoming interested in using astrology as an aid to understanding their patients. It is well known that Carl Jung studied astrology for over thirty years. "I must say that I very often found that the astrological data elucidated certain points which I otherwise would have been unable to understand," he told the Indian astrological authority, Dr. B.V. Raman, in a letter in 1947.[91]

Elucidation is the key word. Ideally, you go to see an astrologer in order to have that which you already know clarified.

Once the basic reading is complete, the obvious question is: "What next?" You breathlessly await forecasts of gloom and doom, or vast, unexpected inheritances. One criticism sometimes leveled against astrology is that a birth chart is supposed to dominate someone for his entire life, and yet people change as they age. In order to describe these changes, astrologers employ various dynamic methods which update a horoscope to any given time period. There are two basic methods to accomplish this, transits and directions.

Transits are simply the planetary positions at the current time. These are taken out the sky, as it were, and placed in the horoscope, where they form new combinations of planets in signs and houses to natal planets in signs and houses. Thus, a planet transitting into a house permits the astrologer to suggest that a particular sphere of activity in your life entered into a particular type of change between certain dates. Or, a planet might transit another planet in your horoscope, producing other combinations of symbols. Since the planetary motions are known well in advance from tables of positions (ephemerides), the astrologer can indicate when a crisis period might arise or come to an end. He or she can outline the general level of tension and change which will be occurring during a given period and perhaps give more specific details regarding these changes.

Directions work the same way, except that they are not real positions in the sky. Rather, they are derived by a variety of methods which do not correspond to actual astronomical motions. The most common method of directing a horoscope is called "secondary progressions." In this method, the first day of life is taken to be symbolic of the first year. The planetary positions of the tenth day are symbolic of the tenth year, and so on. This method really compares two astronomical motions, the daily rotation of the Earth, with its annual revolution of the Sun, in a day-for-a-year formula. Astrologers claim that the cycles which are derived in this fashion represent the major phases of your life cycles. Thus, the Moon takes about twenty-eight days to orbit the Earth. By the method of secondary progressions, then, it would go around the chart and return to its birth or natal position at about age twenty-eight. This is one of the best known and most widely used cycles in astrology, called a "lunar return."

Such cycles in life patterns were once totally rejected as nonsense. But recent studies have shown that there are indeed classical stages in life through which most of us pass at certain ages. Psychologist Daniel Levinson recently published the results of a study of middle age in males, entitled *The Seasons of a Man's Life*, in which he discusses several attempts to describe these stages and determine at which ages they occur. Levinson studied forty men from various backgrounds, born in different years, and confirmed that there are age-linked stages in life, each of which has its characteristic stresses, dangers, and promises.[92] His research became the basis for the bestseller, *Passages*, in which Gail Sheehy described the "trying twenties," the "catch-thirties," the "deadline decade" of the mid-thirties, and so on.[93]

Levinson quotes the Spanish philosopher José Ortega y Gasset who has suggested that there are five main stages in life:

Childhood	0 - 15	years
Youth	15 - 30	
Initiation	30 - 45	
Dominance	45 - 60	
Old Age	60 -	

These phases closely parallel the phases of the progressed Moon in astrology. Remember that the two most important phases of the Moon are the New Moon and the Full Moon, when the Moon, Earth, and Sun are in a straight line together. At the rate of a day for a year, the first full-moon phase of the progressed Moon to its natal or birth position occurs around age thirteen or fourteen. Then, by age twenty-eight, the progressed Moon returns to its birth position. Just as adolescence leads to a flowering of sexuality in puberty, at the first full phase, Ortega y Gasset's middle-age Dominance phase also occurs at a progressed full-moon phase.

If psychologists had been interested in finding out, they would have discovered that astrologers have been working with these life cycles for some time and that their models are quite detailed. The German humanistic astrologer, Alexander Ruperti, who has been studying these phases in his professional practice since 1937, recently published a detailed account of planetary cycles in life patterns.[94] Thus, the general idea of transits and progressions has some scientific support, and with the cooperation of interested psychologists, it will be possible to test them further, with obvious benefits to both psychology and astrology.

Beyond transits and progressions, there are various specialized techniques used in forecasting for desired periods or for looking back at previous periods to see what symbols corresponded with the actual events under study. Whereas transits and progressions are operations added on to the basic natal horoscope, actually drawn on outer circles very often, these other techniques consist of drawing an entirely new chart for a specific moment in time and space. Although the charts themselves are entirely new sets of symbols, they are linked to the birth chart in a special way. For instance, following our example of progressed Moon phases, an astrologer might calculate a horoscope for the moment when the Moon returns to its birth position. This would occur at a specific moment in time, and the new chart is calculated for the time and place where you are located at that instant. Since most of us don't leave our home base very often, it's usually cast for your present place of residence. These charts are known as "returns" and the two most commonly used types are those of the Sun and Moon, hence "solar returns" (a kind of astrological birthday-chart) and "lunar returns." The positions of the planets and angles in these charts are compared to natal positions, and a diagnosis of the period of time covered by the chart can be obtained.

Astrology becomes a kind of oracle through a technique known as horary astrology. Here, the astrologer notes the time at which you pose a question to him and calculates ("erects" is also used) a horoscope for this instant. Sound strange? Remember that astrologers often adhere to the idea of synchronicity, that all events occurring in the same moment of time are somehow connected. From this idea, it would theoretically be possible to find a way to interpret a horoscope for a question, since the question has arisen at a certain moment in the mind of the astrologer (that is, when you posed it to him or her). Horary astrology was far more popular in previous centuries, and today there are few specialists in this field. Most of its applications tend toward business and law, and therefore horary astrology demands a rare sort of client who is well-informed about the various ways in which astrology can be used and can afford to pay a competent astrologer to do them. Since legal or business interests are concerned, the few astrologers who do practice horary astrology regularly tend to charge higher prices for these services. But I must repeat again that I know of few astrologers who earn an adequate income from such services when compared to the earnings of specialists in other fields which demand similar periods of training and apprenticeship.

The rules of horary astrology are complicated and antique. They represent an accumulation of rules developed by seventeenth- and eighteenth-century astrologers, essentially preserved to this day. Unlike the astrology of personal counseling, which is continually adapting to modern psychology and developing new methods and theories, horary astrology is a veritable museum of astrological concepts. A horary astrologer would speak of a "collection of light," "combust" planets, "dignities," and "debilities." For instance, in order to see whether a lottery might be won, a horary astrologer would attempt to balance the "testimonies" found in the horary chart. The "testimonies of loss" would be calculated in this manner:

"[If] the ruler of the fifth [is] separating from the ruler of the first or second and applying to a parallel or other good aspect to the ruler of the seventh, eighth, or to Uranus, Saturn, Mars or the South Node, you may expect to lose."[95]

For obvious reasons, many modern astrologers do not enjoy being associated with horary astrology. They view it as an essentially oracular technique which might involve pure guesswork or possible psychic phenomena on the part of the astrologer.

Another service commonly requested from astrologers concerns the first of our trilogy of concerns — your love life. Many clients are concerned about a potential mate or the progress of an already established relationship. Astrologers are often requested to analyze a relationship as an entity in itself, usually by one of the partners who has obtained both sets of birth data for this purpose. Astrologers take several approaches to this problem. One is called "synastry." In this technique both charts are laid side by side, and the positions of the planets are compared to each other, one by one. A newer technique is that of the "composite chart." Here, both horoscopes are calculated, and the mid-point between each pair of planets is derived in order to draw up an entirely new horoscope composed entirely of the mid-points between the two subjects. Like the horary chart and the various "returns," this chart is held to be symbolic of the relationship between the two individuals. They need not be lovers, of course; they might be employer and employee or any other relationship. "Cookbooks" are available specifically for this application of astrology. Another experimental variation on this theme is the "relationship chart," which is calculated for the mid-point in time and space between the two sets of birth data. That is, if six months and 7,000 miles separate the two births, these are divided and a new time and location is derived so that the relationship chart can be erected. This technique does not appear to be very successful, and it will probably not be widely adopted by astrologers. Counseling astrologers depend on results to make their living, and when a technique does not appear to work reliably, or at all, it is usually dropped after a few years of experimentation. Thus, although it is horribly unrigorous and "unscientific," there *is* a kind of quality control in astrological techniques.

The astrology of health — medical astrology — is even more of a specialty. There are probably only a few dozen astrologers who have really studied the subject, and so it is difficult to say what will become of it. You'll probably recall seeing those medieval drawings of a nude body with the signs of the zodiac attached by lines to different parts. The concept was that if the zodiac is a symbol of the stages through which any given process passes, then the human body might also be seen as a process proceeding from the head down to the toes. Thus, it was held that Capricorn, for example, ruled the knees, and transits or bad aspects to Capricorn might indicate problems with that part of the body. Some of the more traditional astrologers attempt to take this analogy to an extreme and have devised systems of relating various degrees of the zodiac to particular portions of the spine and internal organs of the body.

But like all fields within astrology, medical astrology is not static. New ideas are still developing and being tested. In the 1940s, Dr. William Sheldon developed a theory which he called Constitutional Psychology.[96] Sheldon believed that temperament, psychological and psychiatric profiles, vocational aptitudes, and the tendency to specific diseases all arise from the particular kind of physique you have. He divided the body into five sections, from the head and neck down to the legs, and developed a method of classifying people according to eighty-eight "somatotypes." Each type defined a particular set of body characteristics developed along three main themes — the endomorph, the meso-morph, and the ectomorph. Endomorphs tend to have well-developed digestive systems and viscera, mesomorphs have well-developed bones and muscle, and ectomorphs have well-developed nervous systems and skin. The classical endomorph is the "jolly fat man," the archetypal meso-morph is the Charles Atlas he-man, and the ectomorph is stereotyped as the tall, thin matchstick. Obviously, few people are a pure type, so Sheldon could draw a triangular diagram with a type at each corner, and locate your specific characteristics somewhere in between the three extremes.

In 1977, the American astrologer Ruth Hale Oliver published an interesting analysis of Sheldon's work, showing that by a simple translation of symbols, his somato-types could be related to astrology. From this basis, Oliver was able to show that one can predict the body type from a horoscope! And, by following Sheldon's line of thought, it was possible to relate vocational aptitudes, psychological profiles, and likely physical illnesses to certain astrological configurations. Oliver was no newcomer to medical astrology. She had already published a book on astro-psychiatry with Dr. Harry F. Darling, a psychiatrist and astrologer. So far, she has had little success in interesting medical researchers in testing her theory. Considering the billions of dollars which medical research firms waste every year in essentially cosmetic pursuits, such a test would cost peanuts and possibly open up new horizons. But as we all know, there are no planetary influences, and astrology is nonsense, so there's no point in investigating it, is there?

Astrology is slowly and quietly gaining a foothold in the psychological community, however, especially among therapists with some background in Jungian psychology. Psychologists from other schools are usually too inured in statistical, behavioristic, and materialistic thought to be open to the symbolism of the human psyche. This is one reason why, as I noted above, some psychologists even reject out of hand the whole idea that therapy or counseling can actually accomplish anything. Yet, as we will see later, research is underway at the University of London with promising results for planetary influences in human behavior. Elsewhere, there is a growing number of psychologists, sociologists, and others who are determined to put astrology to the test. Several doctorates are now in progress on astrological hypotheses, with positive initial results. One positive aspect of this movement is that it is precisely the behavioristic and statistically oriented psychologists who are undertaking the best research in the field. The obvious implication is that somewhere down the road a new union of schools of thought may well occur, providing us with a psychology which is simultaneously symbolic, empirical, and responsive to the reality of cosmic conditions.

One astrologer who works regularly with psychologists and psychiatrists is Debbi Smith. Smith maintains practices in London, England, New York, and Philadelphia, in addition to her frequent lecture tours. When I first asked her if I could interview some of the doctors she works with, she told me that although she has written letters of recommendation from them, they were not willing to speak openly of their therapeutic use of astrology:

> *Smith:*   "It's a very peculiar situation, because more and more psychiatrists are coming to astrologers. In fact, I work for seven different doctors, psychiatrists, one psychoanalyst, and a couple of psychologists. And there are other doctors who come quietly for consultations of their own. Now the problem, of course, is that there's still a great deal of superstition against astrology, and most of the people who have degrees are afraid that the AMA or whatever organization may be holding the whip-hand over their salaries will protest and get them in trouble. So although they use astrology, and they use it with their patients all the time, they are very reluctant to come forward in case they get shot down by their colleagues."
> *Dean:*   "Do you think there's any chance that this might change?"
> *Smith:*   "I'm sure it's changing. In another few years so many psychiatrists will realize that they've all been to astrologers, or a great majority of them have been, that once they start talking to each other about it, perhaps the atmosphere will change."[90]

Smith's role in the therapy is to read the patient's horoscope, sometimes in front of the psychiatrist, but usually to the patient himself. The patient takes the tape recording of this reading to the psychiatrist, and in the next session, they listen to the tape together. The astrologer has to be careful with the diagnosis, however, since some patients are not stable. If the possibility of a suicide emerges from the prevailing symbolic trends, the psychiatrist can use this information to advantage, and the patient need not know where it came from.

"I've been rated at 90% accuracy," Smith states. "And the psychiatrists tell me that to have a horoscope done on a patient can save them the first six months of analysis. So it saves a lot of money for the patient as well, because the psychiatrist knows what to shoot for, and what things to sort out, much more quickly."

At some point, the process reverses, however, and the astrologers go to the psychiatrist to learn better counseling techniques, while the psychiatrist learns better astrology. An example of this is occurring in New York City, where a group of counseling astrologers (those hardy souls who put up with their clients' infatuations with their love life, their health, and their finances) meet monthly with psychiatrist, Dr. Bernard Rosenblum. Rosenblum is a classic example of an individual who has overcome his conditioning enough to consider the possibility of astrology. "I had ignored it for many years," he told me, "and toward the end of my medical training, I had certain experiences and heard certain stories which suggested that I had perhaps been limiting my world view. When I finished medical school I started looking into astrology. Finally, I had an astrological-chart analysis done by a New York astrologer which was very informative and expressed a lot of my deeper nature which she couldn't have known at our first meeting, and which indicated some deep validity to astrology. I began to investigate astrology during the next year, and had other readings of my horoscope by other astrologers to further understand my chart and what astrologers can do. I've taken a few courses so I can read charts myself, but it takes many years to understand astrology in its depth and breadth, so I still have many things to learn about it."

Rosenblum meets monthly with his astrological counseling group, where they share their mutual interests in the therapeutic applications of horoscopes. Most astrologers have not had an opportunity to study the basic schools of thought in psychology and psychiatry, just as most psychologists have not had an opportunity to learn about serious astrology. So in each session, a client's horoscope is discussed, counseling strategies are outlined, and readings in the various therapeutic schools are given. The astrologers gain from a training which is officially denied to them elsewhere, while the psychiatrist receives his education in astrology. It's a fair and dynamic deal. And even if astrology is total nonsense, at least the astrologers will emerge as better counselors.

"I've been fortunate in getting to know some of the best astrologers in terms of their overall understanding and world view," Dr. Rosenblum says. "So I don't think I'm dealing with a cross-section of astrologers in my workshops. They themselves agree with me that they need more therapeutic techniques and skills. But their scope is unclear inasmuch as the actual role of the astrologer is unclear. At times, astrological practice seems to be education, at other times it's more counseling, and at other times it's therapy. The astrologer can do a very effective job in terms of the one-time astrological reading if he has a fine mind, and a sense of responsibility."

Rosenblum feels that interest in astrology will gradually increase. It won't be the "in" thing for quite a while, but astrology could become quite predominant in psychology and psychiatry in time.

If it hasn't already been made clear, we find the same spectrum of quality in astrology as it relates to the basic human needs which are popularly known as "sex, money, and health." At one end of the spectrum, we find that many successful, but not necessarily good, astrologers make a point of centering their readings on these concerns, because they are proven money-makers. The public is interested in personal information without paying the price of self-examination. Thus, they are easy marks for someone offering advice in these areas of life.

Beyond this level, there is the bulk of the serious astrological community. These are well-meaning individuals who may well provide some assistance through their readings. But they lack the training which would make them effective counselors to their clients. If their services are sometimes ineffective and not always beneficial, it is society itself which ought to accept the blame. If a child is told he is an idiot all his life, he may end up believing it. Worse, other people might firmly expect it of him. Similarly, astrology and astrologers have suffered derision for so long that it takes a rare brand of courage and insight for someone in the medical profession, for example, to take a hard look at the therapeutic and analytical possibilities.

What may be said at this point is that if astrology is not on the verge of being accepted, it *is* on the verge of being paid attention. Researchers in North America, England, and other European countries are now beginning to seek out interesting astrological ideas in counseling, medicine, and personality theory. Leading astrologers are welcoming these developments, although I suspect it has not become clear to them how many of their preciously held traditions they may have to relinquish. These trends really must be seen as part of a much larger movement among counselors and medical thinkers. Witness the great proliferation of new therapies and psychological systems, particularly since the 1960s. Not to mention all the diet fads, exercise fads, new religious and self-improvement movements.

People everywhere are in search of a greater wholeness in their lives. If they claim to have found some guidance in this search from astrology, no one has the right to deny them that search or to denigrate their experience. We might at least give them a fair hearing, because we might need help ourselves some day.

Your Personal Fortune

If astrology can be used in personal counseling, it can also be used in counseling an employer about his personnel. According to a report in 1977 in *The Globe and Mail,* one of Canada's most prestigious newspapers, astrology is becoming a "closet phenomenon" in American business.[97] Reporter John Picton wrote that "to the 186 scientists . . . who got together to denounce astrology two years ago, [astrology] may sound like nonsense. But it is bucking a growing trend to say so." According to one of Picton's sources, industrialists keep their astrological interests quiet, because "it still has a bit of the witch-doctor status." Picton's report pointed to an interesting fact. While skeptics often refuse to examine astrology until they can be shown how it works, businessmen tend to take a more pragmatic view. If they observe practical benefits from astrology, they will use it.

Personnel counseling for business is an obvious extension of the astrology we discussed in the previous section. Most astrologers can provide this service within the limits of their ability to read a chart without seeing a client, although the thought of being considered or rejected for a job solely according to one's birth data horrifies some critics of astrology. Employers should not rely on the decision of an astrologer, obviously, since many other factors must be weighed in any personnel selection. But personnel astrology does present some interesting possibilities for employers. For instance, the chart of a candidate may be compared with the chart of a business in the same way the charts of a relationship can be compared. In theory, this should describe the nature of the relationship the employee will have with his or her new company. In the case of executives, this kind of information could be critical to a company's future. Then, considering the implications of transit and progression systems in astrology, you can see that it would be possible for an astrologer not only to suggest a good candidate for a position, but also to look ahead and see whether a candidate might be experiencing relative calm or great changes during the next few years. Some companies only count on a five-year tenure with their employees, so someone likely to experience a divorce or severe personal problems during that period should be examined with extra care. On the other hand, companies who attempt to marry their employees for life have the possibility to see what problems a given employee might be facing during a period where his or her productivity is definitely sagging, and when the problems might be relieved. These are all slight modifications of the basic services which astrologers perform as a matter of course in normal public practice.

A few companies go further, however, and hire a staff astrologer. This person might remain hidden, working out of his own office under a contract, or he might be given a desk in the office just like everyone else. One such corporate astrologer is Gary Christen, who was employed by a U.S. steel firm. Christen's employer, the late Jack Savitt, had a background in astrology and even specified the particular techniques which he expected an astrologer to use for him. Christen spent his mornings with a small computer, preparing a day-to-day report which was submitted to his employer, advising him when to act on various business deals. Steel markets were monitored astrologically, and when a key staff member was to attend a meeting, his or her astrological situation was first examined in order to gain maximum advantage for the company.

Christen's other duties as corporate astrologer involved the use of horary astrology, this time applied to offers which might be phoned in during the business day, and general strategy for the company.

"Some people would say that having a staff astrologer in a company would be getting into trouble, not out of it," I said to Christen.

He laughed. "Actually, we get calls from other businesses — some that we deal with and a few that we don't deal with directly — requesting advice from us! We don't run an official service, but if someone is doing business with us, they would consult me through the company." Christen presently works with Astro-Graphics, a New England astrological firm which provides astrological computations and other computer services.

American Express and various large oil interests use astrology, but in a less serious manner. At least one astrological computer-service is currently employed preparing horoscope calculations for advertising campaigns, and the technique appears to be very effective. So many people are interested in receiving a free horoscope medallion or chart, even without an interpretation attached, that initial test marketings have been expanded into national offers across the U.S.

Some clients of astrological computer-services not only request special kinds of print-outs — planetary phenomena which astrologers do not normally even think of using — they also request that the computer services do not release the details on precisely which phenomena are being studied.

Obviously, somebody thinks they're on to a system with regard to the stock markets and doesn't want to let the cat out of the bag.

One business specialist who has released some of his techniques is Sam Crawford, a New York market investment advisor. Crawford publishes a stock market newsletter based on planetary cycles. Formerly a technical analyst for one of the major stockbrokers in the world, Crawford is not an astrologer in the usual sense. He is representative of a group of investors who have become convinced that planetary cycles, sun spots, and other phenomena do have some influence on market conditions and the world economy. But such investigators are often quite incapable of reading a horoscope. One couple I met who have been using essentially astrological methods in stock investment for years found natal astrology extremely puzzling, because dealing with a human being is infinitely more complicated than predicting market behavior. In human astrology, as in psychology, they found everything debatable and subject to other factors, but in their stock market work, they felt they had developed a fairly sure-fire technique which would allow them a predictable rate of success.

Sam Crawford's background was in physics, mathematics, and finance. His approach to finance is statistically oriented. "And when these (planetary cycles) started showing up in my statistics as extremely valuable," he said, "my surprise was as great as anyone's."

On May 15, 1978, *The Wall Street Digest* quoted Crawford as predicting a strong market rally in the summer, contrary to other predictions. "My research will have a good test during this summer," he stated, "as no period in recent memory has such combined cycle force on the upside."

During the summer of 1978, I remember seeing some beaming faces at the biannual convention of the American Federation of Astrologers in Atlanta. As predicted, the stock market had just gone wild, and some people were a few dollars richer.

Crawford's stock market newsletter, *Crawford Perspectives,* was one of the few sources which predicted this market surge. Crawford provides graphs of the Dow Jones industrial data, according to his astrological calculations,

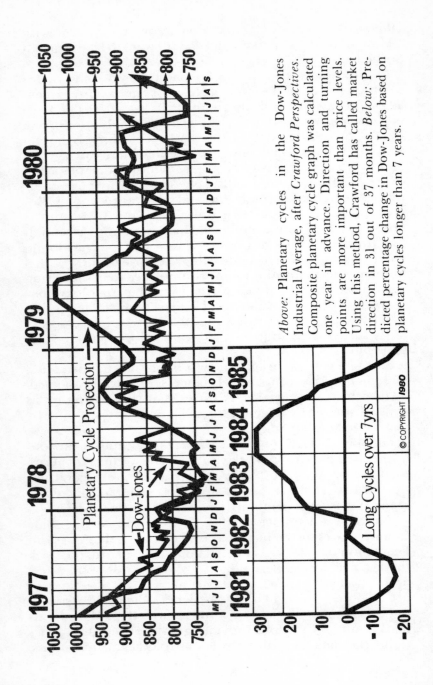

Above: Planetary cycles in the Dow-Jones Industrial Average, after *Crawford Perspectives.* Composite planetary cycle graph was calculated one year in advance. Direction and turning points are more important than price levels. Using this method, Crawford has called market direction in 31 out of 37 months. *Below:* Predicted percentage change in Dow-Jones based on planetary cycles longer than 7 years.

Planetary Cycle Projection ⟶

←Dow-Jones

Long Cycles over 7yrs

© COPYRIGHT *1980*

from nine planetary cycles. By the end of that May, five cycles were up and four were down. In the first week of July, six were up and three down. By July 18, a seventh cycle turned up, and the two that were down "were not down sharply."

"I indicated that there would be a very sharp market rally during that period," Crawford recalled. "For instance, you can take the day of an astronomical event, and then look at the previous time it occurred. You study one day before, two days before, three days before. Or one week before, two weeks before, and so on. By averaging market performance over several such events, you can come up with an idea of how a particular type of astrological event may effect stock prices. It's statistical, so from that point of view, there's no cause-and-effect relationship. But we do have very powerful statistical tools which make a strong case at this point for certain astrological aspects."

Strong enough to convince several hundred investment-specialists to subscribe to his newsletter at $250 per year, that is. And Crawford only publishes nine of his cycles. More than ten others are used in his personal work with gold futures. "Normally, we would not pay much attention to such unsubstantiated prediction were it not for that fact that Crawford predicted almost to the Dow point and day the 1977 decline, its end and reversal," noted one stock market newsletter. Others have added *Crawford Perspectives* to their stable of basic advisory letters. Said one, "Called the bottom — in advance — perfectly!"

For an overview of astrological cycles in stock markets, Thomas Rieder's book, *Sun Spots, Stars, and the Stock Market,* provides a fascinating discussion of the problem and the possibilities.[98] Rieder is a Toronto patent engineer who has stressed the study of astrology in areas where statistics can permit verification. His study of market conditions from 1899 through 1971 led him to conclude that downturns in the market are a result of aspects between Mars and the outer planets. Most of the traditional indicators did not pan out in Rieder's investigation, although for a time it appeared that Saturn passing through Leo and Taurus might be having some effect on the market.

"My system was not intended to make anybody rich," Rieder told me, "but to demonstrate the correlations which exist." Nevertheless, as a result of his cycle analysis he got out of the stock market and into gold and silver several years ago "because I saw nothing but disaster."

Rieder believes that the four-year business cycle follows the cycle of Mars quite closely on a one-to-two basis, since Mars takes roughly two years to orbit the Sun. Cycle researchers, such as Dewey, have found that often natural cycles may skip a beat, invert their phase, or even disappear for a while and return as if they had been there all the time. One of Rieder's most interesting observations is that since the U.S. dollar was cut loose from the gold standard, entirely new factors seem to be at work in the market, and a new analysis may be called for. Currently, Rieder is working on new medical applications of magnetized inert gases.

Other astrologers have found evidence that the zodiac may be involved in market fluctuations. The Washington astrologer and computer specialist, Michael Munkasey, believes that the stock market generally declines when the Sun enters a new sign of the zodiac, as investors take a day or two to adjust to the new astrological and market conditions before resuming normal trading. Between January 2, 1971 and July 24, 1973, Munkasey reports that on the thirty-one occasions when the Sun changed signs, the market generally declined. The probability that such an event was happening by chance, says Munkasey, is over 1,187 to 1.[99]

During the Inquisition, there was a time when effectively all of contemporary Western scientific progress and research was in the hands of Muslim scholars in Spain and northern Africa. The Christian Church managed to suppress intellectual thought much as modern totalitarian governments are doing today. During this period, astronomy and astrology reached new heights, and it is only now that scholars are beginning to survey and translate the immense Arabic astrological literature of this period for clues to astronomical events of that time.

Yet, while the West may have forgotten this interesting epoch, the Arabs did not. So a reporter for *The Wall Street Journal* was surprised, but should not have been, when Arabia's Oil Minister, Sheik Zaki Yamani, offered to cast her horoscope.[100] Yamani is reported to have asked for precise birth-data, including the time of birth, and the latitude and longitude of the city in which the reporter was born — all the information required for a proper and accurate horoscope to be cast. The kind of information someone who knows more than a little about astrology would request.

Think about that the next time you say, "Fill'er up."

Eight

Astrologers All

Astrology presents itself as a science of influences, but it is difficult to understand the condition of modern astrology without some background on the influences under which astrology itself has suffered in modern times. Personal astrology — the astrology of the ego, we might call it — is in itself a modern development. As we have seen, the ancients were concerned with the practical considerations of attuning whole societies to the heavenly cycles they were studying. So far as we can tell, there was no thought of making specific predictions for a given individual — with one exception, the monarch.

Just as the monarch represented a link between the divine powers that be and the world of the commoners, the astrology practiced for ancient monarchs may have provided the vehicle by which the astrology of the individual emerged. By Babylonian and Greek times, mathematics had developed to the point where planetary positions could be calculated with some precision. The stylus and a sheet of papyrus had replaced the pyramids and stonehenges of more ancient astrologers. A portable astrology — as opposed to a monumental one — meant that an individual qualified to calculate a horoscope was no longer tied down to a ceremonial center.

One astrologer who has studied the problem of the origin of horoscopic astrology is Robert Powell, editor of the

British esoteric Christian astrological magazine, *Mercury Star Journal*. Powell suggests that the basic concept behind horoscopic astrology has its origins in the Chaldaean priesthood of Babylon.[101] The library of the Assyrian king, Assurbanipal, which was sacked in 612 B.C., contained an extensive collection of astrological omens, based on general interpretations of planetary and stellar observations. But there is no hint of a personal, ego-centered astrology. After the Assyrian empire collapsed, Babylon returned to its role as the world's leading cultural center. The earliest-known personal horoscopes date from the fifth century B.C. and were calculated by Babylonian priests. The Babylonians believed that souls descended from heaven, passing through each of the planetary spheres until birth in the physical form was achieved in the last sphere of Earth. Once the life had been accomplished, the spheres of planetary consciousness were experienced in reverse order as the soul ascended once more. Thus, the personal horoscope was a diagram of the spiritual laws and forces which had precipitated a particular birth at a specific time and place, for the fulfillment of a soul's evolution.

Powell believes there is circumstantial evidence to indicate that it was in the reign of the Babylonian king, Nabunaid (Nabonidus), which terminated around 539 B.C., that the personal horoscope experienced its own nativity. These were the last years of the Jewish captivity in Babylon, the time of the prophet Daniel. Babylonian mystery schools were active, and Zaratas the Chaldaean, who taught the priesthood, counted among his pupils a young Greek named Pythagoras. King Nabunaid himself had visionary dreams in which he received instruction from the stars and planets. Powell concludes that it must have been in this period, as a result of the Babylonian mystery teachings on the incarnation of the soul, that the doctrine of the horoscope emerged.

The astrology which subsequently developed in Greece is substantially the same astrology which is practiced today. The general meanings of the planets, the houses of the horoscope, doctrines such as "aspects," all seem to have their roots in ancient Greece. Predictions were sometimes easily available from a local astrologer who would calculate a horoscope (often incorrectly) for a few coins and present the client with a clay tablet containing his planetary positions and a rudimentary interpretation. The quality of these prognostications is virtually identical to those found in sun-sign magazines today.[102] By 80 B.C., Greek scientists had even developed a mechanical clockwork device which could calculate planetary positions and eclipse cycles, anticipating by two millennia the advent of the electronic analyst.[103]

But the Greek emphasis on the individual did not survive long. With the European Dark Ages and the subsequent climb to the Renaissance, astrological knowledge became limited to monasteries and royal courts, where scholars were funded and could obtain sufficient expertise to master ancient texts and the mathematics needed for planetary calculations. Although the astrology of the individual had been established for centuries, it remained a luxury available only to the privileged few.

The modern era of astrology began with the printing press. Having developed from attempts to delineate cosmic influences, astrology now collided head-on with McLuhan's Gutenburg Galaxy. By the seventeenth century, Western minds were well on their way to a hypnotic fixation on mechanistic interpretations of the universe, and astrology was gradually shut out from the establishment's version of the universe. Once the jewel of science, art, technology, religion, and culture, astrology was now generally ignored, sometimes berated, occasionally summoned to the witch-hunt. Bright minds who dallied with it found increasing pressure to drop the central concept of an intimate relationship between the Earth and the heavens. Space was to become a black void, a vacuum in which nothing can exist, and through which pass only the known forces of high school physics.

Effectively shut out from the benefits of academic funding and official protection, it is not surprising that astrology suffered. Most of those who were competent to study the then-known Greek texts were no longer interested in astrology. Those who were interested in astrology found themselves outsiders, cut off from their own history and heritage. What today we call the occult sciences could no longer count on a Kepler or a Newton to devote many hours to their study.

Yet, when the printing press arrived on the European scene, bringing with it fresh intellectual breezes, astrologers were as quick as other groups to take advantage of it. Text-books of astrology in everyday language became available, giving rise to an increased number of astrologers. Once astrological teachings became more easily available, a demand for the services of astrologers must have developed, just as many other once-royal prerogatives became common experiences. Modern editions of some of these early authorities are available in reprints today, especially the work of William Lilly.

But as with modern astrology, it was business interests with no commitment to astrology and a beady eye on profit which helped to popularize and debase the celestial science. The Stationer's Company, a trade union of the printing and publishing industry in seventeenth-century England, was granted a monopoly on almanacs as early as 1603. By the middle of that century, there was a booming market for predictive almanacs written by the leading astrologers of the day, Lilly, John Gadbury, and others. As Ellic Howe points out in his history of modern astrology, *Urania's Children*, "The shareholders in the Company's co-operative publishing business there had a vested interest in encouraging and supplying the demand for this kind of ephemeral literature."[104]

On the Continent, Howe maintains, astrology "remained well underground or was almost completely forgotten" until the end of the nineteenth century. But in England, the various astrologers who wrote almanacs for the publishers became the early equivalent of household brand-names. In 1768, Francis Moore's (c. 1657-1715) *Vox Stellarum* sold over 100,000 copies, while the combined sales of five other almanacs that year came to only 13,000 copies. As the early almanac writers died out, publishers tried to maintain their aura by hiring new writers under the old names. The current *Old Moore's Almanac* appears to be the modern descendant of an imitation *Vox Stellarum* which was first published in 1844. Howe believes "It was this annual ration of predictive almanacs that kept belief in astrology alive at a popular level in Great Britain long after it had been more or less completely forgotten in Europe." And as we saw in Chapter Three, this is basically the argument used by sun-sign astrology writers today in defense of their products.

The first purely professional astrological magazine emerged in 1793, when *The Conjurer's Magazine* became *The Astrologer's Magazine*, devoted to "contribute to the revival of Astrology; a science which . . . has been exposed to much calumny and error." Like nearly all serious journals of astrology, it didn't last long. After only seven issues, it folded. By 1814, John Corfield's *The Urania* appeared and immediately died, indicating that time had not increased the interest in a professional journal. Howe records that the British Museum copy contains a note in Corfield's hand-writing saying he was "promised great assistance by pretended Lovers of the Science in the execution of this work, but all failed me; and being left with the editing and expence thereof, it consequently fell into the ground. . . . The letters in it are written by myself to myself for the want of correspondents." Corfield's experience confirms that serious astrology has always represented a tiny minority within a population of curious onlookers who are themselves a minority within society.

But while astrologers were busy attempting to make the public aware of their doctrines and services, astronomers (now no longer astrologers) were busy looking to the heavens for entirely new kinds of signs and portents. Even today, astrology is reeling from a series of discoveries which began with Uranus in 1781. Astrological tradition had been largely confirmed by the contemporary experiences of astrologers with their horoscopes, but many astrologers were not ready for the discovery of a new planet for which no tradition existed! Even today, some astrologers castigate their peers for using Pluto or the asteroids in their horo-scopes.

One delightful tale surrounding the early astrology of Uranus is provided by the life of John Varley, who was a friend of William Blake. Varley, who was a painter and some twenty-one years younger than Blake, was also an astrologi-cal authority. Varley's *Treatise on Zodiacal Physiognomy* is a testament to the emphasis which a painter would bring to astrology — observation of forms, especially the human body. Like other astrologers of his day, Varley must have been excited at the discovery of Uranus in 1781. The opportunity to be one of the first to describe its influence must have been as fascinating as being the first to explore a newly discovered country.

As a result of his early work with Uranus, which was then called "Herschel" after its discoverer, Varley predicted that a serious event would befall him just before noon one day. As noon approached, Varley became greatly agitated, walking up and down his studio, unable to concentrate on anything. A few minutes before noon, he said to his son, "I am feeling all right; I do not think anything is going to happen to me personally; it must be my property that is threatened."[105]

At that moment, someone outside cried "Fire!", and Varley ran out to see what was wrong. His own house was on fire. Varley's son Albert recalled that "He was so delighted at having discovered what the astrological effect of Uranus was, that he sat down while his house was burning, knowing though he did that he was not insured for a penny, to write an account of his discovery. He had timed the catastrophe to within a few minutes. . . . Although he lost everything in the fire, he regarded that as a small matter compared with his discovery of the new planet's potentiality."

The discovery of Uranus was quickly followed by other new celestial bodies. On the first day of 1801, Ceres was discovered orbiting between Mars and Jupiter. The search was on for other tiny planets, and Pallas, Juno, and Vesta were discovered in 1802, 1804, and 1807 respectively. Neptune was not discovered until 1846, and another asteroid was not located until 1845 when Astraea was observed. Yet in 1836, one astrological textbook detailed many of the problems which advanced astrologers of this day are still attempting to work with.

To make this clear, it is first necessary to understand that astrology does not simply deal with the position of the planets *per se*. A planetary position can be expressed in one of several frames of reference besides the usual one of zodiacal longitude. It can be expressed from the point of view of the Earth (geocentric) or the Sun (heliocentric). Important points in a given planet's orbit are also of interest to astrologers. Hence, the Moon's nodes (the place where the

Moon's orbit cuts across the orbit of the Earth around the Sun) are commonly found in horoscopes. The points midway between these events, maximum latitude north and south, are sometimes used. And the place where the Moon is closest (perigee) or farthest (apogee) from the Earth are also studied by some astrologers. Mathematically, all these values are of some use in calculating planetary motions or are derived easily in that process. Astrologers have suspected for some time that it might be possible to detect the meaning of these additional points, as well as the basic meaning and actual position of each planet.

In 1836, J. T. Hacket published his *Student's Assistant in Astronomy and Astrology* in London. His text shows that a dialogue concerning the new astronomical discoveries was well underway among serious astrologers. "Some astrologers say they are of no consequence," Hacket wrote of the asteroids orbiting between Mars and Jupiter, "as they are not easily seen. . . . I am very much of the opinion that the small planets, Vesta, Juno, Ceres and Pallas, ought to be noticed, especially as significators of accidents and hurts." Hacket also considered that the other frames of reference and positions in a planet's orbit mentioned above were worthy of study. He included a discussion of perigee and apogee, heliocentric positions, and even the nodes of the planets.

Hacket was decades ahead of his time in terms of astrological innovation. In 1973, the New York astrologer, Eleanor Bach, published an ephemeris of the first four asteroids, complete with proposed astrological interpretations derived from her study of Jungian psychology and mythology. This was followed in 1977 by a more extensive and accurate ephemeris by Neil Michelsen and Dr. Zipporah Dobyns,[106] so that today, the first four asteroids are almost a commonplace in horoscopes, particularly in North America. Yet their recent astrology was developed in total ignorance of the studies which astrologers had made of them more than a century earlier.

Similarly, the nodes of the planets can be given in either heliocentric or geocentric frames of reference, and some recent authorities such as Dr. Dobyns have attempted to delineate their psychological effects in horoscopes. Yet

Hacket's 1836 textbook contained tables of the planetary nodes, for as he put it: ". . . if the ascending and descending nodes of the moon . . . should signify the effects described by some authors, I can see no reason why that nodes of the ponderous planets Jupiter, Saturn, or Herschel, should not likewise have effect, aye, and those too of Mars, Venus and Mercury. . . ."

The moral of the story is that if the planets move in circles, so do astrologers. Without the benefits of the establishment — funding, scholastic institutions, archives, and libraries — astrologers have left the history and development of their techniques as virtually unexplored territory, a territory which is rapidly crumbling into oblivion. Even today, the best astrological organizations have poorly maintained libraries, and there is no single definitive collection of astrological publications anywhere in the world. Public and scholastic libraries often look upon their astrological collections more as nuisances than fascinating repositories of a proto-science. The Library of Congress refuses to classify astrological works. Astrologers therefore live in a kind of never-never land in which the past is continually forgotten and only the present exists. He who does not remember the past is condemned to repeat it. And so, cut off from their roots, astrologers even today are "discovering" concepts and theories which date back centuries, and in some cases, millennia.

The history of modern Western astrology in the Americas is not well known, mainly because of the preoccupation of historians with the various Christian movements which settled in New England. The American historian, Jon Butler, writes that the commonly held attitude is that astrology and the occult are mundane and practical — that they were used solely for worldly power — while Christianity ultimately triumphed over them due to its ethereal and philosophical superiority.[107] On the contrary, Butler asserts that even before the colonization of the Americas got under way, occult practices were common among even the wealthy, literate upper-class society of England. Records indicate that English astrologers and alchemists visited New England before the English Civil War in the mid-1600s. "It seems likely that [the early] Americans not only read sophisticated occult literature," says Butler, "but contributed to it as well." In 1694, Johannes Kelpius brought a German pietistic Christian community to settle in Philadelphia, where they continued to uphold astrology as a legitimate Christian practice. And just as in England, there were locally published colonial astrological almanacs, giving planetary positions for the year along with gardening and medical advice. So great was public demand for occult information in these almanacs that several New England publishers complained bitterly about the pressure placed on them to publish material which they found objectionable.

By the early eighteenth century, interest in the occult had died down considerably and gone underground within the Masons and other secret societies. Following the English pattern, occult theories were kept alive by outcasts from the establishment mold. The new evangelical Christian movements which replaced witchcraft and occultism in the popular mentality, and the new scientific discoveries which encouraged belief in materialism and the rejection of occult concepts, led to legal movements to ban astrology. Colonial governments moved to steer colonists away from the occult and to make orthodox Christianity the only legitimate religion in the colonies. Maryland's Act of Toleration of 1649 protected Catholics and Puritans from slander, but avoided similarly encouraging sorcerers, "wise men," or witches. By 1727, a Boston almanac-maker complained that his colony's fortune-tellers were not being prosecuted by local officials.

But astrology and occult practices may have survived in the Americas through a curious symbiosis with the Christian groups which had once persecuted them. Christianity has had a long history of permitting heathen gods and ceremonies to exist within its theological framework once its position in a given society has been secured. Butler believes the relationship between Christianity and occult practices among laypersons in America may have been creative rather than hostile. Spiritualism retained strong roots in the Unitarian movement of the northern states, and in the South, evangelism flourished side by side with occultism among both blacks and whites. By the American Civil War, one Unitarian turned spiritualist observed that "When the minister of a cold, conservative church preaches his last closing climax of sermons against spiritualism, he little knows that of the church membership who sit patiently beneath him, more than one half are spiritualists already in their hearts."

The romantic movement of the nineteenth century found astrologers at once reawakening slowly to the depth of the symbolism they held in trust, while they were adapting slowly to the implications of modern scientific (especially astronomical) discoveries. The early history of astrology in the Americas had been forgotten, and few of the early almanacs and texts survived. The transcendentalists sought a new harmony with nature based on their intuition, which reflected some astrological insights and concepts. Walt Whitman spoke of ". . . Speeding through space, speeding through heaven and the stars,/ Speeding amid the seven satellites and the broad ring, and the diameter of eighty thousand miles,/ Speeding with tail'd meteors, throwing fire-balls like the rest,/ Carrying the crescent child that carries its own full mother in its belly."[108] Yet despite the knowledge of astrology which must have survived, at least in folk lore, among North Americans, Ellic Howe reports that he was unable to locate a domestic American astrological literature before the 1840s. In that year, Thomas Hague of Philadelphia published *The Horoscope,* which was succeeded in 1845 by *Hague's Horoscope and Scientific and Prophetic Messenger,* published until 1848. About 1855 Dr. Luke Broughton migrated from Leeds to join his elder brothers in their Philadelphia astrological practices. The Broughton family had already published astrological almanacs in England, and *Broughton's Monthly Planet Reader and Astrological Journal* moved to New York City along with Broughton in 1863. In 1890, Broughton's pupil, W. H. Chaney, wrote in his *Primer of Astrology and American Urania*:

I have already had a taste of New York justice, seasoned with Roman Catholicism. In 1867, when I first began the practice of astrology, while living with my preceptor, Dr. Broughton, at 814 Broadway, we displeased "Boss" Tweed, then mayor of the city, and forthwith he had us sent to Ludlow-street Jail, where

I remained *without a trial,* for twenty-eight weeks and was then *honorably liberated.* . . . Yet before closing this digression I will remark that the law of compensation did not slumber in the case of the Catholic thieves who stole more than thirty millions of dollars from the city, for "Boss" Tweed died in that same Ludlow-street Jail where he had Dr. Broughton and myself confined for the awful crime of being ASTROLOGERS!

Chaney's writings are interesting for the insights he provides into the astrology of the period. "No era in the history of our planet has been more distinguished for investigating the occult in nature than the present," he observed in his preface. Thus, it may well have been precisely the rise of industrialism and scientific technology which encouraged occultists to search through their traditions in the hope that they might recover forgotten clues to new scientific discoveries. In typical American style, Chaney held that "Amid all this search for the wonderful, Americans are among the foremost," yet he was disappointed that "so few are interested in the science and philosophy of the celestial orbs" — clear indication that serious astrology was a minority interest then as now. Some of Chaney's ideas have a positively modern ring, as when he terms comets "mail-carriers from one system of worlds to another." (Fred Hoyle would approve, I think.) He rejected causality as the *modus operandi* of astrology, saying "It is not the heavenly bodies, but antenatal conditions, that make us what we are." Chaney believed that people are born at a time which is appropriate for them, and that their characters were determined before birth. He attacked English astrologers for teaching "that the planets exert an influence over us and cause us to be what we are. . . . Such a doctrine renders man a mere machine, no more responsible for his acts than the buzz saw that clips off a hand."

Chaney's philosophy of astrology came under the attack of *Raphael's Almanac* for 1885. "I have become very obnoxious to some of the English, especially Raphael," Chaney proudly noted, "because I refuse to endorse this stupid philosophy." Chaney called the "Raphael Ring" the "leading frauds in this country as well as Europe," who have "done more to bring astrology into disrepute than all its enemies ever have or ever can. I have determined to diffuse a knowledge of the science throughout America, and to popularise it if possible. This can be accomplished only by exposing the humbugs in it. If Raphael and his gang do not like it, they should blame the planets as the cause of my exposing them." Five pages later, he was still ranting against the English astrologers. "Where is the angelic Jim Cross, who styles himself 'Raphael?'" he demanded. "Let him rise and explain."

Yet Chaney's crusade must have succeeded. If there was little astrology in the United States in the early 1800s, by the end of the century astrological journals were being published in at least New York and Boston, and American textbooks were now available even on such subjects as heliocentric astrology. Astrology stood on the threshold of the modern age. Neomystical movements such as theosophy were active and contributing to the sophistication of astrological philosophy through the 1890s. Small local groups of amateur astrologers were gathering in major cities, and one of them came to the attention of an English commercial traveler by the name of William Frederick Allen. Allen already knew some astrology, and soon came into contact with Walter Gorn Old who wrote under the pseudonym of Sepharial. Old introduced Allen to Madame Blavatsky in London, and he joined the Theosophical Society in 1890, three months before W. B. Yeats resigned from it. Together with his friend, F. W. Lacey, Allen set about publishing a new journal entitled *The Astrologer's Magazine*. Their success, in the face of the discouraging experiences of every other astrological journal, may have been due to their offer of a free horoscope and delineation to new subscribers. Although they made no money from this arrangement, they did manage to keep new subscriptions flowing, so that more than 4,000 free horoscopes were dispatched to new readers in four years. During this period, Allen was absorbing theosophical ideas and attempting to integrate them into astrology. He held that the meanings of the symbols themselves were not understood by astrologers, and that only a study of ancient symbolism could penetrate the veil of the horoscope. Yet it was the same person who held these ideals who was responsible for the invention of the modern cut-and-paste automated horoscope reading!

Alan Leo, as Allen was known to astrologers, became a full-time professional astrologer in 1898, with a reasonably affluent clientele in the Theosophical Society. His business soon expanded to include not only horoscope delineations, but also a magazine, book publishing, correspondence courses, and an astrological society. Leo's staff grew to nine persons and briefly boasted bureaus in New York and Paris. With such a demand for readings, it fell to Leo's clerk to suggest that some use might be made of the copies of delineations which were on file in the office. Readings could now be reused for new clients who had the same planetary positions as former customers. Prefabricated horoscopes were soon prepared and offered to the public for one shilling as "Test Horoscopes." Howe notes that the idea was so successful that three years later, 20,000 Test Horoscopes had been mailed off.

Alan Leo was this century's first important astrologer. Very few in his day, and even in ours, were able to earn their living solely from astrology, let alone employ a staff. Leo's theosophically oriented textbooks are still in print and studied more than sixty years after his death in 1917. His readable texts have been a major factor in the expansion of the astrological community in the twentieth century. Yet the father of modern serious astrology was also the first to flaunt assembly-line astrology.

At this point, the first decades of the twentieth century, astrology began to develop national schools or styles of technique and philosophy, which sometimes existed in ignorance of each other. We shall examine in Chapter Ten some statistical evidence which indicates that astrology has improved steadily as the century has progressed. The doctrines of stellar influences had hardly diverged from their Greek and Arabian heritage for centuries, but now assaults along several fronts attempted to bring astrology into the mainstream of modern thought. As early as 1880, the British astrologer, A. J. Pearce, suggested applying statistics to astrology. But it fell to Paul Choisnard (pseudonym Paul Flambart), a French artillery officer, to become the first to employ statistics in an attempt to confirm astrological tradition. His *Preuves et bases de l'astrologie scientifique* (1908) was a primitive study which ignored the laws of deviation from the average and attempted to show that 123 persons of "superior natures" tended to have Air signs on the ascendant. Choisnard also forgot to allow for the fact that some signs take longer to rise than others, so his positive results were a product of two major errors. In a second study, Choisnard suggested that his statistics proved that Mars and Saturn tend to be in bad aspect to the natal Sun at the time of death. But in a recent replication of this experiment, the French psychologist Dr. Michel Gauquelin failed to find Choisnard's fatal aspects in a sample of 7,482 comparisons between horoscopes at birth and at death.[109] About the same time, Bouche-Leclerq's *Astrologie Grecque* initiated a scholarly interest in the history of astrology. Though most astrologers remained ignorant of Choisnard and Bouche-Leclerq, it is almost certain that the few leading astrologers in other countries nearby would have heard of their investigations. Thus, two of the predominant trends in contemporary astrology emerged: the search for scientific methods which might confirm astrological influences and attempts to reformulate astrological techniques through both radical departures into new methods and a search for an "original" astrology which was supposed to have existed in the ancient world.

The theosophical movement spread into Europe, and several German astrologers visited London to study under Alan Leo. Other German astrologers followed the methods laid down by French astrologers of the nineteenth century. Thus, the majority of German astrologers even to this day adhere to the central tradition of astrology as found in England during the periods we have discussed. However, two groups emerged with quite distinct methods, and it is by their claims of incredible accuracy and radical departures from traditional techniques that German astrology is now known, to the exclusion of the moderate traditional groups which are still alive and well in Germany.

Since the discovery of Uranus, astrologers had been running to keep up with astronomers. By the late nineteenth century it became something of a sport among astronomers to attempt to detect the gravitational influences of as-yet-undiscovered planets through variations in the motions of the known planets. Thus, for an enterprising astrologer in the early 1900s, it would have been an imaginative and daring challenge to attempt to detect a new planet on the basis of horoscopes alone. The story goes that Alfred Witte (1878-1941), whose name most American astrologers mispronounce as "witty," was serving on the Russian front during World War I. Witte attempted to predict the times of enemy artillery barrages, and soon came to the conclusion that there were unaccounted planetary influences operative which might allow for greater predictive precision. His answer was a hypothetical planet beyond the orbit of Neptune. (Pluto was still undiscovered.) Subsequent work with his colleague, Friedrick Sieggrün, led to the "discovery" of seven more transneptunian planets, and "the Hamburg School" or "Uranian" astrology was on its way.[110]

Besides the use of hypothetical planets, Uranian astrology contained several other unique features which became characteristic of the new German astrology. Prediction of physical events and conditions was its main aim, so that even today, Uranian astrologers confidently state that by using their system and undiscovered planets, "orbless" astrology is possible — that is, factors in the horoscopes will match with events without any deviation in time or "orb." Traditional astrologers maintain that as each planetary aspect forms in the sky, there is an orb in which the influence increases and decreases. But for the Uranian astrologer, the additional factors and the techniques in which they are employed demand a high degree of precision. To develop this precision, the zodiac was not drawn in a circle, but was folded into four, as it were, on a 90° dial. This dial allowed all degrees of the zodiac which are in a "hard" aspect to each other to be placed at the same point on the dial. The astrologer would then lay the dial over the redrawn horoscope, and by using the scale provided, he could observe that certain planets were in a given amount of arc to each other. Here the Uranian system differs from traditional astrology with its ancient and well-defined set of aspects. Some modern astrologers believe that Witte's main contribution to astrological theory was not his hypothetical planets, but his emphasis on the recurrence of these planetary arcs, no matter whether they are traditional aspects or not. The Uranian school now flourishes among a small group of American astrologers. The continued use of hypothetical planets despite the lack of a corroborative discovery by astronomers is defended through several arguments, ranging from the possibility of a transplutonian asteroid belt to the suggestion that Witte's "transneps" were simply cycles derived from other known planetary cycles. This latter argument was debunked recently when an analysis of the ephemerides for these planets showed that they were in fact constructed as if the bodies were moving according to the laws of Newton and Kepler.[111] It is safe to say, however, that the vast majority of astrologers view the use of hypothetical bodies as taking things a little too far. Some who have tested these bodies report that while they were able to make some accurate predictions with them, there were also some spectacular failures, indicating that something besides astrological influence is at work.

German astrology also developed a new style of interpreting the data obtained from the 90° dial. Since planetary positions could be reduced to a concise formula, such as Mars=Mercury/Jupiter, it was thought possible to gather numbers of observations of such planetary formulas, in order to base future interpretations on observed conditions. Because the planetary formulas were independent of the more traditional house systems, which in themselves were impossible to represent on the 90° dial, many German astrologers rejected the use of houses as too unscientific. Planetary formulas, it was thought, would lead astrology to greater precision in medical, psychological, and predictive applications, given sufficient careful observations.

The other famous German school which emerged out of this period is known as "Cosmobiology." This system was founded by the Ebertin family, which has been involved in astrology since the World War I. Frau Elsbeth Ebertin was a graphologist in 1910 when she came into contact with works by German astrologers. By the 1930s her son, Reinhold Ebertin, was speaking at astrological conferences, and their particular style of astrology was in development. Frau Ebertin was famous for having made a successful prediction regarding the rise of Hitler, and today the family still produces astrological texts and magazines expounding their techniques. Reinhold's son, Dr. Baldur Ebertin, has an active medical practice and occasionally goes on tour to speak at astrological conferences. Cosmobiology also uses a 90° dial, but eschews the transneptunian planets for its own hypothetical planet, which is called Transpluto. Instead of planetary arcs, Cosmobiology chose to develop a system of mid-points which are found by dividing the zodiacal distance between any two planets. The point in the zodiac which results from this division takes on the combined characteristics of the planets from which it is derived, so that one obtains a broad system of planetary symbolism. When a transitting planet comes into aspect with these mid-points, one obtains planetary formulas which can be interpreted from textbooks. In terms of its predictive orientation, Cosmobiology has developed into a "softer" system than Uranian astrology, but it has been my observation that astrologers attracted to either of these German schools represent a certain personality type within the astrological community. I have found them to be strongly oriented to mathematical procedures and linear logic in their interpretations and oriented to the kind of precision which one might expect from a medical checkup. For them, whether it is consciously admitted or not, a top priority is to see their system work and if it appears to work at the expense of a more traditional system, so much the better.

In England and the United States, astrologers appeared more content with the traditional elements of astrology which they had learned from their predecessors. Their interests lay in improving astrology, certainly, but through refinement rather than reconstruction. Those who did attempt to develop radical new systems of astrology were either mavericks or concerned with nonhuman applications of astrology, such as weather forecasting. The influence of the theosophical movement was not soon forgotten, and meanwhile, the new work of the psychologist Carl Jung appeared to offer a means whereby the rich symbolism of astrology might yield practical fruit in psychoanalysis.

One of Alan Leo's students who carried this movement forward in England was Charles E.O. Carter (1887-1968). At the age of twenty-three in 1910, Carter saw an advertisement for one of Leo's Test Horoscopes. In 1920, he was responsible for reviving the Astrological Lodge of the Theosophical

Society, which had practically collapsed at the death of Leo in 1917. In 1923, Carter began publishing a magazine entitled *Uranus,* and in 1926 he founded the quarterly *Astrology* which is still one of the best examples of traditional astrological magazines. Carter's contribution was not as an originator, but as a synthesizer, as is evidenced in his main contributions to astrological literature, *The Encyclopedia of Psychological Astrology* (1924), *The Principles of Astrology* (1924), *The Seven Great Problems of Astrology* (1927), *The Zodiac and the Soul* (1928), *Essays on the Foundations of Astrology* (1947) — all thoughtful titles in which he attempted to approach astrology with a new clarity and sensitivity. In 1948, Carter became first president of the Faculty of Astrological Studies, one of the diploma schools par excellence for practicing astrologers.

The French representative of this generation of astrologers was Alexandre Volguine, who, like Carter, placed much emphasis on a broad knowledge of the astrological heritage while attempting to integrate new developments in other fields. Born near Alexandria in 1903, Volguine was brought to France after the Russian Revolution and began to study astrology in 1917. In World War II, like many other astrologers, he was arrested by the Nazis and placed in a concentration camp. His journal *les Cahiers Astrologiques,* which he edited from its founding in 1937 to his death in 1977, enjoyed a solid reputation among serious astrologers the world over. Among his many interests were Hindu, Arab, Chinese, Hebrew, and pre-Columbian astrologies, and he emphasized a holistic approach to horoscopes — that is, study of an entire chart as a whole, in opposition to the single-formula analytical methods of the German schools.

In the United States, Dr. Marc Edmund Jones (1888-1980) led the way to the clarification and summation of these trends. Jones's long and colorful career began in the early days of motion pictures, and he was one of the founders of the Photoplay Authors' League, now known as the Screen Writers Guild of America. He discovered astrology, through what he called serendipity, when he met the wife of Frank Woods, one of the first movie critics. Woods's wife read his horoscope in 1913, and astrology became a major concern in his life thereafter. In 1923, Jones founded a new occult movement called the Sabian Assembly. Small groups in major cities around the world still meet on certain phases of the Moon to meditate together, and Jones's more abstruse occult writings in astrology have become standard readings in their field. On the other hand, Jones contributed significantly to the dissemination of astrology through his highly popular works *How to Learn Astrology* (1941) and *Guide to Horoscope Interpretation* (1941), both of which are easily available today. *How to Learn Astrology* remains one of the most accessible introductions to traditional astrology, while in his *Guide*, Jones revealed one of his major contributions to astrological theory — planetary patterns. Following the idea that a horoscope must be examined in its entirety, Jones found seven general patterns into which a horoscope might fall — the splash, bundle, locomotive, bowl, bucket, see-saw, and splay. If the planets tended to be located in all the houses, with no significant bunching in one area, this was the splash type of chart, with its own psychology. If the planets formed a hemisphere along one side of the chart, this was termed the bowl chart, and so on. The major advantage of these seven psychological types is that they are independent of accurate birth-times, and they give the astrologer an excellent place to begin to understand the type of personality he is dealing with. For many astrologers today, the Jones patterns are the starting point for any horoscope reading.[112]

The tendencies displayed in the works of Carter, Volguine, and Jones came into focus and force in the astrological community through Dane Rudhyar, a French philosopher and artist who was significantly influenced by Jones's writing on occult philosophy and astrology. Born on March 23, 1895 in Paris, Rudhyar obtained his baccalaureat at the age of sixteen from the Sorbonne, majoring in philosophy. Arriving in the New World in 1916, he left behind his family name of Chenneviere, and was henceforth known to his friends as "Rudhyar." His abstract dance-drama *Metachory* was performed at the Metropolitan Opera under the baton of Pierre Monteux, but since it played the night the U.S. entered the World War I, there was little notice. Rudhyar spent his time in New York penniless, but avidly absorbing books on Oriental music and philosophy, as well as Western occultism. New Canadian friends invited him to Toronto and Montreal where he lectured in French and recited some of his new poetry. Some months later, he was asked to write a score for a play depicting the life of Christ for the theosophical community which was headquartered in Hollywood, California. While absorbing these occult influences, he worked as an extra in movies and opened an import retail outlet for Javanese art.

After 1927, Rudhyar earned a poor living as a lecturer and recitalist, while writing articles on music and philosophy. He was a charter member of the International Composers' Guild and Charles Ives financed publication of several of his compositions through the New Music Society of California. In the late 1920s, he encountered Marc Edmund Jones at the same time as he was becoming more aware of Carl Jung's psychology, and Rudhyar quickly saw the possibility of a new philosophical synthesis which he first called "harmonic astrology," and later "humanistic astrology." This, then, was the origin, in name if not in spirit, of the most significant movement in modern astrology. By 1931, Rudhyar attempted to publish a small magazine called *Hamsa,* but the Depression, ill-health, and lack of response soon brought it to an end in 1934. But at the same time, Paul Clancy was busy with his new magazine *American Astrology* and encouraged Rudhyar to write about his new type of psychological astrology. Many articles followed on an unusually broad range of subjects for popular astrology magazines, and eventually Rudhyar's writing came to the attention of Alice Bailey, who published a large collection of them as *The Astrology of Personality* (1936).

For many years, Rudhyar's considerable output of writings, compositions, and poetry found no favor with publishers. He remained largely unknown and unpublished except within the small ranks of serious astrologers until 1963, when the Dutch publisher, Servire, began issuing his main astrological works. With the assistance of Tana Rudhyar, a young girl from Edmonton who had corresponded with him and subsequently became his third wife, he set about issuing his writings to the new generation which was turning toward mysticism and Eastern philosophy. If none of Rudhyar's books were in print in 1960, by 1975 twenty-five were available from such publishers as

Doubleday, Penguin, Harper & Row, and the counterculture publishers Shambhala Publications, then of Berkeley. Now eighty-five, he still devotes his time to music, art, and writing.

If Rudhyar accomplished one thing as an astrologer, it was to bring home the realization that astrologers had to accept responsibility for their actions. In his 1968 work, *The Practice of Astrology*, Rudhyar commenced with chapters on understanding the nature and purpose of what one is about to study and assuming personal responsibility for the use of one's knowledge. This sensitivity to the effects of application of astrology *per se* was virtually unheard of. Everyone was so busy trying to outdo other astrologers in predicting events or proposing new techniques like the latest Paris fashion, that hardly any thought was given to what astrology might be doing to those who came into contact with it. If astrology attempts to deal with some undiscovered celestial "radiations," was it not possible that the scattered and checkered careers of so many astrologers were themselves the result of the "influence" of astrology?

For Rudhyar, one had to begin with wholes — holistic philosophy. Astrology existed as an aid to discovering the meaning of a person's life, and even life should be considered as a whole, from birth to death. The birth chart was an indicator of potentialities, not a diagram of physical influences which have determined one's character irrevocably. "Events as such are not the most important factor in a person's life," Rudhyar observed. "What counts is the meaning he gives to them, and what he does with them."[113] Thus, humanistic astrology emerged as the antithesis of the heavily predictive and conditioning-oriented German schools of astrology. Humanistic astrology employed traditional astrological techniques, but to psychological and spiritual ends. Predictions of precise dates and physical events were rejected by humanistic astrologers in favor of studies of the psychological passages through which the individual might grow. Thus, astrology, if it had any basis in fact, was approaching a stage of maturity in dealing with cosmic factors in human experience.

In the 1970s the counterculture movement effectively went underground. Those who grew their hair long and espoused oriental philosophies now had to come to grips with the problem of integrating their vision into society at large. Like other components of the new, emerging society, astrology laid low during the 1970s, and humanistic astrology has neither expanded nor faltered as a movement within the astrological community. Prediction-oriented astrologers still go around attempting to fit the universe on their procrustean bed of astrological theory, while humanistic astrologers continue their counseling. Symptomatic of the situation was Rudhyar's International Committee for Humanistic Astrology, a non-organization which was "founded" in 1968. In order to avoid "partisanship and ego trips" Rudhyar refused to build the committee as a formal organization. Yet years later, some astrologers insisted that they had been elected to its executive!

The real test of astrology is now underway. Increasingly, evidence shows that planetary influences along astrological lines do exist. Psychologists are slowly becoming aware of a growing number of studies which have obtained positive results for astrological hypotheses. And entirely new cosmic influences, unsuspected by astrologers, are being discovered by scientists in many fields. At some point along the spectrum between astrology and these discoveries, there is a historical balance-point at which both astrology and science find fulfillment. What will the new synthesis be like? Will traditional scientists and traditional astrologers be able to accept it? Or will an adventurous group within each community be willing to follow the tide of history and leave the traditionalists behind in their mutually exclusive universes?

This chapter cannot be considered as a history of modern astrology. Too many important schools and thinkers have been overlooked in order to compress this outline into so many pages. It is enough, I think, to be aware that astrology has a rich and fascinating history, and that, as we shall see, it is heading slowly in the right direction. Astrology's biggest problem is that most people are totally ignorant of it, without realizing *how* ignorant they really are. For example, when the media go to cover a specialized field, they usually refer to lists of specialists who know what they're talking about. But when it's time for a prediction on a local election, any old garden-variety astrologer will do. Most people don't even suspect that astrology has its leading thinkers, different schools of thought and technique. You might recognize a difference between Freudian and Jungian psychology, but the gulf between Hindu and Hamburg techniques, or between traditional and humanistic astrology, are not even properly understood among astrological amateurs.

The ignorance in which most people approach astrology is an important issue, because astrology, as the proto-science of cosmic influences in human behavior, will only break out of the closet when this vicious circle is broken. And for this, there must be a greater awareness that astrology has a history and logical direction of development. Unless you begin with the realization that the broad outlines of astrology are being confirmed by modern science, you are soon bogged down in apparent absurdities. Astrology must be seen as a central theme in man's continual struggle to come to terms with his cosmic environment. If astrology and astrologers have accomplished anything, they have kept alive the tradition that there is an intimate relationship between man and the cosmos. That alone is enough to justify all the apparent absurdities which have been perpetrated in astrology's name. Since many have devoted their lives, sat in jail, and even died in concentration camps for their love of astrology, their efforts deserve more compassion than the ridicule which is heaped on astrology at every possible turn.

Should you still entertain the possibility of having your own horoscope read? I would say, sure, why not? It is one of life's little experiences which you will react to in your own unique way (as outlined, no doubt, in your horoscope). The sky will not fall, and civilization will not be engulfed in a black tide simply because you choose to satisfy your curiosity. As long as the astrologer you choose to visit is not a shark, you won't get bitten.

And why are you going to visit an astrologer? That's where this brief exposition of the different schools of astrology comes in. If you still think of astrology as primarily a predictive art and you hope to test it by asking for some specific predictions, then you had better select a fairly competent traditional astrologer, or one who uses techniques from the Uranian or Cosmobiology schools. On the other hand, if you are seeking personal or psychological counseling, obviously a humanistic astrologer is what you're after. I have found that the best humanistic astrologers often have an academic background in psychology, and the cream of the crop have studied Jungian psychology on a post-graduate level. Considering the disdain in which Jung is held by academics these days, they are close to being an endangered species.

If fateful predictions replete with precise details are your cup of tea, you might like to visit a Hindu astrologer, who will easily enter into a discussion of karma and quite possibly read your palm at the same time. Modern Hindu astrology appears to be a collection of Arabian astrological techniques which have survived and slowly adapted to Indian culture. It is not confined to religious Hindus, but is found in any country with historical links to India. There is little, if any, emphasis on psychological development in Hindu astrology, and the most important Indian astrological journal, *The Astrological Magazine,* regularly publishes letters congratulating authors on correct predictions. Most Western astrologers regard this school with some suspicion, although more advanced astrologers recognize that the preserved heritage of ancient techniques is worthy of a close examination by those who can bridge the language and culture gap.

A related movement in the West which employs yet another set of techniques is known as sidereal astrology. Earlier, I mentioned the difference between the sidereal and the tropical zodiacs, which is caused by the precession of the equinoxes. Hindu astrologers use a type of sidereal zodiac, and this is often the bone of contention between them and Western astrologers. The question of a "right" and a "wrong" zodiac was raised again in the West by Cyril Fagan, an Irish astrologer who had spent much time studying ancient Egypt in an attempt to discover the origins of astrology. In a monumental study of heiroglyphs and ancient calendar systems which has subsequently daunted most people and kept them from thoroughly checking his research, Fagan attempted to show that it was Egypt, not Babylonia, which was the birth place of astrology, and that the ancient Egyptians had used a zodiac which he now offered to modern astrologers as the new, improved version of the original.[114] Fagan managed to attract some of the brightest and most technically oriented astrologers of his day to his new zodiac, which became known as the sidereal zodiac. And in order to fortify their theories in the face of the astrological establishment, which still clings stubbornly to its seasonal or tropical zodiac, the siderealists devoted much of their energy to developing techniques which depended heavily upon the unique features of the sidereal zodiac of Fagan, and upon its (in their view) superior predictive performance. Thus, the sidereal movement has largely fallen into the predictive, not the humanistic camp of astrology.[115]

A note to consumers: There is no need for an identity crisis simply because you may be one sun sign in one zodiac, and a different sun sign in the other zodiac. The siderealists were well aware of the possible contradictions of their system with mainstream astrology, and provided adapted interpretations of the signs. Thus, sidereal Scorpio has a different symbolic value than its tropical equivalent sign of Scorpio. It is wrong simply to use the standard *tropical* description of your *sidereal* sun sign. The two systems must not be confused.

It is only fair to observe that the sidereal hypothesis no longer holds the interest of the most advanced astrologers, many of whom have either returned to the tropical camp or passed on to essentially azodiacal forms of astrology, which do not use signs at all. The main areas of interest today center on the search for more reliable techniques which synthesize ancient methods and modern computer power. Both traditional horoscopic and statistical paths are being taken to approach this goal. The most exciting and dynamic period of astrology's development is *now*.

Nine

The Stars and War

Most people knew Winston Churchill as a great statesman. We knew him as a size 46.

Advertisement, Turnbull & Asser,
Men's Clothiers.

Nothing more poignantly underlines the modern condition of astrology than its relationship to World War II. There is no monument for the hundreds of astrologers who died in stinking prisons and concentration camps for their simple faith in the existence of cosmic influences. Astrology became a propaganda tool cynically employed by both the Allies and the Nazis. Astrology's most critical opponents are still attempting to argue that the rise of Nazism in Germany was due to the widespread interest in astrology and the occult which followed the humiliating defeat of World War I. And the suspicion remains that it was not only the Nazi leaders who consulted astrologers.

Of course, for every prominent politician, you can probably find someone who will *swear* that he or she has consulted a nameless astrologer in the strictest of confidence. Many astrologers believe that these same politicians sometimes fabricate new birth-data for themselves, so that any attempt to predict their victories and defeats will not succeed, giving them a transcendental aura. And stories circulate that Sir Winston Churchill kept a stable of up to five astrologers who never knew about each other, and whose predictions were compared to each other and to subsequent developments, so as to give the prime minister an inside edge in the race for victory.

One is prepared to believe all sorts of fantastic ideas about Hitler and his crew. A preposterous crowd to begin with, they came to suitably enigmatic ends, paving the way for all sorts of pulp novels and semifactual histories suggesting that deep in the jungles of South America there may still lurk the heart of Nazi darkness. But Churchill? Can one believe that Her Majesty's first minister was to dally with the advice of an astrologer?

In two words, quite possibly.

For all the thousands of volumes which have attempted to record, analyze, summarize, and comment upon Churchill's role in World War II, it seems to have escaped the notice of historians that a member of his staff — a Canadian-born officer in the British Army who played no insignificant role in the war and subsequent events — was so deeply involved in astrology and psychic phenomena that he later emerged as a leading figure in two astrological movements. And there is suggestive evidence that he acted on occasion as an astrological consultant to Sir Winston.

Roy Charles Whitworth George Firebrace was born at 21:03 hours in Halifax, Nova Scotia, on August 16, 1889. It is unlikely that his birth was recorded so accurately. The time given is most probably that which he derived from rectifying his birth chart. Firebrace joined the British Army at the age of twenty (Canada was very much a British colony in those days) and became a second lieutenant in the Royal Artillery. He rose steadily through the ranks, serving in France and Belgium during World War I, where he was wounded. By the end of the war, he was breveted to the rank of major.

Besides his early and lifelong interest in the paranormal, Firebrace had a real talent for language; he was able to converse in no less than thirteen of them. Because Russian was his best, he was selected for service in the War Office in 1917, and thereafter served in various liaison capacities in France, India, Germany, and Russia. By 1931, Firebrace found himself on the shores of the Baltic Sea, stationed as the British military attaché in Riga. In his spare time, he studied astrology from German and Russian texts which came his way. Five years later, and probably many horoscopes as well, Colonel Firebrace found himself sent to Moscow as British military attaché, with top security clearance. It was the beginning of the most unpleasant episode of his life.[116]

By 1939, World War II was underway, and Churchill was already urging an alliance with the Soviets in order to defeat a Germany which at that time seemed invincible. Through the early 1940s British propaganda built up a sanitary image of a suffering and heroic Russian people, working under benevolent guidance from a government with essentially democratic aims. Stalin — "Uncle Joe" — was portrayed as a man of his word who would certainly hold free and fair elections in the captured territories which today remain behind the Iron Curtain. As the war drew to a close, the general map of Europe was becoming fixed into new boundaries, and the great powers were concerned with defining this new world as soon as possible. Victory in Europe was clearly only a matter of time, and the Allies wanted to obtain Soviet help in the final defeat of Japan. The Manhattan Project was still top secret, its grizzly end-result as yet unsuspected.

As early as 1941, Russian troops had joined with the Germans in order to defeat the Communists. Those who knew Nazism and Communism on a firsthand basis often concluded that Nazism was by far the lesser of two evils. And as the German war effort weakened, it became obvious to the Germans that some of the captured Russians might be encouraged to join hands with them to regain their country. By 1944, the Allies were landing in Normandy, and Europe became a patchwork of prisoners from one country, rescued by an Ally, but still held for repatriation.

The problem was that Russian soldiers were being captured in German uniforms. Were they, therefore, German prisoners of war who should be treated according to the normal procedures, or were they traitors to the Soviet government, who deserved to be brought to justice? The Soviets at once insisted that such traitors did not exist and pressed continually for their return. The question had to be settled at the highest levels, and thus the fate of up to 2 million former Russian citizens was to be decided, after a fashion, at conferences which were held toward the end of the war.

At the Livadia Palace, about a mile from Yalta, on the Black Sea, Stalin met with Churchill and Roosevelt from February 4-11, 1945. Russia had just gained spectacular victories in Poland, and it was dawning on the Allies just what Stalin had really accomplished. Unlike the Western leaders, the Russians attended conferences to obtain recognition of their political conquests, not to negotiate future arrangements. It was during the Yalta Conference, then, that the Allies effectively accepted the Soviet domination of half of Europe.

Stalin opened the conference by reporting that his armies were advancing on German territory. The Germans were digging in to defend Berlin. The final offensives of the war were planned, and the fate of the German people decided. By the sixth sitting, on February 9, 1945, Churchill raised the question of war criminals. How were they to be dealt with once the fighting had ceased? Stalin inquired if prisoners of war could be included in the list of criminals.[117]

"The Soviet Union had an almost obsessive fear of its subjects abroad bearing arms," writes Nikolai Tolstoy in his *Victims of Yalta*.[118] Stalin's crowd felt quite threatened by the fact that despite all his brutality during his early conquests in Russia, "Hitler had succeeded in raising nearly a million anti-Communist legionaries from amongst the prisoners in German hands. What success might not the humane democracies have if they tried the same game?" The Communists viewed everyone who came into contact with the West as suspicious. Even an army which had been surrounded for a brief period by the enemy was viewed as contaminated.

Thus, the question of war criminals and prisoners of war was of great concern to Stalin. Yet he could not admit publicly why. By the eighth sitting of the Yalta Conference, February 11, 1945, Stalin had decided that a section of the British draft of the conference statement had to be deleted. He urged that the leaders agree to a "special decision" in a separate paper. Thus, the Yalta Conference also produced an Agreement on Prisoners of War and Civilians. ". . . each ally was to provide food, clothing, medical attention and other needs . . . until transport is available for their repatriation. Soviet officers were to assist British and American authorities in caring for Soviet citizens liberated by British and American forces in Europe or in the United Kingdom, awaiting transportation to take them home."

The truth of what followed is still being hotly debated. Nicholas Bethell's book, *The Last Secret*, was the first to bring the whole affair to public attention in 1974.[119] By that time, thirty years had passed since the closing days of the war, and the British government was releasing documents which might allow historians and journalists to find out what really had occurred. Several years later, Tolstoy's book added much material from the years just after the Yalta Conference, which had by then emerged from the dusty caverns of official archives. The rough outlines of the story as these two researchers have recorded it follows, with particular emphasis on the role which then-Brigadier Firebrace played.

Russian citizens fell into the hands of the Nazis in several ways. Some were captured on the battlefront, others were acquired while in residence in one of the countries outside Russia which the Germans defeated in the first part of the war. Others had been living in exile ever since the Russian Revolution. Thus, scattered throughout Europe, there was a population of several million Russians, caught, as Bethell explains, "between the devil and the deep blue sea." Those who were prisoners received brutal treatment from their Aryan captors, but once given the opportunity to put on the German uniform and join labor gangs where the food and conditions were better, they had little choice. On the Allies' part, it was not exactly pleasant to fight against Russians in German uniform, then care for them once captured. The flow of prisoners across the channel to Britain, and thence to Canada and the United States, was increasing. The British government was considering the Allied Forces Act, which would organize the Russians in British and American hands into military units which could then be repatriated.

At the same time, Allied troops liberated from prison camps were falling into Soviet hands. The Soviet authorities gave the impression that these troops would be taken good care of, but ignored all subsequent efforts at cooperation. Brigadier Firebrace, as deputy director of the Russian Liaison Group of the Imperial General Staff in London, was sent to drop a strong hint to Major-General Vasiliev of the Soviet Military Mission in Britain. Firebrace explained that if the British troops could not be returned speedily, then the legal procedures involved in defining the status of the Russian prisoners in Britain might be held up. Furthermore, the Allied Forces Act was pending, and this would meet the special problems of the exiled French and Polish governments, who wished to maintain military units on British soil. Firebrace had difficulty explaining the intricacies of the problem to Vasiliev, who could scarely believe that even the British government had to abide by its own laws. The Russians were suspicious. And they wanted their people back before the Allied Forces Act could be passed. After all, the act would result in an armed Russian unit in Britain which was not under the control of Moscow. In various parts of the world, Soviet agents were alerted to see if Russian prisoners were being mobilized by the Allies. In Washington, the young Andrei Gromyko accused the Americans of similar plots, but received only sarcasm in return.

As a result of the Agreement on Prisoners of War and Civilians at Yalta, the Russians in Britain now became members of an Allied military force.[120] But so liberated were they from their former status as prisoners of war, that the Russian general who was sent to organize the repatriation asked Brigadier Firebrace to provide British guards and prison facilities for ten men. General Ratov admitted that they all had refused to return to the Soviet Union, and some had openly threatened suicide. Firebrace reminded Ratov that under the agreement, the Soviets had to provide their own discipline, but he eventually agreed to detain some of the Russians in a British military prison.

By October, 1944, the war effort could spare enough shipping to accommodate 11,000 of the Russians who were to be returned to the Soviets. Sir Anthony Eden, the secretary of state for Foreign Affairs wanted them out of the country before the story became widely known. Scattered in camps across Yorkshire, the Russians were poorly clothed and would return in the dead of winter. The British army provided thousands of sweaters, socks, coats, and toiletries for the voyage. The prisoners were shipped to Liverpool "as inconspicuously as possible." Over 10,000 men, 30 women, and 44 boys sailed on October 31, scheduled to arrive on the anniversary of the Revolution.

On November 14, Tass, the Soviet "news" agency, reported that the people of Murmansk greeted their long-lost cousins. Citizen after citizen spontaneously rose to thank Comrade Stalin for his concern for them. Then those repatriated were provided with food and accommodation before returning to their native cities. However, a report sent to Brigadier Firebrace a few days later recorded that the Russians were marched from their transport under armed guard to a camp outside the city.

In April, 1945, Firebrace received yet another report of the fate of the returning Russian prisoners. While they were being disembarked at Odessa, two salvos of submachine pistols were heard behind a large shack on the pier. The Soviet guards informed a British officer that two "bad men" who had been "sold to the capitalists" had been executed. Driving through the city later, the same officer saw an execution squad shooting a dozen prisoners. His Soviet guide told him they were traitors, and that the other prisoners would be sent to "educational labor camps."

The Russian prisoners in Britain soon got wind of the situation. If they were shown to be Soviet citizens, they were to be forcibly repatriated. Their only hope was to convince someone they were not Russians. Since Britain and the United States had not recognized Soviet domination of the Ukraine, Byelorussia, and the Baltic states at that point, those who could show that they lived outside the Soviet Union before these conquests had a chance to escape the Soviet clutches. Firebrace and General Ratov arranged for a joint British-Soviet commission to examine disputed cases by talking with each of the prisoners who claimed not to be a Soviet citizen. Through Firebrace's knowledge of Russian and other officers who knew the various languages the prisoners spoke, Ukrainians could be sifted out from the

Russians, for example. Much as the various accents in English can distinguish a Scot from a Londoner, a western Canadian from a Maritimer, a New Yorker from practically anyone else, Firebrace and Ratov could tell where the prisoners came from. The Russian delegation at these sessions included a shorthand writer who kept notes of everything the prisoner said.

Firebrace complained to the Foreign Office on April 14, noting that practically every prisoner protested violently at being sent back to the Soviet Union or Poland. They recounted the shootings, arrests, and deportations of families which followed the victory of the Red Army. One young man, said Firebrace, reported having been in prison since the age of twelve until he was released for army service. Some asked to be shot rather than turned over to the Communists. "I have never in my life seen such human misery or such despair," Bethell quotes Firebrace as writing.

But Firebrace's orders were clear, and everyone who knew him describes him as a man of iron discipline. Only once did he admit to intervening in favor of a prisoner who pointed to General Ratov and accused him of killing his parents, his brothers, and requested that he be shot by the British on the spot, rather than return to the Soviet Union. General Ratov at one point threatened to retain fifty British prisoners of war, unless he had more cooperation in selecting the Russians for repatriation. Firebrace calmly told him that unless his comments were a poor joke, they would be reported to higher authorities.

Suicides among the prisoners continued. Prisoners leapt from the decks of their ships. There were efforts to ensure that the BBC and other news media would not pick up the story. It was decided to explain to the public, if the story became news, that some prisoners were afraid because they had openly collaborated with the Germans. In the summer of 1945, 153 Russians held at Fort Dix, New Jersey, made a desperate attempt to forestall their repatriation. They dismantled their metal beds to make crude weapons. When Fort Dix's executive officer arrived to order them on their way, they refused. Tear gas was thrown into the barracks, and the Russians charged the American guards. Nine suffered wounds, none fatal. When the uprising ended, officers found three Russians had hanged themselves in the barracks, and fifteen more nooses were suspended from the ceiling, empty. The prisoners were then shipped to Camp Shanks, New York for final departure. One had to be hospitalized after swallowing a razor blade. The next day, a presidential reprieve was announced. But by the end of the summer, the public furor had died down, and all but seven of the prisoners were shipped into the hands of the Soviets.[121]

The forced repatriation policy continued a year and a half after the war ended. When the new Labor Government came to power in 1945, the new foreign secretary, Ernest Bevin, was told that no violent measures had been used in the action, and there were no suicides. Some involved in these events disagree with the scenarios outlined by Bethell and Tolstoy. Several claim that they were misquoted and that both authors sought out only information which would support their concept of what happened.

Major George Youmatoff, now a retired Anglican priest living near Windsor, Ontario, is one person who worked directly under Firebrace during these events. He plans to publish his own version of the story and points out that the atrocities committed by Russians in World War II were by no means limited to the Communist ranks. Cossack occupations are remembered vividly by their survivors as bloody affairs, and the Cossacks were fighting with the Germans.

Youmatoff was surprised to be informed that his superior was a serious astrologer. But he recalls that "Firebrace could see a long way into the future." When the Russian Liaison Group in London heard the news that the Allies had stopped short to allow the Russians to enter Berlin at the same time, Firebrace wept openly in front of his staff. "This will be a millstone around our necks," said Firebrace, "and it will be there for a long time."

It is more than likely that Firebrace's tears were based on his astrological studies as much as innate foresight. Having already spent years experimenting with horoscopes, knowing many of the top Soviet leaders personally both in Moscow and London, and having sufficient security clearance to obtain any birth data which might not be public knowledge, he was in a perfect position for a political astrologer. Firebrace had close contact with Sir Anthony Eden, as the reporting member of the Russian Liaison Group, and Major Youmatoff remembers "one incident at least" where Firebrace and Churchill had discussions.

Further evidence that Firebrace used his astrology in more than an amateur capacity, and that he had fairly close contact with Churchill, came from his own mouth. Firebrace was apparently one of the first to interrogate Rudolph Hess when he landed in Scotland, and he later shared amusing anecdotes of his conversations over that event with Churchill. A source which was close to him reports that Firebrace did "scads" of charts for Churchill during his period in London. Furthermore, these charts were later published in an astrological journal.

Just as someone who speaks several languages keeps vocabularies in separate mental cupboards, so to speak, Firebrace must have lived an inner life quite hidden from most of those around him. Close staff members apparently did not know about his lifelong interests in astrology and psychic phenomena. Yet Firebrace spent much of his time in retirement at both interests. He was president of a psychic college for a while, but soon began to devote all his energies to astrology. When British astrologers gathered to found the still active and highly reputed Faculty of Astrological Studies in 1948, he acted for a time as vice-president, as well as vice-president of the Astrological Lodge of the Theosophical Society in London.

In 1958, Firebrace played a leading role in founding the Astrological Association, an organization based in London with a worldwide membership of about 1,500 astrologers in 1979. As the British astrological authority John Addey remembers him, "he was a natural choice as the A.A.'s first President, and he filled it with characteristic authority and enthusiasm." Firebrace's wartime subordinates speak of him as a leader who would back you to the hilt in public — and blast you in private. And later, among astrological circles, "the Brig.," as he was called, dug in and helped the association with publication of its journal and with all the small tasks which such organizations require.

It is not clear when Firebrace first came into contact with the sidereal school of astrology. In earlier chapters, I touched briefly upon the difference between the sidereal and tropical zodiacs, and mentioned briefly something of the sidereal school itself. The whole "battle-of-the-zodiacs" debate is often held up by those who are ignorant of astrology and quite critical of it as a proof of the absurdity of astrology. In fact, it is no such thing. The significance ascribed to the *constellations* of the sidereal zodiac differ from those attributed to the *signs* of the tropical zodiac. The founder of the school, the Irish astrologer Cyril Fagan, attempted to reconstruct an astrology which he thought existed in ancient Egypt. Egyptologists are still years behind archaeoastronomers in expressing an interest in the astronomy of the Egyptians, so some years will pass before a truly qualified scholar examines his evidence. No subsequent attempt by astrologers has really dealt with the issue properly, and the sidereal school of astrologers, themselves, quickly became as fascinated with and hypnotized by their new toy as other schools of astrology have been with their techniques. Siderealists have placed much emphasis on charts erected for the time when the Sun and Moon return to its place at birth, and when "the Lights" as they are sometimes called, enter the sidereal constellations. Another astrological theme which they emphasize strongly, and which will be shown to have some experimental verification in the next chapter, is the concept of angularity — that is, when a planet crosses the horizon or the midheaven line of the horoscope.

Firebrace spent thirty-five years working with the tropical zodiac. Then he came into contact with Cyril Fagan and one of his disciples, Rupert Gleadow.[122] Fagan first published his research on the sidereal zodiac hypothesis in 1947, and it happens that Gleadow, like Firebrace, had been engaged at the Foreign Office and air force intelligence during the war. Gleadow and Firebrace both passed away late in 1974, so we can only guess whether they knew of each other's astrological involvements in those days. Nevertheless, they must have hit it off well together, and Firebrace was soon translating his hundreds of horoscopes into Fagan's zodiac.

By 1961, the sidereal movement had gained enough momentum, and caused enough debate and friction in the Astrological Association, that Firebrace decided to resign. This was not the first time he resigned, however, for one

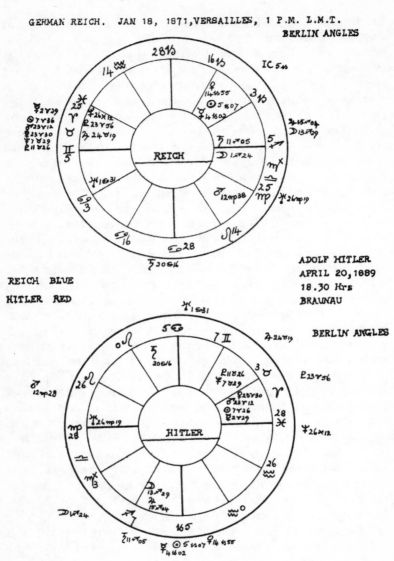

GERMAN REICH.   JAN 18, 1871, VERSAILLES, 1 P.M. L.M.T.
BERLIN ANGLES

REICH

REICH BLUE

HITLER RED

ADOLF HITLER
APRIL 20, 1889
18.30 Hrs
BRAUNAU

BERLIN ANGLES

HITLER

astrologer present during his tenure as president of the A.A. recalled that "he was a great 'resigner' when things didn't go his way." That year witnessed the birth of *Spica: A Review of Sidereal Astrology,* which he edited for thirteen years until his death shortly after publication of the October 1974 issue.

"Firebrace produced *Spica* with unfailing regularity," recalled John Addey, "to make it not merely the only periodical in this country devoted to the problems and techniques of Sidereal astrology, but probably the longest running and surely the most penetrating of any in the West."

It was in *Spica,* named after one of the critical stars in Fagan's zodiac of constellations, that Firebrace eventually published the most important horoscopes which he had originally calculated beginning in the early days of World War II. In volume I, number I, he produced a study of the astrology of Germany in both world wars and suggested that astrological research might best proceed by gathering a thematic series of charts and examining them statistically for significant symbolic trends. "This admittedly presents difficulties with astrological themes," he wrote, "but it should be our aim." From his study of the relevant horoscopes, he concluded that Hitler's chart should be transposed ("relocated" is the current term) to Berlin from his birthplace in order to see how Hitler related to the horoscope of the original Reich of 1871. He was also convinced that Pluto plays a very important role in moments of crisis. He had already published a collection of the significant sidereal horoscopes for both World War I and II.[123] By 1968, he published a new horoscope for the USSR based on his years of research with important events in the history of that country.[124] His horoscope for the death of Lenin contains this interesting observation: "It is curious that both transiting and natal Jupiter are angular, but this could refer to the pomp and ceremony of the funeral. I have noticed this in similar maps, notably in those for Winston Churchill." He admitted feeling dissatisfied with the chart, because he considered that the event could not have been predicted from it.

In that same year, Firebrace published a horoscope for Richard Nixon one month before the election, November 5, 1968. "The result is astonishing," he wrote. "Within two degrees of the angles it gives progressed Jupiter as well as transitting Jupiter. . . . This is fine testimony for a victory and possibly a run-away victory at the polls."[125]

Thus far, the evidence establishes that Firebrace was a competent astrologer who devoted much time to cross-checking his astrological calculations. We know that he was strongly interested in astrology when the war broke out, and we know that he was in close proximity to Churchill in both physical and diplomatic terms, as the Yalta affair involved Churchill and Eden on a personal and continuing basis. We have the statement of a close associate that Firebrace did in fact consult with Churchill on the basis of horoscopes, and those who knew him would not like to think of "the Brig" as telling such a tall story if it were not true.

Turning the tables for a moment, is it really likely that Churchill would have permitted some kind of documentation to exist which might indicate that he had accepted astrological advice? Hardly likely. If such consultations did occur, Firebrace may not even have brought his charts with him, but merely memorized some important points for his discussions with Sir Winston. Firebrace's horoscopes would not be covered with Top Secret stamps, and to an untrained eye, they could be for any event whatsoever.

Even more important is what people try to do with the idea of their leaders using astrology. In Canada, for instance, astrologers insist that Pierre Trudeau, as the longest-standing elected leader in the West, has timed all his elections (except one) so perfectly that he just *has* to have an astrologer. By the same token, gay Canadians insist in perfectly serious tones that their prime minister just *has* to be. . . . Others view with great horror the idea that the world's fate might have hung on the balance of a few symbols in a horoscope. Better to have John Kennedy performing legendary deeds in secret with Marilyn Monroe than consulting the *real* stars!

I think the bottom line is that politicians are a pragmatic bunch at heart. Just like businessmen, they don't care how crazy it sounds, just as long as it seems to give them an inside edge. If we accept even a small portion of the implications of the evidence presented in the next chapter, astrologers may indeed have means to read character and possibly predict the quality of major life-events. Such information could be useful to a politician during intense conferences such as Yalta. Churchill was not likely to ask Firebrace for his opinion without testing it against subsequent events. His interest in astrological consultation might have been more of a corroborative nature, attempting to see if Firebrace's conclusions matched with his own suspicions in any way or clarified his options. This, in fact, is how a humanistic astrologer would like astrology to be used, and how Firebrace is known to have practiced astrology. "Firebrace did not like reading horoscopes in a fortune-like manner," a close associate told me. "Rather, he wished to warn them of the attitude they should adopt towards events coming their way."

No wonder he cried in public when the Allies stopped their advance to the East. Perhaps Firebrace foresaw some events which even today, people insist will never happen.

Astrologers have always been connected to political leaders in one way or another. In ancient times they were employees of the court, and when the court found no further use for them, they then published their horoscopes and conclusions before the public. In 1814 John Corfield was one of several astrologers who published a horoscope for Napoleon Bonaparte in his *Destiny of Europe!!! The Nativity of Napoleone Buonaparte, Emperor of the French.* As with Hitler a century later, no one had an accurate birth-time and there was much inspired guessing as to the correct horoscope. Astrology is often connected with the rise of Nazism, to the point where several facts are lost from sight. Nuremburg Document D-59, signed in 1941 by Reinhard Heydrich, head of internal security for Nazi Germany, states:

> In the present struggle for the fate of the German people, it is necessary to maintain not merely the physical but also the mental health of our people, both individually and collectively. The German people can no longer be exposed to occult teachings which pretend that the actions and missions of the human being are subject to mysterious magic forces.
> Immediate measures will be taken against the following:
> Astrologers
> Occultists
> Spiritualists
> Followers of Christian Science
> (etc.)

The remainder of Heydrich's order specified that all

records and property of such groups was to be confiscated. Simultaneously a search of their houses was to begin, and publishers of such material were included in the order.

> Persons who have devoted themselves to secret teachings and secret sciences as their main occupation, and who have therefore led the existence of a parasite at the expense of the people are to be arrested in every case.... They are to be sent case by case, to a concentration camp or (in less serious cases) through the agency of the Labour Exchanges, to be directed to an occupation more useful to the German people. . . .

That people died for their beliefs is not a matter for mockery. Yet countless writers have made hay out of the supposed connection between all sorts of occult movements and the top Nazi leaders. Those who are convinced that there is not a shred of truth to astrology reason that only a lapse of clarity could lead anyone to accept advice from astrology. Astrology cannot be true, by definition, therefore it is not true, and therefore anyone who believes in it in any way must be fundamentally misled *or misleading*. Thus, it is argued, interest in the occult is dangerous, such believers are to be held in suspicion, and such nonsense must be vigorously exposed and opposed at every turn.

This, in part, is the reasoning behind the current attack on astrology which the media has supported actively since 1975 (see Chapter Eleven). And for these reasons, any evidence which appears to support such a ridiculous (by their definition) idea as astrology is to be vigorously dispatched to the nether regions. Yet astrology will keep on popping up in the most unexpected places. Now I suppose that the rise and victory of Sir Winston Churchill may be blamed on his secret associations with astrology!

Only two documents appear to be of any real value in understanding the role of astrology in World War II, especially on the German side. I have already mentioned Ellic Howe's *Urania's Children,* the latter half of which is devoted to the search for Hitler's astrologer. Although Howe admits in several places in his book that he himself has seen horoscopes work and that circumstantial corroborative evidence for astrology is growing, his tone remains supercilious. He does not view the development of astrological technique and philosophy as a serious subject. One of the most interesting documents written by an astrologer about his work is *Zodiac and Swastika* by Wilhelm Wulff.[126] Herr Wulff recounts how he was forced to practice astrology for Himmler during the war, and gives the reader insight into the astrologer's point of view. Now elderly and retired, he lives in Munich and refuses to discuss his experiences or his astrological techniques with anyone — even astrologers.

Both the critics who attempt to blame the rise of cults such as Nazism on public gullibility engendered by a belief in the occult, and those who believe that astrology is completely true and was probably used by the Nazi leadership, are missing the mark. Jung, in his psychiatric practice, noted that before the war he began to receive patients who were having premonitions of the bad times which were to come. And the simple truth — which I will leave you to consider in your own fashion — may be that the human population is, after all, swayed from time to time by cosmic conditions which lead whole nations toward one mental set or another. As individuals are aware of this, in some way, on an unconscious level, it should not be surprising to find a rising interest in such concepts as astrology just before times of crisis — personal as well as collective. They may be intuitions with a basis in fact if not in detail.

Are the planets somehow related to wars? In Chapter Twelve we'll take a closer look at this question. Meanwhile, from the Totally Unsubstantiated Rumor Department, I present this transcript of an interview I recorded in 1978 and broadcast in 1979 with New York astrologer Barbara Somerfield. Ms. Somerfield told me she believed astrology was used as a tactical weapon during the Viet Nam War.

Somerfield: "Much of this is being done privately within the Pentagon. I've met the astrologers who have done the work."
Dean: "Are you willing to name names?"
Somerfield: "No. It was given to me in confidence."
Dean: "And what did they tell you?"
Somerfield: "Well, there was one fellow who used to order twenty copies of a particular textbook, and it was sent down to one of the Air Force bases. I got very curious why he kept ordering twenty copies, and when he came to visit the shop one

year, we questioned him, but he wouldn't talk about it. Then he retired, and one day over many drinks he told me what he was doing."

Dean: "And that was . . .?"

Somerfield: "Helping to out-guess the Cambodian astrologers and plan bombing missions."[127]

Ten

The Mars Effect

These are the facts. I think it may be said that, as far as objectivity of observation, statistical significance of differences, verification of the hypothesis, and replicability are concerned, there are few sets of data in psychology which could compete with these observations. . . . Should one even consider the possibility of fraud, it must be rejected; there is no possibility of fraud entering into the picture. However much it may go against the grain, I think we must admit that there is something here that requires explanation. Whether that explanation would be along astrological lines is, of course, another question — indeed, astrology really does not furnish us with an explanation at all, it simply asserts the facts (or something very much like the facts) actually found. . . . That there is a relationship cannot be doubted any longer in view of the large body of evidence supporting it. . . .

Prof. Hans Eysenck, *"Biography in the Service of Science: A Look at Astrology,"* Biography, Vol. 2(1), 25-34.

"Consider the dilemma of Dr. Gauquelin," commented *Human Behavior* magazine in 1976. "He set out to debunk astrology, but as far as his fellow scientists are concerned, he might as well have done just the opposite."[128]

Indeed, how would you react if you were an eager young psychologist who had decided to check out astrology and

found some surprising statistical evidence that the planets
do influence human behavior? If you were looking for a nice
cushy career and many favorable comments from your peers,
my advice to you would be to duck quickly and forget the
whole thing as soon as possible. Never admit to anyone that
you might have uncovered what's really behind astrology.
And even better, write a few articles reporting that you
looked into the whole thing, and as expected, found negative
results. Along with your negative results, it would be wise to
include a warning that society is being endangered by the
irrational beliefs people hold these days and that it would be
safer if people would just listen to establishment scientists.

But if you were the kind of young scientist Galileo was,
someone with a thirst for knowledge, a desire to penetrate the
mysteries of nature, a determination not to be brushed aside
or discounted, and the strength to persist for years against the
mockeries of others, then you would be in for an interesting
career, to say the least.

Were it not for the fact that the word "astrology" is in such
disrepute, Michel Gauquelin would be honored as the
greatest astrologer the world has seen for centuries. Unfortunately, no one has invented a better word, and Gauquelin
himself winces when his critics call him a neoastrologer.
For he is, in the true sense of the word, a scientist, one who
seeks to know.

Michel Roland Gauquelin was born in Paris, France, on
November 13, 1928. His father, Roland, was a dental
surgeon, and his mother's name was Lenoir. Although he
would deny it, any astrologer would tell you Michel
Gauquelin is a typical Scorpio.

"At the beginning, some members of my family did horoscopes," said Gauquelin, recalling his early years at home.
"Not for money, but as a hobby. I became fascinated by
that."[129]

Gauquelin's fascination with astrology returned when he
was a student in his mid-twenties at the Sorbonne (University of Paris). He obtained his Ph. D. in psychology in 1954
and married Françoise Schneider, a science writer and
psychologist, that same year. Even though she knew of his
strange researches into astrology, Françoise found Michel
irresistibly attractive. Even today, they still enjoy arguing

over who chose whom first. And to this day, they continue their close collaboration in scientific research and various editorial projects, which leads to some confusion when one refers to "Gauquelin's research" rather than "the Gauquelins' research," and explains in part how so much research could have been performed in so few years.

Why should the critics of astrology become infuriated with this man who wrote in 1968: "However it is judged, astrology loses in serious confrontations. Even if they are cast by renowned practitioners, the individual horoscope and the world prediction appear scientifically as nonsense. Thus there would be nothing more to say, astrology would be only deceit and deception, and the heavenly bodies would have no influence on man."[130]

What has this man done to bring down the unholy wrath of skeptics? Why is this man lumped in with gypsy fortune-tellers, spoon-benders, and flying saucer nuts? Because he has demonstrated that whether astrology is true or not, the position of some planets at our birth has a statistical correlation with our later choice of career, and perhaps even our success in that chosen career. That's why.

"It seemed to me that the only way to prove or disprove astrology was through statistics," Gauquelin tells anyone who asks. "So, I began to gather a large number of birth-data of different kinds of people. And in the beginning, I didn't find any positive results for the main claims of astrology. But one day, in the course of these negative results, I found a positive result. I was somewhat puzzled by that, and surprised, so I tried to replicate [repeat] it. It was the beginning of a new story for me."

And for everyone interested in astrology.

Today, no one can claim to have studied, investigated, or debunked astrology without having examined the work of Michel and Françoise Gauquelin. The evolution of their research into planetary influences is simultaneously a major scientific monument and a perfect example of the treatment which the scientific establishment bestows upon results which contradict its own unscientific biases.

Gauquelin's earliest experiments were designed to detect the traditional astrological components that we saw at work in our study of sun-sign columns and serious astrology —

the sun signs, rising signs or ascendants, moon signs, and major aspects between planets. All tested negatively. Either the astrologers were fooling themselves, or modern statistical methods were still incapable of detecting variables of this kind (statistics is still a young science, after all). Gauquelin's personal training and bias led him to the former conclusion.

But there were some surprises in store for the young psychologist who set out to disprove astrology through statistics, as indeed there are surprises for everyone who decides a priori that planetary influences are impossible.

"I achieved these strange results almost in spite of myself," Gauquelin admitted. "They have been checked by many scientists who have failed to uncover any mistakes. They seem no more at home with reason than with superstition, for my findings are completely without explanation at the present time."[131]

Just when he was about to finish his investigation, complete with its comfortable negative findings which discounted traditional astrology, Gauquelin was confronted by an outrageous statistic. In the birth charts of 576 medical academicians, a certain planetary position was occurring at a frequency far from normal. According to the rules of statistics, this was no chance event. It was highly significant. Having gone this far, Gauquelin could not ignore it.

The initial results showed that eminent doctors tended to be born just after Mars or Saturn had either risen or reached the highest point in its daily travel across the sky. But ordinary people didn't display the same tendency. Could the planets at the birth of these doctors somehow determine the personality characteristics necessary to succeed in medical school?

"This was absurd and embarrassing," Gauquelin admitted. "It was better not to ask too many questions, but to repeat the experiment and see what happens."

So he gathered another group of 508 eminent doctors. Sounds simple? Remember that it took time and money to locate their names, determine their dates of birth, and find out where each of them was born. In many countries, birth data is very difficult to obtain. In North America, for example, there are no laws requiring an accurate birth-time to be recorded. Doctors will sometimes record a time close to the actual birth-time, but there is no telling how accurate a recorded time might be. Often, hospital staff are woefully ignorant of little details such as Daylight Savings Time. The clock in the delivery room could have been a few minutes out, or not working. And the net result is that it is nearly impossible to obtain accurate birth-times for many people. As a result, astrological research and any other research which attempts to deal with possible cosmic or geomagnetic or other influences at birth suffer for lack of sufficient data.

But Gauquelin began his research in France, where Napoleonic law decrees that time and place shall be recorded for each birth. These records are public, and it only remained for Gauquelin to muster the time, energy, and funds necessary to gather photocopies of the original documents. He wrote to the various city halls in each locality where one of the eminent doctors was born and requested the hour of birth. Since he had to assume there would be some mistakes in these records, or that some births might not be recorded accurately in the first place, his methods were devised to take such problems into account. Unlike astrologers, he was not looking for a precise effect, but a *statistically significant* trend in the data.

Mars and Saturn were prominent in the second group of doctors, just like the first! "This happened in 1950," Gauquelin recalled. "I was twenty then, and my enthusiasm forbad me thinking that anything is impossible. Why couldn't these influences have been buried in astrology all these centuries? I had no idea then how much of my life this research would consume, and how much criticism it would receive."

By 1955, Gauquelin had completed and published a study of French celebrities, with similar results.[132] Critics found this interesting, but objected that perhaps only Frenchmen displayed them. They argued that Gauquelin ought to perform his experiments in another country to see what happened there.

Gauquelin agreed, and from 1956 onward, Michel and Françoise spent their holidays in a different country each year, accumulating new data. It is to their great credit that they gathered an incredible 25,000 sets of birth data from Germany, Italy, Belgium, and Holland. During each year, thousands of dollars were spent on postage, tracking down cases which had been missed. Many hours were spent cross-checking and indexing the data, tracing errors and ensuring the best and most extensive data-base possible. And for each person, planetary positions had to be laboriously calculated — those were the days before home computers! The calculations were, in fact, more difficult than those used in normal astrological or astronomical procedures, since they represented a kind of statistical hybrid between the two sciences.[133]

"Naturally, I was well aware of what I was investigating," Gauquelin recalled. "An individual's profession may be determined by the planetary positions at his birth! Only the astrologers had maintained such an idea. And there was, and still is, no explanation of how this happens. But if a fact is well described, the fact *is*. And the explanation will follow, as has happened in many other problems which science has faced."

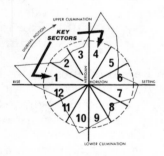

Diagram: If there were no planetary effects, the position of a given planet at birth would be random (dotted circle) in any group of subjects. By observing the positions of planets in the birth charts of successful persons, Gauquelin found they tend to have planets related to their career in the key sectors, or opposite to these sectors. The diagram shows the typical pattern which emerged in dozens of experiments. The distance from the center indicates the number of cases in each sector.

Year by year, the evidence became clearer. In every country they investigated, in every professional group they tested, the planetary influences were there for those who had eyes to see and ears to hear. Local customs, languages, other such factors were ineffective barriers to these apparent planetary influences. The pattern remained the same: the more prominent and successful a given group were in their chosen field, the more they displayed a tendency to have the related planet in particular places in their birth charts. These areas of the sky became known as "key sectors," because of their importance to Gauquelin's hypothesis.

Mars tends to be in a key sector at the births of great doctors, great athletes, or great soldiers. For artists, painters, and musicians, Mars displays a tendency to *avoid* these key sectors at birth. Politicians and actors tend to be born with Jupiter in a key sector, while scientists avoid this Jupiterian influence. Ministers, politicians, and writers tended to have the Moon in key sectors, while athletes and soldiers avoided having the Moon in key sectors.

Even the Nazis fell prey, postbellum, to the Gauquelins' statistical analysis.[134] In 1960, Gauquelin reported his results on a study of 259 high Nazi dignitaries, 130 generals of the Waffen SS, and 119 generals of the German High Command between 1939 and 1945. Against chances of 50,000 to 1, Jupiter was prominent in the charts of the top German military and political figures.

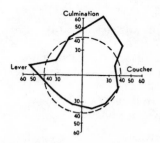

Diagram: The position of Jupiter in the birth charts of prominent Nazis and German military leaders during World War II.

In this connection, it's amusing to note what some astrologers have observed concerning Jupiter. Manley Palmer Hall suggests that the symbol for Jupiter represents an eagle, and this was certainly prominent on the banners carried by the Nazis. In keeping with the Nazi penchant for overkill in just about everything from architecture to social theories, Robert Hand notes that Jupiter "will sometimes just enlarge something or make an action grandiose or overdone. . . . You will be tempted to expand in order to take advantage of your prosperity, but you might leave yourself vulnerable to the more difficult times that will eventually come. . . . If others do not acknowledge you openly, you may feel cheated and go on to assume the station and privilege that you think you deserve. Even if you are recognized, you may act arrogant and smug. This creates a negative energy that could lead to your total downfall. . . ."[135]

Those trite horoscope readings sometimes take on nasty dimensions.

Planet in key sector:	High frequency	Average	Low frequency
Mars	Scientists	Cabinet Ministers	Writers
	Doctors	Actors	Painters
	Athletes	Journalists	Musicians
	Soldiers		
	Executives		
Jupiter	Team athletes	Painters	Individual athletes
	Soldiers	Musicians	Scientists
	Ministers	Writers	Doctors
	Actors		
	Journalists		
	Playwrights		
Saturn	Scientists	Soldiers	Actors
	Doctors	Cabinet Ministers	Painters
			Journalists
			Writers

Moon	Cabinet Ministers	Scientists	Athletes
	Politicians	Doctors	Soldiers
	Writers	Painters	
		Musicians	
		Journalists	

For some planets and some professions, there is a usually high or low frequency of individuals born with a certain celestial body in a key sector.[136]

But finding positive evidence for planetary influences did not make an instant believer out of Michel Gauquelin. Far from it. His early works, in fact, are extremely critical of astrology.

There have been mathematicians who have tracked down chance and brought it to defeat in its own territory. They have discovered that the world, or at least a large part of it, is governed by the laws of probability. Each weekend we can state with statistical certainty that the following Monday a given number of deaths will occur on the highways. But for someone who is actually on the road this certainty has no significance. What he wants to know is whether he himself will have an accident, whether it is his fate to be killed next Sunday if he takes out the car.

The astrologers promise a horoscope for everyone, individual horoscopes with individual forecasts . . . it is high time this came to an end. Every attempt, whether of astrologers or scientists, to produce evidence of the validity of astrological laws has been in vain. It is now quite certain that the signs in the sky which presided over our births have no power whatsoever to decide our fates, to affect our hereditary characteristics or to play any part however humble in the totality of effects, random or otherwise, which form the fabric of our lives and mold our impulses to action.[137]

"Has Gauquelin gone mad?" cried some astrologers. "Can't he see that you actually have to work with horoscopes before you can observe the powers of astrology? Can't he see that his negative statistics prove nothing, since he hasn't really tested astrology itself? What does he think he is

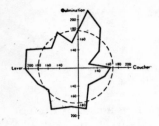

Soldiers: Position of Mars

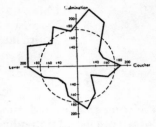

Soldiers: Position of Jupiter

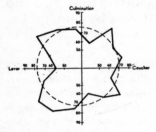

Painters: Position of Mars

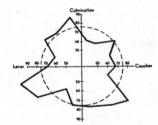

Painters: Position of Saturn

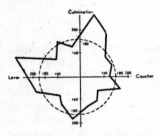

Scientists: Position of Mars

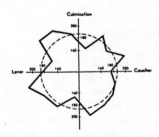

Scientists: Position of Jupiter

Diagram: For each profession and each planet, the diagrams indicate the number of persons born with the planet in each sector. For Mars, note significant excesses in key sectors for soldiers and scientists; artists display a *negative* Mars effect in key sectors. For Jupiter, scientists display a negative effect, soldiers display a positive. Saturn is positive for scientists, negative for painters.

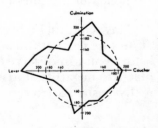

Scientists: Position of Saturn

gaining by proving planetary influences in one breath and attacking astrology in the next?"

"Has Gauquelin gone mad?" cried some scientists. "Can't he see that it's impossible that distant planets could affect human behavior? Gauquelin's calculations are faulty! Surely he is merely encouraging all sorts of irrational beliefs which are threatening the very fabric of our civilization!"

The essential difference between what Gauquelin discovered and what astrologers study is that Gauquelin is speaking of statistical probabilities, while astrologers almost never speak of probabilities in their predictions or character analyses. For most astrologers, the universe operates on the principle of synchronicity, not chance. Carl Jung spoke of synchronicity as an *acausal* connecting principle through which one event does not cause another. Rather, everything which occurs at a given moment is connected through the very qualities of consciousness, time, and space at that instant. To the astrologer, there is never any chance involved in, for example, the manifestation of your rising sign. There would be adjustments based on the many modifications from your genetic, social, and personal background. There would be other adjustments based on the many factors used in horoscope analysis. And there would be the particular interpretational bias each astrologer or counselor has in interpreting a given astrological sign in its context.

But no chance. The very fact that something has occurred means that synchronicity was operative. And to the astrologer, his symbols can be used to determine the meaning of that event. A prominent astronomer, who has papers published in the leading astronomy journals, once told me of his first exposure to synchronicity and the symbolism of Tarot cards, which are related to astrological symbolism. He was visiting California, and friends took him to a rural commune one day, where he met someone who offered to read the Tarot for him. He accepted. Minutes later, he realized that the conversation had gone to great depths, exploring questions concerning his personal life he had not revealed to anyone. The astronomer's conclusion was that however they work, such symbols have great power.

Such powers are irrelevant, of no interest whatsoever, and most probably exist only in your imagination, according to the statistical world view. Did you have a significant dream last night? You must dream the same dream at least a dozen times in a row before it attains a *statistical* significance. Furthermore, if you dream something which comes true, or which you find later to be true, you must be able to do this on demand, like Pavlov's dogs, before any skeptical scientist can accept the reality of such prophetic dreams.

Thus, as we saw in Chapter Two, whether you accept the world of symbols or the world of statistics, depends very much upon your prior experience. If you've had such dreams, you know they exist. But if you haven't, for whatever reason, you'll debate and deny them. But the two worlds can work together. Although Gauquelin's character and career predictions based on planetary positions at birth are thus of a different nature than the predictions of astrologers, we can begin to see that they confirm some of the basic ideas behind astrological symbolism.

In order to comprehend what Gauquelin was observing in his statistics, you have to understand something of astronomy and something of statistics. Remember that the Sun appears to rise and set because the Earth is turning. We know that in our minds, but we're not very conscious of it during the day, because it's hard to sense it. At the same time, as if they were carried along by the sky, each planet appears to rise and set each day. So at certain moments today, for example, Mars will rise in the east, climb overhead like the noonday Sun, and set in the west. If you like, there's a martian morning, a martian noon, a martian evening, and a martian midnight. Or, to put it another way, a marsrise instead of a sunrise and a mars-set instead of a sunset.

Got it? Now let's complicate things!

Remember that the Earth is traveling around the Sun once per year, which makes the Sun appear to travel through the zodiac. Now at the same time, each of the planets is also traveling around the Sun, but at a different speed. It takes a few hours of thought to understand how all this works, but I find it helps if you lie down, close your eyes, and try to picture yourself floating in space. Pretend you're looking down on the solar system, and you can see the planets going around the Sun. See how tiny Mercury speeds around the Sun, while Earth and the slower planets farther out each take progressively longer to make one orbit of their star. It's rather like a stream, where the middle travels more rapidly than the water at the shore. This is the second concept you need; the planets all move at different speeds. Some are fast, and some are slow. Sometimes, when one planet overtakes another, the other planet even appears to go backward for a while, just like the car you speed past on the highway can appear to be traveling back down the highway and away from your car.

Now come down to Earth, and imagine you're standing up, looking to the south. But this time, you're wearing some special glasses which allow you to see right through the blue sky. You can see the planets, large and bright. Remember that as you face south, the Earth is carrying you to the left. This makes the Sun appear to rise, and in your mind, you can see two other planets rising just after it, tiny Mercury and bright Venus. A little later, red Mars rises. They all proceed silently upward toward the south until they are high in the sky.

Now as you are standing, you are defining a very important influence. Your body is roughly defining the line of gravitational attraction. You know without being told which is up and which is down. And you find it rather difficult to deviate from this line. For instance, it's hard to walk along at 45° like a drunk. And if you take this vertical line which your body defines and make it into a plane cutting through the Earth at the north and south poles, you have defined your "meridian." We speak of a "meridian of longitude" which is a measure of how far east or west you are from Greenwich. In astrology, any planet (including the Sun and Moon) which crosses this line is said to be on the midheaven or M.C. (from the Latin *Medium Coeli*). Since this line shows where each celestial body appears at its maximum height during its daily (or diurnal) arc in the sky, Gauquelin refers to this point as the "upper culmination."

So we have this procession across the sky — the Sun, followed quickly by Mercury and Venus, with Mars trailing along. Each proceeds to "culminate," takes a bow, and goes to set in the west. But two months later, things appear

Diagram: Origin of the astrological houses and the Gauquelin sectors.

Upper culmination
Planets appear to move in this direction

Your meridian

Planets set in the west

Earth is rotating in this direction

Diurnal motion

Orbital motion

Planets rise in the east

Upper Culmination

Set

Rise

Lower Culmination

Gauquelin sectors

You are facing south

S
E — W
N

MC

Descendant

IC

Ascendant

Astrological houses

different. By this time, the Sun has moved (really the Earth has moved in its orbit), and each of the planets has also shifted position. From our earthly observation post, we might not see Mercury at all now, because it is hidden behind the Sun. Venus, which followed shortly after the Sun, has now swung around in front and actually rises first! In the pre-dawn glow, you can see it like a tiny spotlight in the distance. Mars has also moved in its orbit and rises much later than the Sun now.

Don't worry if you can't picture this all at once. No one can. Sometimes it's easier to grasp if you take the time to visit your local planetarium. Or at your local science shop they might have one of those small mechanized models of the solar system so you can see the relative motions of the planets around the Sun.

We have two main motions to consider. The first is the daily rising and setting of each planet, caused by the Earth's rotation. The second is the orbital motion of the planets, including the Earth. We have seen that this motion can advance or delay the time a planet rises or sets, as time goes by.

A third factor which affects rising and setting times is your latitude, how far north or south of the equator you are located. Why? Once again, this is something you should ask to have demonstrated at the planetarium. But remember that in most northern countries, the days are long in the summer and short in winter. This is one example of rising and setting times being advanced or delayed by latitude. In the far North, the effect becomes so extreme, that the Inuit experience six months of day and six months of night. In summer, instead of setting, the Sun just goes around the horizon! Then in winter it sets for six long, dark months.

Thoroughly confused? Don't worry. For now, it's enough simply to realize that nothing rises or sets at the same time each day or at the same time for different locations on Earth. It's not too complicated with the Sun, because its annual motion (actually our annual orbit) is quite regular. You can look in your newspaper and read the time of tomorrow's sunrise or look it up in tables for your particular latitude. But the other planetary motions, which we can't observe in the same direct way, complicate things quite a bit.

If it's any consolation, many of the astronomers and scientists who have checked Gauquelin's calculations had to work hard before they could grasp the astronomy and statistics involved. As for the statistical principles involved, we've already briefly discussed the idea of probability. When something occurs more or less than the laws of chance would predict, we begin to look at levels of significance. The statisticians ask, "Is it significant that this is occurring, or is it a normal deviation from what we ought to expect?" For example, if it rains today and not tomorrow, this is what we might expect by chance. One week's worth of rain might be significant, depending on where you live. Seven days of rain would be an interesting statistic, but probably within normal limits for most areas. But one full year's worth of rain would be a very significant sign indeed. You might also have a run of events, such as one day of rain and one of sunshine. At the end of the monsoon season in India, this wouldn't be unusual. But if it occurred in your location for six months steady, the statistics would probably be very significant.

Similarly, what Gauquelin was looking for was any such planetary position which occurred *significantly more than chance,* taking all those planetary motions into account. The statistics and astronomy are quite involved, and the fact that the Gauquelins calculated tens of thousands of cases by hand is something to marvel at.

Gauquelin began by dividing the daily arc of each planet into sectors. These were numbered from the rising point in the east, up to the upper culmination, down to the point of setting, and thence to the lower culmination point. A planet should spend the same amount of time in each sector, and if only chance were operating, over a great number of cases, the planet should be observed equally in each sector once all the astronomy is taken into account.

Astrologers, too, have divided the sky into sectors, but with a different terminology. Instead of sectors, they speak of houses and number them in the opposite direction. The astrological houses are numbered in the direction planets orbit the Sun, so that once the horoscope is erected, the planets move through these houses in the sequence shown, from the first house through to the twelfth. There are dozens of ways to calculate these divisions of the sky, but they all come down to variations on a handful of systems. Each attempts to solve a particular problem in representing a three-dimensional sky on two-dimensional paper or in symbolically representing an aspect of astrology on paper. The houses are mainly used in astrology as symbols of worldly experiences, such as career, partners, the home, the self. The history of these divisions, and how they came to be interpreted as they are today, has never been properly traced. But we do know that perhaps in ancient Greece, the behavior of the symbols on paper became more important to astrologers than the behavior of planets in the sky. To the ancient astrologers, as we saw earlier, what was *visible* was most important. A planet which had just risen was just beginning its cycle and was especially potent. The second most important place for a planet was at the upper culmination, since from there its influence, like the noonday Sun, was most intense. A planet just about to set on the western horizon also had meaning, and somewhere in between the extremes of rising and setting, and opposite to the upper culmination, the planet passed invisibly through its lower culmination, hidden by the Earth. The symbolism of birth, maturity, death, and the underworld is all too plain.

But as the mathematics which deal with planetary motion were developed, astrologer/astronomers became often more concerned with their diagrams themselves. Like weathermen who speak of their graphs, saying "the barometer is rising" rather than "I think it's going to rain," the astrologers lost touch with the observational symbolism and gradually became enamored of the behavior of the symbols they saw on paper. Thus, the place where planets shine bright and fresh over the eastern horizon became known as the Twelfth House, the final rather than the first phase of a cycle, and therefore a place of confinement, restrictions, and past involvements or karma. Instead, the First House, just below the horizon, was now to symbolize the individual himself.

It would be simple to say that the Gauquelins have shown that the system of astrological houses is wrong. And that is what they have insisted in their writings. If we find that a planet is statistically more important after its rise, or after its culmination, they ask, why do astrologers continue to lay the emphasis on the house before the rise, and before the culmination? In fact, the issue is not that simple, and it is probably too early in the history of this research to offer a definitive answer. Dr. Zipporah Dobyns, for example, maintains that the houses indicated as significant by the Gauquelins' research represent a search for the absolute. "Based on the individual's faith in what is true, real, morally right, possible and desirable, goals are formulated and choices made," says Dobyns in her discussion of the astrological houses which correspond to the Gauquelins' "key sectors."[138]

This is a description of how a choice of career is made, and thus it is possible for the traditional astrologer to argue that modern statistics are, in fact, confirming the essence of astrology, not disproving it. History will judge. And even history makes mistakes.

Even though Gauquelin was employed as the editor of a series of psychology books for a French publisher from 1967 and later as consultant to the French edition of *Psychology Today*, he doggedly pursued his research. Twenty years later, he was still the cautious scientist, still triple-checking everything, exploring every possible loophole and error in his methods. Like the Scorpio he insists he is not, the mysterious planetary influences had him hooked. Besides his several popular books, Gauquelin published all his original data in twelve thick volumes commencing in 1970. Over 2,000 sports champions, nearly 4,000 scientists, 3,000 career soldiers, painters, musicians, actors, politicians, writers . . . enough characters were employed in the Gauquelins' celestial drama to put Will Shakespeare to shame. Along with these volumes, two series of booklets were published under the name of their laboratory in Paris, in which the Gauquelins clearly outlined and discussed their results. It is therefore to these more technical documents that critics and the curious must turn for a proper under- standing of these important discoveries. Unfortunately, one can still hear academics, who should know better, condemn Michel Gauquelin's results on the basis of a superficial reading of one of his popular books which are aimed at the general public.

Because his collection of 2,088 sports champions was the

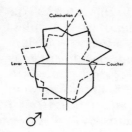

_____ 703 musicians
...... 3142 soldiers

Gauquelin, "Les hommes et les astres."

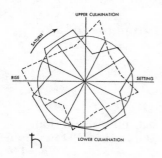

...... 3647 scientists
_____ 5100 artists

Inner circle: 1409 actors
Central circle: 903 journalists
Outer circle: 1003 politicians

Gauquelin,
"Les hommes et les astres."

Gauquelin,
"Cosmic Influences in
Human Behavior."

Diagram: **Comparison of planetary effects on different groups of successful professionals. Mars is positive in the key sectors for soldiers, negative for musicians. Saturn "illustrates the classical antagonism between art and science," notes Gauquelin. For scientists, Saturn is positive in the key sectors, negative for artists. Jupiter displays the same peaks in the key sectors for actors, journalists and politicians — three professions which depend heavily on language and the media.**

first published and because most of the attacks on Gauquelin's work have used the athletes as examples, Gauquelin's theory is often referred to as simply "the Mars effect." It's true that Mars's motion has some peculiarities, as do the motions of all planets. And Mars is close enough to Earth so that if gravity or some kind of radiation were involved, perhaps one could imagine it emanating from a planet close by. Or perhaps the martian symbolism — aggressive behavior, energy, assertiveness, militarism — was very close to the state of mind in which skeptics examined these evidences of planetary influences. Frustration leads to aggression, and when your firm belief that the planets cannot influence human behavior is contradicted, it can get pretty frustrating.

Recalling what we learned about astronomy and astrology earlier in this chapter, we can now observe the Mars effect in this diagram:

Diagram: 2088 sports champions display the "Mars effect." The circle represents chance expectation. The dotted line indicates other athletes, but *non*-champions.

The two high peaks show where planetary effects are most prominent, just after the rise and just after the culmination of a planet. These are the "key sectors" and the tendency of a planet to be found there is called "the (name of planet) effect." If there were no planetary effects, we would expect a fairly equal or random distribution of the positions of Mars in this collection of cases. You can see that the dotted line, representing average athletes, comes pretty close to this. The average athletes only exceed chance expectation in three places, and this is not significant. But observe the two prominent peaks found among the champions. These are the winners, the movers, they are not in it for a comfortable career. And Mars tends to be in its two most powerful positions in their charts. A traditional astrologer would assert that those successful champions who do not have Mars in the key sectors would have other combinations of planets, signs, and aspects to provide them with an assertive, aggressive disposition. Gauquelin would simply put these cases down to fluctuations within a statistically significant tendency to have Mars in key sectors. It all depends upon your paradigm.

For each of the four initial planets which the Gauquelins studied, and for each professional group related positively or negatively to that planet, a similar graph can be drawn. But what could be causing it all, Gauquelin wondered? Shouldn't our disposition, our interests, and our physical capacities be determined by the known factors such as genetics, social background, and our environment?

One way to test this out, Gauquelin concluded, would be to compare the birth charts of parents and children. If the planets had nothing to do with it, one would not expect any relationship between the parents' planetary positions and those of the child. But if "like father, like son" had a cosmic implication, then one would.

Fifteen thousand pairs of data and 300,000 planetary calculations by hand later, Gauquelin was ready to perform his final calculations. This time, he was not out for champion athletes, highly successful doctors, or great military men. It was Joe Lunchpail and Son he was interested in. Carefully, Gauquelin compared the positions of the ten known planets in the birth charts of the parents and offspring. In his earlier experiments, he could only detect the planetary influences of the Moon, Mars, Jupiter, and Saturn.

The results: 499,999 to one! A child tends to have planetary positions similar to the parents'. There is a planetary heredity as well as genetic one. And still no results for the other planets — Mercury, Uranus, Neptune, Pluto, and the Sun. For the first time, however, there was a significant result for Venus. Gauquelin's astrological horizons were expanding.

"Planetary heredity followed rules of a consistency to

satisfy the strictest critic," says Gauquelin. "It appears as much with the father as the mother, with the son as with the daughter, and it also follows certain genetic laws!"

What was your birth like? It's interesting to find out, because you might not have the planetary heredity effect between your birth chart and those of your parents. Why? Because the effect is altered or disappears when the birth is interfered with.

Since the 1950s, many doctors have found the birth process a terrible inconvenience. Rather than wasting hours waiting for a patient to deliver her baby, it's much more efficient simply to induce the birth at any convenient time — say, after the morning coffee break. Thus, increasing numbers of children are born through chemical inducement, cesarean section, and the use of forceps. Obviously, if the time of birth is not natural, you wouldn't expect there to be any planetary heredity effect. It would be the doctor, not nature who is deciding at what time things will happen. And this is what the Gauquelins discovered. Births before 1940 show planetary heredity clearly, but after the war, induced births became increasingly common, and the effect began to disappear from the statistics. To make sure, the Gauquelins gathered together all cases where the birth was by cesarean section. No planetary heredity there. But what about forceps? In this method, the baby is practically pulled out of the womb at the doctor's discretion by a large pair of tongs.

"In those cases," Gauquelin observed, "the planetary effect does not simply disappear, but seems shifted ahead . . . these surgical interventions seem to have shortened the normal delivery, so that the baby was born about one hour before 'the right time.' "

If planetary heredity is a natural fact, an aspect of birth which nature prefers for her own, unstated reasons, then modern medical convenience is getting in the way. It's that simple. Doctors may be fooling with effects and processes of which they have no understanding whatsoever. But after millions of years of evolution, it's in man's character to blithely assume that he can now do better than Mother Nature any time he wishes.

The original planetary heredity experiment was conducted in 1966. And in 1977, the Gauquelins released new results in a second huge experiment designed to confirm their initial findings. Such a repetition, or replication as it's called, is an important component of any modern scientific experiment. Without some assurance that a phenomenon can be observed with reliability, a scientist cannot make any deductions. Without a regular pattern, it is difficult to perceive a natural law at work.

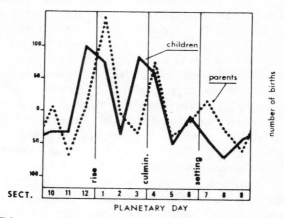

Diagram: The sectors of the planets' daily arc are here graphed along the horizontal axis, beginning with the lower culmination. Peaks in the key sectors for the parents (just after the lines showing rise, culmination, and set) are shifted earlier in time for the children. Combined results for Moon, Venus, Mars, Jupiter, and Saturn. (Gauquelin, *Scientific Documents,* Vol. 2.)

This time, two entirely new sets of data were gathered in the cities of Bourges and Paris. The planetary heredity effect suggests that if a parent has a planet in one of the key sectors the child will tend to have the same planets in one of his key sectors. Which parent does not matter, but the effect is stronger when both parents have the same planetary condition in their charts. Results of the second experiment confirmed the first — planetary heredity exists.

By combining the results of their 1966 and 1976 experiments, the Gauquelins were able to show that in over 172,000 cases, the odds were 10 million to one in favor of planetary heredity! Now they could use their huge collection of birth data to outline more clearly some of the ramifications. Just as the subset of cesarean and forceps births confirmed the planetary heredity effect in a negative fashion, the Gauquelins knew from medical statistics that the average length of labor in childbirth has been decreasing over the years. This is partly due to the methods of intervention we discussed, but it's also possible that young mothers are better prepared for birth than their mothers were. Medical information is much more available, and certainly people aren't embarassed to talk about sex these days.

Knowing that medical statistics indicate births are now occurring after shorter deliveries, the Gauquelins could turn this around and ask if the planetary heredity effect was showing up earlier in their graphs? Bingo! The data shows clearly that where parent and child have the planetary effect, the children have the relevant planet placed earlier in their horoscopes than the parent. If the father, for example, had Mars high in Sector One, the child would tend to have Mars closer to the horizon.

But we're not finished. What could be causing this effect? Astrologers have no idea whatsoever. Some suggest undiscovered radiations or vibrations on higher planes than modern science can detect. Others say the planets do not have any influence because astrology works through synchronicity. It's not a matter of cause and effect, but of symbolic sympathy. The Gauquelins were curious, so they obtained copies of the International Magnetic Character Figure. This is an index of the Earth's magnetic activity since January 1, 1884. When the scale shows 0, it's a quiet day, magnetically

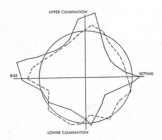

Diagram: Births on geomagnetically disturbed days display more prominent peaks of planetary heredity. Quiet magnetic days seem to spread the effect over longer periods of time.

speaking. But when the scale shows 2, it's a disturbed day with magnetic storms in the Earth's magnetic field.

"We observed more hereditary similarities between parents and children when the children were born on magnetically disturbed days," says Gauquelin. "A high geomagnetic activity seems to facilitate and possibly even accelerate the planetary effects during delivery."[139]

Whatever these planetary influences are, they respond to magnetic fields. This concept has been popular among more technically minded astrologers since the 1800s. In 1910, the British navigator Alfred J. Cooper published a treatise entitled *Solectrics: A theory explaining tempests, seismic and volcanic disturbances and other natural phenomena*, in which he proposed fields of solectric energy emanating from the Sun when it is disturbed by planetary configurations. Several decades later, the American electrical engineer L. Edward Johndro published a two-volume electromagnetic theory of planetary influences, complete with the analogy of a cosmic dynamo mechanism to explain why some passengers survived the sinking of the *Titanic,* but died later as they drifted on life rafts toward more dangerous electromagnetic lines on the Earth.

By now, you will see that the Gauquelins have built carefully and slowly upon the original foundations of their research. At each point, alternatives were explored, and the significance of variations in the data were outlined. They had gone much further than they had ever dreamed possible in 1950, and probably a lot further than you thought they would get at the beginning of this chapter. Their persistence, the quality of their research, and the wealth of detail have been a source of wonder to many scientists and astrologers alike.

By 1973, they were ready to take the next step. What experiments could they design if they took those famous champion athletes and searched their biographies? Might it be possible to describe the effects of Mars on a more psychological basis? To answer these questions, the Gauquelins developed the character-traits method. This is easy to understand if you think about how people describe your fellow workers, classmates, and so on. Suppose you hear a conversation about someone you haven't met. You're told he's a real son-of-a-gun. Naturally, being the level-headed type that you are, you take this with a grain of salt. One opinion doesn't mean much.

But suppose you had three opinions about someone. Or ten. Or 10,000. By then, you'd have a statistically significant case. You could say that it's very likely that so-and-so is, in fact, a son-of-a-gun. Of course, few people have 10,000 biographies written about them. But suppose you had several thousand athletes, each of whom displayed the Mars effect, and each of whom had several published biographies? Then you could go through those biographies and make a note of the words which are frequently used to describe people with a prominent Mars! Those biographers would be describing an astrological condition in all their wide-eyed innocence, even though none of them "believed" in astrology! That's one of the delicious things about planetary influences; just because you don't believe in them doesn't mean they won't work.

In a series of experiments from 1972 and 1977, the Gauquelins pored over thousands of biographies of athletes, scientists, actors, and writers, Each time a word was used to describe their characters, it was recorded. Once it was established that a certain word occurred at a statistically significant frequency, it could be acknowledged as a planetary trait-word. You might think it's rather obvious that a champion baseball player would be described as "an aggressive hitter" in his biography. But scientists can't assume such an idea. They have to go and check it out.

And the Gauquelins are adept at going and checking things out. Forty-six thousand trait-words later, all tabulated along with the planetary positions at birth for each biography, the experiments could begin. For Mars and athletes (the Mars effect), they were able to isolate a list of over 100 words which are used as descriptive terms in a statistically significant way. For instance, athletes were described as "grasping, strenuous, active, restless, aggressive, alert," and so on. Even common phrases such as "an old salt" and "plenty of guts" were found to be used more than chance would predict. The crude nature of some of the terms and the lower number of terms used in sports biographies, due to the hackneyed style often used in sports writing, meant that the portrait of the Mars effect was not as refined as those of the other planets.

For Jupiter in the horoscopes of actors, the Gauquelins found terms such as "briskness," "abundant gestures," "engrossing," "vivacious," and phrases such as "defies the conventions," "pushes himself forward," "likes to disguise himself." While the trait words for athletes filled only one page, those detected statistically for actors filled four pages, in keeping with the greater sophistication and complexity of the arts world over that of sports.

For scientists and Saturn, about one and a half pages of trait words included descriptions such as "analytical mind," "impartial," "imperturbable," "ragged professor," "narrow-minded," "straight," "unsociable," "does not improvise," "seeks perfection," "does not like receptions," and "zealous."

Three pages of trait words described the Moon and writers as "lets himself go," "accessible," "not aggressive," "loves animals," "not authoritative," "genuine," "shows marked attention," "bucolic," "frequents bars," "sense of the universal," "popularizer of knowledge."

And it's true, not all sports champions are aggressive bullies, and not all scientists are the quiet, introverted, ragged professors. But is that an objection to these lists of trait words? No. Because some champions were described as aggressive while others may have been described as weak-willed, the Gauquelins were able to divide their samples in a different way — according to the psychological type *within* each category they had gathered. The planetary effects were once again evident in the statistics. "Iron-willed" champions displayed a greater Mars effect than "weak-willed" champions. "Modest" actors displayed less of the Jupiter effect than "immodest" actors. "Introverted" scientists displayed more of the Saturn effect than "extraverted" scientists. So for each planet, a range of reactions to the planetary effects were established for each professional group.

"Okay," you might object. "So there's a statistical relationship between a few of the planets and a handful of professions. What about the rest of us?"

The Gauquelins began to answer that question in 1978,

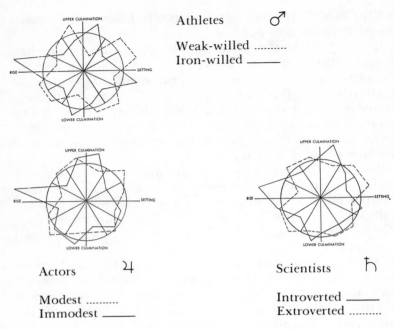

Athletes ♂

Weak-willed ....
Iron-willed _____

Actors ♃

Modest ....
Immodest _____

Scientists ♄

Introverted _____
Extroverted ....

Diagram: Having established that each professional group tends to have a particular planet in the key sectors, the Gauquelins were able to see if the planetary effects were modified in the charts of individuals not typical of their group, such as "weak-willed" athletic champions or "modest" actors. Champions are usually considered to have strong wills, and actors to be outgoing types. The diagrams show that "weak-willed" champions are born less frequently with Mars in key sectors than "iron-willed" champions. "Immodest" actors display a stronger Jupiter effect than "modest" actors. "Introverted" scientists display a stronger Saturn effect than "extroverted" scientists.

when they published yet another study of these trait words. "We still had to prove that the same character traits are always correlated with the same planet, whatever the professional activity of the subjects," admits Gauquelin. "For example, if Mars is related to character-traits that are common among athletes, what is it doing for scientists, actors, and writers who possess the same character-traits?"[140]

The Gauquelins were aiming to prove that the same personal characteristics are always related to the same planet, no matter which group they were studying. That's rather like trying to show that the astrological symbolism of each planet is stable — Mars doesn't mean one thing to you and another thing to me. Mars has a detectable and describable influence, no matter whether we believe it or not, no matter whether we understand how the influence works or not.

Here's the way they worked. Out of the 46,000 character traits they had gathered, about 6,500 were on the list of typical characteristics of champions. But some of these

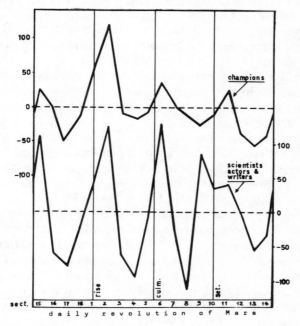

Diagram: Just as Mars was prominent in the charts of athletic champions, it is prominent in the charts of "martian" scientists, actors, and writers. The same trait words used in published biographies to describe champions turn up in the published biographies of those of the other groups who display the Mars effect. Here the Gauquelins have graphed the daily (diurnal) circle along the bottom, and divided into eighteen sectors.

individuals were themselves on the other lists — they were not athletes, but scientists, actors, and writers. So, taking the scientists, actors, and writers who had been described by others as "martian characters," the Gauquelins were able to graph the results for both groups.

Both groups showed the same kind of daily curve, as the graph illustrates. Mars in both groups tends to occur more frequently in the key sectors, and thus it has been demonstrated that the planetary effects are not unique to one profession. When the Jupiter effect on the other groups besides actors was graphed, Jupiterian athletes, scientists, and writers displayed a similar effect. And when the Saturn effect was studied in the other groups beside the scientists, athletes, actors, and writers of a saturnine nature displayed the same effect. The planets affect us all.

Such a virtuoso performance on the part of two private scientists could not go unnoticed for long. And we shall see in the next chapter what treatment the Gauquelins' researches received from a group of True Believers in the scientific community. But more serious scientists had two choices: either study the data and publish their conclusions, whether they liked them or not, or remain silent. The rules of the famous scientific method demand no less.

Enter stage right Prof. Hans Eysenck, "the scourge of psychoanalysis and hypnosis, a man whose record would lead one to expect that he would demolish astrology in one fell statistical swoop. . . ."[141] Prof. Eysenck is also one of the few established scientists who can virtually count on having a demonstration against his research when he guest lectures outside of his London University Institute of Psychiatry. Physically attacked by leftist students at the London School of Economics in 1973, Eysenck was notorious for his 1971 book *Race, Intelligence and Education,* which supported the theory of two American researchers that intelligence is genetically determined and largely unaffected by environment.

But such demonstrations were more examples of emotions trying to deal with unexpected intellectual information, for Eysenck's researches are among the major monuments of modern personality theory. Since 1947, Eysenck had exhaustively researched the idea of extraversion and introversion. "At the time this concept was a most unattractive old thing with a caricature of a face. Most psychologists interested in personality assumed I had attempted to resurrect a corpse," Eysenck recalls.[142]

Eysenck is an experimental behaviorist; that is, he sees intuitive understanding, philosophical speculation, and the intuition which doctors use in their practice as part of an unscientific past. For Eysenck, the scientific history of psychology commenced when facts were established by experiments and personality tests which could be statistically verified. Just as we saw that the Gauquelins differed in their world view from the astrologers, so Eysenck differs from psychiatrists such as Jung. Symbols are not important to Eysenck, because they cannot be measured statistically. Thus, Eysenck has been a major force behind the use of tests such as I.Q. and the kind you were given when you were in high school. One of his tests has been given to literally tens of thousands of British school children over the years, which has allowed him to do massive statistical experiments on the British population. You might say he's a "hard facts" man.

But not a crowd follower, either.

Many modern scientists automatically pooh-pooh early science and consider it beneath their dignity to study its concepts. Thus, astrology and much early medicine, alchemy, and all sorts of fascinating ideas are cast out into the darkness, left for pseudoscientists like astrologers to argue over like dogs over an old bone. One of these outcast concepts is the old idea of the four temperaments which were proposed by the Greek physician, Galen (second century A.D.). Galen proposed four personality types which he called the melancholic, the choleric, the sanguine, and the phlegmatic. Now we say, "I'm feeling very melancholy today," and we hum along to "Melancholy Baby." And in 1979, the latest word in vogue in New York was "sanguine." Everyone was sanguine about something or other, almost as if the word had just been rediscovered like those new fashions which look just like the old ones.

"The theory of extraversion-introversion is intimately connected with this ancient theory," says Eysenck. "It's only laughable to those who don't realize that it embodies lots of excellent clinical observation, without which it would never have lasted longer than any other psychological theory."

A scientist who had thus been unafraid to pursue a lonely avenue of research and see it turn into a major movement in modern psychology, a researcher who had not automatically scoffed at ancient medicine, is obviously the kind of inquiring mind which would at least give astrology a fair hearing.

Enter stage left, British astrologer Jeff Mayo. Mayo had established himself as a leading astrologer through his textbooks and his position as head tutor of the Faculty of Astrological Studies (1957-73) in London, England. The Faculty is the most prestigious and long-standing school of serious astrology, and those who hold its degree are among the best astrologers the world over. Mayo was principal of the Faculty from 1969 until 1973, when the personality differences which are so endemic among astrologers led him to separate and form the Mayo School of Astrology. In the early seventies, astrologers around the world received questionnaires from Mayo, along with a request to participate in a study to validate the signs of the zodiac. Mayo wanted to demonstrate that the positive signs, Fire and Air, would respond differently to his questionnaire than the negative signs, Earth and Water.

Mayo thought his results were positive, so he took them to Eysenck. It pays to go to the top.

"It really started with Mayo writing me a letter saying he'd been testing some astrological hypotheses about extroverts and introverts," Eysenck told me as he recalled how he became involved in astrological research. "He claimed he had found that extroverts tend to be born under the odd astrological signs, and introverts under the even-numbered signs." (Aries = 1, Taurus = 2, etc.) "I wrote back to tell him that you can't really make up your own test like that, and if he really wanted to prove anything, he'd better take one of the standardized and widely accepted tests."[143]

Standardized tests are those which have been tested on a large number of people. Often psychologists may argue what the tests are testing, but whatever it is that they are testing, they know how it behaves. In this respect, at least, they're in the same boat as the astrologers.

"I didn't think I'd hear any more from him," Eysenck continued. "But then, after nine months or so he wrote back to say that he had collected that data using my own test, and he asked me to analyze them for him."

The results of this initial study were published in the *Journal of Social Psychology* in 1978.[144] A clear zigzag pattern was evident as each subsequent group of sun signs tended first toward extraversion, then toward introversion. Before these results were published, Prof. A. G. Smithers of Manchester University realized that a study of 559 British University students he had undertaken in 1966 had shown remarkably similar results. Smithers's paper was published along with the Mayo/Eysenck results in the same journal.[145]

But if the Mayo/Eysenck results looked like a zigzag graph, so did the results of subsequent repetitions of this test zigzag from positive to negative, according to the paradigm of the researcher doing the research! Investigations along similar lines by Dr. David Nias, a graduate researcher working under Prof. Eysenck in London and Prof. Kurt Pawlik in Germany, lead to the suggestion that

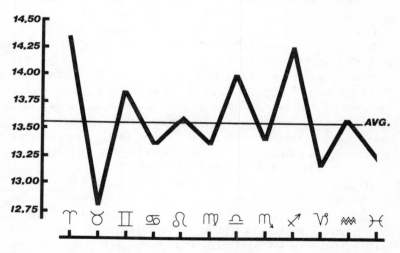

Diagram: Signs of the zodiac compared to extraversion-introversion scores on a psychological test of 2,324 students. A 1966 study obtained similar results. In a test for neuroticism, clear peaks were observed in the Water signs. Results are discussed in the text. After Mayo et al., *J. Soc. Psych.*, 1978, 105, 229-236.

people who answered the tests probably had some knowledge of how their sign ought to answer.[146] In other words,
if you know you're an Aries, you'll probably know your sign
is outgoing and martian. Therefore you would tend to
respond to questions as you think a good Aries ought to.

While discouraging, this still left the mystery of the 1966
results which were obtained prior to Mayo's. The question
is still open.

But at least one refutation backfired in a curious manner.
One researcher suggested that the Mayo/Eysenck results
were simply due to biological rhythms which many people
experience with three crests each year.[147] Other biological
rhythms have been discovered with this pattern, he noted:
Circulatory functions tend to peak in March, July, and
November. So there was no reason "on Earth" to look for
anything to do with the signs of the zodiac. But his paper
instead provided astrologers with a curious correlation with
the signs which they had overlooked. Blood is a fluid, and
the heart is related in astrological tradition to the Sun (hence
circulation). And by a strange "coincidence" in March, July,
and November, the Sun moves from a Water sign to a Fire
sign! So much for off-the-cuff debunking.

The upshot of all this is that some solid research into
astrological influences has been quietly conducted in and
around London, England during the past decade. Several
academics at other universities, students at the University
of London and the London School of Economics and a
number of independent researchers have been paving the
way for a vastly higher level of scholarship and experimentation. Quiet conferences have been held, deliberately
misnamed as gatherings on "biological cycles" so as not to
bring down the wrath of the establishment.

Results with the zodiac have been mixed, but this is not
surprising given the different world views involved in
symbols and statistics. Unless you are prepared to suggest
that some researchers deliberately falsified their results
through bias, it's remarkable that there were *any* positive
results for the signs of the zodiac.

But, to return to our main subjects, the Gauquelins had
been continuing the research we examined earlier in this
chapter. Meanwhile their bread-and-butter work consisted

of editing a series of psychology books for a French publishing house. One of these books contained an analysis and summary of Eysenck's research, so it was natural that the Gauquelins would meet Eysenck at some point to learn more about him firsthand. Given his positive results with Mayo, Eysenck could hardly be blamed at that point for becoming interested in the research of the Gauquelins. It was 1974. By 1975, Eysenck had appeared in the pages of *New Behaviour* magazine, speaking out in favor of their results.[148]

"I started out not really having an attitude toward astrology," Eysenck confessed. "I regarded astrology as such obvious nonsense that I didn't even have to think about it. But when Mayo produced his results I began to think again. And when I looked at the work of the Gauquelins, which of course is really outstanding and first class, I couldn't find anything wrong with it, although I went into the statistics quite thoroughly."

At this point it became possible to unite two streams of psychological research which had been in progress for decades — that of the Gauquelins and the Eysencks. It was decided to see if the three major personality features which the Eysencks had isolated in their research could be related to the planetary effects the Gauquelins had doggedly pursued since 1950. Three planets on one hand and three personality features on the other. Michel and Françoise Gauquelin designed and conducted their experiment with Prof. Eysenck's wife, Dr. Sybil Eysenck, in 1977.

In his *New Behaviour* article, Eysenck had suggested that introversion as revealed by his tests might relate to the position of Saturn, while extraversion might relate to Mars and Jupiter. As for his two other personality dimensions, no one knew at this point what might happen. The Gauquelins gathered the trait words they had discovered through their experiments, and Dr. Sybil Eysenck undertook to assign each word to the categories determined by her research. The personality features were then compared to the positions of Mars, Jupiter, and Saturn at birth in order to see if there was a statistical relationship between the dimensions of personality which the Eysencks had been attempting to isolate over the years, and the planetary effects the Gauquelins had discovered.

Results: Odds of 10,000 to one that the position of the planets was indeed related to introversion and extraversion as detected by the Eysenck personality tests. The second of the Eysenck personality features, neuroticism, didn't achieve any significant results, and results for psychoticism were a mixed bag.

"There appear to be lawful relationships between the two sets of variables," they concluded. And since it is not likely that human personality is determining the position of the planets at birth, they felt it to be a reasonable assumption that the position of the planets at birth is determining some features of personality.

Sounds just like astrology, doesn't it?

One measure of the controversy surrounding Gauquelin's results was the recent resignation of a leading scientist from the editorship of the *Journal of Interdisciplinary Cycle Research*. This journal has published dozens of papers dealing with Biometeorlogy and Cycle Research, detailing the relationships between living organisms and atmospheric phenomena. Under S.W. Tromp, whose work was discussed briefly in Chapter Six, the journal was about to publish several papers dealing with extraterrestrial influences on living organisms on Earth, when a Professor of Astronomy in Frankfurt strongly protested to an official of the publishers, Swets & Zeitlinger, because Tromp wanted to include a paper by Gauquelin in the Proceedings of an International Cycle Symposium. Tromp then attempted to have Gauquelin's paper published in abstract form, rather than as a complete paper, but his request was refused due to the pressure placed on the publishers to maintain their reputation. Publicly, it was admitted only that the controversial papers had to be removed due to lack of funding. They were deleted without Tromp's knowledge and approval, even though he was Editor-in-Chief of the Cycle Journal. Tromp resigned and published his results on possible extraterrestrial influences with another publisher in England.

Probably the most important result emerged the year this book was written, 1980. In that year, the Gauquelins finally pulled the veil entirely away from their secret weapon. During thirty years of criticism and innuendo, no one had found Gauquelin's methods faulty, or more than a handful of errors in his data. How Gauquelin could accomplish such a feat remained a mystery to me until I finally met Françoise Gauquelin. For while Michel Gauquelin sometimes enjoys an astrological joke, Françoise is a careful and serious scientist, precise as a Swiss watch in her methods and criticisms. Yet for all these years, most of their publications had only featured Michel's name.

Now a daring experiment occurred to the Gauquelins, one which would go to the heart of the question: Does astrology really work? Since Michel is somewhat sympathetic to serious astrologers (more so than he used to be, certainly) and since his critics might accuse him of bias, it was decided that Françoise would conduct an experiment on her own. Thus, the seventh in their series of Scientific Documents is entitled *Traditional Symbolism in Astrology and the Character-traits method*, by Françoise Gauquelin.[149]

You already know more or less how the character-traits method of research works. We could call it "the son-of-a-gun effect." And you know how the Gauquelins isolated each planetary effect and established the relationship between the traits and the planets. Now add in to this formula the assertion made by Robert Hand earlier, that modern astrological symbolism is the result of thousands of years of observations of horoscopes. Painfully, discouragingly without rigor. But thousands of years to sense whether the system is working or not.

Well, as you saw in Chapters One and Two, whether the system works or not depends on who you speak to. According to the astrologers, they can make insightful character and event predictions. According to the skeptics, these do not seem to test out very well, and so they reject astrology entirely. But as I pointed out, suppose that the general idea of astrology were correct, while the particular ideas and methods of the astrologers were only approximations? Wouldn't this explain why those who work with the system can sometimes obtain positive results, while those who refuse to take up the problem of symbolism and insist purely on statistical tests cannot obtain positive results (except where the Gauquelins are concerned).

Obviously, given all the research which I've briefly recounted above, the next step would be to go to the astrologers' textbooks and see if they had detected the same descriptive words and character traits which the Gauquelins had isolated statistically. After all, an effect is an effect. And language is language. Unless you have a problem with your vision, you'll agree the sky is blue. So what do the astrologers say about Mars, Jupiter, and Saturn? Do they say the same things which the Gauquelins' statistics say?

The answer is yes.

Yes, astrologers using those silly horoscopes, those fraudulent tools for misleading a gullible public (that's you), those pseudoscientific paraphernalia left over from the Middle Ages and ancient times, astrologers using these antiquated tools have been able, since ancient Greece, to isolate the same personality traits for planets which modern statistics have revealed!

"Our first research efforts were initiated with the aim of disproving astrological traditions," Françoise Gauquelin allows. "We were surprised by the positive results of our tests of planetary positions at birth. Then, later investigations of heredity and personality gave us a better understanding of the planetary effects.

"But an important question remained open . . . even astrology's fiercest adversary in France, Paul Couderc, noticed that our descriptions of the affinity between planets and professions look very much like the traditional astrological symbolism. On the basis of this similarity, Couderc rejected our results!

"Personally, my first impression was that the few analogies I could see between the character-traits quoted by astrologers for the symbolism of certain planets, and those listed in our studies for these planets, were nothing but mere chance."

By 1979, the Gauquelins had decided to spend a year in the United States. Here, they were offered free access to facilities which no university had made available, even though it would have cost them little. The Gauquelins were offered free access to a powerful computer already programmed for planetary calculations and filled with their published collection of birth data. While academics and skeptics were busy naysaying their decades of positive results, Neil Michelsen, a retired IBM executive and Director of Research at the National Council for Geocosmic Research (NCGR), a U.S. astrological organization, offered the Gauquelins the use of his powerful computer. Michelsen's computer service for astrologers, Astro Computing Services, remains the most sophisticated astrological computer facility in the world. You can see a sample page from Michelsen's advanced ephemeris elsewhere in this book. The entire page, including planetary symbols and titles is set by the computer. Several years previous, the NCGR had attempted to experiment with the Gauquelin data, and Michelsen had entered their entire collection of birth dates into his computer. The Gauquelins were not quick to take advantage of this, because the stigma of astrology might have stood in the way of acceptance of their results by other scientists. There's no proof that an astrologer's computer comes up with different results, but to other scientists, the results might nevertheless be tainted by some form of astrological contamination (ie. prejudice against astrology). Later on, when it became clear that serious astrologers were a major source of support and more and more scientists were beginning to accept the possibility of planetary influences, the Gauquelins saw they had little to lose by spending a year in San Diego working on Michelsen's computer. They could simultaneously and rapidly advance several of their research projects, while dealing more personally with some of the U.S. skeptics you will meet in the next chapter.

The experiment went this way: Ten well-known textbooks of astrology were selected, and the key words for each planet were listed as each author gave them. The earliest volume was Ptolemy's *Tetrabiblos* (second century A.D.), one volume was dated 1925, and the remainder were published since 1951. For example, in Jeff Mayo's textbook, *Astrology*, pages 24 to 26 are devoted to the Moon. Out of Mayo's description, Françoise Gauquelin extracted ten key words or phrases:

> mediator between past and present
> habit-patterns
> instinctive
> tends to cling to the past
> rhythm

ebb and flow of sensation
emotional experience
revitalized with sleep
restlessness
changeableness

Out of these, only six had previously been entered in the Gauquelins' catalogs of trait words:

instinctive
likes the past
open to sensation (ebb and flow of sensation)
emotional
restless
changeable

Now it was possible to see if the ten astrologers were using what the Gauquelins had identified as Moon traits to describe the Moon in horoscopes. The results are a fascinating glimpse into the crucible of the new astrology.

First, by synthesizing the observations of the ten astrologers, Françoise Gauquelin showed that the Moon, Venus, Mars, and Saturn displayed "remarkably high frequencies" in the key sectors. The astrologers were doing well! Whatever their methods, and for whatever reasons, the results show that for thousands of years astrologers have been able to detect personality characteristics related to planetary influences. The astrologers have been wrong on some details, and their methods may not meet modern scientific criteria. But again, they may still be valid in other ways, as I've already shown.

The big surprise was Jupiter. For years, I've heard astrologers quietly discussing the problem of Jupiter in horoscopes. Like many features of serious astrology, you won't find this in the textbooks or popular booklets. But astrologers have often mentioned to me that Jupiter is not nearly so positive in its effects as the older astrologers would have it. Jupiter used to be called the Greater Benefic. A transit or progression of Jupiter was often held to be a ticket to Palm Springs. But with a critical reevaluation gathering force among astrologers since the turn of the century, the suspicion that Jupiter was not properly understood had been surfacing. Jupiter was now being accused of "all promise and no product," and "a planet of the future" (pay now, get it later — maybe).

And here, in the results Françoise Gauquelin had before her, showing positive results for the planets which had proven so reliable in earlier studies, here was Jupiter with no significant results. What had gone wrong? Had the astrologers sold themselves a bill of goods? Françoise took a closer look. Most of the astrologers under study had assigned words such as "generous" and "religious" to Jupiter. But these words had been found in the Moon's trait words list. Astrologers were using words for one planet to describe another planet! Going deeper, she saw that most textbooks distinguished between the negative side and the positive side of Jupiter, depending on its aspects to other planets in the horoscope. Would the negative descriptions of Jupiter test out more positively?

Back to the textbooks. This time Françoise Gauquelin made a list of the *negative* descriptions the astrologers gave of Jupiter. Then, she saw where Jupiter was located in the charts of people who were described by those words in her massive data-bank. Despite a drastically reduced sample, her results became statistically significant! At odds of 700 to 1, the astrologers were using the correct description of Jupiter only when they had determined that it was negative in a horoscope!

Other curious results followed. During their thirty years of research, the Gauquelins had never been able to detect an influence of Mercury, Uranus, Neptune, or Pluto. To astrologers, this is a little preposterous, but statistically, the results are not there. In her test, there was the barest hint that there might be some detectable influences from these planets. Their statistical frequencies were all slightly above average, but the peaks were not in the infamous key sectors. Could this be the first hint that the tiniest and most distant planets were beginning to reveal their secrets, just as the nearest and most massive ones had done years earlier? It's too early to say.

As in all their previous research, this study revealed no influence of the Sun. Considering the importance placed upon the Sun in astrology, all the way from popular sun signs through to esoteric theosophical concepts about soul archetypes, this remains a major puzzle. But it was possible to go further with those planets which have established influences. By tabulating the key words which each astrologer used to describe each planet, the Gauquelins could observe that sometimes astrologers were using one word to describe an influence which actually belonged with another planet! In other words, an astrologer might have a particularly saturnian concept of Mars or an especially venerian understanding of the Moon.

For the first time, quality control has entered into astrological literature. It is now possible to see which astrological authors are more accurate in their planetary descriptions, and which planets they do not understand. The astrologers must now admit that their own personal horoscopes can prejudice their observations. And hence, it is no longer acceptable for someone of little training to write books with astrological descriptions of planetary effects. Nor is it acceptable any longer for more experienced astrologers to base their descriptions of planetary effects on their own observations of the charts of clients and public figures. These observations are only meaningful when they are taken as hypotheses for further tests. Many astrologers still refuse to recognize these facts. In the pride which they have accumulated over several centuries, knowing they were right despite all official pronouncements to the contrary, most astrologers have remained quite ignorant of elementary research methods. Widely ignorant of astronomy, modern psychology and experimental methods, they find it difficult to detect when their interpretations are correct. The case of Jupiter illustrates this dramatically.

Another group had better scramble to take cover as a result of these results. Critics and skeptics like Martin Pentecost assert that astrologers are simply copying each other and repeating ancient traditions which have no basis in fact. So some critics feel free to make loud pronouncements against astrology, while others feel free to take home fat royalty payments by writing astrology books which are not clearly and prominently marked as cynical imitations.

"When was the last time anyone did any field work?"

asked Martin Pentecost when I challenged his non-study of astrology.

His answer comes clearly from yet another interesting result of Françoise Gauquelin's research. In order to compare ancient and modern astrologers, she added four more textbooks to her list, along with Ptolemy. These dated from the fourth, twelfth, and seventeenth centuries. Thus, five ancient astrologers could be compared with nine modern ones.

As a group, the ancient astrologers did not do well at all. Their predictions of character based on the planets ran about chance. And things did not improve with time, either. The ancient Greek Ptolemy did as well as Morin de Villefranche, fifteen centuries later. But when the ancient astrologers were compared to the modern ones, a definite trend toward greater accuracy in observation was found. And by listing the astrologers in chronological order, the percentages of correct observations showed an improvement, not a deterioration or a repetition of earlier results.

Now we know who's been doing field work.

Astrology deals with circles: Astrological symbolism originates in the circle, and ultimately returns to the circle and all it stands for. So it is not surprising to find that the two young, skeptical scientists who initially had no sympathy whatsoever for astrology, but who rigorously maintained their scientific standards and pursued the positive results which so amazed them at first, are found some thirty years later concluding:

"[These] results point to useful adjustments for those who advocate the traditional approach, as well as for those who, like us, try to reconstruct a statistically proven science of the relationships between the cosmos and life on Earth, without reference to traditional beliefs. Both points of departure have proven valid for a certain part, but both need also to evolve to take these new results into account."[149]

Cosmically speaking, that's a fair deal.

Summary

While many "proofs" offered for astrology are really circumstantial evidence and lists of possibilities, the monumental research undertaken by Drs. Michel and Françoise Gauquelin since 1950 has established a strong and extensive body of evidence for planetary influences in human behavior. This evidence was gathered in strict accordance with established scientific procedures. Results from data a fraction the size of that which the Gauquelins have gathered is routinely accepted as valid proof of an hypothesis by scientists in many fields. To date, no one has ever found serious mistakes or inconsistencies in the Gauquelins' data. Several objections to their methodology have in fact provided further support for their results.

The objection that planetary influences cannot be accepted because there is no explanation for them is unrealistic. There remains the greater portion of our universe which modern science cannot explain. Today's scientific gospel is routinely discarded in favor of more fashionable explanations. To reject these discoveries for reasons of method or result would be, in fact, to reopen literally thousands of currently accepted scientific facts which have received far less examination and proof.

Since 1950, the Gauquelins have meticulously gathered and explored a body of evidence which has slowly led them to a position quite parallel to astrological tradition:

— Planetary influences exist. This is a central tenet of astrology.

— Particular planets have particular effects which can be distinguished from each other. This, too, is a central tenet of astrology.

— Planetary effects are universal; they are not different for different people, just as colors are not different. This accords with astrological tradition. (Just as some people are color blind, others refuse to accept the reality of planetary influences.)

— The planetary effect varies according to the angle between the horizon and the planet. This has been stated by astrologers since earliest times.

— The most important angular positions for planets are the horizon and the meridian. This is in accordance with astrological tradition.

— The angular position of a planet at birth is significantly related to the personality. This, too, is astrology.

— As the planetary effect increases, a person is more likely to succeed in a profession related to that planet. Astrologers have stated this for centuries.

— There is a demonstrable relationship between the planetary positions of parent and child if the birth was natural. This also accords with astrological tradition.

— By observing thousands of horoscopes over several thousand years, astrologers have been able to isolate some of the planetary effects which have been confirmed by statistics. This accords with the position taken by astrological authorities.

— Modern astrologers make more accurate character assessments based on horoscopes than do ancient astrologers. This supports the assertion that astrology is a developing science, not a mere parroting of tradition.

— The planetary effect is somehow modified by the magnetic field of the Earth. An electromagnetic mechanism for astrology has been proposed by several modern astrologers.

— Certain words in any language can be significantly related to certain planets. This has been widely accepted by astrologers for many years.

— Planetary influences work in combinations to produce many variations. For instance, atypical scientists can be shown to have planets other than Saturn prominent in their horoscopes. This is a universally accepted concept in astrology.

— People in the same profession tend to have the same planet(s) prominent at birth. This is an obvious corollary of astrology.

The discovery of planetary influences must surely rank as one of the major scientific monuments of our century. Once the pervasive negativity toward cosmic influences abates, this recognition will surely follow. Since man will soon spend increasing amounts of his time off Earth, a wider and more intimate appreciation of cosmic influences will be essential to survival. In order to prepare to leave this planet, man will have to come to terms with the many natural cycles which constitute his environment. The implications of this awareness for future science and evolution are only now becoming apparent to a few researchers, although they have been discussed in esoteric literature for centuries. Economic cycles will only be controlled when it is accepted that they are a response to cosmic conditions. Cycles of war will only cease when man realizes that periodic planetary configurations impel nations to aggressive behavior.

To reach a harmony between man and nature, human beings must realize that they live in a cosmic environment, filled with energy and opportunity.

And *that,* my friends, is astrology.

Eleven

We, the Undersigned

The responsibility for change, therefore, lies with us. We must begin with ourselves, teaching ourselves not to close our minds prematurely to the novel, the surprising, the seemingly radical. This means fighting off the idea-assassins who rush forward to kill any new suggestion on grounds of its impracticality, while defending whatever now exists as practical, no matter how absurd, oppressive or unworkable it may be. It means fighting for freedom of expression — the right of people to voice their ideas, even if heretical.

Alvin Toffler, The Third Wave
Copyright © 1980 by Alvin Toffler
(William Morrow & Company, 1980)

Heretics and Heroes

In 1975, the attack on astrology became "official." A statement issued amid tremendous media hype by 186 "leading scientists" condemned astrology as a fraud and a danger to society. If the press in the 1960s were willing to give astrology lots of insincere high-profile coverage without taking it seriously, the more sober climate of the seventies led countless newspapers to publish such statements uncritically, without proper investigation or balancing coverage.

In fact, the press have been demonstrably guilty of

ignoring evidence which shows that they were being taken for a ride in the name of one (allegedly scientific) point of view. Statements and press releases exposing the attack on astrology for what it was were dumped into the waste-paper basket by major American newspapers such as *The New York Times*, the major television stations and wire services, and the major Canadian media such as CBC tele-vision news and *The Toronto Star*.

What follows is a brief account of how Gauquelin's research was treated by skeptical scientists and the media, along with previously unpublished details of the attack on astrology.

There *is* an astrological conspiracy — a conspiracy of silence — reigning over these events. It is a conspiracy of silence among a group of determined critics who will not admit that every attempt to defuse the evidence for planetary influences has, in fact, provided stunning confirmation of their existence. It is a battle for public opinion being waged not on the basis of scientific evidence, but as a public relations problem, complete with a willing and docile press corps assisting in the hush-up.

It's high time the facts were made public.

Not long ago, torture, excommunication, and death were the traditional prescriptions for heretics. It was often the Church (and still is, in some countries, whether it be Italy or the USSR) which decided what was true, based on its chosen scriptures. If you chose to use different instruments to measure truth, you made sure your results coincided with those determined (often for political reasons) by the Church.

Persecution is not a guarantee of sainthood or of being right. It serves only to draw attention to possible sources of fresh insights, no matter how outrageous or heretical. What is at stake are preciously held world-views (paradigms). What is so strongly denied are new possibilities which are considered automatically out of the question in the old world-view. Such so-called scientific debates more often proceed along emotional lines than factual ones. What can be so confusing is to read essentially emotional arguments buried inside supposedly objective scientific terminology, hidden in diagrams and tables of figures, camouflaged by the sacred cow of the "scientific method."

It was therefore inevitable that the research of Michel and Françoise Gauquelin would come under the skeptical and jaundiced eyes of various establishment scientists. Evidence for planetary influences was viewed not as a major break-through but as a major threat to the world view which dictates that planetary influences are simply impossible. What took place subsequently (and is still taking place at this writing) is a story which ought to be told in detail. But it is complex and calculated to produce yawns due to the sheer weight of oblique and verbose jargon found in the original documents. Nor can the story be told from a neutral point of view. Either the Gauquelins are right or wrong. Either planetary influences exist, or they don't. I have made my particular bias quite clear in earlier chapters. Therefore, the concerned reader is referred to the original documents from which he can make up his own mind.

The Comité Para

Scientific method dictates that experimental results should be repeated by some neutral or even skeptical investigator, so that any question of fudged data or calculations is ruled out. Once someone has agreed to the experiment, the result should be published and discussed, regardless. So, even if scientists are sure there are no planetary influences, they are obliged to publish the positive results of their investigations, no matter how uncomfortable these make them. In theory, it's all a gentleman's pastime. But in practice, it more often becomes a matter of character assassination and subterfuge aimed at wooing neutral readers to one side of the debate. As we saw earlier, there is a predisposition to accept negative results in astrological studies.

The first skeptical scientific group to test the research of the Gauquelins was the Belgian Committee for the Scientific Investigation of Reputedly Paranormal Phenomena, founded in 1948. In 1955 Gauquelin sent the Comité Para, as they are called, a copy of his early book, *L'influence des astres*, followed by his 1960 work, *Les hommes et les astres*. But it was not until 1961 that the Comité and the Gauquelins held their first discussions.

For both sides, the experiment had obvious dangers and

clear benefits — provided their particular point of view was confirmed. The Comité, like later skeptics knew that if they could prove the Gauquelins' results wrong, they would have dealt a severe blow to serious consideration of astrological influences. And the Gauquelins knew that if their methods and results withstood a strong skeptical examination, their scientific position was strong indeed.

For skeptics, the Comité Para were rather slow on the uptake. In 1964, they told the Gauquelins they had examined their results and found no fault in the methods which had revealed planetary influences. They wanted to do more work, they said, but new data, for some reason or other, was not available. They would publish nothing for the present. Considering the trouble the Gauquelins had gone to in gathering their thousands of cases, these were enigmatic statements.

By 1967, the Gauquelins had gathered a new group of sports champions. The results were identical to the first experiment, and the Mars effect on sports champions had received its first confirmation. But it was not until 1976, nine years later, that the Comité responded. Their suspicion was that the peaks seen in the graphs used by the Gauquelins were due to some kind of astronomical bias in the data. No one seems to know just what this bias was, but even today skeptics continue to suggest that it exists despite many experiments and papers to the contrary. Nevertheless, the Comité Para was right in seeking an answer in this direction.

And they got it. On a new sample which they gathered of 535 French and Belgian sports champions, they obtained results identical to those of the Gauquelins, highly significant results, according to statistical standards. In order to test further, several different "control" groups were used. These are samples used in statistics to compare an average or random group with the group being studied. Sometimes the control group is a collection of real people, and sometimes it is merely a group created by deliberately altering the original data. The Comité Para chose this last method. By taking the same sports champions and their birth data, but shuffling the times of birth up and down the list from one champion to the next, they hoped to obtain some significant result by chance, as it were. But the Mars effect disappeared!

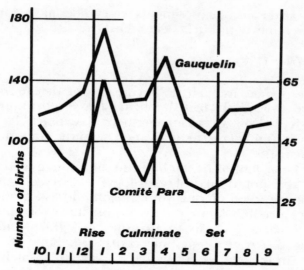

Diagram: Comparison of results for the Mars effect in groups of sports champions. The Comité Para found the same effect in their sample of 535 Belgian sports champions as did the Gauquelins in their sample. Sharp peaks are clearly visible in the key sectors, just after the rise and culmination of Mars.

Could this be chance? The Comité Para repeated this test nine times, shuffling the data this way and that, in a futile search for some explanation of the Gauquelins' positive results. None of their tests approached statistical significance. They were forced to conclude that the Gauquelins were indeed correct in their methods and results.[150] Comité Para papers are never signed; without inside knowledge, no one knows who these scientists are. And in several photocopied prepublication versions of their arguments, Gauquelin claims that false statements were made about his methodology.[151]

The skeptics had obtained the same results — evidence of planetary influences — but they could not accept their implications. The Comité Para's paper on Mars was published with no data which would allow the interested reader to examine the problem further. Three other kinds of sophisticated control experiments were undertaken, but the results were never publicly acknowledged.

Leonardo

Like the planets in their daily courses, the debate moved westward. In 1973, the British journal, *Leonardo*, published an article by an American engineer, Lawrence Jerome, which was highly critical of astrology and the Gauquelins' experiments.[152]

"The latter half of the 20th century has seen a mercurial rise in the popularity of astrology," observed Jerome, decrying the trend among young people to ask questions about the occult. "Many recent authors have attempted to ascribe a scientific basis to astrology in light of modern scientific discoveries," Jerome continued, but "all such attempts in the end are futile for . . . astrology is neither a science nor an art but rather a system of magic divination based on ancient superstitions. . . ."

In other words, that which originates in magic cannot lead to science. Yet Isaac Newton's theory of an invisible "influence" which somehow emanates from the planets and stars, attracting them to each other, has been accepted today. Newton was an occult hobbyist, like many of his contemporaries. And even today, no one can really explain how his mysterious "influences" work. Or does it sound more "scientific" if we replace the word "influences" with "gravity"?

Jerome did admit that there are many known influences impinging upon the Earth. Birds are known to use stars for navigation, and it is possible that some organisms can detect magnetic fields from the Earth. There are the Moon's tides, and all sorts of rhythms tied in with one celestial cycle or another. But astrology can't be true because it is "based on a system of magical correspondences, and *not* on any possible physical influences by celestial bodies. Astrology can never be made scientific, essentially by definition. . . ."

Therefore Michel Gauquelin is wrong, you see.

Like all critics of astrology, Jerome was forced finally to examine Gauquelin's work in order to discount completely the possibility of planetary influences. In one breath, he described Gauquelin's research as "employing impeccable statistical methods" and concluded that Gauquelin had "committed two basic errors in his statistical study." Jerome thought the planets "just happen to be found in the sky at those times" when athletes, scientists, soldiers, etc., are born. The peaks in the graphs are there, but they don't mean anything!

The storm was gathering. One response to Jerome's article came from Prof. Bart J. Bok, University of Arizona, who noted: "From some most unpleasant contacts with astrologers in the past, I have learned that it is almost impossible to argue with these believers in a logical manner."[153] For Bok, astrology-bashing has been a lifetime concern. "I make it a practice of giving astrology a blast every 10 years," he told an Australian newspaper.[154] And indeed, as far back as the 1930s Bok was an outspoken critic.

Sydney Omarr's *My World of Astrology* contains a chapter devoted to one of Bok's early encounters with a leading group of astrologers. On November 22, 1941, Bok was to address an astronomical group in New York City on the fallacy of astrology. Surprised when he found that the audience included a group of leading astrologers representing two major American astrological organizations and several astrological publications, Bok is recorded to have thrown his prepared diatribe away and entered into debate with the audience. The astrologers brought a stenographer along, so the correct transcription of the event could be made public.[155] Bok said it was foolish to continue the endless battle between astrologers and astronomers and called for a research committee composed of scientists and astrologers to test astrology in good faith. He was recorded as saying that the evening of his speech might well mark the beginning of cooperation between astrologers and astronomers.

But something — or someone — changed Bok's mind. In December 1941, he issued a letter to the astrologers present at the November meeting, asking them only to quote from his subsequently prepared summary of his lecture. He now thought ". . . we are 'friendly enemies' and such we shall probably remain for quite a while. In view of this it seems

280 The Astrology Game

that I would make a mistake in associating myself closely with astrologers . . . for the same reason . . . I shall prefer not to join a committee with astrologers among its members."

Meanwhile, "a representative was sent to call on all of the astrology magazine editors," Omarr states. "They were told that if they published Dr. Bok's speech, they would be sued. . . . *Sky Magazine,* a publication for astronomers, also published Dr. Bok's speech. Only there was something wrong. The magazine published the talk Dr. Bok was *scheduled* to give . . . *Sky Magazine* published an attack on astrology, originally intended by Dr. Bok, but said not one single word about the actual speech he delivered."

Time did not lessen the furies Dr. Bok was to unleash against astrology. Here he was in *Leonardo,* thirty-five years later, deploring the fact that so few astronomers speak out against astrology. ". . . they help to produce a climate in which it is easy for the young to believe in astrology and all the nonsense that goes with it," he wrote. "It is high time that more astronomers do their part to make it clear that one's future depends on oneself and not on the planets and stars." (A point which humanistic astrologers have made repeatedly.)

The *Leonardo* debate continued with other papers and responses. Most simply demonstrated how little the average critic knows about astrology and the specialized research techniques needed to detect planetary influences. This is one field where everyone feels at liberty to speak as a self-appointed expert, perhaps because they are convinced no experts exist.

None of these authors deemed it a necessary courtesy to send Michel Gauquelin a copy of the articles in *Leonardo.* Thus, two years after Jerome's original attack, Gauquelin came across back issues and was able to respond.

"Since 1970 the birth and planetary data on more than 40,000 persons have been gathered by our laboratory and published," Gauquelin pointed out. "Jerome could have obtained these statistical data in order to check his idea, rather than invent data."[156] Contrary to Jerome's amateur explanations, the Gauquelins had already shown in several papers that military men do not tend to be born in the "off" hours of the day. With a chance of about one in 5,000,000, notable military types tend to be born after the rise and culmination of Jupiter. Other simple-minded attempts to explain away the evidence of planetary influences bit the dust, as Gauquelin recounted his various experiments and the Comité Para tests.

Jerome's response: "It is clear to me that if the basic assumptions of a hypothesis are not valid, there is no need to collect data to verify it . . . . For modern man, astrology is, and should remain, a historical curiosity."[157]

Gauquelin was not allowed to respond. Coming in at the end of the debate, he found *Leonardo's* editor tired of the matter. It was better to end the whole affair on a negative note.

186 Scientists Object to Astrology

Believe nothing until it has been officially denied.

Journalist's motto

In September 1975, *The Humanist* magazine issued a statement entitled "Objections to Astrology," signed by a group of "leading scientists" and Nobel prizewinners, condemning popular interest in astrology:

> We, the undersigned — astronomers, astrophysicists, and scientists in other fields — wish to caution the public against the unquestioning acceptance of the predictions and advice given . . . by astrologers. Those who wish to believe in astrology should realize that there is no scientific foundation for its tenets. . . . It is simply a mistake to imagine that the forces exerted by stars and planets at the moment of birth can in any way shape our futures. . . . In these uncertain times many long for the comfort of having guidance in making decisions. . . . We are especially disturbed by the continued and uncritical dissemination of astrological charts, forecasts and horoscopes by the media and by otherwise reputable newspapers, magazines and book publishers. This can only contribute to the growth of irrationalism and obscurantism. . . .[158]

To this day, the public has not been adequately informed of the background and nature of this attack.

The anti-astrology campaign underway since 1975 was not based on prior inquiry and available evidence. Two separate investigations revealed that practically all of the scientists who signed the anti-astrology statement had not researched the subject. No sociological studies were produced to show that astrology is a negative influence on society.

Although the media were quick to pick up the attack and give it very good exposure, the other sides of the debate were ignored. Subsequent defections from the anti-astrology camp were not properly covered, and even though reporters for such major networks as the CBC were personally informed of the facts you will read in this chapter, they still insisted on giving the anti-astrology group one-sided positive coverage.

Subsequent investigations undertaken by some of the signatories of the anti-astrology statement have, contrary to their hopes, provided further confirmation of planetary influences. There were several attempts to suppress this evidence and withold it from the public. Major television networks and news services in the United States, Canada, and England ignored documented evidence showing that the anti-astrology attack had resulted in even more positive evidence for planetary influences.

The cover of *The Humanist's* attack issue clearly outlined the problem. It was a cartoon of a giant telescope aimed at the sky, where a rough zodiac had been sketched. Symptomatically, the zodiac was backward, and the representation was astronomically impossible. The cartoon confirmed that the critics knew little, if anything, about serious astrology and the evidence for planetary influences. Most of them were experts in fields which did not permit them to make any competent judgment of the evidence.

Accompanying the "Objections to Astrology" statement were two articles by Dr. Bart Bok, still crusading after thirty-five years of failure to turn the astrological tide, and Lawrence Jerome, repeating his erroneous arguments against Gauquelin's research. (The fallacy of Jerome's argument was later underlined by research undertaken by members of the skeptical group.)

Bok complained that his calls for public statements by

scientists against astrology had twice previously fallen on deaf ears. He quoted a statement endorsed by the Council of the Society for Psychological Study of Social Issues, claiming that faith in astrology is "harmful insofar as it encourages an unwholesome flight from the persistent problems of real life." But it was not pointed out that this is a concern shared by serious astrologers, inasmuch as their writings are replete with discussions of ways to deal constructively with life crises and life cycles.

As for Jerome's reincarnated arguments against Gauquelin, one of the many letters which *The Humanist* received, but did not publish, was that of Hal White, then a postgraduate student of philosophy at the University of Toronto and Chairman of the Toronto Guild of Astrologers. White pointed out that Jerome's article had been published in *Leonardo* in substantially the same form. The original contained a "rough" horoscope for no particular place which was criticized for being inaccurate by none other than Bart Bok himself, who characterized Jerome's attempt to explain horoscopes as "not very well done." Jerome had declined to respond to Gauquelin's careful refutation of his arguments and inserted a new, also facile, criticism. White wrote, "It seems Jerome's strategy is to shoot from the hip, and shift his position later — without bothering to inform readers what has transpired." This was one of many small details which somehow never made it into the pages of the anti-astrology campaign.

The moving force behind *The Humanist's* attack was its editor, Prof. Paul Kurtz of the State University of New York at Buffalo. "We never expected such an enormous reaction," wrote Kurtz in the next issue of his magazine. "Virtually every newspaper in the United States has carried the story," he glowed. Kurtz called on newspapers to publish a warning above their horoscope columns: "Warning! If taken seriously this column may be dangerous to your health!" Three pages of press comments, mostly favorable to the attack, followed.

The astrologers were also allowed three pages of replies. "All serious astrologers agree that newspaper or so-called 'sun-sign' astrology is nonsense," wrote Henry Weingarten, a leading U.S. astrologer. "Yet if such a position were signed by 186 leading *astrologers*, it would surely receive no notice from the press." Weingarten was reminded of a remark by an Indian astrologer who noted that when meteorologists make wrong predictions, they are given more government funding; when astrologers make wrong predictions, they are laughed at.

And Carl Sagan, the famous exobiologist, author, and media personality, wrote to *The Humanist*, refusing to sign the statement against astrology because of its authoritarian tone. The lack of any known mechanism for planetary influences is not evidence against astrology, Sagan said. "Statements contradicting borderline, folk or pseudoscience that appear to have an authoritarian tone can do more damage than good."

By January, 1976, Michel Gauquelin was allowed to respond to Lawrence Jerome (yet again). Gauquelin recounted his statistical methods, his experiments, and his results. He outlined the tests undertaken by the Comité Para and called on Bok to examine his work or have competent scientists look into it for him. "The dignity of science requires that facts not be rejected only because their causes are still unknown," Gauquelin pointed out.

But just across the page was a statement from the Comité Para. Once again, without a name attached, the Comité's statement admitted that it had achieved "analogous results" to Gauquelin's, but now objected to his methods and hypotheses. Unfortunately for the Comité, the hypotheses cited in *The Humanist* were never made by Gauquelin. "Why, having worked for ten years on this problem," Gauquelin asked, "did the Comité neglect to explain how they achieved significant results even in their control experiments? Was it because they confirmed the accuracy of my methods?"

The Zelen Test

One important facet of Gauquelin's character is that he was once a prominent tennis player. Toss a ball into his court and you'll get it back twice as fast as you expect, and at a new angle. He doesn't shy away from a challenge to play. So a new match had begun, by a group of perhaps well-meaning but obviously misguided critics. Taking on the unorganized and ill-educated community of astrologers was one thing, but taking on Michel Gauquelin was another.

The critics appealed to Marvin Zelen, professor of statistical science at Harvard, to design a test which would be definitive. So began the Zelen Test. Zelen proposed that Gauquelin gather a collection of individuals born on the same day and in the same place as his sports champions. Obviously, if there is no effect of Mars on sports champions, everyone born on the same day and in the same place would tend to have Mars in one of those "key sectors." But if they didn't — if their births were spread throughout the entire day — this would confirm that Mars has an effect. Sports champions tend to be born with Mars in a "key sector."

Everyone agreed, and the Gauquelins set to work. After a nine-month research project, they had managed to contact the birth places of 303 sports champions, and gather an incredible 16,756 non-champions born in the same conditions. With speed and efficiency they produced yet another stunning confirmation of planetary influences — ordinary people did not display the Mars effect. The Mars effect was only visible among the sports champions born in those places and on those days under study. The Zelen Test was positive for planetary influences!

During the summer of 1977, I visited Prof. Kurtz at his home in Buffalo. It was during this interview that I first met Michel Gauquelin. The results of the Zelen Test were already known to a few people; Gauquelin had completed them in December, 1976. Yet during our interview, I pressed Prof. Kurtz for his position on the Zelen Test. The transcript of the complete interview was published in *Phenomena*:

Dean: "You've been engaged in testing Dr. Gauquelin's findings. How have they turned out?"
Kurtz: "Well, we're unprepared to say at the moment. We are being pressed constantly. It's interesting that many people in the press worldwide want us to give a pronouncement, you see. But we don't think this is fair. A scientific, cautious, tentative inquiry should proceed. So the inquiry is proceeding and the results are not conclusive, at the moment."
Dean: "But a reporter could say, well, obviously if

Gauquelin's data had failed by now you would have screamed it out loud. So. . . ."

Kurtz: "Not necessarily. He has made certain claims we disagree with, but we want a further investigation. I really should not say, you see. I think it unfair to the public, you see, and this is one of the problems. You get uncritical statements by scientists which are blown out of all proportion. And I can see *The National Enquirer*, for example, taking the least scintilla in any area and blowing it out of proportion. I think it's unfair to do that."

Dean: "And the big question is, if you come up with some study which does show correlations, will it receive equal publicity?"

Kurtz: "Well, we're hoping within three or four months to have completed the initial phase of our examination. And we have one of the leading statisticians of the world, two astronomers and others, and so we will publish a tentative progress report."

Dean: "Now let's go down the road a little bit, and let's say that one or two of these tests turn out to be in favor of cosmic influences from the planets, or something measured by the position of planets. Are you not then obliged to go ahead and follow through on these findings?"

Kurtz: "Well, I've never denied cosmic influences. I mean who could deny cosmic influences? There is constant radiation, you have tides. . . ."

Dean: "Sure, but we're discussing. . . ."

Kurtz: "The real issue is whether the time and place of birth influences the individual. Well, that remains to be seen. I mean. . . ."

Dean: "Now suppose that one test turns out to be positive — let's suppose that the Gauquelin data passes your every test and complaint. What then? Are you not then. . . ."

Kurtz: "Well, we'll have to face that. . . ."

Dean: "Obliged. . . ?"

Kurtz: "If and when that happens we'll have to examine that to see what . . . if that should happen, and I don't think that it has or that it will, but if it should, I say we have an open mind. We'll have to see what the implications are at that time."[159]

It took Kurtz and his assistants a long time to deal with the implications. Initially, he wanted Gauquelin to perform and publish the Zelen Test in just a few months. The

Gauquelins gathered their data and presented their positive results to Kurtz et al in December, 1976. But it was not until November, 1977, nearly one year later, that *The Humanist* released the information.

As usual, *The Humanist* spoke vaguely of the Mars effect not being "uniformly confirmed" by the Zelen Test — whatever that meant. Their inquiry was to continue with "further checking of the original data," and the world was to proceed as if nothing unusual had happened.

Was this scientific caution, or simply a delaying tactic to buy time while looking for a way out or for interest to die? "The situation as it now stands," reported Prof. Kurtz, "is that the Gauquelins maintain that the Zelen Test confirms the existence of the Mars effect. Knowing of the Gauquelins' view, many proponents of astrology have publicized this claim and have urged [us] to make a formal announcement. Yet [we] preferred to proceed with care and diligence."

The "care and diligence" the skeptics displayed was outlined in a letter to Prof. Kurtz from *Phenomena's* associate editor, Eric Tarkington. "I was astounded at the flagrant abuse of statistics," wrote Tarkington. "The basic canons of statistical analysis have been repeatedly violated by the critics."[160] Tarkington pointed out that the critics had to repeatedly break samples down into smaller sub-samples in order to destroy their significance — something which first-year statistics students are cautioned against. The critics claimed that only one portion of the data was responsible for its significance, but *Phenomena* published an elementary statistical test to show that this was not the case at all. Then, the critics decided to remove the *female* sports champions from the data! Nowhere previously had sex been discussed regarding planetary effects, but suddenly women didn't count. And even worse, three of the female champions removed had Mars in key sectors. This left one champion more than chance might predict, so the critics tried to argue that only one individual wasn't enough to support the Mars effect. The joke of the whole matter was that even after all this, the statistics were mildly significant.

Tarkington's letter met the same fate as had White's in 1975. Not surprisingly, *The Humanist* never published it, and no reply was ever received from Prof. Zelen and the astronomer who assisted in conducting the test, Prof. George Abell.

A Committee is Born in Buffalo

During these events, the skeptics emerged as a group of like-thinkers under the aegis of *The Humanist* magazine. By mid-1976, they had formally announced the Committee for the Scientific Investigation of Claims of the Paranormal (CSICOP), devoted to investigating borderline beliefs. Once again, they received much press coverage and praise. Academics rallied to the flag, and the ranks swelled. A new journal, *The Zetetic*, was launched, eventually attaining a circulation far in excess of the meager readership of the serious astrological journals which it loved to criticize. An active campaign of media appearances was initiated, to bring to the public the doctrine that there is no truth in astrology, psychics, UFOs, and other fringe beliefs. All in the name of combating that "rising tide of belief."

The anti-astrology campaign now had two publications. While *The Humanist* was mishandling the Zelen Test reportage, *The Zetetic* proceeded from an initially con- ciliatory position under its first editor to lambaste, debunk, and castigate anything within editorial range, while being encouraged by a sympathetic public media. The Greek word *zetetic* means "to proceed by inquiry," but as Prof. Lynn Rose, State University of New York at Buffalo, pointed out to readers of *The Humanist:* ". . . the trouble with self- appointed idea-killers, whether organized in committees of zetetics or not [is that] they are inclined to denounce first, and to leave investigation until later . . . their minds are already made up anyway. This closed-mindedness is a regression toward sixteenth-century inquisitorial activities, which likewise were all in the *name* of what was good for human beings. Such a comparison is not unjustified: the Greek word *zetetikos* can be translated as 'inquisitorial.' "[161]

The methods used by the CSICOP in their never-ending battle against beliefs which they do not accept was cogently analyzed and exposed in an article by Theodore Rockwell.[162] Originally submitted to *The Humanist,* and like other documents somehow never published or publicly acknowledged, Rockwell's paper showed that *The Humanist* "has traded away its rationalist birthright for a mess of rhetorical pottage." Among Rockwell's points:

— All sorts of minorities were lumped together for criticism in one blow, including Aikido, TM, Jesus Christ, Mohammed, Mary Baker Eddy, encounter groups, yoga, organic gardening, Kirlian photography, and ESP.

— Personal defamation was used to discredit researchers, without an opportunity for rebuttal or correction.

— Most articles published by the CSICOP contained unsubstantiated allegations and generalizations.

— Critics often contradicted themselves. "One critic complained that he received no response to some of his letters," says Rockwell. "Then he says, 'Not responding to a letter is, in my view, irresponsible.' The same critic, several pages later, remarks . . . 'I have a big rubber stamp at home that says, See Your Doctor, and I usually stamp that across [my correspondence] and send it back. I haven't time to fuss with answers to this kind of thing.' "

— Techniques of rumor and innuendo are liberally sprinkled throughout the CSICOP's publications. Dissent is nearly defined as heresy. Apocalyptic rhetoric is widely used to caution against serious consideration of "paranormal" claims (i.e. what is beyond the critics' conception of normal).

Yet the time was obviously ripe for such behavior among scientists. (It must be recognized that science has its fashions, too, which are almost never studied by scientists themselves.) The committee had succeeded in starting a fad. Many science journals took up the anti-pseudoscience campaign with nary a critical look at the evidence being presented — or at the lack of proper investigations — or at the sheer absence of research papers in this field by those who signed the manifestos and statements which were by then being issued with regularity.

New Scientist, the weekly British science magazine, had a brief fling with what it called "parascience." Former Feedback Editor, Dr. Joseph Hanlon, turned (as if by magic?) into the Parascience Editor. But few items on the paranormal ever made it to *New Scientist's* carefully screened pages. Hanlon was aware of the problems the CSICOP faced in disproving Gauquelin's statistics, and in September 1978 I wrote to ask him if he was intending to publish an article on this affair. His terse reply: "It is much more difficult to get an article into *New Scientist* in favor of paranormal research than against, but we are still trying."

By 1978, Hanlon's name had disappeared from the editorial roster of *New Scientist*.

Part of the year-long delay in publishing the Zelen Test results was probably due to the hope that analysis might locate a weak spot in the Gauquelins' statistical armor. As we have already seen, Prof. Kurtz was rather unwilling to admit that this was proving much more difficult than the critics had assumed it would be.

In 1976, a statistics student at Berkeley, J. Stanford Willie, submitted a term project testing the Mars effect. Awarded an A+ by Prof. Elizabeth Scott, Willie had tested some of the CSICOP's statements about the Gauquelin data and concluded "that there does seem to be some evidence that the Mars effect observed by the Gauquelins is statistically significant." In a subsequent paper, entitled "A More Powerful Test of the Gauquelin Mars effect," Willie was a little more cautious, but still concluded that "there seems to be some evidence that it may exist."

Reports of these studies seeped through to interested individuals, and in 1978, *New Realities* magazine reported on them. Later that year, Prof. Kurtz protested against *New Realities'* attack on his attack. Parenthetically, he noted, "I should add that the Department of Statistics of the University of California at Berkeley did not verify [the Gauquelins'] results nor release a report supporting the existence of the Mars effect, as you claim."[163]

Perhaps they didn't, in the strictest definition. It was a student term project, true, and it was not "released," I was informed privately, because Mr. Willie did not enjoy the dubious privilege of having independently confirmed some aspects of the Gauquelins' work. But Kurtz did not go on to inform readers of *New Realities* what *had* happened at Berkeley.

One other important document came from within the

ranks of the CSICOP itself, early in 1977. Astronomer Dennis Rawlins issued a private memo to a handful of committee members concerning some objections which had been raised against Gauquelin's calculation. (In typical CSICOP style, Gauquelin was not allowed the common courtesy of being called "Dr.," "Mr.," "researcher," or "psychologist" — all of which he is. "Neoastrologer" was the term Rawlins chose to describe Michel Gauquelin.) Put simply, Rawlins's memo pointed out that it had been repeatedly suggested that the peaks which appeared in Gauquelin's graphs were due to some peculiarity of planetary motion and social factors. The objection had emerged from several sources, and the CSICOP was now trying to put forward similar objections.

"Some time ago, I examined and rejected this hypothesis," wrote Rawlins in his memo. Yet this document, too, remained under a cloak of silence. Rawlins did not, and still does not, believe in planetary influences. Public release of his memo would have at least advanced the dialogue and saved a lot of fruitless arguments. But, probably afraid that yet another small confirmation of one aspect of Gauquelin's calculations would be taken as supporting planetary influences, which they so fervently believe do not exist, the CSICOP at first refused to acknowledge the existence of the Rawlins memorandum publicly.

In March, 1978, I issued a press release outlining the above facts, and also pointing to possible attempts to interfere with a University of Toronto symposium on astrology.[164] Included were not only details on the current status of the Gauquelin/Mars effect debate, but also reprints of articles from various issues of *Phenomena* outlining various positive tests of astrological ideas by other scientists. "The public must be informed that the CSICOP is deliberately ignoring, misrepresenting and distorting evidence which clearly proves that the planets do have an influence on human behavior," I wrote.

Copies of this press release went out with the latest issue of *Phenomena*, which included critiques by Gauquelin, Prof. Hans Eysenck, several leading serious astrologers, and the interview with Prof. Kurtz quoted above.

Among the recipients: the ABC, NBC, and CBS television networks in the U.S.; the CBC National Television and Radio News in Canada; all major international wire services; *The New York Times; The Toronto Star* (Canada's largest-circulation newspaper, which had been quite critical of astrology through one of its editorial writers, Sidney Katz); *The Globe and Mail* (Canada's most authoritative English-language daily); the Canadian Press; and various independent television services.

No response. Not one single news service saw fit to even direct a researcher to telephone and discuss the story. Gauquelin's plight, and the various other researches which were turning up positive evidence for planetary influences, all went without a single acknowledgment by the media.

About the same time, ABC was preparing a documentary on some aspects of the paranormal and knew of this affair. But since astrology was not central to its theme, no mention of it was made. A BBC documentary on astrology was already in progress, and the BBC was also informed of these events. But the program gathered dust for another year on the shelf due to internal pressure from senior staff in the "Horizon" production unit. Reporters for CBC Radio and Television, two of the world's most sophisticated and extensive media services, were informed personally of the affair. One CBC National Television reporter was offered copies of all the relevant documents and given a verbal outline of the situation, but still insisted on airing a one-sided favorable interview with Prof. Kurtz. His reason: "You guys have had a great deal of favorable publicity, now it's the critic's turn." He would not accept that neither the critics nor the media have distinguished between serious research and popular astrology, nor that by that time, the critics had had three full years of positive press, with little balancing coverage, if any.

Truzzi Quits

If, by now, it is becoming clear to you that there was something rotten in the state of Denmark, this thought was occurring to others close to the CSICOP and *The Humanist* as well. The CSICOP had inherited their journal's name from a newsletter originally published by their first co-chairman, Prof. Marcello Truzzi. As a sociologist, Truzzi had already spent some years studying the "paranormal" and had formulated balanced and reasonable attitudes toward beliefs which he does not share (see Chapter One). For Truzzi, the occult and the paranormal are not so much pseudosciences, as "protosciences," sciences in the earliest, "pre-scientific" stages of development. Truzzi believes groups such as astrologers perform a valuable service by keeping seed-ideas alive during periods of official neglect. We have already seen how close the research of the Gauquelins has come to traditional astrology. Thus, in terms of Truzzi's theory, astrology has indeed performed a valuable function by keeping the idea of planetary influences alive through thick and thin.

In October, 1977, Truzzi wrote to the Fellows of the CSICOP:

> I hereby resign from the Committee. . . . This unpleasant decision does not result from any change in my skeptical views towards claims of the paranormal. It comes about because I find that my views towards both what constitutes a truly scientific attitude toward such claims, and what should be a democratic structure within our Committee are not being reflected in the statements of the Chairman, Paul Kurtz, or the actions of the Executive Council. . . . I see no way in which my original goals for our Committee can be met. These goals included objective inquiry prior to judgment and clear separation between the policies of the Committee and those of the American Humanist Association and *The Humanist* magazine. . . .

Truzzi was unhappy that the CSICOP had not moved for independence from *The Humanist*. There had been some objections to his publication of a paper in the committee's journal which criticized the "Objections to Astrology" manifesto. And to Truzzi and others, the committee was quickly coming under the strong influence of Prof. Kurtz and his emphasis on a high-profile media campaign.

"The CSICOP is dismissing many occult ideas out of hand," Truzzi told *The New York Times* in one of their rare items covering the negative side of the anti-paranormal campaign. "They are tarring everybody with the same brush."[165]

The issue, responded Prof. Kurtz, was over how much emphasis to place on reaching the public through the media. He spoke of this as "an important mission" of the CSICOP. Truzzi preferred to establish a credible body of contrary evidence before publicly denouncing a belief such as astrology. So, in a precedent later to be followed by another ex-fellow of the committee, he appeared in a two-part interview in *Fate* magazine, where he laid out his views on the CSICOP and the occult in general. It's a strange thing to see ex-committee members heading straight for occult publications in an attempt to make their positions known to the public.[166]

So began a crisis within the skeptical ranks. *The Zetetic* was renamed *The Skeptical Inquirer*. Truzzi resumed his scholarly publishing with his new journal, *The Zetetic Scholar*. Members of the American Humanist Association began to dissent strongly against the campaign being waged under the banner of their official publication. Eventually, Prof. Kurtz and leading members of the CSICOP set off on their own crusade and disappeared from the editorial roster of *The Humanist*. *The Humanist* has subsequently returned to its quiet, philosophical, low-profile old self.

The Skeptical Inquirer

Prof. Truzzi was replaced as editor of the CSICOP journal by Kendrick Frazier, a prominent science journalist and former editor of the weekly *Science News*. Readers were never informed of the events behind the change in title. Many important details in the Gauquelin debate, as well as the other battles the CSICOP was waging, never made it into *The Skeptical Inquirer*. The world view which permeates these pages bristles with righteousness. There is no question in the minds of these skeptics that anyone who believes in any kind of paranormal phenomena is simply wrong.

A portion of each issue of *The Skeptical Inquirer* entitled "Psychic Vibrations," is devoted to snappy and sarcastic news items, often highlighting the most ridiculous and negative angles to various aspects of the paranormal. Items from popular news tabloids are often the sources for this section of the journal, such as *The National Enquirer's* annual predictions, which everyone enjoys, but no one (except readers of *The Skeptical Inquirer,* apparently) takes seriously.

But in their attempt to sway readers through sarcasm and innuendo, the polemicists on the staff of *The Skeptical Inquirer* often put their collective foot in their mouths. One example concerned me personally.

In late 1977, astronomer Charles Kowal discovered a tiny planetoid orbiting between Saturn and Uranus. The news created quite a stir in the astronomical community, for no one expected to find an asteroid in that region.

Once the discovery was announced, I set to work with a group of astronomers and computer experts to create an ephemeris for the newly discovered body, which was subsequently named Chiron. An ephemeris, as we have seen, is a listing of celestial positions for an object, and this information is obviously needed if you want to test for any influence or correlation between celestial cycles and terrestrial events. Astrologers had previously suffered with inaccurate and incomplete ephemerides, making it difficult to come to any conclusion about the celestial body in question or the validity of their works. And since astrologers use a different set of coordinates than astronomers usually do, calculating and converting the data was a tedious, tricky, and time-consuming process.

Until a few years ago, astrologers were stuck with whatever data interested the astronomers, which they then converted into their own system. But with home computers, it has become increasingly feasible to produce an ephemeris on even a tiny computer. We decided it would be an interesting experiment to produce a computerized ephemeris of Chiron as soon as possible after its discovery, and then to observe how astrologers go about discovering its significance. Since some astrologers work in other languages, or don't read journals from distant countries, it might be possible in a few years to go back and study the process by which the astrologers reached a conclusion about Chiron's astrological influences, if any. What role does the mythological name (chosen by an astronomer who does not believe in astrology) play? Do the astrologers disagree significantly with each other, or is there a surprising agreement between them? The sociology and psychology of the astrological process are virtually unresearched, and Chiron is providing an interesting case study.

But not to the *The Skeptical Inquirer*.

"The impact of astronomer Charles Kowal's 1977 discovery of the mini-planet Chiron is spreading far beyond the realm of astronomy," they noted. "Phenomena Publications has recently compiled an astrological ephemeris for Chiron . . . the obvious question to be answered is: If astrology is so 'scientific', why did nobody notice the astrological effects of Chiron *before* that planet was discovered?"[167]

If they had bothered to inquire, they might have discovered that at least two astrologers pointed to the probable existence of Chiron long before its astronomical discovery. The leading humanistic astrologer, Dane Rudhyar, discussed a "higher moon" passing between Saturn and Uranus in his famous book, *The Astrology of Personality*.[168] Rudhyar's proposed astronomical characteristics for this "moon" were obviously impossible. He had its orbit entering the photosphere of the Sun and passing out to Saturn in five years. But another astrological authority, Charles Jayne, came much closer.

For years, Jayne has been a leading research astrologer, publishing advanced journals and textbooks. Today, he publishes statistical and philosophical studies of astrology in his journal, *Cosmecology Bulletin*. But under its former title, *In Search*, Jayne published a remarkable article on hypothetical planets.[169] Jayne agreed substantially with Rudhyar's proposed body, and he named it TAU in his work. But unlike Rudhyar, Jayne proposed an orbital cycle of "50 plus or minus two years." Chiron has an orbit of just under fifty-one years.

Jayne also came close on another aspect of Chiron's orbit. All planetary orbits are tilted slightly to one another, and where these planes cross, their "nodes" are located. One node is called "north" and the other "south," indicating in which direction the planet is moving when it crosses its nodes.

Observe this pattern: At the time of its discovery, Uranus was near 24 Gemini and its north node is near 14 Gemini.

Neptune was discovered near 26 Aquarius, not far from its south node at 11 Aquarius. Pluto was discovered near 18 Cancer, and its north node is 18 Cancer.

From this interesting north-south alternating pattern, Jayne suggested that the next planet to be discovered would be found near or past its south node. Chiron was discovered near 3 Taurus, just past its south node at 29 Aries.

Another interesting pattern is found in the position of our own Moon's nodes at the time of these planetary discoveries. Our Moon's nodes travel "backwards" (against the direction of planetary motion) in a cycle roughly eighteen years long. Thus, from the discovery of Uranus in 1781 to the discovery of Neptune in 1846 was roughly three-and-one-half revolutions of the Moon's nodes. Four-and-one-half revolutions later, Pluto was discovered in 1930. In 1781, the Moon's north node was roughly 7 Taurus. In 1846 it was at the cusp of (boundary between) Libra and Scorpio. In 1930, the north node was roughly at 6 Taurus.

From this pattern, Jayne suggested that the next planet would be discovered in about 1975, when the north node would once again be near its location at the discovery of Neptune. Chiron was discovered in 1977, when the Moon's node was in mid Libra, not far from its 1846 position.

Clearly, whoever wrote that *Skeptical Inquirer* item didn't know what they were talking about. It's easier to deprecate something in 100 words than to research it properly. Rather than illuminate its readers on the historical and experimental aspects of the discovery and astrology of Chiron, *The Skeptical Inquirer* raced on to report that "In another exciting development, UFOlogist Wendell C. Stevens, writing in the May 1978 issue of *UFO Report,* contends that Kowal's discovery . . . is nothing less than an extraterrestrial artifact of gargantuan dimension."

"Fantastic as this seems," *The Skeptical Inquirer* quoted Stevens, "I believe Dr. Kowal has discovered the alien star-base."

The Academics Respond

It was not only those sympathetic to astrology who criticized the Objections to Astrology statement and its adherents.

Here again, the media failed to balance their coverage by making it clear that other scientists were not at all happy with the scientific quality of the papers produced by the critics. For example, Lawrence Jerome, of *Leonardo* fame, went on to produce a book entitled *Astrology Disproved*. In a review of this book, Prof. Hans Eysenck wondered why Jerome avoided discussing so much of the available evidence for astrology and simply passed off entire studies by saying "serious questions have been raised" concerning them. "What are these questions?" Eysenck asked. "We are fobbed off with these meaningless verbalizations. This is typical of Jerome's dealing with facts which seem to embarrass his position. . . ."[170]

Paul Feyerabend, a controversial philosopher of science, devoted an entire chapter of his *Science in a Free Society* to the attack on astrology. "The judgment of the '186 leading scientists' rests on an antediluvian anthropology, on ignorance of more recent results in their own fields (astronomy, biology, and the connection between the two) as well as on a failure to perceive the implications of the results they do know. It shows the extent to which scientists are prepared to assert their authority even in areas in which they have no knowledge whatsoever," Feyerabend stated. And he was equally unimpressed with the astrologers: "It is interesting to see how closely both parties approach each other in ignorance, conceit, and the wish for easy power over minds."[171]

While the facts do not support Feyerabend's criticism as far as the majority of serious astrologers are concerned, they are no doubt valid in a minority of cases . . . and among scientists as well.

The U.S. Test of the Mars Effect

Who will be first to disprove planetary influences? For skeptics, this prize looms like a Holy Grail on a distant horizon. Yet the CSICOP still hoped to attain its goal. Several critics had suggested that the Gauquelins might be unable to detect the Mars effect outside of Europe, meaning that their planetary effects might simply be artifacts of European data. So, in July, 1977, Michel Gauquelin met with Prof. Paul Kurtz, Prof. Marvin Zelen, and Prof. George Abell, the CSICOP's chief astronomer, to design a test of U.S. sports champions. Unlike most countries in Europe, birth data in North America is not required by law. And where it has been recorded properly, it is often under the protection of privacy acts, making it very difficult for researchers to obtain sufficient data for experiments.

In the winter of 1979-1980, *The Skeptical Inquirer* published the CSICOP's report on their investigation, a "Four-Part Report on Claimed 'Mars Effect.' "[172] They had followed all the motions, they claimed, and come up with no evidence for planetary influences. "We conclude that the analysis of American sports champions shows no evidence for the Mars effect," Kurtz, Zelen, and Abell concluded.

What had happened? Had the Gauquelins finally met their statistical Waterloo? Accompanying the official results of the CSICOP experiment was a paper by Dennis Rawlins, who had earlier produced a memorandum supporting one aspect of the Gauquelins' calculations. Rawlins, too, claimed that the U.S. test of the Mars effect had been a failure. But in a note added to his original paper, the cracks were beginning to show in the CSICOP's position against the Gauquelins. In tiny print, Rawlins was permitted to note: "The plain fact is that Zelen, Kurtz and Abell proposed their challenge [the Zelen test] in confident expectation [they would] deflate Gauquelin's claims. The actual outcome was a clear success for Gauquelin and should have been openly reported as such."

A committee member now appeared in print, albeit very tiny print in a footnote, stating that the Zelen Test had been positive for the Mars effect. But how had the U.S. test discounted the Mars effect? The third paper of the four-part report was by the Gauquelins themselves, who reminded the committee that the planetary effects appear best when the best subjects are used — Olympic athletes for the Mars effect, for example. The committee had selected its sample from *Who's Who* books which listed most athletes in various fields, including, in some cases, even coaches! By properly selecting the best athletes from the CSICOP's lists, the Gauquelins were once again able to show that the top athletes displayed the Mars effect (Mars in key sectors), while the ordinary athletes did not. Further analyses of U.S. Olympic champions, showed that the more rigorous the standard for champions, the higher the Mars effect.

In the same paper, the Gauquelins announced publication of yet another experiment they had recently concluded — a new replication of the Mars effect with a sample of 432 famous European athletes. Once again, Mars was found in key sectors. The chances against this were 1 in 1,000. But the CSICOP remained unbowed, and the published debate descended into an argument over the criteria for selection of champions.

Such a tale continues over many years, so it is difficult in a contemporary volume to provide the reader with a conclusive summary of the events. Readers truly concerned with the evidence for planetary influences will find their way to the original documents and attempt to make up their own minds.

However, two interesting postscripts may be added. Soon after Rawlins' comments on the success of the Zelen test, an executive meeting of the CSICOP is reported to have been held in New York City. The current executive was dissolved, and a new one elected. But no one, it seems, thought to re-elect Dennis Rawlins, who was not at the meeting. As a result, he is now an ex-executive member of the committee and speaks out forcefully against its tactics. Like other skeptics, Rawlins finds it difficult to accept an honest belief in something which contradicts his own world view. And like Prof. Truzzi, he was last seen heading for the pages of *Fate* magazine, where all good ex-members of the CSICOP seem to go to expose their dissident views.

Meanwhile, during the summer of 1980, the BBC was busy piecing together its on-again, off-again documentary on astrology for the "Horizon" series of science programs. Producer Tony Edwards visited the U.S. to interview the chief skeptics and Michel Gauquelin, who was continuing his research with the assistance of Astro Computing Services in San Diego.

During a filmed interview with the BBC, Prof. George Abell was asked what the end result of belief in astrology might be.

"Jonestown," he responded.

"And what about the U.S. test of the Mars effect?" Producer Edwards inquired.

Abell declined to comment.[173]

The BBC's "Horizon" program is distributed in the U.S. as "Nova." For whatever reasons, the astrology program had not, as of this writing, been scheduled to appear on U.S. television.

When we debunk a fanatical faith or prejudice, we do not strike at the root of fanaticism. We merely prevent its leaking out at a certain point, with the likely result that it will leak out at some other point. Thus by denigrating prevailing beliefs and loyalties, the militant man of words unwittingly creates in the disillusioned masses a hunger for faith. For the majority of people cannot endure the barrenness and futility of their lives unless they have some ardent dedication, or some passionate pursuit in which they can be themselves. Thus, in spite of himself, the scoffing man of words becomes the precursor of a new faith.

Eric Hoffer, The True Believer,
copyright 1951 by Eric Hoffer.
Section 108. Reprinted by
permission of Harper
& Row Publishers, Inc.

Twelve

The Astrology of the Future

Mention astrology and everyone soon thinks of predictions. "Gee, Mr. Astrologer, can you predict my future?"

In a word, No.

Predictions are like sun-sign horoscopes. Nearly everyone agrees they are nonsense, but it's difficult to restrain your curiosity. Sooner or later, you succumb to the wiles of prediction columns, whether they are provided for your entertainment by popular astrologers, political pundits, gossip columnists, sports announcers, or the fellow sitting beside you on the bus.

When you come right down to it, you're just as guilty as the next fellow. Who can say they have never predicted the outcome of a national election, a sports event, a new marriage, or two? Outguessing the future is probably one of the most universal human activities. We all attempt to project current trends into the future as far as possible, in order to prepare ouselves for the possibilities. But predictions are also like those fattening desserts you're not supposed to have. We can dig in and enjoy ourselves, as long as we don't get carried away.

Keep in mind that there are bad astrologers and bad predictions. Just because a prediction you read in the newspaper does (or does not) come true is not a proof (or disproof) of astrology. The best astrologers openly admit that astrology is a system of symbols which do not easily translate into English. Thus, most astrologers only attempt to deal with trends, not specific predictions. As you saw earlier, humanistic astrologers will insist that trends and symbolism are the only legitimate fields of application for astrology.

It is most often in the field of political and social trends that astrologers are requested for public comments. Aside from the annual predictions of pop astrologers in yellow newsrags which no one takes seriously, astrologers are often requested for their analysis of a political election or the world situation during the coming year. This field is called mundane astrology, and it is not for the eager-beaver amateurs who hang their shingle out in your *Yellow Pages*.

It's easy to see why, too. You are an individual, with a particular moment of birth. You were born at a specific time in a specific place. And therefore, you have a horoscope. But the world in general, and many countries in our modern world, did not arrive naked and bawling, anxiously attended by doctors and relatives. So the first problem a mundane astrologer faces is which charts can be used, and how?

Of course, most nations have a certain point in their history where something crucial happened, or when they became a legal nation. But in almost all cases, there are rival charts which other astrologers will hold to be superior. They may be cast for the same instant at a different time, or for a totally different event. In the case of the United States, for example, the precise moment when the Declaration of Independence was signed, if indeed there ever was such a precise moment, was not carefully recorded. Among the several other candidates for the birth moment of the U.S. is a chart for the opening of hostilities against the British crown, about one year previous to the usually accepted date. This chart has performed well in registering the subsequent military adventures of the United States. But even for the official date of July 4, 1776, there are disagreements over which sign was rising at the time. Most astrologers give the U.S. a Gemini ascendant, and the description does seem to fit. The U.S. is a country which seems to thrive on polarization, all the way from the initial confrontation with the parent state, through the Civil War, the racial struggles, and the current clash with the Soviets for world power.

The horoscope for Canada may be cast either for the moment when Queen Victoria signed the British North America Act, which has remained Canada's constitution for more than a century after 1867, or for the time when the act came into effect on July 1, 1867, at noon. The problem is that the Queen's representative, the governor-general, now the head of state for the new country, proclaimed Canada a nation in Ottawa, while the Fathers of Confederation were making merry in Charlottetown. There were no neat standard-time zones in those days, so each place used local mean time. Thus, the two events were not simultaneous, and the horoscopes are slightly different. This is not nitpicking; in some astrological systems such initially small differences are magnified in the course of time by directions and transits. By the time a country becomes 100 years old, the differences can be significant.

Besides using these "birth charts" of nations, mundane astrologers also examine the horoscopes of political leaders, again with much confusion over birth data, as I noted earlier. The charts of the opening of Parliament or Congress can be used, or the moment of an election or inauguration. To each of these horoscopes, the usual methods of directions and transits can be applied, although mundane astrologers tend to lay special emphasis on eclipses, charts for the moment when the Sun enters a sign of the zodiac (technical term: ingress charts), and more rarified methods which demand much calculation.

Keeping in mind that the number of serious astrologers has always been tiny, and that the brightest minds of a given generation have usually been siphoned off toward more lucrative and officially sanctioned careers, it is not surprising that good mundane astrologers are practically on the endangered species list. In 1918, the American astrologer, Marie Pontin, complained that in mundane astrology, "There is but a small volume of information to be had — a few pages in Pearce's Textbook; tiny volumes by Raphael and Leo, and scattered works of the older writers. . . ."[174]

Even in the 1960s someone writing under the pseudonym of "Sepharial" produced a book entitled *The World Horoscope*. The publishers, Foulsham & Co. of England, did not see fit to inform the reader that the original

Sepharial, Walter Gorn Old, died in 1929, when it was still fashionable if not excusable for astrologers to promote themselves to angelic status. By manipulating a kind of astrology based not on actual heavenly motions but rather on fixed recurring cycles much as are used in Japanese and Chinese fortune calendars, the reincarnated Sepharial was able to offer an interesting interpretation of the period 1970-1981. Writing from his vantage of the early 1960s, Sepharial suggested that war might break out around 1973 and last until 1977, when Venus and Libra would rise in his "World Horoscope." From a study of the period, he concluded that:

> . . . Some of the major happenings will revolve around a disturbing of human relationships as a result of a conflict of ideas between peoples. There will be marked political changes throughout the world as a result of the emergence of entirely new and forceful leaders. There will be a realignment of peoples and national blocs with a readjustment of beliefs and also of racial antagonisms. These can broadly speaking be divided into four main blocs, America and the Commonwealth (Western Democracy), Europe, Germanic Fascism, the Communist Block, with China predominant, the Black Races. The odd nation out will be Russia, whose actions will be determined by its then leaders — an enigmatic quality. This decade will also be a period of upheavals, some of a terrestrial nature, especially around 1976 when Saturn and Mars rise in Virgo, bringing in their train an effect upon world crops and thus causing food and population crises.[175]

> W. Foulsham & Co. Ltd.,
> England and reproduced
> with their permission.

Except for a few glaring errors, Sepharial seems to have called current events fairly closely. Iran and Ayatollah Khomeini, the Middle East, South Africa, Mount St. Helens seem to fit. And the Soviet leadership which will take over in the 1980s remains as enigmatic as ever. But a closer examination shows that food and population crises did not emerge in the 1970s. If anything, some United Nations figures indicate that the world population increase might be slowing down as hungry nations finally begin to control their birth rate more effectively. And the hungry have been with us since long before 1970. New leaders have come and gone with regularity in modern times, so it is safe to predict new ones. We are left, therefore, in the same position we found ourselves regarding sun signs. How is it possible to tell when the system is working or not?

This Is the Dawning of the Age of Aquarius

The most common image people have of mundane astrology is the wonderful Age of Aquarius we are all supposed to enter one of these days. Often, it is pictured as a kind of real-life Disneyworld in which we suddenly grow our hair long and commune over herbal teas. As a precise model, such long cycles are questionable. But they may have some explanatory value as outlines of social trends. As Jung explained:

> The influence of the constellations, the zodiac, they exist; you cannot explain why, it's a "Just-So Story", that proves itself by a thousand signs. But men always go from one extreme to the other, either they don't believe, or they are credulous. Any knowledge or faith can be ridiculed on the basis of what small minds do with it. That's stupid and, above all, it's dangerous. The great astrological periods do exist. Taurus and Gemini were prehistoric periods, we don't know much about them. But Aries the Ram is closer; Alexander the Great was one of its manifestations. [A footnote here points out that the Arabic name for Alexander was Dhulqarnein, meaning "two-horned."] That was from 2000 B.C. to the beginning of the Christian era. With that era we came into the sign of the Fishes. It was not I who invented all the fish symbols there are in Christianity; the fisher of men, the *pisciculi christianorum* ... To deny it would be to throw the baby out with the bath-water.[176]

In the new age, Jung called for "A spirit of greater openness towards the unconscious, an increased attention to dreams, a sharper sense of the totality of the physical and the psychic, of their indissolubility; a livelier taste for self-knowledge." Elsewhere in the same volume, he commented that "This atom bomb business, for instance, is terribly characteristic of Aquarius, whose ruler is Uranos, the Lord of unpredictable events.''

Jung's information was that the transition point between the ages would occur in about 150-200 years from the middle of the twentieth century. But as we have seen, the astrological ages are a by-product of the backwards motion of the equinoxes against the star fields of the zodiac. Astronomical authorities give this cycle various lengths, and it is not even clear if it is a regular cycle or one that changes constantly.[177] Since there is no agreement on the precise boundaries of the constellations in these star fields, and no agreement as to where to begin the constellational zodiac, everyone is free to argue for the Aquarian Age of their choice.

My favorite is the model proposed by Frater Albertus, a German-born alchemist who now teaches at his school in Salt Lake City.[178] Albertus has published detailed cycle maps which can be used to analyze historical events.[179] His basic patterns are formed by regular sine-waves of two wavelengths, dividing the circle respectively into seven and twelve periods covering the entire precessional cycle from about 19,000 B.C. By combining the signs of the zodiac with the traditional seven Qabalistic planetary rays, he obtains a symbolic description of each period. Furthermore, his sine waves are in phase in some periods and out of phase in others. Thus, during the Renaissance, both of Albertus's cycles peaked under a Venus phase of the seven-ray cycle. This admirably suits the florid and sensuous image we have of the culture of that period. Unfortunately, the era of the fourteenth century, replete with its crusades and plagues, also occurred during this set of cycles in Albertus's system.

Albertus takes his marker for the transition from Pisces to Aquarius as the first free flight in 1883. He notes that previous to this time, important discoveries and international commerce took place by water. Yet only one century after the earliest flights, the world has changed drastically. Astrologically or not, this is indeed some sort of new age. Yet be forewarned! If each age in Albertus's scheme is represented by a sine wave, it has a negative and positive half. His cycle charts show that the negative half of each age manifests first. And in the case of our time, the Venus phase of his seven-ray cycle is now on the downswing. Until 2500 A.D., both of his major cycles are heading downward into the negative polarity of the Aquarian Age.

Having thus rushed in where more scientific angels fear to tread, I might suggest that the first manifestation of this new age will be a concern with material well-being and supply, quite the opposite of the rapturous, ethereal spiritualism which, as popular myth has it, will infect us all at the magic moment.

It is Albertus's more specific cycle-charts which are of more immediate interest. By dividing each of his cycles into sub-periods, he has interpreted repeating patterns in our civilization. For example, under a triple-Jupiter phase of his cycle system (1733-1748), England became a worldwide colonial power. During the next such sub-cycle (1883-1898), the linotype, photography, and x-rays were discovered. The difference is that the first cycle occurred at the end of the Age of Pisces, while the second was the dawning of Albertus's Age of Aquarius. Under a triple-sun phase (1793-1808), steamships, locomotives, and gas and arc lights were the important developments, while in the next such sub-cycle (1943-1958), we witnessed the birth of atomic power. A triple-moon phase (1808-1823) occurred during the Napoleonic Campaigns, and the next such sub-cycle was from 1958 to 1973, with the Moon landings as the most important events. Just as Napoleon was forced to retreat into exile, even though his conquests had worldwide repercussions, so the Moon landings are now forgotten, though they marked the culmination of the earliest phase of what Timothy Leary calls "post-Terrestrial Man."

Albertus's projections for the next 100 years:

> 1973-1988 - decentralization of world power
> 1988-2003 - establishment of world federation
> 2003-2018 - worldwide economic action
> 2018-2033 - period of fruition of economic policies
> 2033-2048 - consolidation of world's resources
> 2048-2063 - administration of world's resources

The Presidential Death Cycle

One of the most popular predictions of mundane astrology

is the strange pattern which has accompanied the death of U.S. presidents every twenty years since 1840. Just like the hands of a clock, the planets catch up with each other in regular patterns. Saturn and Uranus come to the same place in the zodiac every 45 years, roughly, and Uranus catches up to Neptune every 171 years. The two most ponderous planets of the solar system are Jupiter and Saturn, and these two form one of the most important cycles in astrology, as they come to a conjunction every 20 years.

But these conjunctions are not in the same place in the sky. Think of your clock again. The minute hand goes around once an hour, but to catch up with the hour hand it has to move about one-twelfth of the circle in addition, because while the hour has passed, the hour hand has also moved ahead. This is known as a "synodic cycle," and each pair of planets forms synodic cycles of varying lengths. Since the beginning points of such cycles, the conjunctions occur in different places in each cycle, astrologers have an interesting set of patterns to study. Here are the conjunctions of Jupiter and Saturn from 1800 to 2000 A.D.[180]

16 July	1802	5 Virgo	Earth
19 June	1821	25 Aries	Fire
26 Jan.	1842	9 Capricorn	Earth
21 Oct.	1861	18 Virgo	Earth
18 Apr.	1881	2 Taurus	Earth
28 Nov.	1901	14 Capricorn	Earth
10 Sep.	1921	27 Virgo	Earth
8 Aug.	1940	14 Taurus	Earth
20 Oct.	1940	12 Taurus	Earth
15 Feb.	1941	9 Taurus	Earth
19 Feb.	1961	25 Capricorn	Earth
1 Jan.	1981	9 Libra	Air
8 Mar.	1981	8 Libra	Air
24 July	1981	5 Libra	Air
26 May	2000	22 Taurus	Earth

After each date, the zodiacal degree of the conjunction of Jupiter and Saturn are given, along with the element of the sign in which they conjoin. Now compare this list with the previous one:

U.S. President	Year of (Re) Election	Date of Death	Nearest Conjunction of Jupiter and Saturn
William Harrison	1840	4 Apr. 1841	26 Jan. 1842
Abraham Lincoln*	1860	15 Apr. 1865	21 Oct. 1861
James Garfield*	1880	19 Sep. 1881	18 Apr. 1881
William McKinley*	1900	14 Sep. 1901	28 Nov. 1901
Warren Harding	1920	2 Aug. 1923	10 Sep. 1921
Franklin Roosevelt	1940	12 Apr. 1945	8 Aug. 1940
			20 Oct. 1940
			15 Feb. 1941
John Kennedy*	1960	22 Nov. 1963	19 Feb. 1961
?	1980	?	1 Jan. 1981

*Presidents who were assassinated.[181]

Is there a pattern to these deaths? It has often been suggested that a U.S. president elected in a "zero-year" will not live out his term of office. At first glance, there seems to be some correlation, especially in the cases of Harrison, Garfield, and McKinley. But critics are not satisfied that there is some kind of connection. Two astronomers who have spent some time studying astrology and attempting to debunk it are Dr. Robert Culver and Dr. Philip Ianna. In their recent book, *The Gemini Syndrome,* they note that Jefferson was elected in 1800, a zero-year, reelected in 1804, and died in 1826 at the age of eighty-three. Monroe was also elected for a second term in 1820 and lived to tell the tale.[182] Zachary Taylor, another U.S. president who died in office, was elected in 1848 and died two years later of cholera. Roosevelt's fate took quite a while to arrive, as did Lincoln's. And McKinley died shortly before the 1901 conjunction even occurred.

Confident that they have torn another astrological myth to shreds, Ianna and Culver also note that astrologers run for cover at the sight of the earlier elections in 1800 and 1820, pleading that the cycle was not occurring in Earth signs at the time. You will see from the first table that these conjunctions tend to occur in one element for a while, and then move to a new element briefly. There is usually one more conjunction in the old element before a long series of conjunctions in the new element. Observing this pattern, astrologers have simply suggested that the correlation between deaths in office and these conjunctions may only hold when the conjunctions occur in Earth signs. This is a simple assertion based on the available facts. I have not heard why this should be so, but if the pattern holds, the 1980 president might not die in office. Stay tuned for further details.

Drs. Ianna and Culver believe ". . . the entire process of 'patching up' the Twenty-Year Sequence is totally analogous to the medieval process of stacking additional epicycles onto what was already an impressive array of celestial orbs in order that the insatiable idiosyncrasies of the planets' motions could be temporarily satisfied." But for would-be debunkers, Ianna and Culver display poor scholarship, at least on this issue.[183] Just as one professor of astronomy appeared on television with an incorrectly calculated horoscope, every single date astronomers Ianna and Culver give for the Jupiter-Saturn conjunctions is inaccurate. The conjunction of 26 January 1842 is listed in their book as 26 January 1841. The dates of the other conjunctions in their book vary by about three days from the correct date. And there are at least half a dozen other errors of facts and dates in their supposed debunking of the mysterious death cycle of U.S. presidents. One can only suggest that the low opinion many skeptics have of astrology may become translated into a low quality of scholarship when examining the issues. And therefore, we are entitled to wonder whether the issues have been properly dealt with at all.

The truth of the matter is that the data is far too limited for any kind of acceptable scientific test. In fact, the vast majority of astrological predictions fall into this category. Events such as the deaths of leaders of one particular country are too few and far between for statistics to handle them. Scientists are quite naturally reluctant to accept a projection thus based on extremely skimpy data and a symbolic system which they have already rejected out of hand. Yet this kind of projection of trends is what mundane astrology is concerned with. If the pattern holds, there will be no further untimely deaths of U.S. presidents while in office, due to the conjunctions in Air. Or, if the next president dies, this confirms the cycle, but does not explain the 1820 and 1800 presidents who did not die in office. All astrologers can do is suggest that this pattern has existed for some time, and wait like the rest of us to see what will happen, not knowing *why* it happens. All the scientists can do is to throw up their hands, not understanding why anyone would try to make such precise short-term predictions on such a small data-base. The two world-views are light years apart.

But the problem is not as simple as it might appear. The zero-year factor is not in itself what astrologers are studying — in other words, they are not suggesting that the zero at the end of the year is the cause of the cycle. We saw that the conjunctions of Jupiter and Saturn occur about every twenty years, and we know that U.S. presidential elections take place on a regular schedule. Therefore, the Jupiter-Saturn conjunctions might only be a kind of early-warning that there is a possibility of such a major turn of events. Naturally, any astrologer who simply hangs a prediction on one simple planetary event such as this is probably a rank amateur.

One astrologer who has studied the question of presidential deaths proposes an answer. Jeri Blake's *When Presidents Die* presents an analysis of the horoscopes of all the presidents in question, plus their assassins, and the charts of some of the vice-presidents who were subsequently elevated to the office of president.[184] Obviously, such an elevation in stature would have to show in the horoscope of the vice-president, just as the possibility of an untimely death would have to show in the horoscope of the president. By isolating the astrological factors which were common to all the charts involved, Blake was also able to show why Zachary Taylor died in office, even though he was not elected in a zero-year. The critical factor, says Blake, is not the Jupiter-Saturn configuration, but combinations of Saturn-Neptune and Jupiter-Uranus. These planetary configurations were not operative during the 1800 and 1820 elections, but they figured in each subsequent case, including the Zachary Taylor case which does not seem to fit the zero-year hypothesis.

Blake concludes: "There is no Saturn-Neptune combination in the 1980 [chart], nor is there a Jupiter-Uranus configuration. Thus the conditions for a presidential assassination (if past patterns continue) are not met. There is, however, an effective Saturn-Uranus [aspect] — a pattern which we found in cycles covering two of the four presidential deaths from other causes. A Mercury-Neptune combination (present in 1980) appeared in three of seven unsuccessful assassination attempts." Therefore, the possibility of an assassination attempt during the 1980 campaign was higher than usual.

Whether Blake was right or wrong, the important point here is that a facile examination such as Ianna and Culver present of the death cycle of U.S. presidents simply will not do. As Jung said, any knowledge can be ridiculed on the basis of what small minds do with it.

There's another interesting correlation between the Jupiter-Saturn cycle and social trends. You've probably heard people talk about each decade as if it had a predominant quality or theme. There's the Roaring Twenties, the Booming Fifties, and so on. From time to time, I've heard the suggestion that an odd-numbered decade is often a negative period, while a positive-numbered decade tends to be an outgoing, upbeat, aggressive time. Recalling the ebullient atmosphere of the sixties, which were followed by the dour and tension-filled seventies, the pattern does seem to fit. Furthermore, it has often been noted (by writers with no knowledge of astrology whatsoever) that each decade is a little late in starting up. Rock music critics have noted that the sixties did not get started until 1961 or 1962, and that the seventies did not take over from the sixties immediately.

These are subjective impressions of social trends, but they are also common impressions shared by many people. And they may have a basis in astrological fact. Remember the model of a clock which we used to explain the Jupiter-Saturn cycle. The minute hand turns around the dial until it comes to the same point as the hour hand. This is the conjunction, the beginning of the cycle. From that point on, the angle between the two clock hands increases until they stand opposite each other. (This pattern has nothing to do with the numbers on the dial, it is only a description of the *angular relationship* between the two hands of the clock.) When the two hands are opposite each other, the second most important phase of the cycle, the opposition, is reached. Just as there was a repeating series of conjunctions (see table above), so there is a repeating series of oppositions more or less on the opposite side of the zodiac, gradually shifting around the circle. When the angle between the two planets is increasing, we speak of a waxing hemicycle, just as the Moon appears to us when the angle between it and the Sun is increasing. Similarly, there is a waning hemicycle, both of the Moon and the Jupiter-Saturn cycle. If this appears confusing at first, just try to grasp the essential idea of waxing and waning cycles.

Astrologers attempt to interpret these cycles by noting the natural symbolism of the Moon's phases. At New Moon, you can't see the Moon unless it crosses in front of the Sun during an eclipse. Gradually, a crescent appears in the sky and begins to grow. Halfway between the conjunction and the opposition, the Moon appears precisely half-illuminated, looking like an apple someone has cut in half. Then, the missing half slowly fills out, and at the Full Moon, we see the entire side of the Moon facing Earth as a fully illumined disk. It was the astrologer Dane Rudhyar who was responsible for introducing this symbolism to modern astrology in his book *The Lunation Cycle,* and it is now commonly applied to the interpretation of any similar cyclic phenomena.[185]

Now remember that the total Jupiter-Saturn cycle was about twenty years in length. You have already seen a list of the dates of the conjunctions, or starting points, of these cycles above. So, by dividing the cycle into two portions, it is clear that Jupiter and Saturn take about ten years to go from conjunction to opposition and ten years to go from opposition back to a new conjunction. Since the starting points, as listed in the table above, are near the early years of each decade, it is clear that the opposition points in the cycle also fall near the early years of each subsequent decade. In other words, during this century at least, the two halves of the Jupiter-Saturn cycle are closely synchronized with the decades of our calendar. By recalling the shift in public temperament which occurred between the heydays of the sixties and the early seventies, you can decide for yourself whether the Jupiter-Saturn cycle might not have something to do with the quality of life in each decade.

On the basis of previous decades, it may be suggested that the eighties will be an extroverted decade which will really commence in earnest in 1981. There will likely be a resurgence of some aspects of the sixties, especially counter-culture movements, open confrontations with authorities over military and ecological concerns, and (long-overdue) the return of popular music with a message. Disco, it is to be fervently hoped, will die. In many ways, the confrontations will be more substantive, since many of those who protested in the sixties have now worked their way into the social system. They may now sport pin-stripe suits rather than hip-long haircuts, but they have not entirely forgotten their vision for a new society. Whereas the seventies were concerned with maintaining an increasingly outdated status quo and with a retreat into fantasy and personal indulgence, the eighties will be concerned with the very real need for concrete action on a world scale, in order to avert military and ecological disasters. In the sixties, authorities denied that such actions were necessary. By the seventies, ecology, consumerism, and occupational hazards became accepted concerns, but ones which always received a low priority. The eighties will probably not have such luxuries as the large margins of error which allowed the seventies to muddle about. The issues will be global and immediate, demanding global and immediate solutions. Whereas the seventies placed an emphasis upon refinement and improvement of old technologies such as the automobile, the eighties will place a much stronger emphasis upon new technologies. There will also be a resurgence of new religious movements in response to the social tensions of the decade, as well as renewed interest in the established Oriental teachings.

The Astrology of Jimmy Carter's Tehran Fiasco

Among the most interesting new techniques in astrology, one promises to permit much more accurate forecasting in terms of geographic locations. Cycles such as the supposed presidential death-sequence and the work of Frater Albertus are time-based systems, not tied to any particular place on Earth. But as the research of the Gauquelins has indicated, it is the angle between a local horizon and a planet which is the important factor. In astrology, this is known as "angularity," and a planet which is found "on an angle" is held to be particularly effective. We also saw that astrologers sometimes attempt to move a horoscope from one location to another, as did Brigadier Firebrace with Hitler's horoscope. This has the effect of bringing planets closer to, or farther away from, various angles in the chart, creating a whole new emphasis. But obviously, such calculations and recalculations are quite laborious. One couldn't simply sit down and toss off dozens of calculations to find out where the planets might have been on the angles at a given moment.

Not until computers came along, that is. Computers love this kind of work, and it occurred to a California astrologer, Jim Lewis, to have a program written which would calculate all the places where each planet would be seen on an angle at a given time and draw these lines on a map of the world. Previous to this insight, astrologers usually went through the process of recalculating horoscopes and working with the new house positions which each location would give in a chart. But Lewis decided to investigate what would happen if he drew a line connecting all the places on Earth where Mars would have been "seen" on the horizon at the time of his birth. He followed this process for each planet, and the accompanying map shows the kind of result he obtains. This is called an Astro*carto*graphy Map. Each line relates to one of the planets, such that the curved lines show places where that planet would be seen as rising or setting, and the straight lines show where that planet would be seen as overhead or beneath the Earth. The map is calculated by the computer for a given instant and drawn on a plotting machine. Somewhere on the straight lines, you'll find a small circle, which represents where the planet was precisely overhead at that time. Along the top and the bottom of the map there are abbreviations indicating which planet the line represents.

Once the basic idea was developed, and Lewis's computer

was churning out charts, it became possible to see if these lines had any relationship with personalities and events. For example, the map calculated for the first successful test explosion of an atomic bomb has some interesting features. Astrologers relate Pluto with atomic energy, and in the map for that event, Pluto's lines crossed through Chicago (where the first nuclear chain reaction was achieved) and Nagasaki. All sheer coincidence, of course.

Examining the charts for various presidents of the United States, Lewis then discovered some other interesting coincidences. Roosevelt's Mars line passed through Pearl Harbour. Truman's Mars line passes through Korea, and his Pluto line is almost exactly over the location of the first atomic bomb drop. (Pluto was not discovered until over forty years after Truman's birth.) Truman supported the Shah of Iran when the latter was almost deposed in 1952, and Truman's Mars sets exactly over Tehran. Kennedy was the first president to commit troops to Viet Nam, where he had Mars, Saturn, and Neptune lines. His Pluto line passed through Dallas, Texas. Lyndon Johnson's Mars, Jupiter, and Sun lines passed near Viet Nam. Nixon's Neptune line, traditionally a planet of deception and delusion, crosses through Cambodia and Washington. Gerald Ford's Mars was over Saigon and near where the Mayaguez incident took place. His Pluto line was over San Francisco, where he faced two assassination attempts. All sheer coincidence, of course.

Now we come to Jimmy Carter, whose horoscope and Astro*carto*graphy Map have been computerized and reproduced in this volume. In 1978, Lewis wrote:

> In Carter's map, we find the Mars line through every area we have most reason to fear — Africa and the Middle-East. In fact, the line closely identifies these countries: Union of South Africa; Zimbabwe (Rhodesia); Ethiopia; Saudi Arabia; Iraq; and Iran. . . . Mars appears with Jupiter in Iran, and this calls to mind another chart — that of Harry Truman, whose Mars lines parallel almost exactly Carter's. Does this suggest that Carter may have to deal with some of the outcome of Truman's involvement in Iran? Korea is also a zone where both share Mars lines. . . . If trouble occurs, we can expect it in those areas where Truman also committed troops and material.[186]

ASTRO*CARTO*GRAPHY

JIMMY CARTER

24/25/03 171 © 1980 By Astro*Carto*Graphy

10 1 24 15:00 GMT

In a subsequent article written in December, 1979 and later published in *American Astrology* magazine, Lewis reminded his readers that he had called the problems in Iran and Korea before they became common knowledge. Then he provided this outline of the coming months:

> Early January 1980: Saturn makes its station [stops moving] in exact conjunction to Mars in the chart of the U.S.A. In all likelihood, events (*known or not*) bring the frustration of the American people to a peak of tension. Most projects to release the hostages fail at this time.
>
> Mid-February 1980 sees a solar eclipse exactly on Carter's Mars . . . it is worthwhile to note that this eclipse culminates precisely over Tehran, as does the next lunar eclipse two weeks later. Activating the Ayatollah's Sun, and the deposed Shah's Uranus, these eclipses probably hint at change of government in the near future in Iran, as well as the incredible civil unrest that would engender. . . .
>
> February 29, 1980 sees a station of Uranus in exact aspect to Carter's Mars. This is perhaps the second most threatening of all aspects this year, and shows Carter is forced to act quickly, decisively, and in response to, or with, violence. The President takes an unusual risk, it would seem, abandoning suddenly his circumspect posture, and the world is probably brought perilously close to a major confrontation as a result. . . .
>
> But it is April that sees the most difficult aspect. . . . Mars makes its station in exact opposition to Carter's Jupiter on April 7th . . . this looks ominously militant in nature. It is probably the final stage of the crisis, one marked by considerable tension, and perhaps military involvement. While no responsible astrologer likes to go on record with definite predictions, it nevertheless seems to me likely that April will see a very significant crisis involving Jimmy Carter. . . .

By April 25, the world knew that a rescue mission had been in planning during the previous six months, and that it had failed dismally. Subsequently, there were indeed changes in the government of Iran as the Ayatollah sought to complete his eradication of the Shah's governmental structure and balance the rival leftist and fundamentalist factions. Glancing at the Astro*carto*graphy Map of Jimmy Carter, it is easy to see that his Mars and Jupiter lines cross very near to Tehran and close to where the Soviets have had an army on standby, waiting to descend upon Iran. Even if you can't completely follow the astrological jargon, it is clear that Lewis had called the outlines and timing of a top-secret mission which took everyone by surprise. Like the weatherman, Lewis laid out his data, drew his conclusions, and presented his forecast, but with much more accuracy than we would expect from a weather forecast written five months in advance.

Of course, as we all know, astrology is sheer poppycock. But this is one astrological prediction which came true in a very dramatic fashion.

Carter's "map" indicates where each planet would have been seen on one of the "angles" — rising, setting, on the midheaven, or the I.C. — at the time of his birth. The curved lines are in fact circles, representing the line dividing that half of the globe which lies "under" a given planet, and that half which is farthest from the planet. In terms of the Sun, we speak of the "day" side and the "night" side of the Earth. The small circle visible on the straight lines shows precisely where that planet was directly overhead. Note Carter's Mars lines passing near Korea and Tehran.

Jupiter's "Effect" on One Scientist

Hardy souls that they are, astrologers have been convinced that science will discover the truth of their art ever since they were disbarred from academic circles in the seventeenth century. Thus, any suggestion from scientific circles that planets might actually have some effects on earthly events has been welcomed, if not entirely understood or agreed with.

So it was in 1974 that Dr. John Gribbin, an astrophysicist, author of several popular books on science, and former editor of *Nature,* an elite science journal, joined with Stephen Plagemann to write *The Jupiter Effect.*[187] Complete with a foreword by Isaac Asimov, their book caused quite a controversy due to its astrological overtones.

". . . to the surprise of many scientists," they wrote, "there has come evidence that in one limited respect the astrologers were not so wrong after all; it seems that the alignments of the planets can, for scientific reasons, affect the behavior of the Earth."

Gribbin's and Plagemann's theory caused little controversy when it was first published in the journal *Science* in 1971. They knew that the San Andreas fault in California had been building up to a major earthquake for some time. Other studies had suggested that there was a small but significant increase in seismic activity when the Sun was most active with sunspots. And the solar cycle is known to have a period of about eleven years. Therefore, the next major earthquake might possibly occur at the next solar peak of activity, expected sometime between 1980 and 1984. Said Gribbin, ". . . we got really excited when we found that in 1982 a rare alignment of the planets takes place in a narrow arc on the same side of the Sun. . . . This, we figured, must redouble the strength of the tidal effect, with all the planets, including Jupiter, tugging together. So, on the basis of what has been interpreted as 'astrology,' we predicted a peak of solar activity in 1982 that would set off a ripple of earthquakes in many regions of the Earth, probably triggering the San Andreas in particular."[188]

Once their prediction of a planetary peak *plus* the hypothesis that a planetary alignment could be involved became known, Gribbin and Plagemann were in for a good deal of flak. In more detail, the theory suggests that during part of 1982, all nine planets of the solar system will be lined up on one side of the Sun. This unusual occurrence will generate strong tides on the surfaces of the Sun, which in turn will produce strong solar storms. The increased solar activity will upset the balance of the Earth's magnetosphere and ionosphere, which protects and surrounds the Earth. Thus, the weather will be greatly disturbed, inducing changes in the Earth's rate of rotation. Finally, even a slight change in the rate of the Earth's spin and wobble on its axis might trigger earthquakes along lines which are already highly stressed and ready to let go. Replete with graphs showing various relationships between events on the Sun and events on Earth, *The Jupiter Effect* was, in Isaac Asimov's words, ". . . far more fascinating than the tale of any millionaire found stabbed in any library, locked or otherwise. And far more important, too, — especially if you live in California."

As public knowledge of the 1982 planetary alignment spread, planetariums around the world had to reassure their audiences that the planets will not line up in 1982. No, madam, planetary influences are mere supersition, the world will not end in 1982.

Earthquake researchers such as Dr. Bill Kautz of Stanford Research International, who has been researching planetary influences for some time, have reassured the public that the theory is not very solid.

All but one of the steps are either questionable or incorrect. The planets are not going to be "lined up" in 1982. They will fall within a 65° angle around the Sun — a configuration that happens about every 179 years. Second, the tides which the planets produce on the Sun are very much weaker than the tides the Moon and Sun produce on the Earth. Moreover, only four of the nine planets contribute significantly to the tide-producing effect, and these four are in close alignment much more frequently — about every eleven years. Also, when it comes to producing the largest tides, the bodies involved need not be on the same side of the Sun, but can be lined up on both sides. Third, it is almost inconceivable that solar tides could have any observable effect on the Sun. Despite considerable searching, no evidence has been found to indicate that they have anything to do with the level of solar activity. Studies of planetary positions and the intensity and number of solar storms over a several-hundred-year period have revealed that, although both are highly cyclic in nature, the two cycles do not correspond at all.

On the fourth point, it is now well known that the Earth's magnetosphere and ionosphere are strongly influenced by the level of solar activity. So this step of the argument is correct. However, the effect of solar activity on weather . . .is very dubious. The issue is admittedly controversial but the evidence is far from convincing at the present time. Step six, the effect of weather extremes on stresses in the Earth's crust is also questionable. . . . There does seem to be a correlation between a barely measurable wobble in the Earth's axis and some of the Earth's largest earthquakes, but which is cause and which is effect is still uncertain. Some weak correlations between weather variations and the earth's rate of rotation are known, but these are not presented in the book.[189]

As if that type of rebuttal wasn't enough, somewhere in between the original paper and 1980, astrologers started drawing flak for an idea which they had not originally suggested. Will the planets align in 1982 or not? What did "the stars say" about this period? And so on. People who knew neither the original theory nor astrological projections for the 1980s and 1990s were up in arms at the idea of planetary influences triggering an earthquake. At least one official government research program was set up to evaluate earthquake predictions by any interested individuals using any method, including astrology. Government studies suggested that even if an earthquake were known of in advance, the ensuing drop in property values would have a disastrous effect on the economy of California. Following the Chinese, Dr. Kautz set up a program to determine if animals can provide reliable clues to an imminent earthquake.

By 1980, the Jupiter effect came home to roost. In an article in *Omni* magazine, Gribbin wrote that "A great many people in fringe cults have interpreted the forecast as a prediction of the world's end. . . . Because of the way the book has been misused by cultists who must never have read it, I want to make it clear that there is no reason now to expect any unusual seismic disturbance in 1982 from the causes given in the book."

What changed his mind? By late 1979, it appeared that solar activity had reached its peak, and might begin to decline through 1980. True, there were plenty of small tremors in California in 1979, just as the Sun appeared to be "peaking." But, wrote Gribbin, "In retrospect, some of the accusations that our book was alarmist seem justified. I am older now and, I hope, wiser."

"There's an important lesson here," he concluded, "which may be what our academic critics were trying to tell us: Don't open the door for half-baked cults to latch on to your ideas. The key words *earthquake, planetary alignment,* and *1982* were all that the weirdos needed and all they ever knew about the Jupiter effect. . . . Mind you, as long as the Sun continues to be active, I'm keeping my fingers crossed for the sake of L.A."

As astrologer Alexander Ruperti puts it: "Thus the lesson

of Jupiter on all levels of reality is the importance of limitations. . . . A balloon can hold only so much air before it bursts."[190]

Doom and Gloom, Etc.

Doomsday must be the most postponed and rescheduled event in the history of the world. Yet, like the horror flicks, it keeps us in suspense despite its questionable credibility. Doom-and-gloom forecasts have become so common in many quarters that there is a reactionary movement to remind us all how good things are. Professor Theodore Levitt, of the Harvard Business School, recently addressed some Canadian graduates of his school on the topic "The End of the World Is Not at Hand." Levitt spoke of "unctuous analyzers who write and speak only for and to the mass media, who whip up small facts into big hunks of inevitability, feeding ravenously on life's normal uncertainties, anxieties and troubles."[191]

"What is new today," Levitt told his audience, "is that today's poppycock is so relentlessly advertised for all to hear and read — and is not harmlessly available, as in times past, only to the intelligentsia or the ecclesiastical elite. Today we get it regularly on the six o'clock news." He reminded them about the catastrophes which have still not happened:

— a collapse of the West's economy due to the inability to recycle Arab petrodollars was expected around 1975;
— black militancy was expected to turn American cities into battle grounds in the mid-1960s.

Today's disruptive events will not necessarily become tomorrow's catastrophes, Levitt asserts. And yet, since the Soviet invasion of Afghanistan, there has been a shift in popular sentiment. In the late seventies, people often stated flatly that they thought there would not be another war such as the world wars. By late 1979, a major war had once again become an acceptable topic for social conversation. It was no longer only the fanatics who were bringing up the subject over cocktails. There are many investors who have sold their stocks to purchase gold and silver bullion. I know of one who is burying his gold in his yard, so the government won't be able to seize it if worst comes to worst. R.E. McMaster, editor of *The Reaper Newsletter,* has published a book outlining prophecies of a major war from all kinds of sources.[192] The idea is in the air, and perhaps that's all that counts.

Astrologers have fingered the early to mid-eighties as a critical period ever since the last war. Was it simple coincidence that George Orwell decided upon the year 1984 for his book? Whether these concerns will be substantiated by events in this decade remains to be seen. If the cycles which various researchers have isolated do reap their grim fruit on schedule, we should be prepared to begin the search for ways to deal with the root causes of war. And if they don't, or if we have a narrow escape, a close call, the worst thing we could do is to continue our present arrogance, thinking that the worst will never happen, that somehow we will get by and be spared.

At the same time, it is important to keep a perspective on what war means. Vast areas of the world were untouched by the world wars. In other parts of the world, such as South America, times were good and the outcome of the war was not a matter of life and death. A war in one country can mean a boost to the economy of another country. The question for our generation is how close will the major powers be willing to approach the brink of total nuclear war? And to this question not even the astrologers have an answer. Hope springs eternal in the human heart. Our race is like a reckless teenager. Although we fear for his health and even his life, we know that if he can only get through the next, difficult period, he may become a responsible adult with a fulfilling lifetime ahead of him. With these points in mind, let's take a look at just a few of the cycles which concern the astrologers.

"I think it would be fair to say that the general opinion among astrologers is that the early 1980's will be troublesome in the extreme," Robert Hand told me during an interview in 1978. "The planets are forming into arrangements which have occurred only twice before this century — 1914-1918 and 1940-1945."[193]

Hand was referring to a new type of astrology which has been developed particularly by a group of French astrolo-

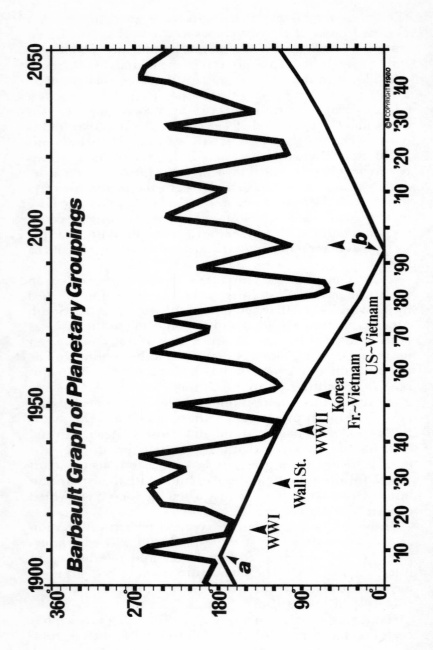

Barbault Graph of Planetary Groupings

The Barbault graph plots the arc between outer planets from 1900 through 2050 A.D. Years are shown at the top and bottom, and the degrees of arc on the vertical axis. For example, the nearly straight zigzag line shows the Uranus-Neptune cycle of 171 years. In 1908, Uranus and Neptune were in opposition (180°) as the peak of the graph (marked *a*) shows. In 1993, they are in conjunction (0°) and the line reaches the bottom of the graph (marked *b*). The sum of all such cycles between the outer planets produces the irregular graph as shown. Computations and programming of the original computer-drawn graph were by Astro-Graphics.

The graph rises and falls as the planets spread out or gather together across the sky. Like irregular breaths rising and falling, major social, political, and economic events are seen to follow this rhythm. What begins at one peak of the graph (maximum spread or in-breath) may end at the following trough (minimum spread or out-breath). Or, as with American involvement in Vietnam, it may await a similar peak in the graph before a new cycle begins. The reader is invited to compare the behavior of the graph with world events by using a reference such as Penguin's *Chronology of World Events*, or an encyclopedia.

Major events are indicated by arrows. The peak at the far left indicates the end of the Boer War, just after the turn of the century. World War I (1914-1918) coincided closely with the next major trough. The postwar economic cycle culminated at the next peak in the graph, when the first downturn since the war led to the Wall Street Crash (1929) and ushered in a world economic crisis. At the next upturn Hitler had become German chancellor (in 1933), and by the next peak in 1936, German troops entered the Rhineland. World War II followed in 1939, ending at the major upswing of 1945. The straight line which follows this period indicates the postwar boom quite clearly. At the peak of 1950, the Korean War commenced. Both the Korean War (1950-1953) and French involvement in Vietnam (defeat at Dien Bien Phu in 1954) ended as the line came to the next trough. The lowest point in 1956 witnessed the Suez Crisis and the Hungarian Revolution. The next peak in 1964 coincides with the Gulf of Tonkin Resolution, which gave Pres. Kennedy almost unlimited powers to "prevent further aggression" in Southeast Asia. The following low-point witnessed the largest communist offensive of the Vietnam War, and renewed strategic bombing of North Vietnam. By the peak of 1976, the Vietcong had entered Saigon. At the same peak, U.S. and Soviet astronauts joined in space. The descending line, to the lowest point in the entire graph (1982), reflects the direction of U.S.-Soviet relations since 1976. The last two arrows on the graph point to 1982 and 1997.

gers, especially André Barbault. Barbault has published several articles outlining the theory in *l'Almanach Chacornac*, his own astrological journal *l'Astrologie*, and his 1979 book *l'Astrologie Mondiale*.[194] What André Barbault has done is studied periods as early as the fourteenth century in order to see what correlations there might be between cultural and political developments and planetary patterns. The idea is quite simple. Just as we found there was an angle between Jupiter and Saturn at any given time, and this angle was constantly increasing or decreasing, so there is a *total angle* between all possible pairs of planets. In other words, if all the outer planets were exactly lined up on one side of the Sun, the total angle between them would be zero. No one was around at that time, and I don't think anyone even knows when that event occurred. But at all other times, there is an angle between each pair of planets. Since the inner planets move so quickly, it is only necessary to work with the slow-moving outer planets to see what happens. You begin by taking the positions of the planets at a given time, say, on the first day of every year. Then, you start with Jupiter, and note the angle between it and Saturn. Then, Jupiter and Uranus, Jupiter and Neptune, and Jupiter and Pluto. Now you take Saturn and find the angle between it and Uranus, Neptune and Pluto. Then Uranus and Neptune in the same fashion. Finally, you total the arcs which you have found, until you have the total arc between all pairs of the outer planets on a given day. Since they move slowly, figures for one day per year are sufficient.[195]

The accompanying graph shows the period from 1900 through 2000 A.D. Put quite simply, when the graph rises, the planets are spreading out in the sky. When the graph falls, they are concentrating gradually in one area of the sky. Barbault says:

> It is difficult not to recognize some striking correlations. The most important characteristic of this graph is that it displays two major drops through the first three quarters of this century; and it is precisely at the bottom of the two falls where we find the two World Wars. In a general way, society unties itself when the curve is descending, and rebuilds when ascending. So the falling graph between 1911 and 1919 illus-

trates the first Balkan Wars until the end of the First World War. The graph again falls between 1935 and 1955, from Hitler's ascension to the end of the Second World War. The reverse cycles from 1919 to 1926 and 1945-1951 correspond to periods of post-war rebuilding. Between the two major drops is a trough of a waning phase, which corresponds to the economic crisis of 1929-1933. The largest rise of the graph in this century, from 1956 to 1964, corresponds to the euphoric growth and expansion which characterized that time. The two other dips in the graph begin with the appearance of the two most significant local wars: the Korean War in 1950, escorted and followed by the decolonization wars in the dip of 1955, and the American intervention in Viet Nam in 1965, which was also an economic crisis. The most recent large dip in the graph, which began in 1975, shows a new economic crisis which is not yet finished.[196]

As for ancient history, Barbault's calculations suggest that two very low troughs in the planetary graph occurred in 1347 and 1485. In 1347-1348, one third of the population of Europe died from plague; and in 1485 a new plague struck Europe and continued for over fifty years. Barbault says that not only the total arc, but also the *rate of change* in that arc is important. The years of maximum decrease are quite interesting: 1914 (start of World War I), 1927 (two years before an economic crisis), 1940 (second greatest decrease of the century, World War II), 1952 (critical year in Korean War), 1966-67 (Cultural Revolution in China). Barbault concludes that the rate of increase or decrease can launch or accelerate a crisis.

The current period, says Barbault, is the greatest drop of the century, and the lowest planetary arc since 1485. When the graph is low, planets tend to be near each other. And therefore they come into conjunction, sooner or later. Now, after nine years without conjunctions of the outer planets, we will have five major conjunctions between 1981 and 1984. You'll recall from the previous section that conjunctions seem to correspond to turning points. They are seed moments in which the stage is set for a new cycle to take place. The first strong concentration of planets occurs from October to November 1980, followed by the all-time low of mid-October to mid-November 1982 (see the sample page from *American Ephemeris*).

Barbault's conclusions: "Since 1975, we have entered the process which is driving us into a large new world crisis. The acceleration of this process is shown for 1978-1980, with the burst of the first obvious manifestations in late 1980. The crisis will fill out in 1981, center about the end of 1982, and end near the beginning of 1984." These conclusions were published as early as 1967. In 1974, Barbault was more specific: "If a third world war occurs between now and the year 2000, there is a great probability that it will fall between 1981 and 1984, 1982-3 being the most critical years of the century."

But Barbault is not entirely of the doom-and-gloom school. He notes that in the late eighties and nineties there are some important conjunctions of the planets which have not occurred for some time. The Industrial Revolution got underway with the Uranus-Neptune conjunction of 1821, Barbault notes, and this 175-year cycle will recur in 1992-1993. Barbault has observed cycles in the political right which correlate with the forty-five-year cycle of Saturn and Uranus. The political left appears to have its ups and downs in rhythm with the thirty-six-year cycle of Saturn and Neptune. Both of these cycles converge in a triple conjunction in 1988-1989. The last time the patterns of 1988-1993 occurred was in the late fifteenth century, when Diaz crossed the Cape of Good Hope, opening a new age of discovery and commerce. By the end of the century, all planetary arcs will be opening up, as in the days when Diaz, Christopher Columbus, and Vasco da Gama undertook to conquer the world. Barbault says, "Can we ask for more, at the dawn of a new century?"

Other astrologers have come to similar conclusions using different graphs. Donn Forrest, a New Zealand astrologer, keeps a chart on the wall of his office. He placed the years going across the top, and the signs of the zodiac down one side, and plotted the motions of the outer planets, Jupiter through Pluto, in a different color.

"It's quite fascinating to see the little groupings that turn up," said Forrest. "And when you start looking back at what was going on when those groupings were there, and looking ahead to see what's likely to happen when they come up again, well . . . the period of 1982-1984, over about an

18-month period we get the same configuration that occurred when Viet Nam was on, it was there when the Second World War was on, it was there when the First World War was on, and it was there when the Boer War was going on, back at the turn of the century. This same little configuration was turning up . . . and in the 82-84 period, it's very tight, runs over a period of only 18 months, and the way the configuration comes up this time, definitely atomics will be involved."

Ever the optimist, Forrest continued: "But then from 1987 to 1997 we have a configuration that turns up very rarely. There's a configuration there which occurred last time in the 16th century, when the European world had an economic collapse. And looking at the way things are going around the world, this is quite a logical thing to see happening. Financial situations and money factors can change completely. The whole way of life can change over."

The differences in the dates which Forrest gives compared to those which Barbault presents are the results of their methods. Forrest's calculations include the signs of the zodiac, whereas Barbault's methods do not depend upon the zodiac at all. Nevertheless, they have both come to similar conclusions and timing. Those astrologers who are still using the zodiac express even more concern about the 1990s than the 1980s. Just as Marc Edmund Jones predicted that the entrance of Neptune into Libra in 1942 would drastically alter the course of history, the entrance of Pluto into Scorpio in 1984 also promises some important developments, quite possibly in the way of a totally new energy source. By the end of the decade, Saturn, Uranus, and Neptune conjoin in Capricorn. Uranus and Neptune remain there until 1998. These are some of the symbols behind Frater Albertus's suggestion that the end of this century will witness forceful efforts toward a world federation, in an attempt to deal with the world's economic problems.

Of course, you don't believe a word of this. I mean, this is *astrology*, and everyone knows it's all nonsense! That's why your eyes have probably been glued to the book for the past few pages. You couldn't restrain yourself — you just *had* to have a prediction or two.

But it's not only astrologers who have concerned themselves with predictions. The late Professor Raymond Wheeler of the University of Kansas undertook a study of wars since 600 B.C. When the Foundation for the Study of Cycles analyzed his data in 1950, they were able to isolate four cycles of war, with periods ranging from 142 to 11.2 years.[197] The combined cycle closely followed the actual pattern of international conflicts up to the present — and the next major peak was projected for 1982.

Surveying much of the work which scientists have undertaken on cycles and possible correlations with planetary events, Bernard Fremerman writes in the foundation's journal, *Cycles:* "Over the years, man has shown an inclination to disbelieve new scientific evidence which later proves to have tremendous influence on the sum of human knowledge. . . . I believe that civilization is on the verge of another major breakthrough in human knowledge, whose effect could be as profound as any heretofore seen." Fremerman then outlines the research into economic cycles alone. In 1801 Sir William Herschel suggested that there is a correlation between sunspot activity and the price of wheat. In 1878, a British economist found a relationship between economic enthusiasm and sunspot activity. In 1881, an English astronomer found a connection between solar radiation and business conditions. In 1959, Edgar Smith, a member of the Royal Economic Study, published *Common Stocks and Business Cycles,* which relates economics to planetary orbits. In 1965, Charles Collins wrote in the *Financial Analysts Journal* that the largest stock market declines since 1871 have coincided with or followed the year in which average sunspot numbers have reached fifty. Says Fremerman: "There are faint hints that some of the longer term economic cycles are trending downward at the present time, and may bottom out over the next 5 to 25 years. If those cycles represent reality, they might well foretell major world-wide economic and social upheavals."

Some cycle researchers believe that the predictions of economic and social upheavals in the near future will be fulfilled. And some are convinced there is nothing we can do about it. As Fremerman puts it:

Preliminary long-term cycle analysis indicates that there is a good probability that we have at the most five or six years before severe world-wide economic recession sets in. The second area of potential catastrophe is the possibility of major international war, also indicated by long-term cycle studies, with a probable occurrence in the early 1980's. . . . It is imperative that immediate consideration be given to undertake careful scientific studies to either confirm or deny the reality of regular periodic cycles in war and economics . . . it is my belief that we are on the verge of becoming aware of the causation. If we can unscramble some of these mysteries, we might be able to ward off or at least limit the destructive effects.

Astrologers have been saying as much. But no one has been listening.

Postscript

As I mentioned at the outset, the many papers and studies which have confirmed one or another aspect of cosmic influences demand a volume (at least) to themselves. There are far more than most people even imagine. They are all hints which appear weak in isolation, but which, when taken together, suggest a larger picture which neither cycle researchers nor astrologers understand. It is clear that in many fields, individuals have been discouraged, silenced, and held back from investigating possible correlations between earthly events and celestial phenomena, simply because it smacks of astrology — and everyone just *knows* astrology can't be true. As Fremerman showed, and as my research confirms, there is a growing number of researchers in many fields who are slowly realizing that the keys to many of the mysteries they study lie in the cyclical behavior of the planets. At some point, this awareness will reach a critical balance, and people will no longer be embarrassed to talk about it. Then, when we have finally begun to accept the fact that we live in a cosmic ecology — a cosmecology — we may discover how and why these celestial and terrestrial phenomena are related. The key point lies in the direction of ecology — the study of living systems. As genetic engineering and the biological revolution take over, we will be forced to accept the concept of organic growth in our civilization and in ourselves. The butterfly may yet emerge from the chrysalis.

It is quite true that much of what appears in the guise of astrology is sheer nonsense. It is equally true that an ignorant public perpetuates this nonsense despite the best efforts of serious astrologers and fanatical debunkers. It is true that the majority of astrologers are quite naive and ignorant of their field, and that astrology still has to catch up with even nineteenth-century developments in science. One could not expect otherwise from a field which has been mocked time and again, which no university in the world admits as a valid field of study even in terms of its history alone, a field which has been "deliberately buried," just as the monolith in Stanley Kubrick's *2001* was described, awaiting the day when new minds would be willing to ask new questions and receive new answers.

The truth about astrology is that it is a fascinating field on the verge of an awakening. It is full of mystery, cultural history, mythology, symbolism, the struggle toward modern science and beyond, and all sorts of characters from the wise to the most conniving opportunist. The truth about astrology is that neither its rabid critics nor its ardent adherents understand what they're talking about. And due to the conspiracy of silence which surrounds important developments in this field, the public has no way of knowing about the situation.

The indications are that a new astrology is already being born, and that the public may now be ready to hear about it. Two groups, especially, will resist these developments — the traditional astrologers and the establishment skeptics. Neither will examine the evidence from a creative point of view, seeking a new synthesis, because this would imply the death and transfiguration of their old world-view. To both groups, my heartfelt condolences.

People sometimes ask me if I am "an astrologer," or would I read their horoscope? The answer is No. I find reading horoscopes *boring*, although I can do it. For me, as a journalist, the real fun comes from covering this field as it develops, and in poking through old astrology books, looking for clues to the history of this neglected facet of our heritage. My role is that of an astrology critic — like a movie critic — who attempts to point out and assess current developments.

Astrology is as vast and complicated as any specialty. I only hope I have managed to pass along an impression of its inner workings, its rich heritage, and its modern condition, without burdening readers unnecessarily. Many interesting stories, leading personalities, and documents have gone unmentioned due to lack of space. It is to be hoped that there will be other occasions for these, as the cycles unfold.

There are no final answers. Most of us are satisfied when a puzzle has been explained, but we are *gratified* when a deeper and greater mystery has been revealed to us in the process.

Toronto, July 1, 1980

Enchantment can only be sustained in those who have it, or regained by those who have lost it, through conceptual inspiration. Nothing could be more exciting than the dawning awareness of the discovery of the presence of another of the eloquently significant eternal reliabilities of Universe.

Buckminster Fuller, Synergetics *204.02*

Appendix A

Basic Books, Journals, and Organizations

Textbooks

Your local specialty bookshop will have a selection, but two widely available, inexpensive paperbacks will serve as an introduction to traditional astrology.

Jones, Marc Edmund. *How To Learn Astrology* (Boulder: Shambhala, 1977). Distributed by Random House in Canada and the U.S.

Mayo, Jeff. *Astrology* (London: Hodder and Stoughton, 1964).

Astrological Reference Books

The American Ephemeris, in various editions covering different time periods. Recommended as most accurate and economical astrological ephemeris.

Devore, Nicholas. *Encyclopedia of Astrology,* Crown Publishers. With additional articles by Charles Jayne. A fascinating and useful introduction to the broad spectrum of astrological tradition.

Dean, Geoffrey et al. *Recent Advances in Natal Astrology, 1900-1976,* distributed by Para Research. First academic review and analysis of this century's astrological literature, replete with references and bibliographical information. Controversial and challenging text, not recommended for casual readers. (Geoffrey Dean is no relation to the author of *The Astrology Game.*)

Journals

Phenomena: The News Journal of Cosmic Influence Research.
Aimed at readers with an active interest in statistical tests of
astrology, its sociology and history, this irregular journal
monitors over 5,000 journals and magazines in a broad spectrum of fields, providing referenced articles on relevant
discoveries and experimental results. Each issue contains lists
of important articles in nearly all traditional astrology
journals, providing constant access to current astrological
writings. Box 6299, Toronto M5W 1P7, Canada.

The Zetetic Scholar. Edited by Prof. Marcello Truzzi after his
departure from the CSICOP, this journal examines the
sociology of occult and paranormal movements and includes
bibliographies for a broad variety of fields. Scholarly and
open-minded. The Editor, *Zetetic Scholar*, Dept. of Sociology,
Eastern Michigan University, Ypsilanti, MI 48197, USA.

The Skeptical Inquirer. For hard-core skeptics and True Disbelievers. Box 29, Kensington Stn, Buffalo, NY 14215, USA.

Crawford Perspectives. Financial newsletter for investors. Not for
the general public. 250 East 77th St., NY, NY 10021, USA. Tel:
212-744-6973. $250 per annum, ten issues.

Astrological Organizations

American Federation of Astrologers. Largest astrology organization publishes a regular newsletter and holds a bi-annual
convention. Box 22040, Tempe, AZ 85282, USA.

Astrological Association. Largely British Commonwealth membership, publishes good journal and holds annual conferences. C/O Charles Harvey, 36 Tweey Rd., Bromley, Kent
BR1 3PP, U.K.

National Council for Geocosmic Research. Holds frequent conferences across U.S. National Council for Geocosmic
Research, C/O 180 N. Michigan Ave., Ste. 732, Chicago, IL
60601, USA.

Computer Services

AstroComputing Services, Box 16297, San Diego CA 92116, USA.
Tel: 714-297-5648.

Astro-Graphics Services, 217 Rock Harbor Rd., Orleans MA 02653,
USA. Tel: 617-255-0510

Astro*Carto*Graphy, Box 22293MD, San Francisco CA 94122,
USA

Appendix B

Bibliography of Publications by Drs. Michel and Françoise Gauquelin

Since it is not widely appreciated how much literature exists on the subject of planetary influences, a complete list of the Gauquelins' writings follows.

Gauquelin, M. (1955) *L'influence des astres, étude critique et expérimentale.* Editions du Dauphin, Paris, 349 p.

Gauquelin, M. (1956) "Influence des astres et Astrologie." *C.A.,* N°62 : 117-122.

Gauquelin, M. et Gauquelin F. (1957a) *Méthodes pour étudier la répartition des astres dans le mouvement diurne* (Préface de Jean Porte, Administrateur à l'I.N.S.E.E.), 112 p.

Gauquelin, M. (1957b) "Der Einfluss der Gestirne und die Statistik." *Zeitschr. f. Parapsychol. u. Grenzgeb. d. Psychol.* 1 (2/3) : 102-123.

Gauquelin, F. (1959c) "L'heure de la naissance." *Population,* 14 (4) : 683-702.

Gauquelin, M. (1959d) "Neue Untersuchungen uber den Einfluss der Gestirne." *Zeitschr. f. Paraspychol. u. Grenzgeb. d. Psychol.* 3 (1) : 10-29.

Gauquelin, M. (1959e) "Propos scientifiques." *C.A.,* N°80 : 119-124.

Gauquelin, F. (1960a) "Chronique des sciences de l'homme : l'heure de la naissance." *Le concours Médical,* I, 25 : 3241-3246 et II, 26 : 3371-3375.

Gauquelin, M. (1960b) *Les hommes et les astres* (Préface du Dr.

Hans Bender, professeur de psychologie à l'Université de Freiburg-im-Breisgau, Allemagne). Denoel, Paris, 268 p.

Gauquelin, M. (1961a) "Die Planetare Hereditat." *Zeitschr. f. Parapsychol. u. Grenzgeb. d. Psychol.*, 5 (2/3) : 168-193.

Gauquelin, M. (1961b) "La latitude zodiacale." *C.A.*, N°92 : 119-129.

Gauquelin, M. (1962a) "Existe-t-il une hérédité planétaire?" *Planète*, 6 : 77-83.

Gauquelin, M. (1962b) "L'hérédité astrale." *C.A.* N°98 : 135-143.

Gauquelin, M. Gauquelin, F. (1963a) *La psychologie au XX° siècle.* Editions Sociales Françaises, Paris, 208 p.

Gauquelin, M. (1963b) "Les astres ont-ils changé le cours de l'histoire?" *Historia*, 203 : 518-525.

Gauquelin, M. (1964) "Le ciel de naissance des enfants morts en bas âge, étude statistique." *C.A.*, N°111 : 189-192.

Gauquelin, M. (1965) "L'Astrologie devant la science." Préface par Aimé Michel, *Planète*, Paris, 255 p.

Gauquelin, M. et Gauquelin, F. (1965) "L'effet planétaire d'hérédité et le magnétisme terrestre." Compte-rendu préliminaire.

Gauquelin, M. (1966a) "Effets biologiques des champs magnétiques." *Année Biologique*, 5 (11-12) : 595-611.

Gauquelin, M. (1966b) *L'hérédité planétaire* (Préface du prof. G. Piccardi, Directeur de l'Institut de physico-chimie de l'Université de Florence). Denoel, Paris, 230 p.

Gauquelin, M. (1966c) "Der planetarische Hereditatseffekt und der irdische Magnetismus." *Zeitschr. f. Parapsychol. u. Grenzgeb. d. Psychol.*, 9 : 69-84.

Gauquelin, M. (1966d) "Les sectes, les pseudo-sciences et les para-croyances en France aujourd'hui." *Planète*, 26 : 11-123.

Gauquelin, M. (1966e) "Las sectas, seudociencias y creencias paralelas en la Francia de hoy." *Planeta*, 12 : 137-150.

Gauquelin, M. (1966f) "Effet possible de la position natale diurne de certaines planètes sur les réponses données à un questionnaire vocationnel." *C.A.*, N°121 : 73-81.

Gauquelin, M. et Gauquelin, F. (1967a) "A possible Hereditary Effect on Time of Birth in Relation to the diurnal movement of the Moon and the Nearest Planets; its Relationship with Geomagnetic Activity." Proc. Fourth Internat. Biometeorol. Congress. *International Journal of Biometeorology*, 11 (suppl.) : 341.

Gauquelin, M. (1967b) *La santé et les conditions atmosphériques.* Hachette, Paris, 254 p.

Gauquelin, M. (1967c) *The Cosmic Clocks* (Préface de Frank A. Brown, prof. de biologie, Northwestern University, Evanston,

U.S.A.) Henry Regnery Company, Chicago, U.S.A., 250 p. (paperback edition : Avon books, New York 1969).

Gauquelin, M. et Gauquelin, F. (1967d) "Un effet héréditaire possible au moment de la naissance en relation avec certains facteurs de l'ambiance cosmique." Relazioni del XIV° Convegno della Salute, Ferrara, 27-28 Maggio 1967 : 69-80.

Gauquelin, M. et Gauquelin, F. (1967e) "A possible effect of subtle timing Synchronizers during the biological phenomena of birth." Society for Biological Rhythm; Ninth Intern. Conf. Wiesbaden, April 6-8.

Gauquelin, M. (1967f) "Note sur le rythme journalier du début des douleurs de l'accouchement." Gyn. Obst. (Paris), 66 (2) : 229-236.

Gauquelin, M. et Gauquelin, F. (1967g) "Un effetto ereditario possibile al momento della nascita in relazione con certi fattori dell'ambiente cosmico." Minerva Medica, 58 (35) : 1658.

Gauquelin, M. (1967h) "Note sur la distribution mois par mois du poids des enfants à la naissance." Population, N°3, 1967 : 544-552.

Gauquelin, M. (1967i) "Tempérament et Caractères (in La psychologie de A à Z) C.E.P.L. — Denoel, Paris : 458-498.

Gauquelin, F. (1968a) "Le cycle annuel de reproduction du macaque Macaca irus." Bulletin Biologique, 102 (2) : 261-270.

Gauquelin, M. (1968b) "L'astrologue paré de l'ordinateur; une expérience de Science et Vie." Science et Vie (Août), N°611, t. CXIV : 80-89.

Gauquelin, M. et Gauquelin, F. (1968c) "A possible effect of subtle timing synchronizers during the biological phenomena of birth." Cycles, 19 (1) : 12-16.

Gauquelin, M. (1968d) "Genetic sensitivity at the time of birth." The Astr. Mag., 57 (1) : 37-40.

Gauquelin, M. et Gauquelin, F. (1968e) "Incidence des conditions de l'accouchement et rôle possible du foetus à terme sur l'effet planétaire d'hérédité." Relazioni del XV° Convegno della Salute, Ferrara, 25-26 Maggio 1968 : 179-187.

Gauquelin, M. (1968f) "Une sensibilité spécifique, d'origine héréditaire, à des facteurs exogènes en relation avec le moment de la naissance; son importance en psychologie. 2nd Symposium International sur les relations entre phénomènes solaires et terrestres en chimie physique et dans les sciences de la vie." 1-7 sept. 1968. Université de Bruxelles.

Gauquelin, F. (1968g) "L'élimination des artefacts dans le problème des relations entre phénomènes solaires et terrestres dans les sciences de la vie. Exemple du rythme nycthéméral des naissances." 1-7 sept. 1968. Université de Bruxelles.

Gauquelin, M. et Gauquelin, F. (1968h) "Incidenza delle condizioni di parto e ruolo possibile del feto a termine sull'effetto planetario di eredità." *Minerva Medica*, 59 (36) : 2143-2144.

Gauquelin, M. (1968i) "L'effet planétaire d'hérédité dans les secteurs du coucher et de la culmination inférieure." *C.A.*, N°134 : 459-473.

Gauquelin, M. (1968j) "L'effet planétaire d'hérédité et le magnétisme terrestre." *C.A.*, N°134 : 459-473.

Gauquelin, M. (1968k) *La nueva ciencia de la salud.* Brugera, Barcelona, Espana, 237 p.

Gauquelin, M. (1968l) "L'astrologie et l'homme moderne." (In: *Le Réel et l'Iréel*). *Le Centurion*, Paris : 73-89.

Gauquelin, M. (1968m) "L'effet planétaire d'hérédité en fonction de la distance de Vénus et de Mars à la Terre." *C.A.*, N°136 : 561-569.

Gauquelin, M. (1969a) *The Cosmic Clocks* (British edition), Peter Owen, London, 250 p.

Gauquelin, M. (1969b) *The Scientific Basis of Astrology : Myth or Reality?* Stein and Day, New York, 255 p. (paperback edition : 1970).

Gauquelin, M. (1969c) "Essai de mise en évidence et de description d'une composante tempéramentale dans l'effet planétaire d'hérédité." Relazioni del XVI° Convegno della Salute, Ferrara, 24-25 Maggio 1969 : 221-231.

Gauquelin, F. (1969d) "Contribution à l'étude de certains facteurs de l'ambiance qui pourraient agir sur le rythme nycthéméral des naissances." Relazioni del XVI° Convegno della Salute, Ferrara, 24-25 Maggio 1969 (à paraître), 8 p.

Gauquelin, M. et Gauquelin, F. (1969e) "Recent observations about a possible hereditary effect and its relationships with some extraterrestrial factors." Proc. Fifth International Biometeorological Congress, Montreux, Switzerland, *Intern. J. Biometeor.* 13 (suppl.) : 145.

Gauquelin, M. (1969f) "Saggio di evidenziazione di una componente temperamentale nell'effetto planetario dell'eredità." *Minerva Medica*, 60 (31) : 1499-1500.

Gauquelin, M. (1969g) *Songes et Mensonges de l'Astrologie*, Hachette, Paris, 250 p.

Gauquelin, M. (1969h) "Un cas particulier de l'effet planétaire d'hérédité." *C.A.*, N°141 : 136-138.

Gauquelin, M. (1969i) "Nombre relatif journalier des taches solaires et l'effet planétaire d'hérédité." *C.A.*, N°143 : 259-262.

Gauquelin, M. (1969j) "Les rythmes." *Science et Vie*, 66, N°622 : 56-67

Gauquelin, M (1969k) "La lune rend-elle lunatique?" *Science et Vie*, 66, N°623 : 53-57.

Gauquelin, M. (1970a) "Image caractérielle des qualités favorables à la réussité professionnelle." *La caractérologie*, 11 : 49-63.

Gauquelin, M. (1970b) *Connaître les Autres*, C.E.P.L. — Denoel, Paris, 250 p.

Gauquelin, M. (1970c) "Le Soleil commande aussi le corps humain." *Science et Vie*, 67, N°628 : 48-54.

Gauquelin, M. (1970d) "Comment un enfant nait et pourquoi au 9ième mois." *Science et Vie*, 68, N°635, 60-69.

Gauquelin, M. et Gauquelin, F. (1970e) "Birth and Planetary Data Gathered since 1949." Laboratoire d'étude des relations entre rythmes cosmiques et psychophysiologiques, Paris. Series A, Professional notabilities : vol. 1, Sports Champions; vol. 2, Men of Science; vol. 3, Military Men; vol. 4, Painters and Musicians; vol. 5, Actors and Politicians; vol. 6, Writers and Journalists.
Series B, Hereditary Experiment: vol. 1, births 1 to 5011; vol. 2, 5012 to 9838; vol. 3, 9847 to 13740; vol. 4, 13741 to 17499; vol. 5, 17500 to 21243; vol. 6, 21244 to 24949.

Gauquelin, M. (1970f) *Los relojes cosmicos*. Plaza y Janes, Barcelona (Espana), 330 p.

Gauquelin, M. (1970g) "Metronom, upravlia iushtshii jizniu. Nauka i jizn." *Science et Vie*, Moskva SSSR 12 : 87-90.

Gauquelin, M. (1970h) *Les Horloges Cosmiques*. Denoel, Paris, 268 p.

Gauquelin, M. (1970i) *Astrology and Science*, Peter Davies, London, 255 p. (paperback edition, Mayflower books, London 1972).

Gauquelin, M. (1970j) *La Astrologia ante la ciencia*. Plaza y Janes, Barcelona (Espana), 255 p.

Gauquelin, F. (1971a) "Terrestrial Modulation of the Daily Cycle of Birth." *J. Interdisciplinary Cycle Research*, 2, 2 : 211-217.

Gauquelin, M. (1971b) "Methodological Model analysing possible extraterrestrial Effects on the daily Cycle of Birth." *J. Interdisciplinary Cycle Research*, 2, 2 : 219-225.

Gauquelin, M. (1971c) "Genetic Sensitivity to external Factors during the daily Cycle of the Deliveries." *J. Interdisciplinary Cycle Research*, 2, 2 : 227-232.

Gauquelin, M. (1971d) *How Atmospheric Conditions affect your Health*. Stein and Day, New York, 188 p.

Gauquelin, M. (1971e) "Het Dossier van de Astrologie, Bres-planète." *Den Haag* (Holland), 27 : 61-84.

Gauquelin, M. (1971f) "Die Beziehung zwischen der Geburtszeit und den Tagesbewegungen des Mondes und der nahen Planeten." *Kosmobiologie*, 42 : 73-80.

Gauquelin, M., De Massard, E. (1971g) "Analyse logique et psychosociologique de Madame Soleil." *Science et Vie*, 69, N°644 : 76-83.

Gauquelin, M. (1971h) "Etude Comparative de deux séries d'observations." *C.A.*, N°154 : 197-203.

Gauquelin, M. (1971i) "Qu'est-ce qui fait gagner les champions?" *Psychologie*, 18 : 25-30.

Gauquelin, M. (1970k) "The Astrologer Electrified." *The Aquarian Agent*, Vol. 1, N°6, : 3-10.

Gauquelin, M. (1972a) *Profession - Heredity, Results of Series A & B.* Laboratoire d'Etude des Relations entre Rythmes Cosmiques et Psychophysiologiques, Paris, 211 pp.

Gauquelin, M. (1972b) "Planeten und Charakterzuge." *Z. f. Parapsychol. u. Grenzgebiete der Psychologie*, 14, 1 : 12-36.

Gauquelin, F. (1972c) "Possible Planetary Effect in Heredity: Refutation of former demographical and astronomical objections." *J. Interdisciplin. Cycle Res.*, 3 (3/4) : 373-380.

Gauquelin, M. (1972d) "Possible Planetary Effect at the Time of Birth of Successful Professionals; an experimental control." *J. Interdisciplin. Cycle Res.*, 3 (3/4) : 381-389.

Gauquelin, M., Sadoul, J. (1972e) *L'Astrologie hier et aujourd' hui.* Editions Retz, Paris, 255 pp.

Gauquelin, M. (1972f) "Psychologie individuelle et action." (in: *Les théories de l'action*), C.E.P.L. — Hachette, Paris.

Gauquelin, M. (1973a) *Cosmic Influences on Human Behavior.* (Foreword by J. Allen Hynek, Chairman, Department of Astronomy, Northwestern University), Stein & Day, New York, 287 pp.

Gauquelin, M. (1973b) *Die Uhren des Kosmos gehen anders,* Scherz, Bern-Munchen-Wien, 220 pp. (paperback edition by Ullstein Buch, Berlin, 1975)

Gauquelin, M. (1973c) *Le Dossier des Influences Cosmiques.* Denoel, Paris, 283 pp. (paperback edition by J'ai Lu, Paris, 1974).

Gauquelin, M., Gauquelin, F. (1973d) *The Mars Temperament and Sports Champions.* Lab. ét. Relations entre Rythmes Cosmiques et Psychophysiologiques. Paris, 388 pp.

Gauquelin, M., Gauquelin, F. (1973e) *Vingt Tests pour se Connaître.* Editions Retz, Paris, 252 pp.

Gauquelin, M. (1973f) *Rythmes biologiques, Rythmes cosmiques.* Editions Marabout Université, Verviers, Belgique, 256 pp.

Gauquelin, M. (1973g) *Wetter-Fuhlig. Einfluss des Klima auf die Gesundheit.* Albert Muller Verlag, Zurich-Stuttgart-Wien, 240 pp. (paperback edition by Doldmann Sachbucher, 1975).

Gauquelin, M. (1973h) "La Lune et le Soleil influencent-ils notre Comportement?" *Psychologie,* N°44 : 7-12.

Gauquelin, M. (1974a) "L'Astrologie devant la Science." *Psychologie,* N°50 : 55-64.

Gauquelin, M. (1974b) "Dieti Solntsa" (in Russian). *Literaturnaya Gazeta,* N°6, February 6, Moscow, SSSR.

Gauquelin, M. (1974c) *Il Dossier delle Influenze Cosmiche.* Astrolabio editore, Roma, 250 pp.

Gauquelin, M., Gauquelin, F. (1974d) *The Saturn Temperament and Men of Science.* Lab. Et. Relations entre Rythmes Cosmiques et Psychophysiologiques, Paris, 395 pp.

Gauquelin, M., Gauquelin, F. (1974e) *The Jupiter Temperament and Actors.* Lab. Et. Relations entre Rythmes Cosmiques et Psychophysiologiques, Paris, 405 pp.

Gauquelin, M. (1974f) *Cosmic Influences on Human Behavior* (English Edition) Garnstone Press, London (paperback edition by Futura Publications, London, 1976)

Gauquelin, M. (1974g) *La Cosmo-Psychologie.* Editions Retz, Paris, 256 pp.

Gauquelin, F., Lampe, H., Paruta, R. (1975a) "Constant Intensity of the Planetary Effect Throughout the 24 Solar Birth Hours." *J. Interdiscipl. Cycle Res.,* 6 (1) : 53-59.

Gauquelin, M., Deloche, R-M., Tanon, F. (1975b) "Temperamental Significance of the Planetary Effect in Heredity. Methodology and Results." *J. Interdiscipl. Cycle Res.,* 6 (1) : 60-70.

Gauquelin, M., Gauquelin, F. (1975c) "Review of Studies in the USSR on the Possible Biological Effects of Solar Activity." *J. Interdiscipl. Cycle Res.,* 6 (3) : 249-252.

Gauquelin, M., Sadoul, J. (1975d) *La Astrologia Ayer y Hoy.* Plaza y Janes, Barcelona, Spain, 250 pp.

Gauquelin, M. (1975e) "Concerning the Possible Influence of Planets on Human Beings." *Leonardo,* 8 : 222-231.

Gauquelin, M. (1975f) "Mars et le Sport 'Agressif': une Statistique Etrange." *Science et Vie,* N°690 : 54-56.

Gauquelin, M. (1975g) "Spheres of Influences." *Psychology Today,* N°7 : 20-27.

Gauquelin, M. (1976a) *Ritmi Biologici, Ritmi Cosmici.* Faenza editrice, Italy, 230 pp.

Gauquelin, M. (1976b) "On Astrology and Modern Science." *Leonardo,* 9 : 259.

Gauquelin, M. (1976c) "The Influence of Planets on Human Beings: Facts versus Fiction." *The Humanist* (Jan/Feb.) : 29-31.

Gauquelin, M. (1976d) "The Influence of Planets on Human Beings" (cont.). *The Humanist* (March/April) : 53.

Gauquelin, M., Gauquelin, F. (1976e) "The Truth about the Mars Effect on Sports Champions." *The Humanist* (July/ Aug.) : 44-45.

Abell, G-O. & A-A., Gauquelin, M. & F. (1976f) "A Test of the Gauquelin 'Mars Effect'. *The Humanist* (Sept/Oct) : 40-45.

Gauquelin, M., Gauquelin, F. (1976g) "The Planetary Factors in Personality." Lab. Et. Rythmes Cosmiques et Psychophysiologiques, Paris, 23 pp.

Gauquelin, M., Gauquelin, F. (1977a) "Replication of the Planetary Effect in Heredity. Lab. Et. Relations entre Rythmes Cosmiques et Psychophysiologiques, Paris, 72 pp.

Gauquelin, M., Gauquelin, F. (1977b) "The Moon Temperament and Writers." Lab. Et. Relations entre Rythmes Cosmiques et Psychophysiologiques, Paris, 252 pp.

Gauquelin, M., Gauquelin, F. (1977c) "The Zelen Test of the Mars Effect." *The Humanist* (Nov/Dec.) : 30-35.

Gauquelin, F. (1977d) "A Possible Correlation between the Lunar Day and some Factors of the Personality." *J. Interdiscipl. Cycle Res.*, 8 (3/4) : 291-292.

Gauquelin, M. (1977e) "The Planetary Effect in Heredity as a Reproducible Fact. Results of Two Recent Experiments on 36,000 Deliveries." *J. Interdiscipl. Cycle Res.*, 8 (3/4) : 291-292.

Gauquelin, M. (1977f) "Planets, Career & Personality. The Dartington Society: new Themes for Education annual Conderence." (UK).

Gauquelin, M. (1977g) "A Possible Mars Effect at the Time of Birth of Superior Athletes." Proceedings IV Intern. Congress. Soc. Sport Psychology, Prague (Czechoslovaquia).

Gauquelin, F. (1977h) "The Mars Factor in Personality among Sports Champions." Proceedings IV Intern. Congress. Soc. Sport Psychology, Prague (Czechoslovaquia).

Gauquelin, M., Gauquelin, F. (1978a) "Statistical Tests of Zodiacal Influences; Book 1: Profession & Heredity." Lab. Et. Relations entre Rythmes Cosmiques et Psychophysiologiques, Paris, 62 pp.

Gauquelin, M., Gauquelin, F. (1978b) "The Venus Temperament, a Tentative Description. Lab. Et. Relations entre Rythmes Cosmiques et Psychophysiologiques, Paris, 26 pp.

Gauquelin, M., Gauquelin, F. (1978c) "The Planetary Factors in Personality; their Permanence through Four Professional

Groups." Lab. Et. Relations entre Rythmes Cosmiques et Psychophysiologiques, Paris, 32 pp.

Gauquelin, M., Gauquelin, F. (1978d) "Diurnal Positions of Sun, Mercury, Uranus, Neptune, Pluto (Profession — Heredity)." Lab. Et. Relations entre Rythmes Cosmiques et Psychophysiologiques, Paris, 40 pp.

Gauquelin, M. (1978f): *Cosmic Influences on Human Behavior* (new revised edition). New York, A.S.I. Pub., 319 pp.

Gauquelin, M. (1978g): "Critical Review of Krafft and Van Deusen's books." *The Skeptical Inquirer*, 2(2), Spring/Summer 1978, 118-128.

Gauquelin, M. (1978h): "Getting the facts straight: The Committee and the Mars effect." *Phenomena* 2.2, Mar.-Apr. 1978, 7-8.

Gauquelin, M. (1978i): "Reply to Dennis Rawlins." *The Skeptical Inquirer*, 3(2) Winter 1978, 70-72.

Gauquelin, M and F., and S. Eysenck (University of London) (1979a): "Personality and Position of Planets at Birth, An Empirical Study." *Brit. J. Soc. and Clin. Psych.*, 18, 1979, 71-75.

Gauquelin, M. (1979b): *The Mars effect and Sports Champions, A New Replication.* Laboratoire d'etude des relations, etc., Paris.

Gauquelin, M and F. (1979c): "Star U.S. sportsmen display the Mars effect, A comment on the Kurtz-Zelen-Abell experiment." *The Skeptical Inquirer*, 4(2), Winter 1979-80, 31-43.

Gauquelin, M. (1979d): *Dreams and Illusions of Astrology.* Buffalo, NY, Prometheus Books.

Gauquelin, M. & F., Eysenck, S. (University of London): Personality and Position of the Planets at Birth. An empirical Study. The British Journal of Social &: Clinical Psychology (to be published in 1978).

Gauquelin, M. (1978f) Cosmic Influences on Human Behavior (new revised edition). A.S.I. Publ. New-York, 319 pp.

Gauquelin, M. (1978g) Critical Review of Krafft & Van Deusen's books. *The Skeptical Inquirer*, Spring-Summer.

Gauquelin, M. (1978h) Reply to Dennis Rawlins. *The Skeptical Inquirer*, (Spring-Summer or Fall-Winter issue).

Gauquelin, F. (1980a): *Traditional Symbolism in Astrology and the Character Traits Method.* Laboratoire d'etude des relations, etc., Paris.

Gauquelin, M. (1980b): "The "Mars effect": A Response from M. Gauquelin." *The Skeptical Inquirer*, 4(4), Summer 1980, 58-82.

Gauquelin, M. (1980c): *The Sphere of Destiny.* London, Dent, 250 pp.

Notes

Only the first reference to a particular author or source has been given a footnote number. To identify the origin of subsequent quotations, the reader should refer back to the first mention of the author's name in the text.

One: Who's There?

1. "Interview with a sceptic: Prof. Paul Kurtz," *Phenomena* 2.2, Mar.-Apr. 1978, 14-16.
2. CP, Sept. 22, 1970.
3. Darrach, Henry B., "Up Horoscope!", *Life*, Feb. 22, 1960, 97-106.
4. Even according to traditional astrology, that astrologer would have been well advised to consider the position of Venus as well, since that planet is traditionally connected with the tangible quality of possessions. Venus also "rules" Taurus, a sign connected with the second house, and its faster motion would have allowed the astrologer to time his actions more accurately than Jupiter's slow motion would have allowed. Darrach picked up a little astrology in his research, but not enough.
5. Clausen, Oliver, "Astrology: An ancient cult on a billion-dollar binge," *Globe Magazine*, Nov. 25, 1967, 7-9.
6. "Astrology: Fad and Phenomenon," *Time*, Mar. 21, 1969, 65-70.
7. Gauquelin, Michel, *Dreams and Illusions of Astrology* (Buffalo: Prometheus Books, 1979), p. 9.
8. Gauquelin, pp. 13-14.

9. *France Soir,* Jan. 24, 1963. Summarized and discussed in: Gauquelin, op. cit.; Tiryakian (see below); De France et al. "Le retour des astrologues," *Cahiers de Club du Nouvel Observateur* (Paris: 1971).

9a. Gauquelin, p. 13, from Fuffa, J.-C., "Les Français et l'astrologie," *Ires Marketing,* May 22, 1968.

10. Fullam, Francis, "Popular 'belief' in Astrology: Public opinion polls," *Phenomena* 2.5, Sep.-Oct. 1978, 15.

11. Maitre, Jacques, "The Consumption of Astrology in Contemporary Society," *Diogenes,* 53 (1966), 82-98.

12. Tiryakian, Edward, "Toward the Sociology of Esoteric Culture," *Amer. J. Soc.,* 78(3), 1972, 491-512.

13. Benz, Ernst, *Les sources mystiques de la philosophie romantique allemande,* (Paris: 1968). Discussed by Tiryakian, above.

14. Bakan, David, *Sigmund Freud and the Jewish Mystical Tradition,* (Van Nostrand Reinhold, 1958). Discussed by Tiryakian, above.

15. Schoch, Russell, "The Myth of Sigmund Freud," *Science 80,* Jan.-Feb. 1980, 22-27.

16. Truzzi, Marcello, "Towards a Sociology of the Occult: Notes on Modern Witchcraft," in Zaretsky and Leone, *Religious Movements in Contemporary America* (Princeton: Princeton University Press, 1974).

17. Truzzi, Marcello, "The Occult Revival as Popular Culture: Some Random Observations on the Old and the Nouveau Witch," *Soc. Quart.* 13, Winter 1972, 16-36. See also his "Astrology as Popular Culture," *J. Popular Culture* 8(4), 1975, 906-911.

18. *Toronto Star,* 21 Mar. 1978, p. 1.

19. Wagner and Monnet, "Attitudes of College Professors Toward ESP," *Zetetic Scholar,* 5, 1979, 7-15.

20. Goodstein, L.D. and Brazis, K.L., "Psychology of Scientists: XXX. Credibility of psychologists: an empirical study," *Psychological Reports,* 27, 1970, 835-838.

21. Weingarten, Henry, *Astrology '79,* 5(9), Winter 1979, 4.

22. Editorial history of *Horoscope:* Philip Sandoval, 10/35 - 5/37; Grant Lewi, 6/37 - 7/46; Edward Wagner, 8/46 - 5/73; Julia Wagner, 6/73 - present.

23. Chanakya, "News and Views," *The Astrological Magazine,* 68(12), Dec. 1979.

24. Steiner, George, "Age of Unreason: Why the West Seeks Solace in the Saucer in the Sky," *The Globe and Mail,* Dec. 28, 1977, 7.

25.   Louaisel, Patrice, survey published in *Astrolabe*, 1(1), 1975, 11-15.

Two: The True Believers

26.   Gauquelin, *Dreams and Illusions of Astrology*, p. 11.
27.   *Toronto Star*, Sept. 22, 1975, ex. *Los Angeles Times*.
28.   Dean, Malcolm, "Astrology: The Cosmic Conspiracy," *Ideas*, CBC-FM, Jan. 4, 1979.
29.   Bok, Bart J, "A Critical Look at Astrology," *The Humanist*, Sep.-Oct. 1975, 6-9.
30.   Fuller, Buckminster, *Synergetics*, 502. 10-11, (New York: Macmillan, 1975).
31.   Fuller, p. xxxi.
32.   Dean, *Ideas*, Jan. 1, 1979.
33.   *Science News*, 117, 8 March 1980, 148.
34.   Hoyle, Fred and Wickramasinghe, N.C., "Primitive grain clumps and organic compounds in carbonaceous chondrites," *Nature*, 264, 4 Nov. 1976, 45-46. Also see *Nature*, 268, 610-613; 269, 674-676; 270, 701-703.
35.   Hoyle, Fred and Wickramasinghe, N.C., *New Scientist*, 17 Nov. 1977, 402-404.
36.   *New Scientist*, 1 Dec. 1977, p. 593.
37.   Butler, E.J. and Hoyle, Fred, "On the effects of a sudden change in the albedo of the Earth," *Astrophysics and Space Science* 60, 1979, 505-511.
38.   Hoyle, Fred and Wickramasinghe, N.C., "Influenza from space?" *New Scientist*, 28 Sept. 1978, 946-948.
39.   *Comet News Service*, 78-4, p. 2, MacDonnell Planetarium, St. Louis, Mo. 63110.
40.   Tyrrell, D.A.J., "Unorthodox epidemiology," *Nature*, 282, 8 Nov. 1979, 158.
41.   Whipple, Fred, "Origin of the Solar System," *Nature*, 278, 26 April 1979, 819.
42.   Dixon, Bernard, *Omni*, May 1980, 20.
43.   Watson, Lyall, *Lifetide* (New York: Simon and Schuster, 1979).
44.   The search for a "unified field theory" which does not take consciousness into account is akin to the search for the Holy Grail as a physical treasure hidden somewhere on Earth. Both quests failed to obtain a balanced point of view.
45.   Fritjof, Capra, *The Tao of Physics* (Boulder: Shambhala, 1975).
46.   Howe, Ellic, *Urania's Children* (London: Kimber & Co., 1967), p. 4.

47. The Hamburg School is much in vogue amongst the more technical astrologers today, especially in the United States, where it is called "Uranian" astrology. It was founded by Alfred Witte (1878-1941) who developed a system of planetàry formulas based on angular arcs between planets, along with several hypothetical planets. See Chapter Eight.

48. Ratzan, Lee, "The Astrology of the Delivery Room," *The Humanist*, 25(6), Nov.-Dec. 1975, 27.

49. Mijangos, A.C., *Causas mecanicas en la produccion de los fenomenos geofisicos y de las manchas solares*, 2nd rev. ed. 1975, Government of Mexico.

50. Dror, Sadeh, and Wood, Kent, "Periodicity in Lunar Seismic Activity and Earthquakes," *J. Geophys. Res.*, 83(B3), 1245-1249.

51. From his article based on the book, *Saturday Review*, 10 Dec. 1977, 21.

52. d'Espagnat, Bernard, "The Quantum Theory and Reality," *Scientific American*, Nov. 1979, 158-181.

Three: Your Daily Fix

53. Snyder, C.R., "Why horoscopes are true: The effects of specificity on acceptance of astrological interpretations," *J. Clinical Psych.*, 30(4), Oct. 1974, 577-580.

54. Dean, Geoffrey et al., *Recent Advances in Natal Astrology, 1900-1976*, Analogic, 1977. Distributed by Para Research, USA.

55. Williamsen, James S., "Issues in Astropsychology - 1," *Cosmecology Bulletin*, 3, Dec. 1975, 1-13.

56. See Nolle, Richard, "Will the Aquarian Age bring the Day of Reckoning?", *Dell Horoscope*, July 1978, 34-38.

57. Browning, Norma Lee, *Omarr: Astrology and the Man* (New York: Doubleday, 1977).

58. Browning, p. 181.

59. See also Omarr's semi-autobiographical *My World of Astrology* (Los Angeles: Wilshire, 1965).

60. For a discussion, see Dean, Geoffrey et al, pp. 79-83.

Four: The Sign of Baloney

61. Pentecost, Martin, *Sex and the Stars* (Toronto: Kakabeka, 1973).

62. Dean, Malcolm, "Astrology: The Cosmic Conspiracy," *Ideas*, CBC-FM, Jan. 1, 1979.

63. Davis, T. Pat, *Sexual Assaults: Pre-identifying Those Vulnerable* (Florida: Davis Research Reports, 1978).

64. Rachleff, Owen S., *Sky Diamonds: The New Astrology* (New York: Hawthorn, 1973).

65. Rachleff, Owen S., *The Occult Conceit* (New York: Bell, 1977); *The Secrets of Superstitions: How They Help, How They Hurt* (New York: Doubleday, 1976).

66. van Deusen, Edmund, *Astrogenetics* (New York: Doubleday, 1976).

67. *Phenomena* 1.6, Sept. 1977, 8.

68. See Wright, Larry, "Biorhythms and Beyond, A New Alternative," *Phenomena* 1.8, Nov. 1977 through 2.5 Sept.-Oct. 1978.

Six: Archaeoastrology

69. Reprinted 1964, MIT Press, Cambridge, Mass.

70. Lockyer, in his time, had not located a temple oriented toward the traditional zero-point of the modern zodiac, the vernal equinox.

71. Thom, A., *Megalithic Sites in Britain* (Oxford, 1967).

72. Dean, Malcolm, "Astrology: The Cosmic Conspiracy," *Ideas*, CBC-FM, Jan. 2, 1979.

73. MacKie, Euan, *Science and Society in Prehistoric Britain* (New York: St. Martin's Press, 1977).

74. Michell, John, *A Little History of Astro-archaeology: Stages in the Transformation of a Heresy* (London: Thames and Hudson, 1977).

75. See also Michell, John, *The View Over Atlantis* (London: Sago Press, 1969).

76. Tompkins, Peter, *Secrets of the Great Pyramid* (New York: Harper and Row, 1971).

77. Dean, Malcolm, "Ancient Egypt: The Pyramids," *Ideas*, CBC-FM, Mar. 16, 1977.

78. Marshack, Alexander, *The Roots of Civilization* (New York: McGraw-Hill, 1972).

79. Marshack, Alexander, "Implications of the Paleolithic Symbolic Evidence for the Origin of Language," *American Scientist*, 64 (1976), 136-145.

80. *J. Hist. Astron.*, 8(2), June 1977, iii.

81. Kelley, David H., *Deciphering the Maya Script* (Texas Press, 1976).

82. Aveni, ed., *Archaeoastronomy in Pre-Columbian America* (Texas Press, 1975).

83. Aveni, ed., *Native American Astronomy* (Texas Press, 1977).

84. Dean, Malcolm, "Astrology: The Cosmic Conspiracy," *Ideas*, CBC-FM, Jan. 2, 1979.

85. Tromp, S.W., *Medical Biometeorology* (Amsterdam: Elsevier, 1963).

86. Tromp, S.W., *Progress in Human Biometeorology* (Amsterdam: Swets and Zeitlinger, 1973).

87. Tromp, S.W., *Biometeorological Review, 1973-1978* (London: Heyden and Son, 1979).

88. Dewey, Edward R. with Og, Mandino, *Cycles: The Mysterious Forces That Trigger Events* (New York: Hawthorn, 1971).

Seven: Sex, Money, and Health

89. Dean, Malcolm, *Ideas*, Jan. 1, 1979.

90. Dean, Malcolm, *Ideas*, Jan. 3, 1979.

91. Quoted in: Omarr, *My World of Astrology*, p. 82.

92. Levinson, Daniel, *The Seasons of a Man's Life* (New York: Knopf, 1978).

93. Sheehy, Gail, *Passages: Predictable Crises of Adult Life* (New York: Dutton, 1976).

94. Ruperti, Alexander, *Cycles of Becoming: The Planetary Pattern of Growth* (Davis, CA: CRCS Publications, 1979).

95. Davis, Geraldine, *Horary Astrology* (Los Angeles: First Temple of Astrology, 1970).

96. Sheldon, William H., *The Varieties of Human Physique* (Harper & Brothers, 1940); *The Varieties of Temperament* (Harpers, 1942); *Varieties of Delinquent Youth* (Harpers, 1949); *Atlas of Men* (Gramercy, 1954).

97. *Phenomena*, 2.1 Jan.-Feb. 1978, 11.

98. Rieder, Thomas, *Sun Spots, Stars, and the Stock Market* (Toronto: Pagurian Press, 1979). Rev. ed. of *Astrological Warnings and the Stock Market*, 1972.

99. Munkasey, Michael, "Void-of-Course Market Phenomena," *The Astrological Review*, Spring-Summer 1974, 33-36.

100. *Wall Street Journal*, July 18, 1978, 1

Eight: Astrologers All

101. Powell, Robert, "The Astrological Paradigm and the Origin of Horoscopic Astrology," *Mercury Star Journal*, 4(1), Easter 1978, 4-10.

102. See Neugebauer, O. *Greek Horoscopes*, Amer. Phil. Soc., 1959.

103. See De Solla Price, Derek, *Gears from the Greeks*, Science History Pub., 1975.

104. Howe, Ellic, *Urania's Children* (London: Kimber Co., 1967), Chapter 3.

105. Lister, Raymond, *William Blake: An Introduction to His Life and Works* (London: Bell and Sons, 1968), p. 162.

106. Bach, Eleanor, *Ephemerides of the Asteroids, Ceres, Pallas, Juno, Vesta, 1900-2000* (New York: Celestial Communications, 1973); Michelsen, Neil and Dobyns, Dr. Zipporah, *The Asteroid Ephemeris, 1883-1999*, (Los Angeles: TIA Publications, 1977).

107. Butler, Jon, "Magic, Astrology, and the Early American Religious Heritage, 1600-1760," *Amer. Hist. Review*, 84(2), April 1979, 317-346.

108. "Song of Myself," 33.

109. Gauquelin, Michel, *The Scientific Basis of Astrology* (New York: Stein and Day, 1969), 137-41.

110. The name "Uranian" astrology is not a reference to the planet Uranus. It probably originated from a reference to the Age of Aquarius, which is ruled by Uranus. Hence the name might imply to astrologers that this system is the latest development, a harbinger of a "scientific" astrology. Also see note 47.

111. Neely, James, "The Orbits of the Transneptunians," *J. Geocosmic Res.*, 2(2), 1978.

112. I am indebted to Helen Weaver, Charles Harvey, and Charles Jayne for some of these biographical details.

113. See *Human Dimensions*, 4(3) for biographical details.

114. Fagan, Cyril, *Zodiacs Old and New* (Los Angeles: Llewellyn Foundation for Astrological Research, 1950).

115. It is interesting to consider what Fagan might have done with the evidence we found in Chapter Six, especially in Sir Norman Lockyer's work, which showed that the ancients were well aware of the precession of the equinoxes and turned their temples in response to the shifting positions of the stars. In the mid-1900s Lockyer's work was little known and difficult to obtain, yet copies must have been available in London libraries, where Fagan did research.

Nine: The Stars and War

116. Obituary, *Astrological Journal*, 17(1), Winter 1974/75, 1-2; *Quarterly Army List*, Jan. 1942, 95-96.

117. *The Tehran, Yalta and Potsdam Conferences* (Moscow: Progress Pub., 1969).

118. Tolstoy, Nikolai, *Victims of Yalta* (London: Hodder & Stoughton, 1977).
119. Bethell, Nicholas, *The Last Secret* (New York: Basic Books, 1974).
120. Various astrological sources insist that Firebrace acted as translator at Yalta, but I was unable to locate any references to him in the various histories and transcripts. Major George Youmatoff, a Russian-born Canadian who worked directly under Firebrace, recalls his presence in London at the time of the Yalta Conference.
121. *New York Times*, Feb. 24, 1980, p. 34.
122. Gleadow, Rupert, *The Origin of the Zodiac* (New York: Castle Books, 1969).
123. Firebrace, Brig. R.C., *Wars in the Sidereal*, Moray Series, No. 2, 1959.
124. Firebrace, Brig. R.C., "A New Horoscope for the U.S.S.R.", *Spica*, 7(2), 1968, 15-27.
125. *Spica*, 8(1), Oct. 1968.
126. Wulff, Wilhelm, *Zodiac and Swastika* (Tierkreis und Hakenkreuz), Bertelsmann Sachbuchverlag Reinhard Mohn, Gutersloh, 1968. Translated 1973 by Arthur Baker, Ltd., London. Amer. Ed., Coward, McCann and Geohegan, New York, 1973.
127. Dean, Malcolm, "Astrology, The Cosmic Conspiracy," *Ideas*, CBC-FM, Jan. 3, 1979.

Ten: The Mars Effect

128. *Human Behavior*, Nov. 1976, 56-62.
129. Dean, Malcolm, op. cit., Jan. 4, 1979.
130. Gauquelin, Michel, *Dreams and Illusions of Astrology* (Buffalo: Prometheus Books, 1979).
131. Gauquelin, Michel, *L'astrologie devant la science* trans. *The Scientific Basis of Astrology, Myth or Reality* (New York: Stein and Day, 1970).
132. Gauquelin, Michel, "L'influences des astres: Etude critique et experimental," *Le Dauphin*, Paris, 1955.
133. See Gauquelin, Michel et Françoise, *Methodes pour etudier le repartition des astres dans le mouvement diurne*, Paris, private publication, 1957; English translation, Phenomena Publications, Toronto, 1981.
134. Gauquelin, Michel, *Les hommes et les astres* (Paris: DeNoel, 1960), pp. 112-114.
135. Hand, Robert, *Planets in Transit* (Para Research, 1976), p. 265, 308.
136. Gauquelin, Michel, *Les hommes et les astres*, p. 200.

137. Gauquelin, Michel, *The Scientific Basis of Astrology*, p. 55, 145.
138. Dobyns, Dr. Zipporah, *Finding the person in the horoscope*, TIA Pub., 1973, p. 33.
139. Gauquelin, Michel and Françoise, *Replication of the Planetary Effect in Heredity*, Laboratoire d'etude des relations entre rythmes cosmiques et psychophysiologiques, Paris, 1977.
140. Gauquelin, Michel and Françoise, *The Planetary Factors in Personality*, Laboratoire d'etude des relations, etc., Paris, 1976, p. 3.
141. Cohen, David, "Stars and Planets," *Human Behavior*, Nov. 1976, 56.
142. Eysenck, H.J., *Readings in Extraversion-Introversion* (Staples Press, 1970).
143. Dean, Malcolm, op. cit., Jan. 5, 1979.
144. Mayo et al., *J. Soc. Psych.*, 105, 1978, 229-236.
145. Smithers, A. and J. Cooper, *J. Soc. Psych.*, 105, 1978, 237-241.
146. Pawlik, K., *Zeit. fur Socialpsych.*, 10, 1979, 54-69.
147. Wendt, H.W., *J. Soc. Psych.*, 105, 1978, 243-247.
148. Eysenck, Hans, "Planets, Stars and Personality," *New Behaviour*, 29, May 1975.
149. Gauquelin, Françoise, *Traditional Symbolism in Astrology and the Character-Traits Method*, Laboratoire d'etude des relations, etc., Paris, 1980.

Eleven: We the Undersigned

150. Comité Para, *Nouvelles Breves*, Vol. 43, Sept. 1976, 327-343.
151. Gauquelin, Michel, "The Influence of Planets on Human Beings," *The Humanist*, Mar.-Apr. 1976, p. 53.
152. Jerome, Lawrence, "Astrology and Modern Science: A Critical Analysis," *Leonardo*, 6, 1973, 121-130.
153. Bok, Bart J. Letter, *Leonardo*, 7, 1974, 188.
154. *West Australian*, 19 Sept. 1978, p. 10.
155. Omarr, Sydney, *My World of Astrology* (Los Angeles: Wilshire, 1965), 104-114.
156. Gauquelin, Michel, *Leonardo*, 8, 1975, 229-231.
157. Jerome, Lawrence, *Leonardo*, 8, 1975, 270-222.
158. *The Humanist*, Sept.-Oct. 1976, p. 4. For the entire debate see issues through 1978.
159. "Interview with a skeptic: Prof. Paul Kurtz," *Phenomena*, 2.2, Mar-Apr. 1978, 14-16.
160. Dated Jan. 5, 1978 and acknowledged Jan. 24, 1978.

161. Rose, Lynn, Letter, *The Humanist*, Sept.-Oct., 1976, p. 61.
162. Rockwell, Theodore, "Irrational Rationalists: A Critique of The Humanist's Crusade Against Parapsychology," *J. Amer. Soc. Psychical Res.*, 72, 1978; reprinted in *Phenomena*, 2.2, Mar.-Apr., 1978, 22-27.
163. Kurtz, Paul, Letter, *New Realities*, Vol. 1(5), p. 6.
164. See *Science Forum*, Jul.-Aug. 1978, 21-24 on this latter point.
165. *New York Times*, June 25, 1978, p. 21.
166. Truzzi, Marcello, "The Crusade Against the Paranormal," *Fate*, Sept. 1979, 70-76; Oct. 1979, 87-94.
167. *The Skeptical Inquirer*, Vol. 3(1), Fall 1978, 14-15.
168. Rudhyar, Dane, *The Astrology of Personality* (New York: Lucis, 1946), p. 306; reprinted by Doubleday, 1970, 283.
169. Jayne, Charles. "Are there hypothetical planets?" *In Search*, Spring 1961, 7-19.
170. Eysenck, Hans, Review, *Books and Bookmen*, 1978; reprinted in *Phenomena*, 2.2, Mar.-Apr. 1978, 9-11.
171. Feyerabend, Paul, *Science in a Free Society* (New York: Schoken Books, 1978).
172. *The Skeptical Inquirer*, 4(2), Winter 1979-80, 19-63.
173. In another interesting incident with the media, Abell appeared on the "Merv Griffin Show" with Sydney Omarr, where he gave a facetious reading of his own horoscope. Omarr showed that Abell had made a mistake of four hours in the position of his Moon, to which Abell responded "Well, maybe I have a better ephemeris than you do." See Browning, Norma Lee, *Omarr: Astrology and the Man*, (New York: Doubleday, 1977), p. 197.

Twelve: The Astrology of the Future

174. Pontin, Marie Muliette, "Mundane Astrology," *Yearbook of the American Academy of Astrologians* (New York: Hermetic Pub. Co., 1918), pp. 47-53.
175. Sepharial, *The World Horoscope* (London: Foulsham and Co. Ltd., 1965), p. 71.
176. McGuire and Hull, eds., *C.G. Jung Speaking*, Bollingen Series XCVII, (Princeton: Princeton Univ. Press, 1977), pp. 375, 412-413.
177. *Science News*, 115(7), Feb. 17, 1979, p. 99.
178. Dean, Malcolm, "Albertus Spagyricus: Interview with an Alchemist," *Phenomena*, 2.1, Jan.-Feb. 1978, 15-18.
179. Albertus, Frater, *Men and the Cycles of the Universe* (Salt Lake City: Paracelsus Research Society, 1970).

180. MacCraig, Hugh, *Ephemeris of the Moon: A Supplement to the 200 Year Ephemeris* (New York: Macoy Pub. Co., 1951).

181. Source: *Cadillac Modern Encyclopedia* (New York: 1973).

182. Culver, R.B. and P.A. Ianna, *The Gemini Syndrome* (Tucson: Pachart Pub. House, 1979), p. 94.

183. Just as *The Humanist* magazine attempted to lampoon astrology in its original anti-astrology issue (1975) with a cartoon of a huge, well-funded telescope trained on a backwards zodiac in space, Culver and Ianna's book has a childish cartoon on the cover showing a spaceship using ray-guns to blast objects out of space. The objects being fired upon look like coins which are emblazoned with the zodiac and the planetary symbols. In the center of each "coin" there is a large dollar sign. Back to the erroneous impression that astrology is a surefire path to big bucks. Ianna and Culver clearly do not have their facts straight on this score, either.

184. Blake, Jeri, *When Presidents Die* (New York: Doubleo Publications, 1980).

185. Rudhyar, Dane, *The Lunation Cycle* (Servire: 1967).

186. Lewis, Jim, "Astrology Predicts the Next Likely War Zones," *Dell Horoscope, 44(7), July 1978, p. 57.*

187. Gribbin, John and Stephen Plagemann, *The Jupiter Effect* (New York: Macmillan, 1974).

188. Gribbin, John, "Jupiter's Noneffect," *Omni*, June 1980, p. 20, 121.

189. Kautz, Bill, "Jupiter and the Great California Earthquake?" *Earthquake Watch Newsletter*, May 1980, SRI International.

190. Ruperti, Alexander, *Cycles of Becoming*, CRCS Pub., 1979, p. 114.

191. Ross, Alexander, "The back page," *Canadian Business*, June 1980, p. 126.

192. McMaster, R.C., *Cycles of War*, War Cycles Institute, 1978, Box 1673, Kallispell, MT 59901.

193. Dean, Malcolm, "Astrology: The Cosmic Conspiracy," *Ideas*, CBC-FM, Jan. 5, 1979.

194. Barbault, Andre, *L'Astrologie Mondiale* (Paris: Fayard, 1979).

195. There are several ways of calculating this graph. The graph shown here was not produced by the same method as Barbault used in his book (ref. 194.), but the results are identical to the eye. Computations and programming were by Robert Hand of Astro-Graphics. Hand notes that during the nineteenth century, the graph does not correspond well

with events if Pluto is included. Without Pluto, he feels, there seems to exist clearer correspondences. The "Pluto effect" on the graph only becomes apparent during the waxing Uranus-Neptune hemicycle, due to the position of Pluto either within or without the Uranus-Neptune arc. This should please some observers who note that Pluto has been found to be so small that astronomers are on the verge of demoting it to the status of an asteroid. Without Pluto, the graph for this century, however, is substantially the same as shown, and would then be based on the groupings of the four most massive bodies in the solar system.

196. Barbault, Andre, *l'Almanach Chacornac*, 1978.
197. Fremerman, Bernard, "Cyclical Phenomena — Possible Relationships Between Terrestrial and Extra-Terrestrial Events," *Cycles*, 28(2), Feb.-Mar. 1977, 43-46.